ECONOMIC SYSTEMS

Dr. S.S.M. Desai

Mrs. Nirmal D. Bhalerao, M.A.

ISO 9001:2015 CERTIFIED

First Edition : 1980
Edition : 2000
Edition : 2009
Edition : 2013
Edition : 2025

Published by : Mrs. Meena Pandey
for **HIMALAYA PUBLISHING HOUSE PVT. LTD.,**
"Ramdoot", Dr. Bhalerao Marg, Girgaon, Mumbai - 400 004.
Phone: 022-23860170, 23863863; **Fax:** 022-23877178
E-mail: himpub@bharatmail.co.in; **Website:** www.himpub.com

Branch Offices :

New Delhi : "Pooja Apartments", 4-B, Murari Lal Street, Ansari Road, Darya Ganj, New Delhi - 110 002.
Phone: 011-23270392, 23278631; Fax: 011-23256286

Nagpur : Kundanlal Chandak Industrial Estate, Ghat Road, Nagpur - 440 018. Mobile: 09325409992, 09325908881

Bengaluru : Plot No. 91-33, 2nd Main Road, Seshadripuram, Behind Nataraja Theatre, Bengaluru - 560 020.
Phone: 080-41138821; Mobile: 09379847017, 09379847005

Hyderabad : No. 3-4-184, Lingampally, Besides Raghavendra Swamy Matham, Kachiguda, Hyderabad - 500 027.
Phone: 040-27560041, 27550139

Chennai : No. 34/44, Motilal Street, T. Nagar, Chennai - 600 017.
Mobile: 09380460419

Pune : "Laksha" Apartment, First Floor, No. 527, Mehunpura, Shaniwarpeth (Near Prabhat Theatre), Pune - 411 030.
Phone: 020-24496323, 24496333; Mobile: 09370579333

Cuttack : Plot No. 5F-755/4, Sector-9, CDA Markat Nagar, Cuttack - 753 014, Odisha. Mobile: 09338746007

Kolkata : 3, S.M. Bose Road, Near Gate No. 5, Agarpara Railway Station, North 24 Parganas, West Bengal - 700 109.
Mobile: 09674536325

Printed at : Geetanjali Press Pvt. Ltd., Nagpur. On behalf of HPH (P).

PREFACE TO THE FOURTH REVISED EDITION

Since the Third Edition of our Economic Systems was published in June 1989, a number of systematic (*i.e.*, structural) changes have taken place, both in India and outside the country. These systematic changes are of vital importance and need their proper understanding, along with their short-term and long-term implications for India.

For example, in the case of India there is a radical change in approach towards Public Sector which had occupied the central place in the Indian Economy since 1956. Similarly, far-reaching liberal systemic changes are proposed in the Indian Economy by the New Economic Policy statement of July 1991.

In the international sphere, almost revolutionary changes have been taking place. The last decade saw unprecedented recession in developed economies of Western Europe and in the United States, the worst since the Great Depression of 1929-33.

There has been the disintegration of the former Soviet Union with retreat of communism in the former Soviet Union and East European countries. There is an end to the cold war which has left the United States as the only super power in the world. The United States has been trying to dictate economic policies both of developed and of developing countries through pressure from the World Bank the IMF and the GATT which are dominated by the United States. Even communist China after the Tiananmen Square explosion in 1989 appears to be gradually moving towards economic liberalism and free market economy, leaving its long isolation.

All these domestic and international systemic changes have vital bearing on India.

An attempt has been made in this Fourth Edition of Economic Systems to analyse direct and indirect as also short-term and long-term implications of these domestic and international systemic (*i.e.*, structural) changes for India and Indian people.

It is hoped that this revised and updated Fourth Edition of our Economic Systems will be found instructive and useful by the student world and teaching faculty in different universities in India.

Any suggestions for improvement in usefulness of the book would be welcome. There is always room for improvement.

We are extremely thankful to Shriman D. P. Pandey of Himalaya Publishing House, Bombay, for his encouragement and persistent pressure on us to revise and bring out this Fourth Edition of our Economic Systems.

Poona, **Authors**
Date: 1st January 1994

PREFACE TO THE FIRST EDITION

In recent years, comparative study of different Economic Systems functioning in different countries of the world has been assuming increasing importance.

The English Classical School headed by Adam Smith, propounded and provided the foundations of the Capitalist System which for quite some time came to be looked upon and accepted as the most natural economic system and therefore endurable, with all its shortcomings pointed out by classicists like Malthus and David Ricardo, J.B. Say, the French classicist, gave finishing touch to this classical edifice, by logically proving that competition and the Law of Markets automatically ensured stability of the capitalist economy at the full employment level and was crisis-proof.

Observing *laissez-faire* capitalism functioning in several countries of Western Europe and the evils or defects which eventually surfaced, early socialists of the 19th century raised some serious doubts and challenged some of the assumptions of capitalism which had come to be assumed *a priori* as valid. But essentially theirs was only a voice of protest and their attempts to rebuild or suggest an alternative system were tentative, fragmentary, sketchy and experimental. But they did raise the voice of protest and tried to think along new lines and thus paved the way for building an alternative economic system.

The credit for putting capitalism on the defensive and suggesting a comprehensive and viable alternative economic system must go to Karl Marx whose philosophy and thoughts hold sway over more than half the population of the world at present. The Marxian process of thinking and his efforts culminated in the October Revolution of 1917 in Russia and a new Economic System came to birth and started functioning.

The immediate result was confrontation and conflict between the two underlying philosophies and Economic Systems of Capitalism and Socialism. J.M. Keynes tried to find out a via media between the two system, retaining the fundamental or basic tenets of capitalism and absorbing in capitalism some of the features of socialism. It may broadly be said that it is the Keynesian model of capitalist system that is prevailing in the West European countries, the USA and Japan at present.

Both Capitalism and Socialism were essentially international in their approach and there was for long no reconciliation between the two. Prejudices and dogmas die hard and the basic conflict, sometimes overt, sometimes covert, continued, the extremes on either side believing in the ultimate destruction of the rival economic system and triumph of their own. This trend continued with temporary co-operation between the two systems forced by the abnormal conditions of World War II. But the suppressed basic conflict between the two philosophies and systems asserted itself immediately the World War II was over and burst out with all the fury into an atmosphere of the cold war between the two. John Foster Dulles and Joseph Macarthy on the one hand and Joseph Stalin on the other during the immediate post-war period represented the culminating point of the confrontation and conflict between the two philosophies and systems.

Two developments of fundamental nature that took place during the post-World War II years however may be said to have brought about a radical change in the attitude of thinkers, governments and people towards different economic philosophies and systems. The break-through which the USSR achieved in nuclear technology and emergence on the scene of a large number of the Third World countries which were not fanatically attached to either of the two economic systems forced a reappraisal of the whole attitude of looking upon other economic systems than one's own with only suspicion and distrust. If different countries with different economic systems must think in terms of coexistence because of the nuclear threat which if executed might annihilate the entire mankind, why then not live in healthy competitive atmosphere in various fields outshining the rival economic system in socio-economic, political and cultural fields and winning over people and countries to one's philosophy and system?

On the intellectual plane this has led to the objective and scientific study of various economic systems and the factors that evolve and mould them. It is being increasingly realised that like flora and fauna of a country, an economic system grows in the soil and changes or gets modified with changes in environment. It is not an artifice that can be borrowed wholesale and foisted upon a country and its people. Economic system is a social organism which must naturally grow and get its nourishment from the soil and culture of the people. In the present-day dynamic world, economic and political institutions must change and will change, but the change must be natural and in tune with the basic thoughts and value-system of the people in a country. Borrowed systems, like borrowed garments, will not fit well.

India may be said to have learnt this bitter lesson (has it?) to its/great cost. While there is no denying of the favourable impact left by the British rule over India, their attempts, may be unconscious and with the best of intentions, to foist their own institutions on a country with different geography, history, culture and value-system, and on our part, blind imitation and acceptance of whatever was British — their language, their parliamentary democracy, their universities and educational system, their medical system, their various economic institutions and even their sports and games — have been to a great extent responsible for the growing plight of the country more than 38 years after the country became free during which time some of the countries like West and East

Germany and Japan almost totally destroyed by war have not only rebuilt their economies but are being counted as major powers in the world, whereas India with its vast and varied resources, natural and human, continues to be counted among the poorest of the poor countries!

Economic prosperity (on which depends political and military strength) of a country depends on a sound ideology and/ability to build and manage Economic System with its various sub-structures in harmony with that ideal. Dynamic changes, especially in the technological field, are taking place in the world and failure to continually readjust and modify the economic system would mean the danger of losing in the international competitive field from which no country has the option, in the second half of the 20th century, to opt itself out. And therefore economic institutions making the totality of the economic system of a country, must change not only in response to changing domestic needs and challenges but also as a response to changes in the economic systems of the other countries in the world. Failure to perceive and to act in accordance with this dynamics of social change would result in the concerned country being swept off the feet and going under or be dominated by those countries which have successfully adjusted their social and economic systems in accordance with the above doctrine. This would explain the disappearance of civilisation and culture of Greece which produced more than 2,000 years ago Aristotle and Alexander than whom no greater philosopher and warrior-general respectively, are yet born! That explains the downfall of Sparta, of Rome, of Carthage, of ancient civilisations of China and India, in fact of the whole of Asia (except Japan), which fell an easy prey to dynamic cultures of European countries which from the 17th century onward learnt to move in step with the changes taking place in the world.

Now that partly by their own efforts and partly by force of circumstances these countries have become free and independent, the lesson before them is clear and unmistakable. As Charles E. Lindblom in his 'Politics and Markets' has pointed out, "If we are to have any control over futures, understanding our institutions well enough to reshape them is on some counts more necessary than predicting a future on the assumption that we are wholly powerless to form it." That is how we acted for centuries and that is how we must not act hereafter because the race for survival and mastery is every day becoming more and more fiercer. Any failure to move fast enough would mean being swept off or be trampled under the successful ones. We have no choice in this respect.

And so not only we must understand our own economic system, its functioning, its strong and weak points and the reforms needed, but we must be equally aware of other economic systems adopted by other countries in the world and changes taking place therein. And hence the importance of the comparative study of Economic Systems.

There is one possible danger or shortcoming that is likely to adversely affect our study of Economic Systems, if we are not on our guard. Our strong emotions, predilections, prejudices, biases, consciously or unconsciously, are likely to cloud our views study, preventing us from undertaking objective analysis and reaching right conclusions. In this respect we are all ostrich-like. But as Carl Landauer has pointed out, "It is bitter but necessary to realise that an economic system that is a product of hostile ideology may have some points on which its technological performance is superior to that of our system. It is a false loyalty to blind ourselves to this possibility. For in a struggle of rival ideologies, victory is not likely to go to those who refuse to see the strong points of the opponent and to lean from him."

I must express my heart-felt thanks to Shri D.P. Pandey of the Himalaya Publishing House, Bombay, whose endearing and repeated goadings left me no choice but to give high priority to the writing of this book.

26th January, 1980 **S.S.M. Desai**

CONTENTS

CHAPTER 1

WHAT IS AN ECONOMIC SYSTEM ? MEANING, FUNCTIONS AND CLASSIFICATION

1. INTRODUCTION

Different sciences use the concept of a system in their own way. For example, the science of biology views 'human body' as a 'system'; the science of astronomy views the entire universe with the sun, the stars and planets as a system. In politics, we come across democracy as a political system and we have also monarchy and aristocracy as different political systems.

In the same way, when man tries to satisfy his numerous wants by producing various types of goods and services with the help of various productive resources, he builds a number of institutions. Together all such institutions constitute 'an economic system.'

In order to understand the meaning of an economic system in a proper way, it is necessary that we understand one or two additional concepts.

The term 'institution' refers to the way of thinking, taking decisions and doing various things some way or another. Thus we speak of banking institution, educational institution, caste institution, marriage institution and so on.

All those things that concern production of goods and services, their exchange and their consumption may be called 'economic institutions.' Thus factories, banks, trade unions, market places and their functioning, bullion market, peasant proprietorship and landlords, cooperative societies, etc., are all 'economic institutions.'

The concept or term 'system' is defined as "an aggregate or assemblage of objects united by some form of regular interaction or inter-dependence, a group or diverse units so combined by nature or art as to form an integral whole and to function in unison."

Thus various economic institutions together constitute 'an economic system.' An economic system is an assemblage or aggregation of the numerous economic institutions, some tangible and some intangible, which are concerned with production, exchange, distribution and consumption of various goods and services or in other terms wealth.

Thus the present economic system of India is made up of peasant proprietorship and other systems of landholdings, rural moneylenders and cooperative credit and non-credit societies, village fairs and urban markets, land legislation, private and public sector industries as also small-scale industrial establishments in rural and urban areas, banks, railways and so on.

Every country has one total or comprehensive system covering every aspect of an individual's and community's life — social, political, ethical, cultural and of course economic. Each of the above aspects has its own system and these may be described as sub-systems of the total or comprehensive system. From this point of view, 'an economic system' may be said to be a sub-system of the total and comprehensive system. Similarly the political system of a country with its various political institutions, laws, and customs and conventions may be said to constitute a sub-system of the comprehensive or total system.

What needs to be noted is that all these sub-systems are closely interlinked and have deep influence on one another. To give an example, generally democracy (a political system) seems to encourage capitalist economic system with its emphasis on personal freedom to consumers and producers, on competition and on private property, whereas fascism (another political system) generally favours socialism or communism or in some cases a feudal type of economic system.

2. DEFINITIONS OF AN ECONOMIC SYSTEM

Before we undertake the study of different economic systems operating in different countries and the manner in which they are functioning to solve the problems referred to above as also the degree of success with which they have been in a position to deal with or solve those problems, it is essential in the first instance to know the definition and meaning of an economic system, its main features, and the forces which mould and influence it.

Definition of an Economic System

Jan. Prybyla has given the following definition: "An economic system may be defined as the sum total of devices which through their interaction give effect to economic choice, *i.e.*, which translate choice from an idea into action. Action in this context means the actual movement of resources towards the

Mrs. Joan Robinson writes: "Any economic system requires a set of rules, an ideology to justify them, and a conscience in the individual which makes him strive to carry it out."

Manual Gottlieb defines an economic system as follows:

"An economic system is an evolving pattern of complex human relations which is concerned with the disposal of scarce resources for the purpose of satisfying various private and public needs for goods and services."

W.W. Loucks has given the following definition:

"... an economic system consists of those institutions which a given people, a nation, or a group of nations, have chosen or accepted as means through which their resources are utilised for the satisfaction of human wants."

Gregory Grossman explaining the concept of an economic system writes:

"An economy in which individuals and families are substantially interdependent is usually called a social economy. In order to accomplish its tasks, a social economy resorts to what the social scientist calls institutions — an institution in its broadest sense being a set of norms, rules of conduct, or established ways of thinking. Property, the business corporation, the family household, the government, money, the income tax, share-cropping , the tipping of waiters, planning, profit-making, the labour union—these are all examples of economic institutions.

The set of institutions that characterizes a given economy comprises its economic system."[2]

Carl Landauer defines an economic system as follows:

"An economic system may be defined as the sum total of the devices by which preferences among alternative purposes of economic activity is determined and by which individual activities are co-ordinated for the achievement of these purposes."[3]

If we carefully study and analyse the above definitions of an economic system given by various authors, certain broad features stand out prominently.

An economic system would be seen to consist of various individuals who constitute society, of various economic units (like households, firms, labour unions, employers' unions and so on), and of various economic agents (such as consumers, entrepreneurs, savers, investors, planners, etc.,) who perform some economic function or functions.

In abstract, an economic system embodies the way different individuals are related to one another in the economic sphere, the way they are related to various economic resources used for productive purposes (*i.e.*, whether an individual firm or an individual owns these resources, or whether there is state ownership or there is a mixture of the two), preferences of the people and the manner in which they are expressed and various ways in which resources come to be allocated for satisfying certain wants in preference to others.

In concrete terms, an economic system includes various individuals and their economic institutions. For example, in the case of India, her economic system would include all the individuals who are carrying on some sort or other of economic activities, various agricultural institutions like Zamindari, Mahalwari and Royatwari systems, and various land legislations and cooperative credit and non-credit societies; on the industrial side, the economic system of India would include various industrial institutions like large-scale industries, some owned by private individuals and some by the State; it would include small-scale and cottage industries, their ownership pattern and the manner of their functioning with state assistance; it would include banking institutions, transport and communication systems and the manner of their functioning; it would include planners and the manner in which five-year plans are being formulated and implemented; and above all India's economic system would include how the wealth annually produced in the country is being shared by different sections and individuals in the community.

India thus has its economic system; so have other countries like the United States, Great Britain, France and West Germany; and so have countries like the Russia and the East European countries; and so have Latin American countries and countries in Africa. The point to note here is that it is not only developed countries which can have an economic system; even the least developed or most backward countries can have their own economic systems. Thus even the most backward countries consisting of illiterate and poor tribal communities have their own economic systems. Only the content, type and functioning of their economic systems will be different from those in developed countries.

It should also be obvious form above definitions of an economic system, that whatever the type of an economic system which a country adopts, it has and must have an institutional base and also a psychological or idealistic base or foundation.

3. FUNCTIONS OF AN ECONOMIC SYSTEM

All economic systems have got to take the following important decisions or perform the following important economic functions:

1. *What to Produce.* It is a well-known fact that human wants are unlimited in number. No sooner a particular want or desire is satisfied, another want or desire appears and man continues to be ever-dissatisfied. On the other hand, the resources (namely, land, labour, capital goods and organisational ability and skills) are, in relation to wants, always limited. Man cannot produce unlimited number of commodities and services of all types with relatively scarce resources. The society therefore with its relatively limited resources at its disposal, has to take decisions as to what commodities and services it is going to produce, and what commodities it is going to sacrifice, may be temporarily or for longer period.

Thus no society, however it is organised, can avoid taking decisions on this important issue. Fascism (Nazism) under Hitler gave higher priority to guns than to butter; the former Soviet Union for long gave emphasis on production of capital goods and lower priority to consumer goods; in a capitalist country like the United States, there appears to be as much emphasis on capital goods as on consumer goods, both of which are being produced in certain proportions. In the case of a mixed economy like that of India also, we have to take decisions regarding whether we are going to produce luxury and semi-luxury goods or wage-goods; whether we are going to produce capital goods or consumer goods; and if both, in what proportions. This decision becomes inevitable in view of the fact in relation of unlimited wants of individuals living in a society, resources required to produce goods and services are relatively limited.

2. *How to Produce.* Having decided what commodities and services to produce and what not to produce, or in what combination or proportion to produce them, the society has to take decision on the next important question (which is rather technical in nature) as to how to produce those goods and services. Thus if top priority is given to the agricultural sector and decision is taken by society to produce more of agricultural commodities, what is the method or technique of production which the society is going to prefer out of the many possible technical ways open for producing more agricultural commodities? Is agriculture going to be organised on the US model where a private individual can own vast land and cultivate it with various types of agricultural machines? Or is society going to prefer the former USSR system where land is owned by the state and is cultivated collectively? Or is society going to prefer, as in certain parts of India, peasant proprietorship with certain ceiling on landholding?

The question 'how to produce' also includes other technical decisions such as capital-intensive technique versus labour-intensive technique of production, large-scale co-operative farming versus small-scale individual proprietorship farming, extensive farming versus intensive farming, chemical fertilisers versus natural manure and so on.

Thus there are alternative methods of producing practically every commodity and society will have to take decisions as to how it is going to produce the combination of goods and services on which it has set its heart.

Incidentably, this technical question also involves. 'where' the goods and services will be produced. Is the society going to concentrate its industries in a particular locality (as in Bombay, Calcutta, Delhi, Ahmedabad and Kanpur) or is it going to bring about dispersal of industries? What is the most suitable location for an industry? No society, however it is organised, can avoid this question.

3. *Maintaining Internal Consistency.* While deciding what to produce, how and where, the society has to take care to see that since all the processes of production are closely interdependent, there is proper balance between

different processes of production and also among different commodities and services produced. "Let one integral part of this co-operative process of social production lag behind, and potentially all the other parts will suffer. This applies to the supply of raw materials, of intermediate goods, of trained labour, and even consumer goods, since without adequate supply of consumer goods labour may be less efficient than before."[4]

Different economic systems, as we shall see, try to maintain this internal balance in the process of production of goods and services in different ways, with greater or less success. For example, in capitalistic countries like the USA, the task of achieving internal, balance is left to market mechanism or price system governed by free play of the forces of demand and supply; in communist countries like the former USSR and China, the sectoral and commodity balance is sought to be achieved through the system of economic planning.

4. *How are Goods and Services Produced by the Society to be Shared among Different Sections and Members of the Community?* After a society decides what to produce, in what proportions commodities and services should be produced, how to produce and where, the society, whatever the form of organisation it adopts (capitalist, communist, or mixed economy or fascism), has to decide how and on what basis the commodities and services annually produced are going to be distributed among different sections and members of the community. What would be the share of annual national wealth that would go to labourers, employers, agriculturists? What would be the share that would go to each member of society? Society tries to find out a satisfactory answer to this question, because it is on this decision that, among other things, the welfare of the society depends.

We shall see that different economic systems have adopted different methods of distributing national product among different sections and members of society. For example, in the USA, though there is certain amount of intervention by the state, it is mainly the competitive forces in the market and bargaining strength of different sections and individuals that determine the question of how national production will be distributed. On the other hand, in China, it is not the market forces but it is the state that takes decisions as to what portion of wealth will go to what section of the community and also what share of wealth each individual will get. It will be seen that the principles followed in distributing annual produce among different sections and members of the community are different in USA and China, each claiming merit for its system. Anyway, every society has to take decision regarding the principle and manner in which annual produce will be distributed among different sections and members of the community. It is a vital decision, because welfare of a community depends not only on what is produced and how and where, but also on the share which each individual is going to get out of the annual wealth produced by the community. Also, the principle followed in distributing wealth will have influence on the rate at which wealth is produced in a country.

5. *What about Provision for the Future?* Man is the one animal who thinks not only of his welfare for the present but also of his and his children's welfare for the morrow. Since this is so, society has to take the important decision of how much of the existing resources will be used for the production of consumption goods to be currently enjoyed, and how much of the resources to be diverted to the production of capital goods which add to production of consumption goods in future. Diverting of present resources for the production of capital goods involves sacrifice of satisfaction of current wants for the sake of future satisfaction of wants and welfare. Whatever the economic system community adopts, it has to and does think of the future and takes decisions, regarding how much of current resources are to be utilised for the production of consumption goods and how much for capital goods (*i.e.,* decision regarding level of current consumption and future consumption level). In one sense, the question is implicit in the first question, namely what to produce; but it is better to draw special attention to this problem which vitally affects the standard of living of the people at the present and in future.

6. *Is the Economy Growing?* Man wants to continually raise his standard of living. Demonstration effect plays a vital role in this. Also, population of every country is bound to grow in future and more and more goods will have to be produced at a rate faster than the rate at which population is growing annually. Also, there are international rivalries among different nations and occasionally there are wars. That requires ever-increasing goods and services of all types and raising the rate of their production in a country.

Whatever the economic system a society adopts, capitalist, communist or mixed economy, it will have to decide the rate at which its economy is to grow in future, how efficiently it works so that the highest possible growth-rate is attained and that proper system of incentives is provided to different sections of the community (agriculturists, industrialists, labourers, people from various services, etc.,) and to individuals so that no resources are wasted or inefficiently utilised and they are in a position to give their best and see that the economy works with maximum efficiency and grows at the highest possible rate.

One or two things need to be carefully noted.

Though for purposes of simplification of analysis the six questions which every economic system will be called upon to decide are shown under independent and separate headings above, it should be noted that all the above six questions or problems are closely interrelated and decision on any one of them in a particular way is bound to have its repercussions on all the other questions, decisions or problems. For example, answer to the question what to produce will influence answers to the problems of how to distribute, making provision for the future and future rate of growth of the economy. Similarly, answer to the problem of providing proper incentives to people will influence their efficiency and future rate of growth of the economy. It should therefore be noted that the six problems on which community will have to decide are not in different water-tight compartments but are closely linked with one another. Answer to one will influence answers to all the other problems. This implies that answers to all the above six problems must carry logical consistency among themselves. This also means that it entails the danger that wrong answer to any one of the above six problems will have its unfavourable repercussions on all the others. Whatever the type of economic system, different sectors of the economy are closely interlinked and inter-dependent and any misjudgement or misdirection in one sector will have its repercussions on all the other sectors of the economy.

Secondly, it again needs to be emphasised that whatever the type of economic system a community adopts (laissez faire capitalism, managed capitalism, socialism, fascism, communism, or mixed economy or any other conceivable pattern that prevailed in the past or may come into existence in future), every community will be called upon to take decisions on every one of the above questions. As we shall see later on, every community takes decisions on the above issues in the light of its historical traditions, culture, available resources, value-system and its vision of the future.

The different economic systems adopted by the Americans, Russians, Chinese, Swedish, Indians, etc., are based on their beliefs that the economic systems which they have come to adopt provide best answers to the above six problems.

It may also be noted that if a particular economic system adopted by a community fails, due to one reason or another or due to dynamic changes taking place in the world, to provide satisfactory answers to the above problems, or if a system is found unable to solve satisfactorily any one or other of the above problems, the community will bring about suitable adjustments in its economic system (as for example West European countries gave up laissez faire capitalism of the 19th century and introduced in its place managed or regulated capitalism with greater role to the state than envisaged by Adam Smith and Ricardo), or in extreme cases replace the economic system which failed to solve the above problems satisfactorily by a totally new economic system as the former Soviet Union did in 1917 when the prevailing Russain capitalistic system was completely replaced by the communist system.

To summarise in the words of Gregory Grossman: "... every economy (*i.e.*, economic system) has to accomplish certain basic tasks: determine what, where, how and how much is to be produced; allocate the aggregate amount of goods and services produced (the 'gross national product') between private consumption, collective consumption, replacement of capital stock used up in the course of production, and further growth of the economy; distribute its material benefits (the 'national income') among the members of society; and maintain economic relations with outside world. It may do these things spontaneously, with no central direction or planning or with some measure of central control, but to do them it must be functioning economy."[5]

4. FACTORS THAT INFLUENCE AND MOULD ECONOMIC SYSTEM OF A COUNTRY

Prof. Loucks and Prof. Whitney have mentioned that the "concrete nature of a nation's economy (*i.e.*, economic system) is determined by five sets of moulding forces:

1. the historical sources of its people's ideas and ideals, desires and attitudes;
2. its natural resources, including climate;
3. the philosophies which some or many of its people possess and advocate;
4. the past and present theorizing of its people about how to achieve chosen ideals and goals; and
5. the trials and errors of its people in seeking the desired economic ends."[6]

It would be instructive to discuss how the above factors (not necessarily in the same order), and some additional ones influence and mould an economic system of a country. Certain concrete illustrations which are provided will help students understand this aspect better.

1. *Natural and Climatic Factors*. Natural and climatic factors play directly and indirectly a vital role in moulding an economic system of a country. Fertility of soil, nature of rivers and climate, mountains, minerals and other resources, nearness of sea and nature of coast line have all deep influence on the economic system of a country. For example, these natural factors explain at least partly why India is predominantly an agricultural country and why West European countries have become industrialised countries. If a country is vast, certain amount of decentralised type of economic system becomes inevitable. If a country has varigated natural resources, then such a country is likely to adopt an economic system where agriculture, industry, trade and commerce all assume almost equal significance. Climate very greatly influences character of people of the country and through them their economic system. People in mountainous region (as for example in Nepal and Afghanistan) are sturdy and independent-minded and this would definitely produce its impact on the economic system adopted by people of such countries.

English Channel and sea-faring traditions of the British people made them independent-minded and this certainly has had its impact on the economic system of Great Britain.

To take another illustration, vastness of agricultural land in the United States and comparative scarcity of labour led to private farming on a large-scale, first with the aid of slave labour (especially in the Southern States of the United States) and later to mechanisation of agriculture. On the other hand, relatively plentiful supply of labour and scarcity of land and other natural resources have led in Japan to intensive method of agriculture and emphasis on industrialisation by importing necessary raw materials from other countries as the country lacks industrial resources. International trade becomes a sort of life-line of the economic systems of England and Japan; but it is not of the same importance in the case of countries like the United States, Russia, China and India which have varigated natural resources.

2. *Historical Traditions and Associations.* Like geography, history also leaves its deep impact on and influences the economic system of a country. This can well be illustrated by the historical association of India with Great Britain for over two centuries. It was the English (Lord Cornwallis) who introduced the Zamindari system in Bengal and other parts of Northern India. Also, emergence of private capitalism, managing agency system, commercial banking system, prevalence of laissez faire policy on the part of the state for quite some time, the railway system and the international trade pattern which persisted in India for long were all due to our historical association with Great Britain. Though attempts are being made to change the features of the colonial economic system after the country became independent in 1947, there have appeared many obstacles in changing the colonial features of the economic system on account of long-standing character of the institutions and traditions established and the emergence and opposition of the vested interests created during the days of the British rule in India.

The same can be said about the economic systems prevailing in countries of Africa which for centuries were colonies of various European countries.

3. *Philosophy of the People and their Value-system.* Philosophical attitude towards worldly affairs and the value-system which people cherish ardently have great influence on the economic system of a country. If people have faith in themselves and their efforts, instead of blind faith in God with fatalistic attitude, if people value dignity of labour, personal freedom and are self-reliant resenting excessive interference in economic affairs by the State as people in the United States and West European countries are, economic system built in such countries — Capitalism — comes to embody all the above characteristics of the people's philosophy and their value-system.

On the other hand, blind faith in God and fatalistic attitude towards life, indifference to material pleasures which are considered as sin, and acceptance of the Maya and Karma philosophy by majority of people in India have had deep impact on the economic system prevailing in India from time to time and even at the present. The typical Indian attitude is fatalistic and submissive with the consequence that we find even at present existence of the system of bonded labour to a considerable extent, and exploitation of tribal agricultural workers by money-lenders-cum-traders in rural areas of the country. Indian cultural values do not regard poverty as a sin and a degradation that can be removed by concerted human efforts. No wonder, such a philosophy and cultural value-system (which is only gradually getting transformed) have had deep impact on the economic system of India.

Similarly, tribal rivalries and the old-world value-system prevalent in many newly independent countries in Africa have had deep impact on the prevailing economic systems there where traditional type of agriculture, hunting, small-scale handicrafts, and little trade still predominate.

What is to be noted in this connection is that changes in philosophical attitude and value-system of people in a country generally come about in a very gradual way (unless there is engineered a violent upheaval as in Russia in 1917) or in China in 1949 by a determined group of dedicated leaders) which means that changes in prevailing economic system in a country can be brought about only gradually in consonance with changes in philosophical attitude of the people and in their value-system.

4. *Role of Eminent and Charismatic Leadership.* Dedicated, intelligent, determined, selfless and charismatic leadership with great appeal among masses of people can bring about changes in the prevailing economic system in a country. Thus Adam Smith dealt a mortal blow to the Mercantilist system that was prevailing in Great Britain for about three centuries and along with Ricardo laid firm foundation of laissez faire capitalism in Great Britain from where it spread to other countries in Europe. Marx and Lenin by their fierce criticism of capitalism succeeded in destroying capitalist system in Russia and replacing it by a new economic system, namely communism. Pandit Jawaharlal Nehru may be said to have laid the foundation of 'a mixed economic system' in India and of democratic socialism.

5. *Trial and Error Method.* Man is a rational animal and can and does learn from his past experience and mistakes. He possesses some capacity of viewing the prevailing economic system objectively and scientifically and make efforts to remove glaring defects in the prevailing economic system and set it along right path. Thus people in Great Britain and many West European countries have come to accept the existence of public sector and increasing role of the State (to which they were opposed vehemently at one time) as necessary part of their economic system to stabilise it at the higher level of employment and for removing fluctuations that characterised laissez faire capitalist economic system causing immense misery to people, as for example, evidenced in the Great Depression of 1929-33.

In India, policy-makers have come to realise some of their mistakes since the era of economic planning commenced in India in 1951. In the light of the past experience, policy-makers have been reshaping their policies and redrawing their priorities, giving greater emphasis on agricultural sector rather than heavy industries sector emphasised by Nehru. They are now emphasising medium and minor irrigation works rather than gigantic irrigational projects like Bhakra-Nangal for which Nehru had great fascination. The policy-makers are now laying greater emphasis on dispersal of industries and balanced regional development. All this will have deep impact on the economic system of the country.

The above discussion should make one thing clear about economic system in a country. An economic system in any country is not a rigid and unchanging system lasting forever. There are various dynamic forces operating inside the country and outside which produce their impact on the economic system of a country and bring about lesser or greater modifications or sometimes even its complete replacement by a new system. But in most cases transformation is gradual. This transformation in the prevailing economic system of a country takes place because of several internal factors like change in the attitude and value-system of the people, discovering of new raw materials or better techniques of production, new scientific discoveries and inventions, emergence of new leader or of formation of military or economic blocs in the international world, or strained or improved relationship with neighbouring countries, attitude of major powers towards other countries and especially developing countries, role played by world organisations like the World Bank and the International Monetary Fund and so on.

It might broadly be said that the success or survival of people in a country depends to a great extent on their ability to change their economic system in consonance with changing times, challenges and dynamic forces that are operating inside and outside any country.

5. CLASSIFICATION OF ECONOMIC SYSTEMS

Jan S. Prybyla has classified economic systems as follows:

(A) Perfectly Competitive Market Model

The perfectly competitive market model, according to Jan S. Prybyla, has the following four basic characteristics:

(*a*) Individual economic units like households and firms own all the factors of production.

(*b*) These household units of firms "autonomously or voluntarily enter into exchange relationships on terms mutually acceptable to the parties to the exchange." To give some details, these households and firms sell their land, labour, capital, and skills to producing units or establishments, from which they derive incomes to purchase goods and services produced by various producing units. The market is the exchange nexus and markets exist for all types of goods and services.

(*c*) While entering into exchange relationship, the main guiding force is the relative prices which are solely influenced by freely operating market forces of demand and supply. In this model, it is assumed that all economic units, namely individuals, households, farms and firms have perfect knowledge of market conditions and of the economy.

(*d*) It is claimed for this model that the freely fluctuating price-mechanism not only allocates various resources according to consumers' preferences (expressed through prices which they are willing or unwilling to pay), but allocates various resources most efficiently. Each economic unit attempts to maximise its returns and this results in the most efficient allocation of community's resources. Thus, freely fluctuating price-mechanism in the perfectly competitive model is not only "a co-ordinating device concerned with internal consistency, but also an optimising instrument."

Thus, the perfectly competitive market model includes elements such as institution of private property, individual freedom, and freely fluctuating price-mechanism which achieves both internal consistency and maximum efficiency in the use of community's resources. This implies that in this model there is no interference by the government in the economic affairs or activities of the people and the perfectly competitive market model is supposed to achieve automatically both maximum satisfaction of consumers on the one hand, and most efficient use of community's resources on the other.

(B) The Absolute Command Model

According to Jan S. Prybyla following are the important characteristics of the absolute command model of economic system:

(*a*) It is the government or central authority that owns all factors of production.

(*b*) It is the central authority which determines the allocation of community's resources and determines what commodities will be produced in what proportions, by what techniques and at what cost or process and at what places; it also sees that all these orders are executed through its administrative machinery.

(*c*) The distribution and consumption of goods and services by people is through the system of physical rationing which is determined by the central authority.

(*d*) The central authority determines the allocation of labour among different occupations and services as also their rewards and the length of hours of work and leisure.

(*e*) Though in such an economy, there is theoretically no place for money, money is introduced ; but money acts only as a unit of account and is used for calculating the efficiency of different units of production.

Thus it would be observed that the essential characteristics of an absolute command model of an economic system are public ownership of all factors or means of production (which implies absence of the motive of personal profit in production), central authority with wide powers to decide all matters concerning production of goods and services and their distribution (naturally this implying comprehensive and centralised economic planning), and translating social decisions into realities and maintaining internal consistency by the central authority.

Thus if in the perfectly competitive market model, it is the people who make of their free will all important economic decisions in regard to production and distribution, in the absolute command model, it is the central authority (may by the government or specially created planning authority by the Government) which makes all these decisions. If in the first model decisions are made with the help of freely fluctuating price-mechanism expressing people's preferences; in the second model, these decisions are made administratively and expressed in physical terms and orders are executed through physical controls. In the absolute command model theoretically the preferences are those of the central authority and there is no regularly established machinery to ascertain preferences of people in respect of consumer goods and services. In theory, in an absolute command model, the assumption is that the central authority, with all its wisdom and expert knowledge at its command, is a better judge to decide what people should consume and what they should not, instead of leaving these matters to free choice of people themselves.

The main features of perfectly competitive model (*i.e.*, pure capitalism) and absolute command model (*i.e.*, pure communism) are put down side-by-side in the following tabular manner to facilitate comparison between the two models embodying opposite features.

Features or Characteristics	*Perfectly Competitive Market Model or Pure Capitalism*	*Absolute Command Model or Pure Communism*
(1)	*(2)*	*(3)*
1. Role of Government	Laissez faire policy with least interference by government in the economic activities of people, government undertaking only functions like defence, law and order, dispensation of justice and some public works.	Government is all powerful and decides all economic matters concerning production, distribution and consumption of goods. All people carry on all their economic activities at the command of the State.
2. Fixing objectives of economic system	People are free to decide and try to attain their objectives. Normally objectives set by individual producer is to maximise personal profit and by consumers to maximise their satisfaction or welfare.	Central government or State fixes all the goals or objectives of the economic activities of the people and of the economic system of the country.
3. Resource Allocation	Each individual consumer and producer decides how to allocate his own resources. It is decided at the individual and firm level. No central planning in allocation of resources.	Rigid central planning setting both goals and allocation of resources among various sectors of the economy by the State.

4. Ownership of resources	All the factors of production like land, capital, etc. are privately owned.	State owns all productive resources of the community.
5. Price Mechanism	Freely fluctuating price mechanism representing preferences of consumers and producers.	All prices are administered prices and are fixed by the State.
6. Competition	Consumers and producers freely compete among themselves for various goods and services which are freely exchanged in markets.	Total absence of competition because of all pervasive role of the State in matters concerning production and consumption of goods and services which are distributed among people through physical rationing.
7. Motives and incentives	Maximisation of personal profit and maximisation of personal satisfaction or welfare.	Maximisation of the welfare of the community as perceived by the State.
8. Income distribution	Distribution of income among various factors of production (*i.e.,* among their owners) based on competition and bargaining strength of different parties in the market.	Shares of income going to different sectors of the economy and to individuals fixed by the State.
9. Savings and Investment	Decisions regarding how much of income is to be saved and to be invested are taken by each individual and firm.	All decisions regarding level of saving and investment to be done by the community are taken by the State.
10. Sovereignty	Sovereignty is of final consumer whose freely expressed preferences decide how producers are going to allocate their resources and what goods they would produce.	Sovereignty rests with the State which decides all matters regarding production and consumption of goods and services.

PURE AND MIXED SYSTEMS

Jan S. Prybyla has observed, and this is also what is noticed by all, that in actual or real world of today, neither the perfectly competitive market model nor the absolute command model is found. Operational economic systems are seen to depart considerably from the above two pure models. In actual life, the economic systems based on the first model mentioned above may contain to a smaller or greater extent various elements of the second model and vice versa. From that point of view, all economic systems today are not pure systems. Prybyla observes: "But whatever the degree of imperfection, the point of departure and assumptions of each real-life economy are extremely important." There are in the world today various economic systems which, however, imperfect, are fundamentally derived from the assumptions of the perfectly competitive market model and there are other economic systems which however market-oriented (as in the case of Yugoslavia) are derived from the fundamental or basic assumptions of the absolute command model. While all economic systems at present are imperfect manifestations of the two pure models and combine elements of both models to a smaller or greater extent, the above aspect must be carefully brone in mind.

We have thus the following classification of various economic systems prevailing in the world at present :

1. Capitalism	(A)	Democratic capitalism (as for example in the United States).
	(B)	Totalitarian capitalism (as under Hitler's Germany and Mussolini's Italy).
2. Socialism	(A)	Market socialism (as in Yugoslavia).
	(B)	Totalitarian socialism (as in the former Soviet Union, East Germany, China, etc.)
3. Mixed Economy		As in India, Sweden, etc.

6. SCOPE OF THE SUBJECT

In this book we begin our study with the description and analysis of Feudalism — an economic system which prevailed throughout Europe for about thousand years (*i.e.*, from roughly 5th to 15th century). We begin with feudalism because it is out of this system and its eventual decay that modern capitalism emerged.

We will analyse the ideology behind modern capitalism and show how laissez faire capitalism emerged. There is special discussion of the capitalist system in the United States which for long has symbolised capitalist development. We analyse the achievements and failures of laissez faire capitalism.

Because of serious failings or evils that were associated with laissez faire capitalism, it came to be gradually transformed into welfare capitalism. Welfare capitalism, the circumstances under which this economic system emerged and the ideology behind the economic system are all explained.

It was out of the failure of laissez faire capitalism that Marx and Marxian Socialism (and communism) emerged. The emergence of Marxian Socialism, with its ideology and theory is explained. Also achievements and failures of Marxian Socialism are analysed.

In the course of time, Marxian socialism and communism invited criticism because of some serious theoretical and other defects that came to be associated with that economic system. This gave rise to market socialism in countries like Yugoslavia. Market socialism, its ideology and its institutions are all explained.

The Chinese adopted their own brand of socialism or communism. Socialist or communist system in China has been explained.

After the end of the Second World War there merged Third World developing countries. Like India most of them have adopted what is described as a system of Mixed Economy. Mixed economy combining features of capitalism and socialism has been explained as also its ideology and institutions. Some of the important problems faced by mixed economy have been analysed.

There is a special reference to Indian economic system which is characterised as mixed economy, to economic planning, to Gandhian economics and to Sarvodya.

The different economic systems under modern technological pressure appear to be facing some common problems and adopting practically similar measures to solve those problems in the process developing some common features. The different economic systems appear to be converging towards a common economic system. The convergence thesis is explained and criticall' examined.

Throughout the analysis, the approach is analytical and scientific all with a view to gain as much knowledge as possible about economic systems under which different peoples of the world have been living at present.

7. APPROACH TO THE STUDY OF ECONOMIC SYSTEMS

The study of different economic systems (that is the comparative study where we analyse different economic systems and compare them with one another) is of great theoretical and practical significance and importance, if we bring correct approach to this study.

The correct approach to the study of economic system comprises of the following points:

1. The student of economic systems or of this comparative study must not start with any bias or prejudice against or in favour of any ideology or an economic system. Our common failing is generally to regard our own economic system as the best and consider all other economic systems as inefficient or unethical or unworthy of close study.

If this study is to be useful, it is necessary that we shed all these personal prejudices to the maximum possible extent against ideologies and economic systems other than our own.

This would mean that the student should approach the study with as much open mind as possible.

2. We must bring scientific and critical approach to this study. We must critically and scientifically analyse and examine each economic system, the ideology behind the system, the geographical, historical and cultural factors that influence the economic system and so on. To properly understand an economic system embraced by a country, it is necessary to know the political developments in the country. Thus the Russian Revolution of October 1917 and emergence and perpetuation of communist system in the Soviet Union can be appreciated properly only if we know the history of the Czarist regime in Russia with extreme exploitation of the masses.

Thus the critical mind should approach the study with open mind ; but we must be critical enough and should be free to point out and criticise logical inconsistencies in any economic system or lack of balance among various institutions that go to make an economic system or contradiction among different objectives which a particular economic system aims to achieve in the short or long run.

3. To understand properly different economic systems, we must study scientifically the different ideologies underlying different economic systems. Without the study of an ideology, we will be unable to understand fully the working of an economic system based on that ideology.

4. When in this comparative study of different economic systems, we compare the achievements and failures of different economic systems, we must take care to see that such comparisons are appropriate. Thus it would be wrong to say that because the economic growth rate in the Soviet Union was smaller than that of the United States, Soviet Communism or economic system was inferior to the United States or capitalist economic system. This is not scientifically correct comparison. It is possible that the United States is endowed with better and more abundant natural resources and therefore produces more wealth and records higher economic growth rate than the former Soviet Union. It is also possible that capitalism has been in operation in the United States for more than 150 years whereas communism or socialism came to the Soviet Union only in 1917. Thus when comparing different economic systems one must be very careful.

5. Different economic systems have a number of objectives which they hope to achieve in the long run.

It would therefore be wrong to condemn an economic system because of short term failures which may be due to natural calamities and disasters or unfavourable international environment. An economic system must be judged in terms of its ability or failure to achieve the stated objectives in the long run.

6. There are certain ideals and objectives which all mankind values. For example, in this fiercely competitive and hard world there will be trade wars and cut-throat competition to capture foreign markets. There would be even

open wars to gain certain ends. This is yet an imperfect world. And therefore everyone wants that his country records the highest growth rate annually. Similarly every individual wants stable employment with rising real income or standard of living. Similarly every individual wants to enjoy maximum freedom as a consumer and producer because freedom is extremely valuable and man resents restrictions by his very nature.

These — higher annual economic growth-rate, full employment, rising standard of living, maximum personal freedom — may be said to be absolute values which all people intensely desire and want to enjoy.

We can compare different economic systems by the extent to which they have succeeded in achieving the above objectives.

But assessing achievements of an economic system may not be an easy tasks. For example, people in India under her mixed economic system may be enjoying freedom but without bread, clothing and shelter as evidenced by nearly 33 per cent of India's total population living below the poverty line whereas in China people may not have the same degree of freedom as consumers and producers but may have guaranteed employment and at least minimum standard of living. In such cases it would be very difficult to arrive at any definite conclusion as regards which is a better economic system. We may have to think of some trade-off point and then decide which is a better economic system. But it is very difficult to find out that trade-off point. Similarly 10 per cent annual economic growth rate under an economic system in a particular country may be accompanied by great amount of pollution and stresses and strains on the people whereas another country with a different economic system may be achieving only half that annual economic growth rate but with minimum pollution and stresses and strains. How do we compare these two economic systems ? What is the trade-off point between growth rate and degree of pollution ? All that a student can do or should do under such circumstances is to try to view the position as critically and objectively as possible and form his own judgement.

If a student bears the above points in mind and approaches the study of different economic systems in a critical spirit, the study would greatly benefit him and give him comprehensive ideas regarding working of different economic systems in the world.

8. IMPORTANCE OF THE STUDY OF ECONOMIC SYSTEMS

We derive the following advantages from the study of different economic systems or in other words due to the under-mentioned reasons, the comparative study of different economic systems assumes great significance.

1. By critically studying different economic systems, we gain a better understanding or knowledge of our own economic system. Thus as G.N. Halm has pointed out : "By comparing it (our economic system) with other systems,

we see it as a whole and become aware of its framework, working mechanism, distinctive features."

2. Study of different economic systems helps us to understand in a better or more comprehensive way certain theoretical questions and institutional arrangements.

Thus while some people in the United States believe that only free market forces, the institution of private property, personal profit motive and competition among consumers and producers can ensure most efficient use of the community's scarce economic resources, the citizens of China believed that replacement of free market forces by central economic planning, of the institution of private property by State ownership or the community's ownership of all productive resources, and of personal profit motive by social welfare motive can alone help the community attain the most efficient use of community's resources and its maximum welfare. Only a comparative study of the principles and institutional set-up in the United States and China will help us to see properly the soundness of the theoretical frameworks and institutional arrangements in the two countries.

3. The study of different economic systems helps us to acquaint ourselves with economic systems which are different from ours. If we are objective enough, we can learn much by understanding defects of our economic system and merits of the other or rival economic system and improve our own economic system by trying to incorporate good features of the rival economic system into our own if such features can be properly absorbed into the system.

At present there appears to be a sort of rivalry between the capitalist countries led by the United States and the socialist countries led by the Russia and China. Each country can and is trying to improve its economic system and its efficiency by learning from the rival system. Thus the United States by an act in 1946 has guaranteed employment to all seeking employment and Russia is trying to provide more and more scope to free market forces and to profit motive.

It would thus be worthwhile for the United States to enquire why its economic system is plagued by inflation and rising unemployment and how socialist economies managed to enjoy stable prices and full employment. The United States government will have to take steps to curb inflation and rising unemployment because some people in the United States, especially those affected by inflation and unemployment are bound to raise the question of non-existence of inflation and unemployment in the socialist countries and why those afflictions should be tolerated by people in the United States.

Similarly people in the socialist countries will come to know about the higher growth-rate, rapid technological advancement and ever-rising standard of living in the United States and are bound to enquire why Russia should not achieve these things. Thus it is as much essential to know other economic systems with their strong and weak points as to know our own economic system. The study of different economic systems helps us to precisely achieve this objective.

4. In the real world, with fierce competition and rivalry raging between the United States and capitalist countries on the one hand and the communist and socialist countries on the other, it is essential to know what others think about our economic systems. Thus it necessary that people and government of the United States know what the people and government of China think of the economic system of the United States. This is because Chinese policy towards the United States will depend upon what Chinese think about the United States. The same is true of the people and government of the China knowing about the economic system of the United States and what people and the government of the United States think of China, its economic system, people and the government. Almost as a universal rule it might be stated that it is much more important to know what others think about us as we think and know about ourselves. The study of different economic systems helps us to do this. This would mean that Indians must carefully study economic systems of other countries, especially of its neighbouring countries like Pakistan and China with whom she will have to live either in peace or occasionally face conflicts.

5. Study of different economic systems gives a warning to us all not to take our economic system for granted or that we can easily substitute our economic system by another system with all its advantages or that we can introduce an economic system by borrowing good features of both socialism and capitalism getting rid at the same time of the disadvantages of both the economic systems.

The study will tell us that no economic system is sacrosanct or holy and that with the changes in time and environment we will have to bring in suitable changes in our economic system.

Thus after the Great Depression of 1929-33, it was realised by the capitalist countries that laissez faire policy (that is policy of least interference by the State in the economic affairs of the people) would result in trade cyclical fluctuations with their depressions, unemployment and mass misery. This has resulted in abandnonment by countries like England and France of the laissez faire policy and government playing a substantial role in the economic affairs of the people.

Also it was realised that competition leads to increasing inequalities of income and wealth in capitalist countries and since these increasing inequalities would one day become intolerable and lead to instability or even violence, the State must take some steps or measures to see that income and wealth are equitably distributed among people in the country. Thus to avoid the evil consequences of extreme inequalities, laissez faire capitalism (which was prevailing at the time of Adam Smith and Ricardo' thought of as an ideal economic system) has undergone much institutional changes. Even in the

United States the government takes the responsibility of providing employment to all or pay unemployment insurance to all those forced to remain unemployed.

Similarly economic system of Russia which at one time was considered holy by the orthodox Marxists has been undergoing substantial changes, increasing role being assigned to market forces and to private profit motive.

The study of different economic systems tells us that it is not easy to replace one type of economic system by a brand new economic system which may catch the fancy of some political and social reformers. Economic system of a country with delicate balance of its different parts is an organic growth and cannot be dismantled overnight and another brand new economic system transplanted in its place.

Thus after the October Revolution, the Soviet Union abolished 'money' thinking that money is a capitalist device through which capitalists made profits and exploited workers. They realised that abolition of money is not so easy and soon money was reintroduced in the Soviet economic system. The same is happening in Russia in respect of the institutions of private property, competition, foreign trade and so on.

6. The study of different economic systems prevailing in different countries would help to improve international relations. The study will tell us that people of different countries have their own history, culture, value-system and factor endowments and are entitled to build their own economic system as they think would help them to realise their socio-economic goals just as we have the right to do that in our own country. The study thus helps us to understand other economic systems which are different from ours and thus help build bridge between people of different countries with their own economic systems.

7. The study of different economic systems prevailing in different countries definitely would make us less dogmatic in our attitude towards our own economic system and more tolerant of other people with their different economic systems. The study will thus broaden our viewpoint and approach which will serve as basis of better relations among different countries of the world.

REFERENCES

1. Jan S. Prybyla — Meaning and Classification of Economic System, An Outline: in Comparative Economic Systems (Edited by Jan S. Prybyla), page 10.
2. Economic Systems — Gregory Grossman (Third Edition).
3. Contemporary Economic Systems—A Comparative Analysis—Carl Landauer, page 2.
4. Economic Systems — Gregory Grossman (Second Edition), page 2.
5. Economic Systems — Gregory Grossman (Second Edition), page 3.
6. Comparative Economic Systems — Loucks and Whitney, page 4.

CHAPTER 2

DIFFERENT TYPES OF ECONOMIC SYSTEMS AND THEIR BROAD FEATURES

1. INTRODUCTION

Since the functioning of important economic systems is to be undertaken later in the book, in this chapter reference is made only to the main features of each economic system.

Feudalism was in existence in different European countries for over a thousand years after the collapse of the Roman Empire. Feudalism gradually gave place in many West European countries to Mercantilist system by about the 15th century. Mercantilism in its turn gave place in most West European countries to capitalist system of economy as a consequence of the changing times, new challenges and mood of the people and powerful advocacy of that system (*i.e.,* capitalism) by the English Classical School. Gradually there appeared reaction to the capitalist system of economy on account of the various evils which came to be associated with it. Marx was a powerful critic of capitalism which in many countries came to be subsequently replaced by communism. Theoretically it is possible to conceive of pure models of capitalism and communism. But in the actual world we never find these pure models either of capitalism or communism or pure models of any other economic system in operation at any time. Each model has tried to borrow consciously or unconsciously because it found it advantageous, some features of the other economic system. Since no country starts with an absolutely new slate, the heritage or traces of the old system which is being modified or even entirely replaced linger on.

For example, even in the hey-days of 'pure' capitalism or *laissez faire* capitalism, even Adam Smith made exceptions and allowed interference by the state in the economic affairs of the people, for example, for breaking the power of monopoly, in the sphere of international trade to take retaliatory measures, for fixing rate of interest and so on. With the progress of time and under-changed conditions, the so-called pure or *laissez faire* capitalism departed more and more from its theoretical model as presented by Ricardo and borrowed various features such as public sector and increasing role of the state in the economic affairs of the people. Thus pure capitalism does not exist even in the United States at present; possibly it never operated in any country even in the past.

The same can be said of the pure model of communism. In fact, human nature and psychology being what they are, it is just not possible to entirely destroy the old economic system and institute in its place a totally brand new system. This would imply that there never was in operation 'pure' communist system even in the former USSR and China at any time. The remnants of the old economic system persisted along with the newly established system.

Later on when the shortcomings of the so-called pure communist system surfaced, the communist countries reintroduced some of the features of capitalism. Thus at present in Russia farmers who generally work on collective farms are given small plots of land which they can cultivate on their own and keep the profits for themselves; also consumers are being given greater scope to show their preferences to provide guidance for production of goods and services which is planned; greater scope is being provided to factory managers to show individual initiative and so on.

To sum up, though theoretically it is possible to conceive of pure models of different economic systems, in actual practice, these 'pure' models have never been in operation. From that point of view all economic systems may be said to be 'mixed economic systems.' (It is in this sense that Prof. Samuelson calls US economy 'a mixed economy').

2. BROAD FEATURES OF DIFFERENT ECONOMIC SYSTEMS

Though it has now become a common practice to broadly divide economic systems into three broad categories, namely 'Capitalism,' 'Communism,' and 'Mixed Economy,' it would be convenient to look at different economic systems historically along with those that prevail at present and also to pay attention to sub-systems and their characteristics.

3. FEUDALISM AND ITS FEATURES

After the break-up of the Roman Empire, it was Feudalism or Feudal System that came into existence and remained in existence practically in the whole of Europe from about 5th century to 15th century.

The main features or characteristics of Feudalism or the Feudal System were as follows:

We can illustrate the features of Feudalism by taking the illustration of England and the type of economy that prevailed there under Feudalism. (It should be noted that for all practical purposes this analysis holds good in the case of other countries also where Feudalism was prevailing during 5th to 15th century).

There was during the Feudal days hardly any feeling of nationalism or national unity among people of England. England was divided into several Manors and there was a Manorial Lord in each case. Agriculture was the chief occupation of the people and the Manorial Lord was for all practical purposes the owner of the land in the Manor (though it was supposed to be held on behalf of the King of England whose authority was for all practical purposes only nominal). As noted already, agriculture was the main occupation of the people and each Manor as far as possible tried to be self-sufficient both because of the extremely unsatisfactory state of the means of transport and communications, and also because of rivalry and continual welfare that used to go on among neighbouring Manorial Lords.

The Manorial Lord got the land in his Manor cultivated with the help of vassals some of whom enjoyed certain rights but most of whom belonged to the class of serfs. Agriculture was carried on in the traditional manner with a view to make the Manor or sometimes even villages self-sufficient in respect of important foodgrains. Agriculture was of the open-field system. All land was divided into two or three strips, each being left fallow every year to enable land to recover its fertility. Naturally agricultural productivity was very low.

The vassals and serfs were closely bound to the Manorial Lord to whom they paid annual rent partly in the form of services. In return the Manorial Lord gave serfs livery and maintenance and it was his responsibility to see that they did not face undue hardships or distress. A Manor was thus a close-knit and more or less self-sufficient economic unit with agriculture as the predominant occupation of the people.

In each Manor and even in every village there were small-scale industries producing mainly for the local market essential goods like cloth, pots and pans and agricultural implements. Markets were mostly local and limited and therefore production of goods was carried on in households and on a very small scale.

Since no village or manor could be self-sufficient in all respects, there were held weekly bazars on specified days at specified places and often there were annual fairs where agriculturists sold their surplus for various articles like salt and metalware not available locally. Prices of most goods were governed by tradition. All disputes were settled in Manorial courts where the Manorial Lord presided often with wide powers over his vassals and serfs sometimes including the power of sentencing a person to death for specified crimes.

Once the harvesting season was over, there was generally continual warfare among different Manorial Lords, the vassals and serfs being required in duty-bound to render military service for specified number of days in return for the Manorial Lord's land which they were permitted to cultivate.

Continual political disturbances and mutual warfare, predominance of traditional type of agriculture, small-scale industries mostly producing for local markets all meant that during thousand years or so of Feudalism, the economic conditions in different countries of Europe where Feudalism prevailed were for all practical purposes stagnant. Agricultural and industrial efficiency was very low and majority of people on the whole lived a miserable type of living compared to present standards of living in Western Europe.

4. MERCANTILIST SYSTEM AND ITS FEATURES

Feudalism came to be gradually replaced by Mercantilist System in most of the countries of Europe by about the end of the 15th or beginning of the 16th century and was the dominant economic system in European countries till about the middle of the 18th century. It is important to know the main features of the Mercantilist System because it was as a reaction to this system that *laissez faire* capitalism arose in most countries of Western Europe after the second half of the 18th century.

Following were the main features of the Mercantilist System:

By about the end of the 15th century and certainly by about the beginning of the 16th century, feudal organisation that prevailed in different countries of Europe gave place to the emergence of 'National States.' Hereafter England, France, Spain, Portugal, etc., were no more assemblage of people grouped in Manors and fighting among themselves but emerged as Nations. Those countries gradually emerged as National States; people in those countries being united by the feeling of nationalism generated on account of common ancestry, common language, culture, religion and common economic interests. It should be understood that while nationalism is a unifying force it is also a divisive force — distinguishing England as a nation from Spain, Portugal and France as different nations and those people as of different nationalities.

Emergence of National States in Europe therefore immediately gave rise to national rivalries and national wars which came to characterise the 16th and 17th centuries.

The major problem therefore was how to make the Nation strong so that it may prove victorious in wars over other nations. It was also at about this time that the old subsistence and barter economy that prevailed during the days of feudalism was gradually giving place to money-economy, money mainly then consisting of gold and silver. If only a nation came to possess gold and silver, it could purchase anything at home and abroad, raise armies, build navies and make the Nation strong. Extent of the possession of gold therefore became the foot-rule or measure of the strength of a Nation.

How to get gold, especially if a country like England which had no gold mines, therefore became the major economic problem. The only way to get gold was by exporting manufactured goods to other countries and not importing goods at all from those countries or importing as little as possible. The question of exporting perishable agricultural commodities did not arise then because oceanic transport was very much underdeveloped and slow and incapable of carrying speedily bulky and easily perishable agricultural commodities. This meant to boost up exports and to cut down imports (thus forcing the other country to make payments in gold for exports), the country must promote export industries.

The consequence of all this was that the state intervened and regulated every economic activity of society. It regulated in a comprehensive way the prices of industrial raw materials, wage rates, quality of manufactured goods, their home consumption, navigation and so on, all with a view to promote exports and cut down imports with the objective to get gold with which to strengthen state politically and economically.

Thus, to summarise, the features of the Mercantilist System were: emergency of Nationalism and National States; national rivalry and national wars; objective of making the Nation strong; National strength lay in the acquisition of gold; international trade (and not agriculture) became the main instrument of getting gold from abroad by exporting manufactured goods to the maximum possible extent and completely avoiding or cutting down imports to the minimum and thus forcing the other country to part with gold with which to build navy, standing army and making the Nation relatively stronger than others ; and to achieve all these objectives State control and regulation over every economic activity of the people in the country. Rivalry between Elizabethan England and contemporary Spain and eventual destruction of the Spanish armeda and Spanish power and emergence of England as the most powerful National State typically embody all the above Mercantilist principles and practices.

5. CAPITALISM

Capitalism as an economic system has undergone substantial changes since it emerged in West European countries and in the USA after the second half of the 18th century. Broadly we can say that it was '*Laissez Faire* Capitalism' that prevailed between 1815 (end of Napoleonic war) and 1914 (the beginning of World War I). After 1914 and especially after the Great Depression of 1929-33, the type of capitalism that has come to prevail in Western countries and even in the USA may be called 'Managed Capitalism,' or 'Guided' or 'Regulated Capitalism' or 'Welfare Capitalism.'

We shall describe here the main features of both the types of capitalism.

6. MAIN FEATURES OF *LAISSEZ FAIRE* CAPITALISM

Following are the main features of *laissez faire* capitalism that prevailed in West European countries and in the USA in the 19th century:

1. *Individual is the Best Judge of Self-Interest.* It is assumed that every individual is the best judge of what is in his best interest and therefore he should be left free to do what he wants to do as a consumer and producer, as a saver and investor and so on. He should not be dictated by the State to do this or not to do that, either as a consumer or as a producer.

2. *Consumers' Sovereignty.* The above thing implies that under *laissez faire* capitalism consumer with his unlimited freedom to spend his income as he likes is sovereign and decisions by numerous producers as to what to produce and what not to produce are taken on the basis of preferences expressed by free choice of consumers.

3. *Freely Functioning Price Mechanism.* Consumers express their preferences through freely operating price-mechanism. Consumers are prepared to pay more for goods for which they have higher preferences and less for goods of lower preferences. Price-mechanism thus acts as a signalling system indicating to the producers preferences of consumers and influencing allocation of resources of produces.

4. *Profit-Motive and Freedom and Private Enterprise.* Under *laissez faire* capitalism all production is carried on with a view to maximise personal profit. Naturally it would be in the interest of producers to produce those goods and services for which consumers show higher preference than goods of lower preference as the former would help them maximise personal profit. Personal profit motive is the most powerful incentive under *laissez faire* capitalism that influences the allocation of resources among various alternative uses.

Thus freely operating price-mechanism while on the one hand ensures maximum satisfaction to consumers, on the other hand, ensures the most efficient use of community's scarce resources.

5. *Institution of Private Property.* Freedom of producers and entrepreneurs assumes existence of private ownership of means of production. Under *laissez faire* capitalism the institution of private property (in land, capital and other sources of production) is sacrosanct. Under *laissez faire* capitalism owners of private property are free to use their resources as they like and there is no restraint on such use by the State.

6. *Existence of Competition.* Competition among consumers and among producers is the very soul of *laissez faire* capitalism. It is only if competition among consumers to secure through consumer goods maximum satisfaction and among producers to produce goods with a view to make maximum personal profit prevails that it will ensure efficient functioning of price-mechanism and ensure both maximum satisfaction of consumers and most efficient use of community's scarce resources.

7. *Harmony between Personal Interest and Interest or Welfare of Society.* Even as each individual works for maximising his personal profit under competitive regime (say by producing new commodities or inventing new processes to produce old commodities cheaply and sell them at lower prices in competitive market, or by trying to become the best doctor, or surgeon or architect), he will, at the same time, as said by Adam Smith, through unseen hand of providence, be serving the cause of maximising social welfare which was no part of this intention. Thus under *laissez faire* capitalism where each individual tries to carry on activities for his own interest under competitive regime, there appears to be perfect harmony between individual welfare and welfare of society. There appears to be no conflict between the two.

8. *Non-Interference by the State (or Laissez Faire).* If under *laissez faire* capitalism an individual acting for his personal interest or profit automatically ensures maximum social welfare, if there is thus no conflict between individual welfare and social welfare, and if freely operating price-mechanism under competitive system automatically ensures maximum satisfaction of consumers and the most efficient use of community's scarce resources, there is no point whatsoever in State trying to interfere and regulate economic activities of the people. People should be left free as consumers and producers, as savers and investors to do what they like without any direction of interference by the State. *Laissez faire* capitalism is thus 'a planless economy' where millions of consumers and producers take their own decisions in their personal interest.

But under *laissez faire* capitalism, the State may be called upon to do certain essential public functions like defence of the country and maintenance of law and order, and civil works like roads and bridges which private individuals may not be forthcoming to undertake as they may fear that profits in these ventures may not be maximum or actually there may be losses.

Under *laissez faire* capitalism, the State is thus called upon to do minimum functions such as defence of the country, maintenance of law and order (to see that institution of private property remains intact and there is peaceful atmosphere for individuals to carry on their economic activities smoothly) and construction of certain civil works like roads and bridges which because of large investments involved and long gestation period, private producers may not be interested in undertaking. (It is worth noting in this connection that in England even construction of roads, canals, railways and shipping activities were undertaken by private individuals out of profit motives).

7. FEATURES OF 'MANAGED' OR 'REGULATED' OR 'MODERN' CAPITALISM

As *laissez faire* capitalism started on its march gradually but inevitably its shortcomings and serious defects began attracting the attention of its critics.

For example, it became evident that some of the assumptions of *laissez faire* capitalism were not valid, or became invalid in rapidly changing world. Thus it was not true that man always knows what is in his best interest; it also came to be realized that at least in the short-run there can be serious conflict between individual interest and interest of society. It came to be observed that price-mechanism which was supposed to work smoothly and flexibly under competitive conditions ensuring maximum satisfaction for consumers and most efficient allocation of community's resources did not work as expected. On the contrary competition and competitive rivalries among producers gave rise to monopoly, duopoly and oligopoly which were in a position to control market, production and supply of commodities and prices. For example, a monopolist would purposely create artificial scarcities by keeping resources idle, charge higher prices and make huge monopoly profits, all at the cost of welfare of the society. Competitive capitalism gave rise to monopoly capitalism which meant neither maximum satisfaction for consumers nor most efficient use of community's resources.

There were also other evils of *laissez faire* capitalism. In a competitive regime with minimum State intervention, those with productive assets and skills were in a strong bargaining position compared to those with no assets and with only unskilled labour to sell at whatever price in the bargain, as some income at any cost is necessary for their daily subsistence. Thus *laissez faire* capitalism gave rise to great inequalities of income and wealth so that in course of time, society came to be divided into 'Haves' and 'Have Nots.' There was class hatred and jealousy and fear of class conflict or class war disturbing social peace and political stability.

The greatest single factor that shook the faith of even the ardent believers in *laissez faire* capitalism was the Great Depression of 1929-33 and the publication of 'The General Theory' by J.M. Keynes in 1936 with his severe attack on the shortcomings of *laissez faire* capitalism and therefore inviting to some extent State intervention and regulation.

It had come to be assumed that in a competitive *laissez faire* economy wage levels will be completely flexible and therefore the economy would automatically attain the level of full employment and stabilise. Say'sLaw of the Markets was one of the corner-stones of *laissez faire* capitalism. It stated that demand creates its own supply and therefore there will never be general glut of commodities in the market and continually falling prices creating unemployment.

But it had come to be observed that automatic functioning of *laissez faire* capitalism not only did not provide full employment of resources, especially of labour but on the contrary came to be visited by economic fluctuations (*i.e.*, booms and depressions) which became almost a regular feature of *laissez faire* capitalism. The Great Depression of 1929-33 was so severe that almost a quarter of working population in the USA and West European capitalist countries lost their jobs and income and savings (due to bank failure as State intervention in any economic sphere was not permitted under the philosophy of *laissez faire* capitalism). Naturally, this meant tremendous loss of opportunities to create much wanted wealth and incalculable misery for the vast unemployed who had for long to live on State aid and in a state of moral and material degradation.

It was against this background that J.M. Keynes published his book 'The General Theory' in 1936 and showed that *laissez faire* capitalism would not automatically and necessarily provide full employment and much less stabilise economy at the level of full employment.

In order to remove some of the serious defects and evils of *laissez faire* capitalism, Keynes advocated some degree of State intervention and regulation while at the same time maintaining the fundamental features of capitalism, namely, personal freedom, personal profit motive, price-mechanism and competition. It is this book which created profound effect in all capitalist countries where *laissez faire* capitalism gradually gave place especially after World War II to what may be called 'Managed Capitalism' or 'Controlled Capitalism' or 'Regulated Capitalism' or 'Welfare Capitalism.'

Main Features of 'Managed' or 'Regulated' or 'Welfare' (or Modern) Capitalism

Since the Great Depression of 1929-33, and especially after the end of the World War II, most of the West European countfies as also the USA are moving more and more away from *laissez faire* capitalism and the State has been using various devices to 'manage' or 'regulate,' or 'guide' capitalism in such a way that while retaining as far as possible the fundamental features of capitalism such as the institution of private property, personal profit motive, freedom of consumers and producers, competition and freely operating price-mechanism, the above-mentioned evils of *laissez faire* capitalism are either reduced or if possible eliminated. Following are the main features of 'Managed' or 'Regulated' or 'Welfare' capitalism:

1. *Anti-Monopoly and Anti-Trust Laws.* Since competition is the soul of capitalism and since monopoly, duopoly, and oligopoly come in the way of maximising consumer satisfaction and most efficient use of community's productive resources, attempts are made through legislative measures to prevent emergence of monopoly power and break such monopolies where they have already made their appearance. For example, in the USA the Sherman Anti-Trust Act of 1880, the Celler-Kefauver Anti-Merger Act of 1950, and Mcguire Act of 1952 were passed. All these legislative measures aim at preventing industrial combinations and emergence of or breaking monopoly, power of industrial establishments.

2. In the USA, 'The Small Business Act' was passed in 1953 and the same year 'The Small Business Administration' was set up. Financial and technical

assistance is made available by the State through this institution for starting and running of small-scale industrial units. In the USA, 'The Small Business Investment Act' was passed in 1958 with a view to help development of small-scale industries.

3. In most capitalist countries, agricultural sector is being helped by devices such as support prices, encouraging their export through bilateral trade agreements to ensure better prices to agriculturists, providing cheap credit and so on.

4. As a measure to fight trade-cyclical fluctuations that characterised *laissez faire* capitalism, monetary policy (with its instruments of quantitative controls, namely, the Bank Rate Policy, the Open Market Operations and the Variable Reserve Ratio and various qualitative or selective controls) is being used in most capitalist countries to a greater and greater extent.

5. Along with monetary policy and possibly as a more effective instrument to remove many of the evils of *laissezfaire* capitalism, greater and greater use is being made in all capitalist countries of Fiscal Policy (*i.e.*, Taxation and Expenditure Policy of the Government or Budgetary Policy). It is being utilised not only as an anti-trade cyclical device but also as an effective instrument to reduce extreme inequalities of income, to bring about development of depressed area (which exist even in developed countries like the USA) by offering tax concessions and tax holidays to entrepreneurs ready to start industries in such areas and by providing various infrastructure facilities through appropriate government expenditure policy.

6. The capitalist countries have all given up the free trade policy which they had come to adopt during the days of *laissez faire* capitalism and have instead adopted protectionist policies to help and develop domestic industries in the face of foreign competition. Thus instead of Free Trade Policy, protectionist trade policy is being used to an increasing extent by capitalist countries to ensure development of industries, use of domestic resources and maintain and raise level of employment at home. Thus prohibition of import of some items, import duties, quota fixation, export duties and bilateral trade agreements are being increasingly used as part of positive trade policy by capitalist countries instead of free trade policy of *laissez faire* days.

7. Most of the capitalist countries have, mainly as a consequence of the advocacy of J.M. Keynes, brought into existence 'public sector' with which to have some sort of control over the predominant private sector. Thus in the USA, the Government undertook the Tennessee Valley project for development of a backward region. In the United Kingdom, the Bank of England was nationalised and so also coal and iron industries so that by controlling these strategic heights it should be possible to exercise control over the private sector and achieve important socio-economic objectives such as maintaining higher level of employment and output, reduction of inequalities of income and wealth and

avoidance of trade cyclical fluctuations. In France also four major commercial banks came to be nationalised for achieving similar socio-economic objectives.

8. Many capitalist countries like the UK and France came to adopt some sort of planning. The type of planning adopted is not of the type adopted in communist countries but is of different type. It is democratic planning where people's willing co-operation is sought in the formulation and execution of the plan. As regards the method of implementation of the plan, the insistence is not on command as in the case of communist countries but on various inducements whereby private sector enterprises are, through various inducements such as tax concessions and monetary subsidies, persuaded to move in a particular direction so that plan policy and plan targets are broadly attained. This sort of planning is known as 'democratic planning' or 'indicative planning' or 'planning by inducements' (instead of planning from the Centre or planning by command or direction as in the communist countries).

The USA may not have adopted planning as such but it has detailed regulations governing important and essential industries. The USA has also passed an Act in 1946 guaranteeing employment to everyone seeking employment failing which he is paid by the State maintenance allowance till he gets a job.

9. Since the Great Depression, it has come to be realised how an individual by himself is powerless in the face of complex and diverse forces influencing capitalist economic system. Since 1930s and much more so after the World War II, the USA and other capitalist countries of Western Europe have introduced (gradually though) comprehensive welfare schemes. These welfare schemes generally known as Social Security Schemes aim at providing cash benefits when regular monetary earnings are cut off because of unemployment, retirement due to old age, death, total disability, etc. Thus, the welfare measures or social security include schemes covering unemployment insurance, workmen's compensation in case of accidents, maternity benefits, children's allowances, and special assistance in the case of blind, disabled, dependent children and low income group families not covered by any of the above schemes. In addition, in some capitalist countries (as for example, in the USA) there are veterans' benefits, public health programme of immunisation of children and maternal health, recreation facilities, educational loans, public housing and subsidised home-ownership at favourable mortgage rates. The entire concept behind these welfare measures or Social Security is that no individual in a capitalist economic system should suffer for no fault of his and that it is the moral responsibility of the society to see that every citizen is guaranteed tolerable minimum standard of living under even the most adverse conditions from the point of view of an individual or a family.

From the description of the characteristics or features of 'Managed' or 'Regulated' or 'Welfare Capitalism' of modern times, it should become clear how far and in what direction former *laissez faire* capitalism has been transforming itself into a new form of capitalism attempting to preserve at the same time, the basic or fundamental features of capitalism to the maximum possible extent. Modern capitalism in West European countries and the USA shows the above features.

8. FASCISM AS AN ECONOMIC SYSTEM: ITS MAIN FEATURES

As we have already seen, Karl Marx and other communist critics mounted a serious attack on *laissez faire* capitalism and its functioning. They were particularly severe on the exploitation of labour in the form of surplus value pocketed by the employers. They pointed out the inner contradictions of capitalist system and its eventual but inevitable collapse. Marx also made an appeal to the workers to organise themselves and bring about destruction of capitalism, if necessary by revolutionary and violent methods.

One consequence of this criticism was that trade union organisations and labour parties got established in all capitalist countries including Germany and Italy. It was however in Russia that peasants and workers brought about in the October Revolution of 1917 complete destruction of capitalistic system (or whatever the form of capitalism had assumed) in the former USSR.

It was in response to this attack by labouring classes on capitalism with the eventual aim of its destruction that put capitalism in some of Western European countries on the defensive. Desperate attempts by capitalists to save capitalism it assumed the form of Nazism in Germany and Fascism in Italy, both sharing the same fundamental features.

The man features of Nazi or Fascist (the two terms are practically interchangeable) economic system were as follows:

1. The institution of private property was allowed to remain in existence; but the allocation of private resources into various lines of production was done by the State according to priorities the State deemed fit. (Since Hitler after coming to power in 1932 had the aim of waging war against its erstwhile enemies England and France and later on against its mortal foe, the former USSR, Germany naturally preferred production of 'guns to butter').

2. The State put national interest above private interest and assumed authority to decide all economic matters regarding what to produce, where, how and how the produce would be distributed among different sections and individuals of the community. Private profit-making was allowed ; but the State determined the rate of profit to be made by private property owners.

3. Since the greater emphasis was on nationalism, no room was given to ideas like class-war prevalent under capitalism and communism. Both workers and employers were to put forward their joint efforts for making the Father Land strong so that it can have its due place in the sun.

4. Though the institution of private property was maintained, every aspect of economic life, namely production, choice of occupation, distribution of income, international trade and foreign exchange operations, banking and so on were all regulated with extremely complicated system of regulations which together came to form a National Plan. Thus economic planning became an important feature of Nazi or Fascist economic system. Fascism or Nazism is often defined as dictatorship of the rightist forces and desperate efforts by capitalists to protect capitalism through the dictator and appeal to the sense of nationalism against communism which represented dictatorship of the left (*i.e.*, of workers).

Can we call Nazi economic system or National Socialist Economy under Hitler a capitalist economy or a socialist economic system?

The following points are put forward to prove that Nazi or Fascist economic system was a sort of capitalism:

1. Private enterprise economy was maintained. Attempt was made to preserve basic institutions of private property, private enterprises and private profit.

2. In several instances, the National Socialist Party (*i.e.*, Nazis) believed that they were returning or reintroducing a free enterprise economy rather than centrally planned economy. "The destruction of the labour unions, the increasing power of the employer as 'leader' in all labour relations, the refusal to nationalise the banking system and the importance of big business in the administration of industrial production — all these were interpreted as evidence of a purer form of capitalism."[1]

3. For many years, the National Socialists continued to think "in terms of a private enterprise economy." They were often not aware of the "economic implications, possibilities and potentialities of the system of controls they had created." (For example, we have also seen the steps taken by Hitler for the elimination of free pricing process, his wage controls and enforced distribution of labour among different occupations and services, his investment controls and controls over foreign trade and foreign exchange transactions).

On the other hand the following arguments are brought against National Socialism (*i.e.*, Nazism or Fascism) to prove that the economic system could not be identified with Private Enterprise Economy or Capitalism:

1. Free market forces in the case of most of the spheres like pricing, allocation of resources, saving and investment, foreign trade and foreign exchange transactions were to a very great extent suppressed and replaced by direct controls.

2. Though much of capitalist facade was maintained outwardly, Fascist or Nazi economic system was in fact "a command economy." For example, though the Nazi or the Fascist regime was eager to give the appearance of

personal freedom of choice in occupation, in reality citizens had not much choice in this respect whatsoever. Thus membership of the Labour Front in Germany was supposed to be voluntary; but it was also a fact that unless a worker was a member of the Labour Front it was for all practical purposes impossible for him to get any job.

3. According to Halm, "The regime could easily have become a true command economy." For example, because prices, wages, and profits did no longer guide production, there was no need to maintain the income distribution of the private enterprise system.

4. The National Socialist System cannot qualify as a private enterprise economy, when under a regime of ruthless dictatorship citizen's individual freedom was suppressed and minds were tried to be controlled by massive propaganda machine of the State.

By way of conclusion, it may be said that Nazi or Fascist economic system (which had most intense hatred for Soviet communism) may be said to be capitalism preparing for functioning under total war conditions. Thus what all rules and regulations were adopted under Nazism and Fascism by Hitler and Mussolini during their regimes came to be adopted during World War II in the United Kingdom noted for its capitalist system.

9. SOCIALISM AS AN ECONOMIC SYSTEM: ITS MAIN FEATURES

There are many definitions of socialism, each emphasising according to the subjective or personal preferences of the persons who define that the term, emphasising one or the other aspect of socialism in terms of ownership of factors of production, or planning or income distribution.

There are many brands of socialism. There is the orthodox socialism; there is 'democratic' or 'liberal socialism.' We shall consider the features of 'democratic' or 'liberal' socialism later. Here we shall mainly deal with 'orthodox' model of socialism.

We may refer to some well-known definitions of socialism as an economic system and then describe its main features.

H.D. Dickinson defines socialism as follows:

"Socialism is an economic organisation of society in which the material means of production are owned by the whole community and utilised according to a general economic plan, all members being entitled to benefit from the results of such socialised planned production on the basis of equal rights."[2]

Sidney and Beatrice Webb write thus about socialism: "The essential feature in socialisation is that industries and services, with the instruments of production which they require, should not be owned by individuals and the industrial and social administration should not be organised for the purpose of obtaining private profit."[3]

Before we describe features of socialism, it would be worth noting the reasons or background against which socialism emerged.

By the beginning of the 19th century, evils of capitalism began to come to the surface. It came to be observed that capitalism tended to give rise to monopoly, economic wastages, increasing inequalities in the distribution of income and wealth, instability, and above all exploitation of workers by employers. Socialism arose as an alternative method to organise production of wealth and its distribution in such a way that the defects of capitalist methods of production and distribution are removed. Against this background it would be now easy to describe the main features of socialism.

From the above two definitions of socialism the following prominent features of Socialist economic system may be said to distinguish that system.

1. *Social Ownership of the Factors of Production.* Social or collective ownership of the means of production distinguishes socialism from capitalism where ownership of the various factors of production vests in private individuals; under socialism, society as a whole or collectively owns factors of production.

2. *Production Guided not by Private Profit but by Social Welfare.* The fact that factors of production are owned not by private individuals but collectively by society implies that unlike under capitalism where the motive of private profit guides production of goods and services, under socialism it is directed towards attaining and maximising social welfare. This means that unlike capitalism where private entrepreneurs take decisions regarding what to produce, where and how and how the production is to be distributed, mainly with a view to maximise personal or private profit, under socialism all these decisions are taken by the public authority (*i.e.,* by the State) in the interest of society.

3. *Existence of Planning.* H. D. Dickinson states that planning implies "the making of major economic decisions — what and how much is to be produced, and to whom it is to be allocated — by the conscious decision of a determinate authority, on the basis of a comprehensive survey of the economic system as a whole."[4]

Since all factors of production are owned by the State and since it has to take all the important decisions such as what to produce, where, how and how to distribute the wealth produced, the socialist economic system necessarily implies acceptance of economic planning. Under capitalism where factors of production are owned by private individuls who produce goods and services for maximising private profit, reliance is placed on freely fluctuating price mechanism which brings about automatic allocation of various resources among alternative lines of production and therefore no planning is deemed necessary under capitalism. But under socialism with collective ownership of factors of production and with the responsibility of managing them to achieve maximum social welfare, economic planning becomes inevitable.

4. *Economic Equality.* One of the evils of capitalism where means of production are privately owned and used for maximising private profit was great inequalities in income and wealth and economic power.

Socialism was critical of extreme inequalities of income and wealth and naturally the consequence of social or collective ownership of the means of production and also the objective of maximising social welfare imply that socialism aims, if not at complete equality in distribution of income, at least that there would not be extreme inequalities of income and whatever inequalities there are, would be functional and not because of private ownership of means of production. Some inequalities would be there under socialism because different persons are called upon to perform different functions according to their abilities and because they are contributing differently to national production.

Also not only will there be greater equality in distribution of income but every individual will have equal opportunity for the development of his faculties and personality so that he can make his maximum contribution to national product and social welfare.

10. 'LIBERAL' OR 'DEMOCRATIC' SOCIALISM

The working definition of democratic or liberal socialism is stated as follows:

Democratic or liberal socialism refers to "the movement that aims to vest in society as a whole, rather than in individuals, the ownership and management of all capital goods used in large-scale production to the end of increasing national income and distributing it more equally without materially destroying the individual's economic motivation or his freedom of occupational and consumer choice."[5]

Liberal socialism as an economic system is characterised by the following features:

1. Liberal socialism lies somewhere midway between private enterprise economy or capitalism on the one hand, and authoritarian communist economy on the other.

2. With free enterprise system (*i.e.,* with capitalism), liberal socialism "shares freedom of occupational choice and consumer's sovereignty, the use of prices to direct production and to assign productive resources, some inequality in income distribution, and belief in the necessity of decentralisation of management of production. On the other hand, it (*i.e.,* liberal socialism) resembles the collectivist character of authoritarian socialism because it consciously strives for social and economic goals. Under liberal socialism, the government owns at least the strategically important material means of production, and tries to make income distribution more equal. A central

economic authority determines the rate of capital accumulation and somehow provides necessary guidance where automatic market forces cease to operate."

"Liberal socialism mainly differs from the private enterprise system because it provides for state-owned industries which are not operated for private profit."[6]

Democratic or liberal socialism is clearly non-Marxian and is generally associated with the growth and development of democratic institutions in West European countries. If Marxian socialism held the view that there is no possibility of socialism evolving out of capitalism whose basic institutions, according to Marx, existed to protect interests of owners of the means of production, and therefore must be destroyed by violence, the democratic or liberal socialists hold the belief that with the establishment of democracy and parliamentary form of government with free elections, it is possible to achieve socialism by voting to power the working class.[7]

11. COMMUNISM AS AN ECONOMIC SYSTEM AND ITS FEATURES

Often the terms 'Socialism' and 'Communism' are used interchangeably as if both mean the same thing. Thus the former USSR called itself Union of Soviet 'Socialist' Republic. Many refer to the former USSR as a Communist country. While there are many features common to both (such as society's or collective ownership of the means of production, planning, absence of private profit motive, emphasis on social welfare and so on), often distinction is and should be made between socialism and communism. Following are the points of difference between the two:

1. Communism believes that so long as the institution of private property and private ownership of the means of production, and production for profit exist, the society will be divided into two classes, the 'Haves' and 'Have-Nots' and class-war appears inevitable. The interests of the two classes being in conflict and class-war, being inevitable, the final aim of communism is elimination of the institution of private property, of the private ownership of means of production, of production for private profit, and thus complete elimination of the bourgeoise class of property-owners.

2. The communists advocate violence to overthrow capitalism and its substitution by communism.

Unlike socialism, communism believes that unless violence and revolutionary methods are used, capitalism cannot be destroyed. Hence they appeal to workers to be ready for violent revolution (and do not believe like socialism in parliamentary and evolutionary method of introducing communism in place of capitalism).

3. While socialism is compatible with nationalism, communism believes that workers of all countries have common interests and therefore they must

combine to give common fight to destroy capitalism wherever it exists and stop exploitation everywhere. Communists believe that workers of the world must unite because capitalists of all countries will collaborate among themselves to protect their class interests. Thus communism is essentially international in outlook and appeals to all workers of the world to combine, irrespective of their nationalities.

4. When capitalism is overthrown, and when working class acquires control over the State, since workers are not trained as yet in the art of administration, there will have to be for a temporary period, dictatorship of the proletariat, in order that resistance of bourgeoise class and all anti-communists to communism is successfully destroyed.

5. The policy formulation and implementation of economic plans which will come to be introduced under communism will have to be in the hands of trained and disciplined workers of the party, *i.e.,* Communist Party.

6. Once communism is established and institution of private property is abolished, the State as constituted at present by the capitalists for the preservation of the interests of the capitalist class will just wither away in the face of existence of classless society and elimination of exploitation of one class by another. The classes of 'Haves' and 'Have-Nots' come into existence solely on the basis of existence of private property. Once the institution of private property is destroyed, there will be classless society. "There will vanish all need for force, for the subjugation of one man to another, one section of society to another, since people will grow accustomed to observing the elementary conditions of social existence without force and without subjugation."[8]

12. MARKET SOCIALISM IN YUGOSLAVIA

Yugoslavia broke away from Russia and gradually evolved its own system of economy having realised the serious shortcomings of the Soviet type economic system of communism. "... in reaction (to Soviet type communism) the Yugoslavian government set up to develop a system of workers' control in a communal economy."

Yugoslavia developed its own peculiar and highly distinctive economic system — "a socialist market economy with workers' management and planned economic growth." By experience it has proved to be quite workable with some marked advantages over the Soviet type communism.

The distinctive features of the 'Market Socialism' in Yugoslavia may be said to be as follows:

1. There is better and faster mutual adjustment of demand and supply, thanks to the existence of 'market mechanism.'
2. There is greater attention paid to the needs of the consumers, of-course, within limits of resources allotted to consumption.

3. There is much wider scope to economic initiative whether in the field of consumption or production.
4. Consequently there is much less administrative pressure from the authorities on all facets of economic activities of the community.
5. As a result, though there is authoritarian political control over the society in general, there is definitely more relaxed atmosphere both among consumers, and among workers engaged in the process of production.
6. There is avoidance of the wasteful method of the system of collectivised farming.
7. Considerable measure of industrial democracy is introduced in the system. (Where each individual industrial enterprise can take certain important decisions with the help of participating workers in that establishment).
8. Welfare measures have been introduced by the State for the benefit of workers on a considerable scale.

"With all its defects and handicaps — inadequate competition on the domestic market, price control, foreign exchange control, and so forth — the market mechanism in Yugoslavia seems to have functioned reasonably well in bringing both not only growth but also technological and organisational innovations, satisfaction of consumer demand, and flexible adaptation to export requirements."

"Thus during 1950 and 1970 gross national product tripled which meant an annual growth rate of 5.6 per cent and 4.5 per cent per capita income growth. Personal consumption also increased sharply."[9]

13. MIXED ECONOMY

Introduction

As capitalism and its opposite economic system, namely, communism developed and were in operation for some time, it was observed that while both economic systems had certain remarkable achievements to their credit, it was also observed that some undesirable and serious defects were associated with both the systems.

Thus, as already noted, capitalism (and especially *laissez faire* capitalism) showed defects such as trade cyclical fluctuations with its booms and depressions and unemployment, misdirection and misuse of community's resources for the production of luxury and semi-luxury goods because there was demand for them and as they yielded maximum profits, while neglecting goods needed by masses as such production did not yield high rate of profit as in the case of former type of goods, neglect of social welfare, emergence of monopoly and wastages associated with it, especially exploitation of consumers by keeping resources idle and, creating artificial scarcity of monopolised goods and raised prices to make high monopoly profits, wastages of competition, inequalities of income and wealth in a competitive regime where labourers with only labour to sell possessed poor bargaining strength with employers commanding vast productive assets leading to exploitation of labour, division of society into two classes of 'Haves' and 'Have-Nots,' and class conflict and class-war leading to social tensions and political instability and often to revolutions.

Communism, on the other hand, meant complete suppression of individual freedom as consumers and producers, arbitrary decisions by a small body of planners or government agency regarding allocation of resources resulting in production of goods and services often not preferred by people and thus misdirection and misuse of community's resources, predominance of bureaucracy and regime of rules and regulations making economy extremely inflexible and therefore incapable of quickly adjusting itself to changing times and needs, and above all lack of adequate incentives to people (in the absence of personal profit motive) to put forward their best efforts and therefore general inefficiency of communist economic system.

'Mixed Economy' or 'Mixed Economic System' came to be evolved as an economic system (combining some features of capitalism and some of communism) that would avoid the defects of both capitalism and communism (mentioned above), while at the same time combining merits of both (*e.g.*, combining the efficiency of capitalism on account of the powerful incentive of personal profit motive, ability of the people to take risk to make higher profits, their inventiveness and so on with merits of communism such as systematic and planned use of community's resources with a view to achieve maximum social welfare, avoidance of wastages of resources, avoidance of economic fluctuations with the aid of economic planning, guarantee of employment and of minimum standard of living to all, absence of a class of people living on unearned incomes, greater equality in the distribution of income and wealth and so on).

Features of a Mixed Economy

Following are the important or basic features of a mixed economy :

1. *Co-existence of Public and Private Sectors.* Mixed economy is based on the idea or philosophy that in an economy there is room for existence and profitable operation of both the public sector and the private sector. Public sector is made up of those industries and financial institutions which the State considers as of vital importance and therefore nationalises them. In the public sector therefore there are generally basic and heavy industries of vital and strategic importance which are owned and managed by the State and profits of which accrue to the State which uses them for augmenting welfare of society.

At the same time there is substantial private sector (for example, in the case of India consisting of most consumer goods industries, small-scale and cottage industries, most of agricultural sector, most of retail trade, part of banking, transport and financial sector and so on) where ownership and management are in private hands and profits are appropriated by private individuals or private companies.

It ought to be noted that the term 'Mixed' in the phrase 'Mixed Economy' is a rather flexible concept and the size and proportion of the public sector and private sector and the way they are 'mixed' may vary from country to country accepting the mixed economic system as also circumstances prevailing in the country.

The main point to be noted and which is basic to the concept of a mixed economy is the acceptance of both public and private sector on both ideological ground and on grounds of practical consideration as the best possible system for the country and impartial and equal treatment given to both the sectors, the two sectors not harbouring any ill-will or jealousy against each other but in fact heartily co-operating with each other.[10]

2. This brings us to the second feature of a mixed economy, namely, existence of some sort of planning. According to Prof. Learner, in a mixed economy, instead of isolated decisions and activities by the public and private sectors and unrelated legislation for each sector, there would have to be proper co-ordination between activities assigned to each sector. This means there will have to be some sort of economic planning and all enterprises, whether owned by government or by private persons or companies, would have a well-defined place and functions in an integrated plan.[11]

At present a mixed economy seems to many countries as a way out or method of avoiding defects of both capitalism and communism. It would ensure scope for individual initiative and enterprise and ensure efficiency by providing scope for private profit motive in some sectors of the economy without permitting economic instability, unemployment and insecurity and gross inequalities of income and wealth due to existence of public sector. According to Prof. Learner, "the fundamental point of the mixed or controlled economy is that it recognises neither collectivism nor private enterprise as an end or principle of economic organisation." Both of them are to be used as means or instruments of policy to secure previously determined socio-economic ends.

Experiments in mixed economy are being tried in the UK and India and one additional advantage of this is that the system of mixed economy is being worked in a way that is compatible with political democracy which both the countries have accepted.

REFERENCES

1. Economic System — (Current Thought Series No. 10), George Halm, page 167.
2. The Economics of Socialism — H.D. Dickinson, page 10.
3. The Decay of Capitalist Civilisation — Sydney Webb and Beatrice Webb, page 2.
4. The Economics of Socialism — H.D. Dickinson, page 14.
5. Comparative Economic Systems — W.N. Loucks and W.C. Whitney (Ninth Edition), page 165.
6. Economic Systems — George Halm, page 94.
7. In England some of the important democratic or liberal socialists were: Arnold Toynbee, G.B. Shaw, Sidney and Beatrice Webb, Graham Wallas, H.G. Wells, R.H. Tawney, John and Barbara Hammond, G.D.H. Cole and Harold Laski.

The British democratic socialists formed a parliamentary party in 1890s with roots in working class trade unions and consumers' co-operatives. The democratic socialist movement spread upwards among fabians, intellectuals and universities. The British Labour Party achieved majority in the British Parliament in 1945.

As noted already, the democratic or liberal socialists, unlike Marxist socialist, were committed to parliamentary democracy and winning power by votes of working class which formed majority in the community.

Before the Labour Party achieved majority in the parliament, they advocated for half a century before 1945 short-term proposals which today we all accept policies of Welfare State — that the government should assume responsibility for alleviating poverty and expanding social services, unemployment pay, health and educational services.

The long-term policy of the British Labour Party were socialist: nationalisation of industry, and in some sense, economic planning to displace autonomous market determination of output and distribution of income.

Source: Economic Systems and Society — George Dalton, page 91.

8. The State and Revolution — Lenin.
9. Economic Systems — Gregory Grossman (Second Edition), pages 158 and 159.
10. Even in a capitalist country like the USA, in modern times, government is trying to regulate economic activities of the people and there is the existence of the public sector. In the USA, for example, there are controls on quality of food products, controls on monopolistic undertakings; atomic weapons are manufactured by the government; the Tennessee Valley Authority, a public authority, has constructed dams, canals, and power stations in the Tennessee Valley and supplies power, irrigation, water and other needed articles to residents in that area. On this ground, Prof. Samuelson claims that the US economy is a 'mixed economy.' If this is accepted then since during modern times there is in every country existence of some public sector industries and State regulations, there would hardly be any distinction between Capitalism and a Mixed Economy.
11. It is for this reason that Prof. Learner has suggested the use of the term 'Controlled Economy' instead of 'Mixed Economy,' though the term 'Mixed Economy' has come into common use.

CHAPTER 3

INCENTIVES IN DIFFERENT ECONOMIC SYSTEMS

1. INTRODUCTION

In order to carry any type of activity, man requires certain incentives. A glance at history would show that different people at different times and under different systems have acted or were inspired to act due to different motives or set of incentives.

Different motives or incentives that have made or compelled or inspired people to undertake activities have been — sense of duty, love for humanity, religion, patriotism or nationalism, desire for reputation, sacrifice, adventure, competitive spirit, pride, job-satisfaction, revenge, self-reliance, power, self-interest and so on and so forth. Possibly in the case of most people, it is not just one among the above motives or incentives that compel them to work; it is generally a combination of different motives or incentives listed above that moves men to work hard and harder.

2. INCENTIVES UNDER CAPITALISM

The main or the chief incentive on which free enterprise system or capitalism is based is 'private profit'. It is this desire to make more and more profit that makes farmers to work harder on their fields; shopkeepers to run their shops more efficiently; industrialists to try to take risk, invent new goods or services or try to find out new processes, all with a view to increase their profits so that accumulation of their private property would have increased ensuring them and their progeny comfortable standard of living. Capitalism is based on the conviction that of all motives, private profit (*i.e.*, self-interest) is the most permanent and most powerful incentive that will bring the best in man as labourer, farmer, as inventor, as industrialist. Thus, in the case of the USA, it was self-interest which made early settlers take great risks and clear jungles and enter unknown lands; it is this which has inspired men to go to the bottom of the ocean to find sea foods or oil; go in search of gold or minerals to distant and dangerous mountains and undertake all types of risks. Capitalism is based on the conviction that while other motives such as love for humanity, duty, patriotism, etc., are important and do influence man's conduct, in the economic sphere no incentive is as powerful and constant as private profit (which is another name for self-interest).

But as stated already it would be incorrect to say that under capitalism it is only self-interest or private profit motive that provides incentive to people to work hard and do their best. No doubt, private profit and attempts to maximise private profit is the main incentive under capitalism; but it cannot be said to be the only incentive under capitalism. There are other incentives which are also goading capitalists to work harder and do their best. For example, there is creative joy of finding a new product or a new and better process of producing the existing commodity; there is the joy of taking risk which normal person would shrink from, and succeed; there is the joy of job-satisfaction; there is the joy of competing with others and coming out successful; there is the joy of accepting new challenges and finding solutions to them; and there is of course the joy that out of private profits made by individual enterprise, one can do great service to society by donating to construct schools and hospitals, libraries and museums; and there is thus the joy of gaining esteem and love of fellow human beings in society.

As critics of capitalism have done, it is wrong to consider all capitalists as unscrupulous bandits out to take maximum advantage of every possible opportunity of the distress of people and ruthlessly exploit them and their weak position for personal gain. There may be a few such capitalists as every profession and every economic system has black sheep. But were all capitalists (farmers, traders, wholesalers, shareholders, bankers, industrialists and so on), as unscrupulous as described by their critics, the Western European countries, the USA and Japan would not have recorded the all-round progress which under the capitalist regime they have done.

3. INCENTIVES UNDER SOVIET COMMUNIST SYSTEM

The problem of incentives assumes different nature in Soviet communist system than under capitalism. While discussing the problem of incentives in the Soviet system, it should be kept in mind that there is practically no private ownership of the means of production; there is little private enterprise ; there is virtually no unemployment, and there is guarantee of employment to all; and there is fairly well-developed system of social security.

Thee are two types of incentives in Soviet communist system:

1. *Moral Incentives.* "The operation of these (moral) incentives is based on a worker's social consciousness in contributing to society's welfare, on his

interest in his occupation, his sense of satisfaction from the work performed and pride in his status."

In order to appeal to and arouse their moral incentives among Soviet workers, and citizens, methods such as " Political appeals, slogans, boards and books on honour in factories, awards or pendants, badges, medals and orders and holding of self-criticism sessions are well-known instruments utilising these sentiments to spur workers to better production performance."[1]

2. *Material Incentives.* Material incentives under Soviet communist system consist of "rewards in money or kind according to the quantity and quality of work performed or economies achieved. In addition to the differentiation of standard wage and salary rates, they include individual and group bonuses or benefits out of special incentive funds."[2]

Marx and Lenin believed that material incentive was antisocial and relic of capitalism; they believed that the material incentives would gradually be replaced one day by a system of moral incentives. Experience of 50 years or so shows that the assumption is not correct and the most significant reform that has taken place in the USSR and East European countries which have adopted communist system has been the extension of and strengthening of material incentives. It is now widely recognised that higher the stage of communist economic development " the greater should be the differentiation of earnings." Though in the early stage of communist economic development, income of poor classes may have to be raised to the minimum, if necessary by preventing excessive consumption of higher income-group people, in advanced stage of communist economic development, "a wide scale of material incentives must be provided if centralised planning, direction of labour and a decline in the rates of growth are to be avoided."[3]

In the beginning for quite some time incentives were determined on the basis of "reaching and exceeding of planned quantitative targets." This was especially applicable to management personnel and were also part of incentive system for workers. But what started happening under such incentive system related to output was that enterprises purposely tended to state officially low target proposals, demand more machinery and capital goods, labour force and raw material inventories, and later turn out larger output than stated in the original proposal. Even today, it is thought that the incentive system for managerial personnel in the USSR is not satisfactory and does not bring the best out of them.

"The new system of material incentives to labour is chiefly based on a 'synthetic" criterion, *i.e.,* on enterprise profits. Part of the profits of an enterprise is channelled into the "material incentives fund". This is described as " an essential factor dynamizing the economic activity of the enterprise today". A part of the profits is allocated to the "socio-cultural and housing funds". The material incentives fund is distributed among personnel of the enterprise in the form of individual bonuses whereas "the socio-cultural and housing funds" is used for group welfare amenities and services.

The aim of the system of incentives that is built up in the Soviet Union is "to spur the management and workers not only to greater output but also to reduce waste, improve quality and produce articles for which there is demand."

There is now increasing departure in the USSR from early piece-wage system to time-wage system. This is not much different from the system in West European countries.

Incentives to managerial personnel have also been increased in recent years differing from one communist country to another. It used to be for quite some time 5 per cent of the basic salary. Today it varies between 10 - per cent in Rumania to 33 per cent of basic pay in the Soviet Union. Naturally actual proportion in the case of individual manager varies depending upon the nature of industry, responsibility, etc. For example, in Poland, in the case of managerial personnel it may reach a maximum of 80 per cent of basic salary, whereas in the case of economic and technical personnel, it varies usually between 15 to 20 per cent. It is observed that in some countries (for example, Yugoslavia, Bulgaria, Czechoslovakia and Hungary) not only incentive bonus margins but even basic pay-scales are made dependent upon the performance of the enterprise.

It will thus be observed that these days, the system of material incentives plays an important role in communist countries though that is supplemented by "system of moral incentives". It may also be noted that what an individual manager or worker is going to get as his total emoluments (basic wage or salary plus bonus) depends upon the performance not just that of the manager or worker individually but on the performance of the enterprise as a whole to which they all belong as a team.

In recent times Soviet economists have admitted the role which private profit motive plays in the process of production. Somehow, the agricultural sector has not made progress as anticipated and the collectivised farm system has failed to reach planned targets with the consequence that the Soviet Union is forced to import foodgrains from the United States. They have therefore been allotting small patches of land which farmers working on collective farm can cultivate during spare time and keep for themselves profit which they make by selling produce grown on those small plots in the market."[4]

If one visualises retrospectively, one sees how radical changes have taken place in the system of incentives in communist countries. During the Stalinist phase, the main incentive to work was fear of severe punishment in case of failure to attain allotted targets and many managers and workers were banished to Siberia for failure to attain the targets. Even Molotov who failed to record expected results as minister of agriculture was demoted and practically disgraced.

From fear, banishment and punishment as 'incentives' to work, the Soviet Union and other communist countries have travelled a long way in evolving a new system of incentives based on a combination of moral and material awards.

But one unfavourable thing needs to be noted. The fact that the State under the communist regime guarantees minimum standard of living to all, whatever the extent of his efficiency, efforts and contribution to national product and national welfare, is bound to have some unfavourable and disincentive effects. Since one is guaranteed the minimum standard of living, one may put forward the least effort (especially if no positive punishments are provided for failure to reach minimum targets).

4. INCENTIVES UNDER NAZI (NATIONAL SOCIALIST) OR FASCIST SYSTEM OF ECONOMY

Under the Nazi economic system in Germany and Fascist system under Mussolini the main incentive that was provided to people to work and give their maximum to the nation was appeal to the spirit of nationalism and call to people to do their utmost and if necessary sacrifice everything for the sake of the nation.

Under the Nazi Germany thus the incentives were essentially non-material though care was taken to see that appropriate employment opportunities were secured to most and social security was provided to workers, and there were appropriate wage and salary differentials.

But the main motive or incentive was moral. Firstly, Germany was to take revenge against its erstwhile enemies, namely, England and France, for the humiliating treaty of Versailles imposed upon her. Also the USSR with its hateful ideology and system of communism was to be destroyed and so also the Jews. Secondly, appeal was made to German people that they belong to the superior Aryan race whose destiny it is to rule over the world and undo the injustice done to the German people by depriving them of colonies by other European nations. By massive propaganda, right from the childhood, these values were inculcated in the minds of German people who also with the encouragement provided by increasing employment opportunities came forward not only to work hard for the nation but if necessary to die for the Father Land.

The same could be said of Fascist economic system in Italy under Mussolini who appealed to Italian nationalism and the superior Italian race which at one time under the Roman Empire were the masters of the world. Italy must regain that past glory. This along with fair amount of economic security under Fascist planning provided the system of incentives.

5. INCENTIVES UNDER MIXED ECONOMY

We have already examined the features of a mixed economy. In the light of that, it is comparatively easy to analyse the system of incentives that operate under a mixed economy.

Insofar as the private sector exists, there are the usual incentives (that are referred to under capitalism), namely personal profit motive, self-independence and self-reliance, job-satisfaction, taking risk and meeting new challenges, to come out on top in a competitive system, and attain status and honour among fellow human beings.

In a mixed economy at the same time there is the existence of public sector. People in the private sector are encouraged because public sector enterprises are ready to help private entrepreneurs by providing infrastructure facilities like roads, communications, market information, power, finance and so on. Private sector entrepreneurs are also encouraged to come forward to do their most because with the help of public sector, the State tries to avoid economic fluctuations and to stabilise economy, provide price-support and if necessary monetary subsidies and other concessions, protect home industries by suitable international trade policies and so on. Public sector in a mixed economy thus creates favourable and stable conditions wherein private entrepreneurs get increasing scope for the development of their potential abilities.

In a mixed economy there is public sector. Managers in the public sector as also employees enjoy security of tenure, better conditions of work (*e.g.*, railway employees get annually some free travel passes in India; the nationalised bank employees get concessional loans for housing), pension and gratuity and so on. Naturally these favourable conditions help them (or should help them) to put forward their best efforts in their field of activities. There is also added incentive that they are not working for any individual and to help him to enhance his profits but are working for the public sector the profits of which are going to be utilised for the welfare of society.

But it may also be noted that security provided for employees in the public sector, the regular pay-scales and promotions, difficulty of removing them or stopping their promotion even if they are found inefficient because of the great many difficulties in proving charges of inefficiency, and absence of personal profit motive all have also disincentive effect in the case of employees of public sector.

Also, the fact that government will come to the assistance of the private sector in a mixed economy in case of their difficulties with finance and other protective measures reduces the incentives of managers and personnel in the private sector. The case of more than 100 sick cotton textile mills in the private sector taken over for management by Government of India to prevent unemployment that would result in case they are closed down illustrates the point.

6. INCENTIVES UNDER LIBERAL OR DEMOCRATIC SOCIALISM

The incentive system under liberal or democratic socialism is practically the same as in the case of a mixed economy which has already been referred to above.

There is however one additional factor that may be mentioned.

Under liberal or democratic socialism, people are closely associated with the process and formulation of economic plans for the country. Such a plan is therefore more likely to reflect the aspirations, needs and priorities of people right from the village level upwards. This close association of people at all levels with the formulation of the plan will make the people feel that it is their own plan (and not a plan imposed upon them from above as in the case of central type of planning in communist countries). Since the democratically formulated plan is more likely to lead to the satisfaction of urgent needs and aspirations of the people at different levels, there will be greater incentive among people to play their part both in the process of formulation as also implementation of the plan (than in the case of centralised type of planning in communist countries).

REFERENCES

* *The Economics of Socialism* — J. Wilczynski, page 108.

1. *Ibid*, page 108.
2. *Ibid*, page 108.
3. J. Kleer — *Op. Cit.*, page 95.
4. A visitor to the USSR has described how he found distinct qualitative difference in tomatoes kept in two baskets being sold by a farmer. On enquiry he was told that the inferior ones were those grown on collective farms and those of better quality in the other basket on patches allotted to farmers out of which they could keep profits for themselves.

CHAPTER 4

EFFICIENCY OF ECONOMIC SYSTEMS

1. GENERAL CONSIDERATIONS REGARDING EFFICIENCY OF ECONOMIC SYSTEMS

The term 'Efficiency' may be interpreted in a narrow sense as well as in a broad sense.

In the narrow sense, 'efficiency' of an economic system refers to 'technical efficiency'. It refers to the ability of an economic system to make the best and most efficient use of available resources of the community, and to avoid or keep to the minimum, all sorts of wastages.

'Technical efficiency' has also short-term aspect and 'long-term' aspect. Thus technical efficiency of an economic system may be viewed in a static manner (*i.e.,* the manner in which the given resources are utilised at any particular point of time); it can also be viewed in a 'dynamic' manner, namely flow of inventions and changing level of efficiency with which resources of the community come to be utilised in the long run.

It is claimed on behalf of capitalist system that from the point of view of technical efficiency, it is the most efficient system, both in the static sense as well as in the dynamic sense. It is claimed on behalf of capitalism that under the incentive of private profit, entrepreneurs try to make the best use of available resources, providing at the same time maximum satisfaction to consumers. Also, competitive forces compel entrepreneurs to attain maximum efficiency.

According to the proponents of capitalism, this applies in the case of capitalism not only in the static sense and in the short run; but it holds good in the dynamic sense and also in the long run. Capitalism, they say, is therefore, from the technical point of view, the most efficient economic system, ensuring both maximum satisfaction to consumers on the one hand and most efficient allocation of resources of the community, on the other. This is exemplified by continually rising standards of living of people in capitalist countries which are definitely much higher than those in the case of communist countries and in countries with a mixed economy.

The communist critics of capitalism point out that the above claims, made on behalf of capitalism, might be true in its abstract model or in case of capitalism working under ideal conditions. But the reality is different.

According to the critics, there is enormous technical wastage of resources under capitalist system both in the short run and in the long run. There are booms and depressions and unemployment both of seasonal, frictional and chronic type. Even at present both in the USA and West European countries rate of unemployment ranges anywhere between 4 and 10 per cent. This is waste of resources. Also, ideal competitive conditions rarely obtain under modern capitalism. This means the productive scene is characterised by monopolies, duopolies and oligopolies. These monopolistic enterprises try to create artificial scarcities (which means keeping productive resources purposely idle), raise prices and make higher monopoly profits, sacrificing both higher satisfaction of consumers and efficient use of community's resources.

Even where there is competition, there are enormous wastages of competition. One has just to think of the vast real resources spent on advertisement by rival producers, which mostly neutralise the effects of rival's advertisement. From the community's point of view, it is net loss of real resources which could have been used to produce desirable goods and services.

Another wastage which takes place under capitalism is that under pressure of effective demand from richer sections of the community, production of luxury, semi-luxury goods as also of harmful drugs and strong liquors etc., is encouraged, whereas production of mass-consumption goods needed by poor sections of the community comes to be neglected.

As regards technical efficiency of capitalism in the long run, critics point out that entrepreneurs try to keep as their secrets new inventions through laws governing patents, so that other rival producers cannot make use of those patented processes. This deprives the community in the long run of the advantages which would have flowed by wide spread inventions.

There are certain exhaustible and non-renewable resources like oil and minerals which must be used with long-term perspective and keeping the needs of future generations in mind. Under capitalism due to the desire to maximise profits as quickly as possible, these resources come to be used away in the short-term to the great long term disadvantage of the country.

It is claimed on behalf of socialism and communism that as under them, production is planned (taking into account these days preferences of consumers), the sort of technical wastages which occur in capitalist countries both in the short run and also in the long run due to various factors referred to above do not occur under socialism and communism where productive resources are fully made use of with due regard to the true welfare of the community. There are no wastages on account of unemployment, monopolies, competition and laws regarding patents. In socialist and communist countries research is conducted in State-owned laboratories and the fruits of research are made available to all. Rising standard of living in socialist and communist countries and the fact that the Soviets could also reach the moon and develop nuclear power or make remarkable technological advances in all other fields show that it is not private profit motive alone that can bring about technological progress either in the short or in the long run.

The critics of communism point out that it is the dictatorship that characterises communism; planners are not popularly elected and therefore they do not represent wishes and aspirations of the people; therefore the decisions of the planners are arbitrary decisions or Party decisions which may not correspond with the wishes and aspirations of the people. This may result in enormous wastage of resources under socialism and communism both in the short and long run when goods and services which occupy lower priority in the minds of consumers but higher priority in the minds of planners may be produced, resulting in both sacrifice of consumer satisfaction and wastage of resources.

Communists are aware of these defects in their system and attempts are being made to ascertain the preferences of people and arrange production of goods and services accordingly.

2. EFFICIENCY IN THE BROADER SENSE

Efficiency of an economic system traditionally comes to be measured in a very narrow sense and in terms of annual growth rate of Gross or Net National Product, and more especially by rate of annual increase in per capita income. For example, on this basis, it is claimed that economies of the USA, West European countries and Japan are most 'efficient' than either the economic systems of the communist countries or countries with mixed economic system.

It should be obvious that the rate at which the GNP or NNP or per capita income grow, cannot be said to be the most satisfactory index of 'efficiency' of an economic system. This is because, as is well known, while calculating national wealth and rate of its increase, commodities which are harmful to society (drugs, liquor, cigarettes, services in night clubs, etc.), also come to be included and per capita income comes to be calculated on that basis.

But it would be better and more justifiable if 'efficiency' of an economic system is interpreted in a broader sense and measured in broader terms.

For example, the following considerations should be taken note of. Along with the growth rate of the economy and per capita income, care must also be taken to consider, 'the composition' of the annually produced national wealth.

Further, growth rate of the economy may be rising; but along with it whether the increasing wealth is being equitably distributed among the participating factors of production or whether it is getting concentrated in fewer hands leaving the vast majority of poor and many unemployed, must also be taken note of. Justice in distribution should also be an important criterion for determining efficiency of an economic system.

Is growth accompanied by stability or with inflationary pressures which would press very hard on the poorer sections of the community? Is growth taking place with stable employment and fairly stable price level?

Is the economic system such as would ensure security both at present and in future for all? Or is increasing growth rate accompanied by increasing tensions, anxieties, cares and uncertainties?

Does growth make rational use of resources, especially of those scarce and exhaustible resources which cannot be renewed? This means, is the economy moving along right lines ensuring better living for the future generations?

Does the economy and its growth mean rising national prestige among the nations of the world? Or is it making the nation dependent upon others so that under certain circumstances they may dictate what policies the country should follow? This means, is the economic system aiming and attaining self-sufficiency and becoming self-reliant in matters of vital goods and services?

We have now realised that economic growth has to pay a price in terms of pollution and disturbance of environment or ecological balance. Is the economy paying intolerably higher price by destroying pleasant natural environment and economical balance?

And finally, is the economic system adopted by a country contributing to the development of fundamental virtues like individual freedom, love for humanity, regard for truth and beauty, sympathy for the unfortunate and a peaceful and contented life for all?

If efficiency of an economic system is to be defined in the broad sense (as it should be), all the above and possibly many other factors may have to be taken account of.

It is difficult to give appropriate weightage to various factors that make for efficiency in the broad sense of an economic system. And yet all those factors count.

Since people in different countries because of differing history, tradition, culture and value-system, are inclined to give different weightage to the above factors, from this broader point of view, it would be difficult to give final judgement on whether capitalism or communism or a mixed economy or any other conceivable economic system is more 'efficient' than other economic systems and if so, to what extent.

CHAPTER 5

ECONOMIC SYSTEMS AND BASIC FREEDOMS

1. INTRODUCTION

Man by nature is free. He is inclined to oppose restraints that take away his freedom. But is obvious that in any type of society, no individual can have absolute freedom. No sooner man begins to live in society, society almost automatically imposes certain limitations (may be in the form of customs and conventions and later by legislation) on his conduct and behaviour, as otherwise social life would become impossible, if freedom or liberty comes to be equated with licence to do what one pleases.

Thus the concept of freedom is to be interpreted always in a relative sense. If a man can enjoy freedom to choose from a number of alternatives or if circle of his choice in any field is wider, we say that the individual enjoys greater freedom; if on the other hand, the individual's circle of choice or alternatives open before him out of which he can choose is limited, we say that he enjoys less freedom. If an individual is left no choice at all, we say that such an individual enjoys no freedom; it is slavery.

In our discussion here we are mostly concerned with economic freedom that exist under different economic systems.

2. MEANING OF ECONOMIC FREEDOM

Economic freedom (or economic freedoms) broadly refers to the following:

Every individual is a consumer. We say that consumer enjoys economic freedom, if he is free to spend his income as, when and where he likes, and on commodities and services which he likes, the aim in all this being maximisation of one's satisfaction. He may save part of his income for future use or he may spend the whole of it on current consumption. Greater the extent of his choice in all these matters, greater is the economic freedom that individual enjoys as a consumer.

An individual is also a producer either of commodities or of services — may be as a farmer, a wholesale or retail trader, as a doctor or an engineer or a manufacturer or in any other capacities. A producer is supposed to enjoy economic freedom, if he is free to use his productive resources (land, labour, capital and organisational ability) in whichever line he likes, in whatever place he likes, produce a commodity or service that he chooses to produce, and market the produce where and when he likes and at a price not regulated by government.

Thus economic freedom refers to individual freedom as a consumer, as a producer, as a saver and investor and so on. Greater the choice to an individual in these respects, we can say that greater is the economic freedom that he enjoys.

3. ECONOMIC FREEDOM UNDER CAPITALISM

Economic Freedom of Consumers. Since *laissez faire* capitalism nowhere exists at present (not even in the USA), we shall concentrate our attention on the degree and extent of economic freedom under capitalism as it exists or operates at present (*i.e.,* economic freedom under 'modern', 'managed' or 'regulated' capitalism).

One of the claims made on behalf of capitalism is that 'consumer is sovereign', and he enjoys maximum freedom as a consumer under capitalism.

It is maintained that under capitalism, consumer enjoys freedom to spend his income as and where he likes, and on assortment of goods and services out of thousands of them available in the market. It is claimed that under capitalism 'consumer is king' and his choices and preferences direct productive resources into those lines of production for which he has shown preference.

On the face of it, under capitalism, a consumer, say in the USA, does appear to be a king with great amount of freedom as a consumer. It would be instructive to examine the proposition that under capitalism consumer is king.

If we consider the proposition, namely consumer is sovereign under capitalism closely, we find that at present there are several restrictions that have come to be imposed upon his freedom of choice that he once enjoyed during the days of *laissez faire* capitalism.

Following are the main considerations that may restrict his choice as a consumer under the modern capitalism.

In the first place, it is possible that due to economic instability or recession or dynamic changes taking place, a consumer may lose his job and therefore his income. He may have to live on government allowances. Reduction or loss of income puts a limit on his choice as a consumer.

Secondly, modern governments impose heavy taxes (direct and indirect) both to meet increasing government expenditure, as also to realise certain socio-economic objectives like reduction of extreme inequalities. In capitalist countries at present thus anywhere from 25 to 40 per cent of people's income is taken away by taxation.

Thirdly, government puts restrictions on production and consumption of harmful commodities or prohibit production and use of goods such as hasish, opium and so on or puts restrictions on hours during which night clubs may operate or areas where they may operate and so on.

Fourthly, under modern capitalism, there have emerged monopolies/duopolies/oligopolies which have greater or smaller degree of control over market forces. They can determine what quantities of goods to be produced and at what prices those goods are to be sold and where. This leaves very little choice to consumers. Some 200 such giant industrial establishments dominate the US market and may be said for all purposes to dictate to consumers who in the case of those commodities are practically left no choice.

Fifthly, there is the high pressure advertisement through TV, radio, press and other media through which producers can manipulate the choice of consumers. Consumers these days mostly go by brand-names hardly stopping to enquire into qualities of similar commodities produced by competing producers.

Sixthly, there is consumer's ignorance. In modern times, the number of commodities produced and the number of varieties available are so great, that even if a consumer is given completely free choice, he hardly has time, energy, resources and knowledge at his disposal to decide what is the best commodity for him and what quality of that commodity, and where he gets it, and at prices and so on. Thus on practical grounds, consumer's choice becomes restricted to a few commodities and only a few varieties which come to be influenced mostly be customs and conventions or advertisements.

Seventhly, even in capitalist countries like USA, scarcities of some commodities are being felt (*i.e.,* petroleum) or such scarcities do occur temporarily. Under such circumstances, government intervenes directly by rationing the commodity or indirectly by imposing heavier taxes on such commodities with a view to raise their prices and curtail their consumption to the level of supply.

Eighthly, Government often puts restrictions on commodities to be imported from abroad (*e.g.,* restrictions on cloth to be imported by USA from India, or various electronic goods from Japan). These restrictions may be direct or indirect through taxation. Naturally consumers are forced to replace them by domestically produced goods, may be of inferior quality and priced at higher level than those of imported goods.

Also government may impose restrictions on travel facilities, forbidding citizens to visit certain countries (as USA did for long in the case of China).

From all these, it will be seen that consumer is no more sovereign under modern capitalism and that the circle of his choice of goods and services is, due to various factors, getting narrower and narrower. All the indications are that this trend will continue and possibly get reinforced in future in capitalist countries.

And yet with all these limitations and restrictions, it would still be true to say, as we shall see, that an individual does enjoy greater freedom as consumer under capitalism than under any other economic system such as communism and mixed economy.

Economic Freedom of Producers. It is claimed that under capitalism, the institution of private property is sacrosanct; and that individuals are free to use their productive resources to produce any commodity or service of their choice. Nobody dictates to him to produce this commodity or not to produce that commodity. (The only factor that a producer has to consider is the preferences of consumers expressed through price-mechanism). It is therefore said that under capitalism, producers enjoy maximum freedom.

It would be instructive to examine the above proposition. Yes, compared to communism and mixed economy, under capitalism producers do seem to enjoy greater freedom. But then here also there are appearing a number of factors which are limiting an individual's freedom as a producer to a greater and greater extent.

Under modern capitalism, though theoretically producers are supposed to enjoy maximum freedom in the use of their various resources of production, in actual fact, a number of restrictions are being imposed upon them reducing to a greater and greater extent their economic freedom as producers.

For example, producers are forbidden to use their productive resources for production of certain commodities either because State has the monopoly of it (as in the case of generation of atomic energy in the USA) or because their production is deemed harmful to society.

Even in the case of those goods and services which private enterprise is permitted to produce, number of restrictions are increasing. Thus for practising various services such as medicine, engineering, surgery, architecture, etc., rigorous qualifications are prescribed, without which individuals will not be allowed to practise those professions.

Then there are professional associations and trade unions and often the policy of closed shop is followed (*i.e.,* unless one is a member of those associations, he will not be allowed to be recruited into a particular factory or profession).

In the case of production of commodities, there are various restrictions such as control over location of factories (*e.g.,* industrial units may not be allowed to be started in the midst of a civil locality), various factory legislation and acts regarding minimum wages, quality control, payment of taxes, conditions governing conditions and hours of work in the factory, regarding payment of provident fund, bonus and gratuity and so on. At present government is imposing severe conditions regarding steps to be taken for reducing or elimination of pollution of air, water and environment and to prevent even noise pollution.

Also, the power of trade union in most of the capitalist countries is growing and therefore producers' freedom to do what they like is getting restricted because of increasing bargaining strength of trade unions with their weapons such as strikes, and go-slow methods.

In countries like the USA, freedom of small producers such as a small farmer or a retailer or a small tailoring firm is getting more and more restricted because of their inability to face competition with giant undertakings which are coming to existence in all fields. Thus there are chain-stores spread over large parts of the USA which are in a position to offer various concessions to purchasers. This makes local small shop-keeper unable to compete with them. The same is true in respect of small producers in many other fields.

For political reasons, producers are prohibited to export goods to certain countries, (*e.g.*, prohibition on export of strategic goods by the USA to China for long).

Also savers may be forbidden to invest their savings in certain countries which are considered alien or producers may be forbidden to start factories in those countries either on their own or in collaboration with the nationals of those countries.

In times of scarcities, government steps in, compulsorily procures part of the production of factories, introduces price controls and rationing.

It will thus be observed that under modern capitalism, economic freedom of producers is also getting restricted more and more.

Thus, it may be concluded that economic freedom enjoyed by consumers and producers, by savers and investors during the days of *laissez faire* capitalism of the 19th century is getting more and more curtailed under modern capitalism.

4. ECONOMIC FREEDOM UNDER COMMUNISM

Consumer's Freedom. Since all production is planned under communist system, one is possibly under the impression that there is strict rationing of all goods and therefore consumers have absolutely no choice and therefore they hardly enjoy any economic freedom as consumers.

This may or may not have been true at one time in Soviet communist system; but at present among the assortment of goods and services produced, consumers do enjoy freedom of choice to some extent. There may not be thousands of varieties of textiles to choose from as in the USA; but out of the limited number of varieties produced, consumers in communist countries do enjoy some degree of choice. This is also true in respect of different consumer goods, say, icecream or cigarettes or cinema pictures, though the circle of choice may not be as wide as in capitalist countries. If people prefer a certain commodity, say, A to B, and therefore if shortages of commodity A begin to occur whereas inventories of commodity B go on accumulating, planners see that suitable adjustments are made in planned production of consumer goods. It is therefore wrong to say that under communism with planned production, distribution of consumer goods is also rigidly planned and therefore there is always a perpetual system of rationing of consumer goods under communism and therefore consumers have absolutely no freedom. But the fact remains that the circle of choice of consumer goods is definitely wider under modern capitalism than under modern communism.

Producer's Freedom. Since all productive resources are owned by the State since all production takes place in enterprises owned by the State, it follows that theoretically there is no producer's freedom whatsoever under communist system in the sense in which that freedom exists under capitalism. No private individual can start a factory, manage it and appropriate profits out of it. Theoretically every productive activity takes place in factories, establishments and farm owned by the State.

But that does not mean that under communism, an individual has no freedom at all in the process of production.

For example, within the broad framework of manpower, planning based on the present and future requirements, aptitude tests are taken and as far as possible people enjoy freedom of choosing occupation of their choice. But as stated above, all this freedom of choice of individuals to enter this line or that line of production is broadly circumscribed by the broad plan framework.

Also, within the factory or establishment, the management is at present enjoying some freedom of taking decisions on their own in some matters and not necessarily wait for decision in all minor matters from the central planning authority. This freedom on the part of management and even workers who are free to suggest changes or improvements is to be found to a greater extent in Yugoslavia than any other communist countries. There is no doubt that in view of growing complexity of modern production, increasing decentralisation of decision-making is taking place in communist countries.

This aspect is to be particularly noticed in the case of agricultural sector where vagaries of nature play a dominant role. Managers of collective farms are therefore these days enjoying greater decision-making power than formerly, though all this must take place within the broad framework of the national plan.

It has also been noted that even in the USSR many farmers who have to work on collective farms are now given small plots of land in the backyard of their households and there they enjoy greater freedom to decide what to produce there and at what price to sell the produce and to retain the profits made on those farms for themselves.

To sum up, the old rigidity where every one as producer was required to go by the decision and direction of the central planning authority is gradually giving place on account of the dynamic changes in the circumstances to greater freedom of decision-making and sharing of authority by management and working personnel with the higher planning authority. But all this takes place within the broad framework.

But it should be clear that producers enjoy greater freedom as producers under modern capitalism than under modern communism.

Under communism, what portion of the community's annual income will be or should be saved is entirely determined by the government and also how that is to be invested. And therefore in communist countries, individuals hardly have any freedom as savers and investors generally enjoyed in capitalist countries as well as in countries with a mixed economy.

5. A NOTE ON COMPARISON OF CONSUMER'S FREEDOM UNDER COMMUNISM AND CAPITALISM

Consumer's sovereignty is to be judged by the extent to which he influences production of goods and services.

At the one extreme, in the case of centralised planning (during, for example, Stalinist time or War communism), "consumer patterns are simply imposed on the consumer from above by means of specific, non-transferable, fixed period validity rationing."[1]

Naturally under such conditions under communism, planners are sovereign and consumers have absolutely no choice.

This sort of situation was in existence in the USSR during the War Communism (1917-21), the early Plan Era (1928-36) and in European Socialist countries up to early 1950s.

But it should be noted that this sort of tight controls over consumer's choice operates under conditions in total war in capitalist economy also (as for example during World War II).

But in European Socialist (Communist) countries at present, the situation can be described as 'a liberal' form of consumer's free choice. On the one hand, total consumption and its broad structure are laid down by the Central Planning Authority. The long-term investment programme for major developments in consumer goods industries is also determined centrally in communist countries. "On the other hand, the precise composition and distribution of the output in the consumer goods sector are determined by individual consumers registering their preferences in the market."[2]

Consumer's sovereignty is simply impossible under centrally planned communist economic system. Communist planners also believe that such free choice for consumers is not desirable. "As a result of prejudice, habit and imperfect knowledge, many consumers' preferences are irrational, such as an excessive preference for drugs, alcohol and luxuries which the economy cannot afford, a lack of appreciation of external economies and diseconomies and a predilection for immediate consumption." Instead of allowing complete freedom to consumers, the central planning authority intervenes whenever there is conflict between private and social interest. Additionally planners under communism try to appropriately shape the pattern of consumption of the consumers.

Thus J. Wilczynski concludes that "a planned economy whether of a centralised or decentralised type, cannot and should not, permit absolute consumer's sovereignty, but it is in a good position to ensure rationalised consumer's sovereignty."

But the critics of communism wonder "whether the Central Planning Authority's preferences really reflect those of the consumers as members of society". The planning authority is likely to follow Party's preferences rather than of consumers. There never have been free elections in communist countries to prove that the Party in power represents the majority of consumers.

But from experience gained during 1960s and 1970s, it may be said that in communist countries "the consumer is allowed to perform useful function in perfecting economic planning and the capacity of the more developed Socialist economies has sufficiently improved to allow higher standard of living."[3]

Communists also maintain that the concept that under capitalism 'the consumer is king' (ensuring rational allocation of resources) is more a fiction rather than a reality.

Accordingly to communist critics, monopolies, large inequalities of income, high pressure salesmanship by a constant battery of sales promotion with a view to maximise profits — all combine to impose consumption pattern on consumers, rather than its being determined by free and rational choice as is claimed in text books written by believers in capitalism.

The communist critics conclude: "Besides, some consumers' preferences are inherently irrational which in the absence of government intervention produces adverse long-run effects on consumers themselves, as well as society in general. In the Socialist economy, either such irregularities do not exist, or otherwise there is a unique machinery to counteract such tendencies which is conducive to higher levels of social welfare."[4]

6. ECONOMIC FREEDOM IN A MIXED ECONOMY

It has already been noted that a mixed economy (like that of India) combines in varying proportions the features of capitalism (with its institutions of consumers' free choice, institution of private ownership of the means of production, private profit motive, competition, etc.) with certain features of communism (such as public sector with State ownership of factors of production, appropriation of profit by the State, system of economic planning with planned production and distribution and so on).

From this it follows that economic freedom of people (as consumers and producers, as savers and investors, etc.,) in a mixed economy lies somewhere midway between economic freedom enjoyed by people under capitalism and under communism.

Consumer's Freedom.

Under a mixed economy, in respect of commodities produced in the private sector, the consumers enjoy freedom to purchase goods and services as they like. Of course, restrictions regarding payment of taxes out of their income, restrictions on purchase of prohibited goods, payment of regulated prices in case such price regulations are imposed directly or indirectly (as by government fixing procurement prices) all curtail to that extent consumer's freedom as also by his ignorance, high pressure advertisement, monopoly and so on. But consumers in a mixed economy do appear to enjoy relatively greater freedom than consumers under communism, but relatively less than consumers under capitalist countries like the USA, West Germany and Japan.

In respect of goods and services produced and provided by industrial establishments in the public sector (for example, in the case of India, railway and air services, bus transport, water from government irrigational projects, some of the consumer goods like bread produced by government owned bakeries, fertilizers, electricity, etc.), consumers have no choice but to purchase those goods at prices regulated by the government. There is no competitive market for those commodities and consumers enjoy hardly any freedom in regard to sources from which to purchase or prices to be paid for them. This is unlike in the USA where most consumer and capital goods are purchased by private enterprises and are sold in competitive markets, giving greater freedom to consumers.

Producer's Freedom.

In a mixed economy, there are again a number of restrictions on freedom of producers.

Naturally, private enterprise or private companies cannot start or manage industries which are reserved for the public sector or which may, according to the policy of government, be nationalised and taken over by the government. In a mixed economy like that of India, most of the basic and heavy industries as also those providing infrastructure facilities (like transport, energy, finance etc.,) are in the public sector, where private enterprise is not permitted to enter.

In respect of the sector which is open to private enterprise, producers in a mixed economy do enjoy producer's freedom, subject of course to all laws and restrictions which are already mentioned in the case of producer's freedom under capitalism. In a mixed economy also producers like manufacturers are subject to various rules and regulations passed by the government. For example, in the case of India, there are the licensing policy, capital issue control, foreign exchange regulations, factory legislation, minimum wages laws, laws regarding rights of trade unions, payment of bonus, prevention of pollution, quality control, location of industries and so on. As modern society is becoming more and more complex, naturally, rules and regulations concerning private sector (whether agriculture or manufacture) are increasing and getting more and more complex. Even agricultural sector which is mostly in the private sector often comes in for certain amount of regulation in regard to crops to be grown, government procurement regulations and so on, though on the whole there appears to be greater producer's freedom in the agricultural sector than in the industrial sector.

In a mixed economy there is one more aspect that imposes some additional restrictions on private enterprise and on producer's freedom. Since in a mixed economy public and private sector co-exist, there has inevitably got to be established a certain amount of coordination in respect of their policies, production plans, pricing policies and so on, because both the sectors are very closely inter-dependent. Naturally this brings in a number of restrictions on the freedom of producers in the private sector in a mixed economy.

Increasing strength of trade unions and consumer associations are also resulting in direct or indirect curtailment of producer's freedom in a mixed economy, as in the case of capitalism.

As stated already, producer's freedom in a mixed economy is not as great as under modern capitalism; but they certainly enjoy more freedom than under modern communism.

The same can be said about an individual's freedom to save and invest. Since in a mixed economy, there exist the private sector and the institution of private property, individuals enjoy freedom to save smaller or greater part of their income and also enjoy freedom to invest in any of the industries or productive activities reserved for the private sector. In this respect also, their position lies somewhere between individual's freedom to save and invest under capitalism and that under communism.

REFERENCES

1. *The Economics of Socialism* — J. Wilczynski, page 95.
2. *Ibid.*
3. *Ibid.*, page 97.
4. *The Economics of Socialism* — J. Wilczynski, page 97.

CHAPTER 6

ECONOMIC SYSTEMS AND SOCIAL JUSTICE

It is very difficult to define the concept of 'social justice.' The content of the concept of social justice or answer to the question 'what is social justice,' has changed from time to time depending upon the ethos of the age. "Some are born slaves and some are born masters" declared one of the wisest among the Greeks, Aristotle; and for long it was accepted and acted upon. Today it would be condemned outright as a preposterous proposition. This shows that content of social justice has vastly differed from time to time.

Clearly at present, social justice has something to do with sharing of income, wealth and power with mass of people. Would social justice be secured if all are given equal income, wealth and power? Some critics would say that under such circumstances, the lazy and idolent would get as much reward as the intelligent and industrious and this would not only mean injustice to the latter but would also encourage laziness and indolence among members of society, reducing the rate of growth of the economy. Also giving equal share to the weak and old as much as to young and strong would be wasteful, apart from being unjust.

This mean social justice under any economic system will have to admit some degree of inequality in the distribution of income, wealth and economic power. If this inequality is in proportion to the contribution that individuals make to national wealth and social welfare (*i.e.*, if inequality is on purely functional ground), it would appear socially just as it would discourage indolence and laziness and encourage individual efforts to do his best. There thus appears to be a feeling that certain amount of inequalities in income, wealth and power based on merit and contribution would not only be socially just but would also encourage higher rate of growth of the economy.

Even while admitting inequalities, the concept of social justice, at present, implies that nobody, whatever his merit, status and contribution to production and social welfare, should get below a minimum that would be required to satisfy his basic needs and help him provide for the future, relieving him of the anxiety regarding tomorrows bread; but nobody however significant and high his contribution should also get beyond a certain maximum. There has however not been agreement as to what the proportion should be between the minimum and maximum, the figure varying from 1 : 30 to 1 : 300.

While inequalities of income are admitted even in communist countries, what is generally agreed among social scientists while discussing content of social justice is that inequalities arising out of unearned income (out of ancestral property or savings, etc.,) should as far as possible be reduced, if not eliminated. Complete elimination of such unearned incomes would mean that at the death of every individual all his savings and accumulated property would revert back to the State and the new generation will have to begin the race on equal footing. There is some justice in this concept; but since the institution of family continues to be a basic unit, love and provision for one's off-springs is a powerful incentive to increase efficiency and production. Any attempt therefore at complete elimination of unearned income at present (especially in capitalist countries as also countries with mixed economy) would produce adverse effects on production of national wealth. In case of complete elimination of ancestral property and unearned income, social justice would then require that the State takes full care of the retired and disabled persons, children, their maintenance, education and such other things which are being done at present by family institution. This appears unlikely and also impracticable under capitalism or mixed economy.

But one thing is certain and it is that whatever the type of economic system, in order that it is socially just, the system must provide equal opportunities of development to all so that each individual is in a position to develop his potentialities to the fullest possible extent.

(In a country like India, where harijans and tribals have come to be neglected for thousands of years, provision of equal opportunities for all would also mean providing some special financial and other assistance to them as also reservation of jobs for some years to come because due to long neglect, they would find it impossible to compete with better-off classes on equal terms).

Regarding sharing of economic power (apart from income and wealth), modern thinking and therefore the content of social justice in this regard is that big modern industries, whether they are in public sector or in private sector, are joint ventures wherein all participants — managers, technical personnel and workers — play their role. Roles of all are essential, if the industrial enterprise is to be efficient and successful. And therefore it is contended that just as in a political democracy every one has a single vote whatever his wealth, intelligence and status in society, similarly justice in the economic field requires economic democracy where each individual irrespective of his position and status should have a voice in the management of the enterprise. At any rate each should be provided an opportunity to co-operate in decision-making at appropriate levels. It is this kind of participation which will remove barriers that exist at present between the class of managers and workers and get both of them completely involved in the enterprise of which they will feel they are an indispensable part. This will naturally increase efficiency of the industrial establishment and of the economy as a whole.

CHAPTER 7

ECONOMIC INSTITUTIONS AS MEANS AND ENDS

Human actions are guided or influenced by certain ideological consideration. Man has certain moral and material vision before him that he wants to attain.

For example, in the economic sphere man wants to satisfy as many material wants as he can, consistent with the resources and technological knowledge and organisations ability available in the community. He wants to raise continually his standard of living with new inventions and new processes of production. He wants to live materially prosperous and contented life. He wants to be above, as far as possible, material wants.

When once these material wants are satisfied, man aims at higher values of life. He wants to get as many opportunities as possible for developing his personality; he wants opportunities to develop his creative faculties. He wants to co-operate with fellow human-beings and live happy, creative, contented and all-round life in a world where all arts and sciences get maximum scope for development.

Translated in economic terms, the community aims at raising economic growth rate of the economy, wants to ensure minimum living conditions for all and go on raising it; the community in modern times wants reduction in extreme inequalities in income and wealth and thus more equitable distribution of wealth in the community so that no individual or section of a community has command over the economic lives of others. There is also the idea that each citizen should have voice in the management of the economic life of the community. It is when these economic conditions are guaranteed or material base is secured for all citizens that they then turn their attention to higher attainments in the cultural and creative field — literature, music, painting, architecture, travel and so on.

Every man and every community in the world have these inner urges. These are the ultimate ends to attain which man along with his fellow human-beings strives perpetually.

From that point of view it might be rightly said that economic organisation or economic system that a group of people or a community adopts is only a means to attain the above objectives. Economic system is nothing more or less than means helping the community to attain the above ends.

Thus economic institutions together constituting an economic system get established in consonance with the philosophy and material and moral ideas of the prevailing times. For some time they act as quite effective 'means' to help the community realise its material and non-material ideals.

But in course of time, because of the dynamic changes which are taking place, conditions change, so do man's aims, objective and visions. (For example, nationalism came to replace local loyalties and in course of time internationalism has come to replace nationalism; or there took place shift from monarchical form of government to democratic form; and inequalities which were tolerated once appeared thoroughly unjust).

But by then, the economic system which was appropriate at one time and in consonance with the desires and aspirations of the people develops vested interests who begin to oppose any changes in the economic system necessitated by changing times. This means economic system which came to be established at one time to attain certain ends, ceases to be a means and begins to be viewed as an end in itself. Thus as in the economic sphere, in other spheres 'also' there takes place the usual confusion between 'means' and 'ends.' What were established as 'means' becomes 'ends' in themselves, and vested interests who stand to gain by the established economic or non-economic system oppose all changes on the ground that the system is sacrosanct. (Thus in the case of India, there was opposition to abolition to Zamindari system, to introduction of ceiling on land, to nationalisation of commercial banks and so on and so forth on the ground that they are old and therefore sacrosanct institutions).

But one lesson that history teaches us it that every community must always make clear distinction between 'means' and 'ends'; and as, due to dynamic changes, 'ends' go on changing or new visions appear on the scene, the old institutional set-up or economic system must be changed by bringing suitable adjustments. Any attempt to hold on to the established economic system rigidly as if it was an 'end' in itself would mean disaster for the country. In fact, this applies not only to economic system but also to political system, educational system and so on. One reason why Asian countries which have old civilizations have remained backward in spite of their vast natural and human resources has been their inability to regard their institutions mainly as 'means' but to consider them as 'ends' in themselves, though the times have vastly changed and a totally new national and international environment is facing them.

CHAPTER 8

DIFFERENT STAGES IN THE EVOLUTION OF CAPITALISM

1. INTRODUCTION

An important feature of the medieval period was that growth of commerce gave rise to the origin, growth and expansion of towns. As trade and commerce continued to expand during the medieval period, more and more towns came into established along the banks of rivers or at important cross-roads or some such convenient places from the point of trade. In such towns, there usually used to be a cathedral and fortified place known as 'Burg' which afforded protection in times of disturbances. As more and more merchants flocked into a town, they built in course of time a wall around the town that could afford protection both to merchants and to their merchandise.

As we saw, it was trade and commerce that gave rise to growth of towns during medieval *i.e.*, feudal age. The merchants flocked together because they were all interested in making money by exchanging goods (*i.e.*, by trading), not as producers of goods.

The merchants who flocked into emerging towns discovered that their strength lay in union. When travelling from place to place with their goods to be sold in different markets, they would join together to protect themselves from brigands and on seas against pirates.

Trade and commerce require and flourish in an atmosphere of freedom. Trade and traders naturally abhore restrictions of any sort.

It was therefore natural that traders and merchants who flocked into medieval towns to carry on their trading activities resented various feudal restrictions by which they found themselves bond at each and every stage of their activities. The merchants and traders resented and found oppressive the manorial lord's rules and regulations governing their activities in towns in that particular manor. Thus a sort of conflict developed between the manorial lords and traders and merchants in towns. Traders and merchants wanted freedom from feudal regulations and conventions to carry on their trading activities in towns. They found that their strength lay in union. They therefore established their associations, called 'Guilds' or 'Hanses' to win freedom from feudal rules and regulations.

2. MERCHANT GUILDS

Life in feudal or medieval age was essentially communal (*i.e.*, community-based) and co-operative. It was therefore to be expected that merchants in medieval towns formed their own associations. They were known as 'Merchant Guilds.' Merchants in each town thus had a merchant guild.

In general members of a merchant guild enjoyed certain privileges. They alone had the monopoly of wholesale and retail trading in the particular town where the merchant guild was established and functioning. The merchant guild had practically complete control over buying and selling activities in a town. All such activities had necessarily to be conducted through the merchant guild.

The main objective of a merchant guild in a town was to establish fair trading practices. The merchant guild saw that the merchants in the town sold various goods at 'fair prices', a 'fair price' being based on cost of production. The merchant guild also saw that various unfair practices were not resorted to by merchants in the town.

For example, the merchant guild was opposed to 'Regrating' *i.e.*, the practice of buying goods in the same market with a view to sell again at a higher price without adding anything to the usefulness of the goods. Such a practice was strictly forbidden by the merchant guild. The practice of 'Forestalling' which consisted in purchasing of goods on the way to the town-market or immediately on their arrival before the market opened or commenced its activities according to established conventions, with a view to get such goods cheaply and make higher profit was also prohibited. The merchant guild was also opposed to the practice of 'Engrossing' which meant storing of goods in anticipation of possible shortages or as protection against possible rising prices.

It would thus be observed that objective of a merchant guild in a medieval town was 'fair trade'. — fair to other merchant in the town, and fair to customers buying various commodities in the town market.

Merchant guild regulated different aspects of training activities in the town. It checked quality of goods sold in the market; goods of unsatisfactory quality were confiscated and owners were punished by the merchant guild. Buyers of various goods in the market town were protected by the merchant guild from various possible dishonest practices of merchants and those found practising such dishonest tricks were dismembered from the merchant guild. Thus a merchant guild kept watchful eye on weights and measures, on quality of goods, on their prices and so on. If a merchant made extraordinary profits in a transaction, he was made to share his profits with other merchant-members of the merchant guild. Thus a merchant guild aimed at establishing fair competition among its merchant-members and put a check to emergence of monopoly of merchants.

The merchant guild also did an important function of settlement of disputes among its members regarding repayment of debts or settlement of mutual obligations, etc. The merchant guild by convention had acquired powers to enforce its decisions on its members.

A merchant guild was not just performing functions regarding commercial activities of its members. It was also concerned with social and religious aspects of the lives of its members. It came to the assistance of a member who was overtaken by misfortune or rendered assistance to children and widows of diseased members of the merchant guild. A merchant guild was a sort of professional-cum-social club in those days catering to various needs of its members and thus occupying a very important position in the day-to-day life of its members.

Organisation of a Merchant Guild

As we saw, in each town there was a merchant guild. Alderman was at the head of such a guild, and he was assisted in the management by about four wardens who constituted a council. The guild held periodical meetings wherein new members were admitted to the guild, new rules and regulations were made, if felt necessary, and other important business was transacted.

There was a Guild Court which held occasional meetings for the settlement of disputes among its members. Its decisions were binding on the members. The guild court also tried offences committed by guild members against its rules and ordinances.

It should be noted that there was no opposition or opposing interests between the merchant guild in a town and the town itself. Most of the guild-members were burgesses (*i.e.*, town people) and practically all the important town people (burgesses) were members of the merchant guild in the town. The same people were active in the affairs of the merchant guild and of the town. Rich merchants held offices both in the merchant guild and in the body that looked after administration of the town. In course of time the merchant guild and government of the town tended to merge into a single organisation.

Rise of towns and merchant guilds in a manor posed a threat to the power of lord of the manor and clergy who generally supported him. The town people, merchants and merchant guild found feudal rules and regulations oppressive and wanted freedom to carry on their trading activities as also other affairs of their town. But it should be remembered that the towns in a manor did not aspire for complete independence but only freedom from feudal rules and regulations which if observed or obeyed would have hampered expansion of trade and administration of towns in the manor.

In course of time, towns, merchant guilds, townsmen and merchants did manage to secure varying degrees of freedom from the authority and feudal regulations of the manorial lord. This freedom varied from town to town and from manor to manor. For example, in Italy towns became practically independent republic totally free from the authority of feudal lords. In other places towns became free communes with varying degree of independence from feudal regulations and with varying degree of authority for self-government. But some towns, for all practical purposes, still continued to be under the dominance of feudal lords. Of course, all these changes came about very gradually and not all at once.

There is however no doubt that growth of commerce, emergence of towns, merchant guilds and government of towns brought about in course of time considerable changes in the feudal organisation in most countries of Europe.

In place of land and agriculture which dominated the feudal age, slowly commerce and trade assumed importance as a source of wealth. Merchant with his commerce and wealth in terms of money began assuming increasing importance in place of traditional feudal landlords with their landed property.

Thus in the feudal age it was landlord, landed property, cultivation of land with the help of serfs who were exploited, immence power and prestige enjoyed by landlords and clergy that dominated the feudal scene. Slow transformation was taking place in this. Commerce and trade were assuming increasing significance. Instead of depending on land, a new class of middlemen was emerging who were living on trade and commerce; wealth in terms of money was assuming increasing significance in place of land as a source of wealth; the middle class town people who were gradually emerging started claiming and did manage to get increasing freedom from feudal rules, regulations and obligations, and they started enjoying greater power in the administration of towns.

3. CRAFT GUILDS

One impact of the growth of commerce and towns was that it brought about structural changes in the economy of a country. People in a town generally engaged themselves in commerce, trade or industry and depended for foodgrains on rural areas. Thus there gradually appeared division of labour, urban areas and people specialising in trade, commerce and industries and rural areas and people generally concentrating on agriculture.

But it should be noted that industries in towns were carried on mostly in households. Also the main purpose of carrying with production of industrial goods was satisfying the needs of the family. Thus in a family there used to be spinning, weaving and stitching of clothes for members of the household concerned. It took quite some time before markets in towns expanded sufficiently permitting craftsman to specialise in different crafts and producing for various markets.

Rise of towns gradually led to craftsmen in rural areas give up agriculture and migrate to towns and specialise in the production of commodities like candle-stick baking butchering, etc., and produce those goods for expanding markets. Specialisation thus started taking place instead of household production meant for satisfying needs of each households. Of course, the whole process, it must be noted, was very gradual. As markets grew, there came about growing degree of specialisation by craftsmen in towns.

The establishment of a typical craftsman at this stage of evolution was fairly simple. He produced goods in his own house; and if he had requisite skill he could successfully sell his goods in market or the town. He worked with small amount of capital and with the help of family labour. If demand for his goods was found increasing, he took assistance of one or two helpers whom he hired for work. Thus in this stage of evolution of industry, professional craftsmen who owned tools and raw materials began producing goods to be sold in outside markets, instead of the old method of household production meant to satisfy the needs of members of the family.

Gradually craftsmen engaged in the same trade or producing the same commodity formed themselves into a 'Craft Guild.' In this they were following the model already set before them by merchant guild in each town.

Thus all craftsmen practising the same trade (*i.e.,* producing the same commodity) formed themselves into a fairly close-knit association known as craft guild.

Everyone doing the same work in a town became a member of that particular craft guild. There was the master craftsman, journeyman and apprentice. All these three categories were members of their craft guild. There was no distinction between one master craftsman and another master craftsman; and the same was true in respect of journeymen and apprentices. Master craftsman, journeyman and apprentice represented not different social status but three stages in the career of a craftsman. He would start as an apprentice under a master craftsman; become in course of time a journeyman; and if capable, would after due experience become a master craftsman setting his own establishment.

Thus there was craft guild for each trade or industry; all members, whatever their professional status, were members of their respective craft guilds.

Gradually each craft guild developed into a sort of monopolistic organisation with more or less complete control over its particular trade. It formed regulations regarding output to be produced, its quality and price at which the commodity was to be sold. The particular craft guild also had control over the entry of people in that particular trade. If need was there, an individual was allowed to enter a particular trade as an apprentice serving under a master craftsman. Normally an apprentice had to serve in that capacity for about seven years. Throughout this period he lived in the house of the master craftsman who housed him, clothed him and fed him, in addition to training him his particular craft. Each master craftsman was permitted by the craft guild to take only a limited number of apprentices under him.

After serving the requisite number of years as an apprentice, a person could set up himself as a master craftsman if he had the necessary capital, skill and ability to satisfy the conditions laid down to become a master craftsman by the particular craft guild.

In case an apprentice was not in a position to become a master craftsman, he could become a journeyman under his craft master going from place to place with finished goods for purposes of selling them and also for learning the tricks of his trade. After sufficient experience and after accumulating sufficient capital, a journeyman aspired and very often became in due course of time a master craftsman.

After the selected individual served as an apprentice under master craftsman for a specified number of years and later, if necessary as a journeyman, as we saw, he could aspire to be a master craftsman in the particular craft. But to become a master craftsman, he had to satisfy rigorous conditions laid down for the purpose by the particular craft guild. To become a master craftsman and set up his own individual establishment, the individual must possess adequate experience in the craft, necessary skill to manufacture the commodity, skill to teach his apprentices; he should be married and with a house of his own with adequate capital to invest in his business and thus having capacity to house, feed and clothe apprentices when he became a master craftsman. If he satisfied all these conditions, he was allowed to be a master craftsman and share in the monopoly in respect of producing and selling his particular commodity at a fair price.

A particular craft guild put severe restriction of all its master craftsman. The whole idea was to establish equality among them.

All master craftsmen in the trade were required by the craft guild to employ the same technique of production. No one was allowed to introduce any change in technique unless approved by the craft guild, as that would make competition among them unequal. All master craftsmen were required to work with the same amount of equipment in the forms of tools. Master craftsmen were not permitted to advertise their goods or do anything special to attract customers. And they were required to sell their goods only to people in the particular town where they had set up their workshop and at prices regulated by their craft guild. Thus craft guild put severe limitations on all those practising the particular trade and saw that all the conditions laid down were strictly followed by master craftsmen, journeymen and apprentices in that particular trade.

Thus a craft guild of a particular craft or industry controlled the industry. The aim of the craft guild was to secure fair dealings. Prices were to be fair and were to be based on cost of production. There was to be no variation in prices on account of scarcity or otherwise of that commodity in a market. It was the function of the craft guild to ensure satisfactory living to its members. But the craft guild was more interested in maintaining its reputation for satisfactory workmanship and fair dealing rather than in promoting individual interest of members of the craft guild. But though in control of the industry, it functioned under the control and authority of the government of the town where the craft guild existed.

Organisation of Craft Guild

Organisation of craft guild was similar to that of merchant guild. A number of wardens headed a craft guild; these wardens were elected by members appointed by the Mayor of the town. The function of wardens was to supervise workmanship of members of the craft guild and see that goods produced were of satisfactory quality. Goods of inferior quality were confiscated and often fine was imposed on the workman who produced such inferior quality goods. The craft guild prescribed rules and regulations regarding various aspects of the industry and it was the duty of wardens to see that these rules and regulations were properly enforced and obeyed by all the members of the craft guild.

A craft guild was also intimately concerned with social, religious and philanthropic activities of its members. Members of a craft guild generally worshipped the same patron saint of the craft guild. The craft guild provided assistance to its members when they were in difficulties. It looked after children and widows of diseased members of the craft guild. Some of the wealthier craft guilds established schools for children of their members and maintained almshouses for the maintenance of the poor, aged and sick out of the funds contributed by their members. Thus a craft guild served also a social club where members often met, exchanged views and tried to solve problems whether of social or some other nature. Thus a craft guild played a dominant role in the life of members not only in respect of their professional activities but also social and cultural activities. It was a vital institution of the day.

Decline of Craft Guilds

It might broadly be said that the system of craft guilds reached its peak in the first half of the 14th century. After that, the system might be said to be on the decline. Following were the factors responsible for the decline of the craft guild system which was a powerful institution during the feudal age.

The craft guild system catering to town market and with equality prevailing among master craftsmen and journeymen started facing difficulties when markets started expanding.

As markets became wider, production of goods began to be made on a larger scale than before. This required more capital. The wealthier craft masters naturally were the ones who had the capital. Majority of journeymen did not possess the necessary amount of capital. And therefore the chances of journeymen becoming a master craftsman diminished. There appeared inequality of status among master craftsmen and journeymen. Once these two were stages in a career. Now the position was different and there appeared inequality of status between master craftsmen and journeymen who now occupied lower status.

Also with expanding markets and large-scale production of goods, master craftsmen who once were themselves craftsmen manufacturing goods, stopped producing goods but became employers of craftsmen from whom they got goods manufactured. Thus the class of employers of hired labour gradually emerged.

Also if in a small town-market the concept of 'fair price' based on cost of production was important, with ever expanding markets, the concept of fair price gave place to fluctuating price of the same commodity depending upon the prevailing market conditions.

Thus there appeared conflict of interests between master craftsmen and journeymen who began to be employees of the former. The master craftsmen complained that journeymen were idle and inefficient not doing their work properly; the journeymen complained that master craftsmen who employed them were oppressing journeymen. Thus there developed conflict of interest between the two. After all unity among master craftsmen, journeymen and apprentices was the sound basis of craft guild. That unity no more existed thus undermining the craft guild.

Master craftsmen obstructed promising journeymen from becoming master craftsmen. They reserved this position for their sons and near-relatives.

The journeymen who felt that they were oppressed by master craftsmen who now started employing them broke away from the traditional craft guild and started their own journeymen's guild with a view to protect their interest. But craft guilds now made up mostly of master craftsmen who were wealthy and powerful opposed these guilds of journeymen and often compelled town authorities to put obstacles in their way.

Towards the end of the middle ages (*i.e.*, by the middle of the 14th century) as the markets started expanding and spirit of competition started prevailing, craft guilds became narrower and narrower caring little for fair practices and fair dealings in the market. Each member of a craft guild was now seeking more after self-interest.

With the coming of Tudors to power (1485) craft guilds further declined in their importance. Regulations of craft guilds began to be considered as obstacles in the way of industrial progress. New towns developed with new industries where from the beginning craft guilds did not exist or were not permitted to come into existence. Many craftsmen tied to the rules and regulations of craft guilds in old towns left those towns for new ones where industries were flourishing because of the absence of regulations of craft guilds. Thus craft guilds in older towns became weaker and weaker with diminishing number of membership, loss of status and disappearance of traditional functions.

Craft guilds had a positive role in town economy when production was on a small-scale and for town market and relations were based on co-operative basis.

But with the emergence of large-scale production consequent on a number of inventions, with increasing requirement of capital and production for ever-expanding markets, craft guilds under these new circumstances found themselves playing decreasing role. It was a case of new environment making an institution useful at one time out dated.

Emergence of nation-state was another cause of decline of craft guilds in various towns. With the emergence of nation-state, the central power over the entire territory that constituted a nation came to be concentrated in the king. He made all the legislation and the so-called free towns lost the power of governance once enjoyed by them. Craftsmen hereafter were required as citizens of a nation to owe their loyalty to the monarch and abide by his laws and not by those of craft guilds. Naturally this resulted in decline of craft guilds.

4. PUTTING-OUT SYSTEM

Guild system was an institution suited for a small local market. As markets became wider breaking local barriers, there emerged a class of middlemen whose main function was to ensure that goods made by workers reached consumers in far-flung areas and regions.

The craft master in the guild system used to perform a number of functions. For example, he used to act as a merchant when he used to purchase raw materials to be worked into finished products. He was an employer under whom worked journeymen and apprentices. The craft master was also a foreman in that he supervised the work of journeymen and apprentices working under him. He also acted as a shopkeeper in that he sold the finished products.

The new emerging class of middlemen took over master craftman's functions of merchant, leaving him the other functions of employer and foreman and worker. The middleman started bringing raw materials to craftsman and when the goods were ready would return and take away goods from him for being sold to consumers. As the market was rapidly expanding, the middlemen brought to craftsmen raw materials in increasing quantities and took away finished goods in ever increasing quantities to be sold in near and distant markets.

This method whereby a middleman provides raw materials to craftsmen who work on those raw materials at their homes and hand over finished products to the middleman was known a "putting-out system." It should be noted that emergence of middlemen and of "putting-out system" made no difference to techniques of production. The craftsman still worked at his house with the same tools and implements. The emergence of middlemen only brought about changes in the marketing of finished goods. Middlemen specialised as merchants.

Though the class of middlemen did not bring about any fundamental changes in techniques of production, they however brought about reorganisation of the process of production. It was in the interest of middlemen to increase output of finished goods. He soon realised that if each craftsman specialised in a particular process instead of himself undertaking all the processes of production, such a specialisation or division of labour had favourable effect on production which increased as a consequence of specialisation. Specialisation was found to save time and speed up processes of production. Each craftsman was employed in that process for which he was best fitted. This resulted in increased efficiency of craftsmen in general and therefore in significant increase in output. Specialisation also meant economy in capital goods. Thus in textile industry, different craftsmen specialised in different processes like carding, spinning, weaving, pressing, packing and so on. When each did the same process repeatedly, his dexterity and therefore efficiency increased with favourable effect on output in which the middlemen was mainly interested.

It should be noted that the craft guild wanted to maintain the monopoly in respect of both production and selling of goods. There was thus clash of interest of the class of middlemen and craft guilds. The middlemen found the extremely detailed and rigorously enforced regulation regarding every aspect of production — right from purchase of raw materials to the sale of finished goods — hampering their methods of work which they were devising to meet demands of ever-expanding markets. Of course, for long the class of middlemen worked within the broad framework of the craft guild system and it was only gradually that the class of middlemen undermined the various regulations of craft guilds and emerged as an independent class of middlemen.

When, for example, middlemen found it difficult to break the rules of craft guilds, they moved outside the town and sometimes in rural areas where guild rules did not apply and got goods produced. Craft guilds naturally objected to such practices of middlemen but the craft guilds were facing a losing battle in the face of ever expanding markets and necessity of the class of middlemen to link producers with consumers spread over wide areas.

Especially in textile industry, the middlemen brought increasing quantities of cotton sometimes even to craft guilds which were ready to receive the raw material to be woven into cloth. Often the middlemen gave cotton to peasants and rural people to make cloth out of it. As due to enclosure movement, many peasants had lost their lands, they found it convenient to work at home on raw cotton supplied by the middlemen and earn some badly needed income.

In course of time, some enterprising middlemen instead of supplying raw materials to craftsmen to be worked at home, started employing master craftsmen, journeymen and apprentices who all worked at one place or under the same shed. These people were hired to produce goods and they all worked at one place, the employer being the enterprising middlemen who got the work of production done and arranged for its being sold in expanding markets. This was the forerunner of the factory system in England and other West European countries after two or three centuries.

It should be noted that under the craft guild system capital played a minor role. Under the "putting-out system," the middlemen had to purchase raw materials on a large scale and also arrange for sale of finished products on a large scale. Such a middlemen therefore required substantial amount of capital both to purchase large quantities of raw materials and arrange sales over wide markets. Naturally it was only a rich middlemen who could afford to do this.

Broadly, it might be said that from 16th century to 18th century the independent craftsmen tended to gradually disappear and their place gradually came to be taken by hired workers working for a capitalist employer — the middlemen entrepreneurs.

5. THE FACTORY SYSTEM

Between roughly the middle of the 18th century and 1830 England first experienced what is generally referred to as 'Industrial Revolution.' From England the industrial revolution spread to countries of Western Europe and to the United States.

The Industrial Revolution might be said to have begun with a number of inventions first in the cotton textile industry and then in other industries like coal and steel. These inventions mostly took place first in England and from there quickly spread to other West European countries and then to be United States

Some of important inventions of this period in the textile industry in England were: John Kay's Flying Shuttle (1733), James Hargreave's Spinning Jenny (1967), Richard Arkwright's Spinning machine called Water Frame working on water power (1769), Samuel Crompton's Mule (1776) and Edmund Cartwright's Power-loom.

Invention of Steam Engine by James Watt in 1765 was a landmark from all points of view. Steam engine and steam power could be used for a variety of purposes such as pumping water from mines, for operating cranes, for continually driving machines of various types, for railways which became mode of transport of goods and passengers at a fast speed over long distances.

Along with above mentioned inventions in textile industry, steam power which could work, unlike human being, in a tireless way, brought about large-scale production in cotton textile industry. To run steam engines ever-increasing quantities of coal was required. And therefore at about the same time a number of inventions took place in coal industry making possible much needed large-scale production of coal. For making various types of machines needed by inventions in textile industry, for machines to be used in coal industry and for making increasing number of steam engines to be used in textile and coal industries and for making railway engines, there was increasing demand for iron and steel. Naturally a number of inventions took place almost simultaneously in iron and steel industry — better processing method, smelting of iron, making of steel out of iron ore by removing carbon particles by improved processes and so on.

Large-scale production in textile industry required improvements in methods of bleaching, colouring, etc. As a consequence, simultaneously a number of inventions took place in the chemical industry.

As we saw, large-scale production required fast and cheap movement of raw materials, of coal, of iron and steel and of finished products. This brought about a number of changes and inventions in the field of transport and communications.

Thus invention in textiles, coal, iron and steel, chemicals and transport between roughly 1730 and 1830 first in England and later in West European countries and the United States brought about what is referred to as the 'Industrial Revolution.'

These inventions, use of more and more machines, large-scale production and rapid distribution of goods through fast means of communications like railways and steamship changed the mode of production from household production and "putting-out system" into factory system of production.

Since machines required huge amount of investment, only rich entrepreneurs came forward to establish factories wherein machines were installed and large-scale production took place. Since small-scale domestic producers of cotton textiles and other goods could not compete with factory production, they came to these factories as workers in search of jobs. Thus a new working class came into existence. Under the factory system large number of workers were employed under the same roof by the factoryowner who supplied to workers raw materials and tools. He paid them wages for their work. Workers no longer owned as under guild system either raw materials or tools. Workers no longer required skills needed under the guild system or under the system of domestic production. This was because of increasing division of labour requiring each worker to do only one process of one out of several parts of a product.

A new class of entrepreneurs who had vast capital to invest in machines, and factories and to pay wages to large number of workers came into existence.

Society gradually came to be divided into the class of capitalist employers and wage-earning workers.

Thus under the factory system vast number of workers worked under the same roof for capitalist employer who supplied to workers raw materials and machines and paid them wages for their work, got produced goods on a large-scale and managed to sell them in different markets — all with a view to make maximum profit for himself.

The factory system of production with machines, division of labour, vast number of workers working under the same roof, with large-scale production, workers working for wages and capitalist entrepreneur providing raw materials and machines and arranging selling of goods in different markets — this factory system first came into existence in England (this was designated as the Industrial Revolution) and then later spread to other West European countries and to the United States.

Industrial revolution produced great social and political changes. It divided society into two classes of employers and workers. The capitalist entrepreneur class became all powerful in the political field replacing landed gentry who during the feudal age wielded tremendous political power and social status.

—

CHAPTER 9

CAPITALISM

(WITH SPECIAL REFERENCE TO THE USA)

1. INTRODUCTION

Capitalism has undergone great many changes from its emergence in the second half of the 18th century. Broadly, capitalism as it functioned until about the beginning of the First World War (1914-18) may be said to be *laissez faire* capitalism. It was the nearest that capitalism could approach the pure theoretical model of capitalism.

Since then, and especially since the Great Depression of 1929-33 and much more so after the World War II (1939-45), capitalism has undergone in many respects great many changes. Modern capitalism as compared to the *laissez faire* capitalism is referred to as 'Managed Capitalism' or 'Welfare Capitalism'.

We shall analyse the fundamental features of capitalism, especially of *laissez faire* capitalism of the 19th century, or of the pure theoretical model of capitalism and then later make an attempt to trace the changes which have come about transforming *laissez faire* capitalism into 'Managed,' 'Regulated,' 'Guided' or 'Welfare' capitalism.

2. PROBLEM OF DEFINING CAPITALISM

The market economy based on the institution of private property came to be referred to as 'Capitalism'. But since 'capital' as factor of production is as much used under socialism communism and other economic systems, the term 'capitalism' might create confusion by implying that capitalism is a system that make use of 'capital' as a factor of production, it is better to refer to the system (*i.e.*, capitalism) as 'The Private Enterprise Economy'. Also, since the criticism of capitalism by Karl Marx, 'capitalism' as an economic system has come to be closely associated with 'exploitation of labour'. As we shall see, this is not fundamental feature of capitalism and may or may not be true of modern capitalism. On all these counts, the term 'Private Enterprise Economy' is preferable to the term 'capitalism.'[1]

If the above implications are kept in mind, it will not matter very much if the terms 'capitalism' and 'private enterprise economy' are used interchangeably.

3. IMPORTANT FEATURES OF *LAISSEZ FAIRE* CAPITALISM

Following are the basic features of capitalism:

1. *Self-Interest and Private Profit Motive.* Every institution has to have sound psychological foundation. Under capitalism, the basic foundation is that man is the best judge of his interests, and therefore he should be left free to follow what he wants to do, without being dictated by any one including the State. Similarly, among all the incentives, private profit motive is the most powerful motive. Individuals should therefore be left free to pursue that which they feel is most profitable to them and would serve their self-interest to the maximum possible extent.

2. *Absence of a Central Plan.* Absence of a central and comprehensive plan is a basic feature of capitalism or private enterprise economy. The economy of the USA and West European countries is characterised by decisions of millions of consumers and producers taken independently and without there being any conscious co-ordination or consciously created co-ordinating machinery to correlate all those millions of decisions into a definite pattern. Under capitalism, co-ordination among these millions of decisions taken independently by consumers and producers get co-ordinated through freely fluctuating price-mechanism which acts as a signalling system and brings about a sort of co-ordination between the decisions of consumers as regards what commodities they want, how much quantity of each and at what prices, with the allocation-decisions of millions of producers regarding what commodities to produce and in what quantities and at what prices to sell them in the market.

(Freely fluctuating price-mechanism working under competitive conditions is one of the corner-stones or foundations of private enterprise. It is this mechanism which acts as a substitute for comprehensive economic planning. But insofar as, as we shall see later, monopolies come into existence and there is departure from competitive conditions, prices began to get fixed by monopolies or trade unions and to that extent price-mechanism fails in its attempt to bring about proper co-ordination between decisions of millions of consumers and thousands of producers. This started happening especially after the end of World War I).

But when it is said that there is no planning under capitalism, what is meant is that there is no comprehensive and deliberately drawn plan on a national scale or even for a sector of the economy. There is however 'planning';

but it takes place at the micro-level only, *i.e.*, at the household level or firm or company level.

Another point that should be noted is that when it is said that there is no planning under capitalism, it does not imply that there is no government interference in the economic affairs of the people. Under capitalism (even during the days of *laissez faire* capitalism), government did undertake certain functions such as provision of certain essential goods and services to satisfy community's wants and taking steps to ensure that competitive conditions were maintained in capitalistic countries.

(Under managed or modern capitalism, as we shall see later, government interference is growing due to various reasons as also to realise various socio-economic objectives. This has naturally been producing far-reaching consequences).

3. *Consumer's Sovereignty.* Under private enterprise economy or capitalism, "Consumer is King." This is referred to as 'Consumer's Sovereignty.' Under capitalism, the consumer, after payment of taxes, is free to spend his income on any commodity of his choice or on one assortment of goods and services rather than on another. He is not directed by any authority either to purchase this or not to purchase that commodity or service. The consumer thus gets a chance to maximise his satisfaction because of this freedom that he enjoys as consumer under capitalism.

Under capitalism, 'consumer is king' in another sense also. "When the purchases are made they are seen as 'dollar ballots' cast at the market place in favour of one product or another." It is the expression of consumers' preference expressed through their willingness to pay higher prices for goods for which they have greater preference (than goods of lower preference) that influences the future pattern of production and allocation of resources of producers.

It should be noted that even in a centrally planned communist economy, consumers with money incomes may enjoy certain freedom as consumers to purchase this or that consumer goods at regulated prices. But as remarked by G. N. Halm, "Only when the effects of these purchases on consumer goods prices are used as a guide for future production can there be complete consumer sovereignty."[2]

(Whether under modern capitalism the consumer is really sovereign or not or the question whether the consumer should be allowed free choice in the selection of goods and services are questions which we shall analyse later. But under pure classical model of capitalism or free enterprise economy, consumer's sovereignty is a fundamental aspect of capitalism).

4. *Freedom of Saving and Investment Decisions.* When we say that under capitalism or free enterprise economy, people enjoy freedom of choice as consumers, this automatically implies that they also enjoy freedom of saving whatever part of income they can or wish to save. This is because freedom to

save, in effect, means freedom to choose buying of consumer goods now or buying them in future. Freedom to save implies freedom to sacrifice immediate consumption for future consumption by onself or by members of the family or by those to whom the savings are transferred to. Thus freedom to save includes freedom to accumulate wealth and transmit it to successors.

It is obvious that freedom to save, to accumulate and to transmit and inherit wealth are also part of the institution of private property which, as we shall see, is sacrosanct in capitalism or free enterprise system.

Under capitalism or free enterprise economy, people also enjoy right to invest their savings in any manner they like. For example, they can put their savings in savings bank account or in fixed deposits, or purchase government bonds or use them for creation of any productive asset. When we say that capitalism or free enterprise economy is an unplanned economy this in a sense implies that individuals, households and firms enjoy the right of investing their savings in the manner they like within the alternatives legally available or outside the country.

5. *Freedom to Choose One's Occupation.* Under free enterprise economy, individuals are theoretically free to enter any line of occupation (of course, provided they have ability) and the central authority is not going to order any individual to enter this occupation or that. Thus free choice of one's occupation is fundamental to the system of private enterprise economy.

(The question as to whether one should enjoy such freedom of choice of occupation, or whether under conditions of depression the workers are really free to choose their occupations, and whether and to what extent under modern capitalism an individual truly enjoys the freedom of choice of occupations are questions which shall be taken for discussion later when we consider transformation of *laissez faire* capitalism into managed or regulated or welfare capitalism).

6. *Institution of Private Property.* The institution of private property is fundamental to capitalism or private enterprise economy. The institution of private property "involves the right of an individual to acquire, use, or dispose of something of economic value in any legitimate way the owner wishes and the right to enjoy the economic rewards that result."[3]

Under capitalism, private ownership of property is a matter of right. It is the responsibility of government "to define the scope and nature of this right and, in the event of its violation, to enforce and protect the owner's claim."

It needs to be noted that the institution of private property which is fundamental to capitalism does not include only tangible things like land, buildings, machinery and factories but also intangible things such as contracts or patent rights. "Contracts are legally enforceable agreements for the performance of economic activity."

But it should be noted that the right to use private property as one likes or for the production of goods of his choice and at a place which he might be owning has never been unrestricted. Thus government has always reserved even during the days of *laissez faire* capitalism of the 19th century "The right of eminent domain" whereby government can compel any person to part with his land or property for satisfying a compelling public need, even though the owner may not be willing to sell it. Of course, government will pay reasonable compensation for it. Generally government in capitalist countries has always been imposing some limits on the use of private property in such a manner that it is not injurious to public welfare. Thus "A Philadelphia owner, for instance, is still forbidden to construct a soap, candle, glue starch, lamp-black, bone boiling or skindressing establishment, blacksmith shop, slaughter house, cattle pens, piggery, or other buildings for offensive purpose or occupation on his property." Each generation, in view of its technological conditions, defines in its own way what are 'public nuisances.'

One function of the institution of private property is accumulation of savings essential for the creation of capital goods. Under capitalism, private property provides the greatest incentive to private or corporate capital accumulation and thus plays a vital role in the growth of the economy.

The institution of private property as existing under capitalism also includes the right to transfer wealth through inheritance. Thus law of inheritance and succession is an essential part of the institution of private property. Since the family unit is a basic unit of any economic organisation, law of inheritance and succession becomes a powerful instrument of accumulation of saving and capital formation.

It should thus be noted that even in a purely theoretical approach to capitalism, right to private property cannot be regarded as unrestricted, and as we shall see, though the existence of the institution of private property raises a number of issues in regard to equality and competition, the institution of private property is the cornerstone of free enterprise system or capitalism, and in a sense it may be said that "The other institutions of capitalism derive from and depend upon the cornerstone of private property to a large extent."[4]

7. *Freedom of Enterprise.* The concept of freedom of enterprise is implicit in or follows from the institution of private property. Freedom of enterprise gives the owners of private property" to select the type of economic activity in which their resources will be employed."

But what needs to be noted is that the concept of freedom of enterprise does not include only the right of property owners to use their resources in any one of the different avenues open; but the concept in a broadest sense "also includes the freedom of every individual participating in any kind of economic activity whether as a worker or as holder of liquid resources or any other productive resources." Under capitalism they all enjoy freedom of enterprise.

It is the basic tenet of free enterprise economy that every one (acting either as an individual or as a corporate body) is the best judge of self-interest. And therefore if there is freedom of enterprise, the owners of resources will use their resources in the best manner possible with a view to maximise profit. Owners of productive resources who enjoy freedom of enterprise will direct their resources towards their most efficient and profitable use. This, as we shall note, has a great bearing on efficiency of free enterprise system.

Joseph Schumpeter's entrepreneur and the role assigned to him by Schumpeter—finding a new product, inventing a new machine or finding a new technology, or a new structure of business organisation or a new market to take risk and make profits if successful or suffer losses if unsuccessful no more characterises advanced stage of capitalism. In developed form of capitalism, freedom of enterprise expresses itself through business corporations. Big business corporations represent "a collective form of an 'economic man' intent on profit maximization like the solitary, decision-making entrepreneur."

8. *Existence of Competition or Competitive Markets.* Competition is another cornerstone of capitalism or free market economy. Competition refers to existence of a number of independent buyers and sellers of a commodity or product or service in a market. Competition among independent buyers and sellers assumes that nobody or no authority brings any sort of coercion on any one of them as a buyer or seller either to sell or buy any commodity at any particular place or price. Existence of competition implies that price of a commodity or service will be determined by competitive forces of demand and supply operating in the market.

It should be noted that under capitalism, competition exists both in consumer goods markets and capital goods markets. Competition exists among sellers of consumer goods, capital goods and various types of services (*i.e.*, among workers, employers and entrepreneurs) as also among buyers of above commodities and services. In brief, competition exists both in factor markets and in product markets.

In a competitive market where a number of sellers and buyers are competing among themselves to sell or purchase a commodity, it follows that at any given time, there will be only one price at which a particular commodity will be sold.

Existence of competition also implies that if due to any reason (such as changes in taste, or season, or increase in population or income, etc.,) demand for a particular commodity increases, the price of that commodity will rise relative to prices of other commodities. Under competitive conditions this will serve as a signal to producers to shift their resources to the production of those commodities price of which are rising, with a view to take advantage of rise in price and maximise their profits. If, on the other hand, price of a commodity falls because of decrease in demand due to any cause (decline in population, in income, change in taste or fashion, etc.,) this would mean decline in profits of producers of that commodity who will try to shift their resources from production of that commodity where the margin of profits is declining to production of that commodity where margin of profits will be the maximum. Existence of competition thus brings about most efficient allocation of community's resources on the one hand, helping producers to maximise their profits, and on the other hand, providing consumers commodities and services they most desire, thus helping them to maximise their satisfaction.

The above analysis hold good in the case not only of commodities but also in the case of labour markets. If doctors begin to earn more than professors, the tendency among parents would be to send their children into those lines where they will get highest income instead of into those lines where the levels of incomes are relative lower.

(The above analysis applicable to the theoretical model of capitalism makes a number of assumptions such as producers and consumers have full knowledge of what is happening in the market, that producers and sellers do not misjudge market conditions and above all, the assumption that factors of production are perfectly mobile and can move quickly and smoothly from production of one commodity to another and factors of production are technically capable of producing this or that commodity, and above all, competition among sellers and buyers does not give place to monopoly. It will be observed that the above assumptions often do not represent reality and therefore all the advantages of competition are not realised.)

9. *Harmony and Absence of Conflict between Individual Interests and Interests or Welfare of Society.* The Classical School and more especially Adam Smith who provided foundations for the theoretical model of capitalism believe that there is no conflict between interests of an individual (whose economic activities are guided by self-interest) and interests or welfare of society of which he is a part. On the other hand, they believed that even as an individual is trying to follow his self-interest in the economic sphere, he will be automatically and even without his knowing, promoting the welfare of society.

For example, an individual to promote his own interests will try to become, let us say, the best doctor in the locality, or the best teacher or best architect. He will be doing this entirely to promote his material interests. If in the competitive world he succeeds in achieving his aim, he will make maximum material gain of which he is capable. But at the same time, society will be getting the services of the best doctor, or teacher or architect which would promote welfare of society. Under competitive free enterprise economy, only the best will survive in every line and those who fail in a particular line will have to seek other avenues where their abilities will stand the test of competition and succeed. And thus society will have gained the services of best people in every line and naturally this will be in the highest interest and maximum welfare of society.

To take another illustration, in the field of production, capitalism assumes existence of many producers of a commodity competing among themselves. Each for the sake of his own interest and to succeed over his rivals, will try to invent a new process of production to reduce his cost of production, or increase his efficiency with a view to maximise his personal profits. In a competitive regime in order both to survive and make maximum profits, the other competing producers will also have to make maximum efforts to attain maximum efficiency. The result will be increase in efficiency, new inventions, maximum profits for successful entrepreneurs, elimination of the inefficient ones; while at the same time from the viewpoint of society, this competition among producers and continual efforts to increase efficiency to maximise personal profits would mean lower prices of goods, goods of better quality and with better services leading to the maximisation of consumers' satisfaction and welfare.

Thus one of the fundamental features of the theoretical model of capitalism or *laissez faire* capitalism was that the interests of an individual and those of society not only do not conflict, but actually coincide.

(But in order to understand the shortcomings of capitalism which will be discussed later on in the book, it must be stated that the Classical School which provided foundations of capitalism or free enterprise system was always thinking of long-term and not short-term).

10. *Laissez Faire or Non-Intervention by the State.* If there is no conflict between individual interest and interest or welfare of society, and if also freely fluctuating price mechanism secures at the time both maximum satisfaction for consumers and most efficient allocation of community's resources, it follows that the State under capitalism or free enterprise economy has hardly any role to play in the economic affairs of the people. The State should leave things to people themselves and economic affairs of the people will go on smoothly without State intervention. Under capitalism, therefore, the State is supposed to leave economic activities of people to themselves and capitalism will automatically function smoothly without requirement of any sort of active or positive intervention or planning by the State.

There was also another reason why the policy of *laissez faire* was advocated and broadly followed during the 19th century in capitalist countries.

According to Adam Smith, in all 'ordinary cases', "the natural action of private self-interest leads to the most perfect organisation of social and economic relations and to the greatest welfare of all." According to him, not only *laissez faire* policy is the best due to above reason but in his opinion, government is unfit by its very nature for performing economic functions. Adam Smith's conclusions follow from three incontrovertible facts:1. spendthrift propensities of government; 2. remoteness of government control; and 3. inefficiency of administration because of the negligence and thriftlessness of agents of government.

The founders of the Classical School therefore restricted functions of the State: 1. protection against foreign States; 2. the administration of law and justice; and 3. the establishment and maintenance of certain public works and institutions like streets, canals, embassies, school system, etc., because in these cases due to huge investments required and long gestation period, private individuals interested in maximising personal profits may not be forthcoming to undertake those tasks.

Barring the above few exceptions, the general policy in regard to State should be that of *laissez faire.*[5]

REFERENCES

1. George, N. Halm states that the terms 'Free Enterprise Economy' or 'Individual Enterprise Economy' would be preferable to the terms 'Capitalism.' But according to him, the term 'Free Enterprise Economy' perhaps exaggerates the uncontrolled character of the private section of the market economies of the West. The adjective 'individual,' on the other hand, may create the picture of an economic system that existed before the days of big private corporations. On these accounts, according to G. N. Halm, the term 'Private Enterprise Economy' is preferable to other terms like 'Capitalism' or 'Free Enterprise Economy' or 'Individual Enterprise Economy.'
2. *Economic Systems* — G. N. Halm, page 28-29.
3. *Comparative Economic Systems* — W. N. Loucks and W. G. Whiteny, page 22.
4. *Ibid.*, page 23.
5. Even in respect of *laissez faire* policy, it needs to be stressed that, for smooth working of capitalism or free enterprise economy, existence of the State with sovereign powers is essential. "In this sense government *per se* is an institution of capitalism."

   For example, Milton Friedman, a staunch advocate of minimum role of Government in the economic activities of people in the United States, writes as follows:

   "As government maintained law and order, defined property rights, served as a means whereby we could modify property rights and other rules of the economic game, adjudicated disputes about the interpretation of rules, enforced contracts, promoted competition, provided a monetary framework engaged in activities to counter technical monopolies and to overcome neighbourhood effects widely regarded as sufficiently important to justify government intervention, and which supplemented private charity and the private family in protecting the irresponsible, whether madman or child such a government would clearly have important functions to perform."

   It would thus appear that "Restriction on the institutions of capitalism, even in its purest theoretical form, are essential to keep those institutions from destroying themselves. Without the government's regulatory framework individual self-interest would "play havoc destroying all the values for which capitalism stands or which capitalism embodies."

   From '*Capitalism and Freedoms*' — Milton Friedman, 1962 edition, page 34.

CHAPTER 10

ACHIEVEMENTS AND FAILURES OF CAPITALISM

1. INTRODUCTION

It might be said that so far we described the world of pure capitalism or of free enterprise system with its various fundamental features such as consumer's sovereignty, freedom to choose one's occupation, freedom to save and invest, institution of private property, freedom of enterprise, existence of competition, freely fluctuating price-mechanism influenced by market forces of demand and supply and *laissez faire* principle. Under such pure form of capitalism, it was claimed that maximisation of satisfaction of consumers and most efficient use of resources are almost automatically ensured.

But history of capitalism or free enterprise economy tells us that capitalism in the real world has departéd considerably, the extent of this departure differing from one capitalist country to another. And yet, broadly, it can be said that capitalism in its purest form never existed in any country at any time. The capitalism in the 19th century came nearest to the pure form of capitalism. Since the end of World War I and especially after the Great Depression of 1929-33 and much more so after the end of World War II, capitalism has moved more and more away from the pure model and has, transformed itself into 'Managed' or 'Regulated' or 'Welfare' capitalism. Why did capitalism or free enterprise system undergo such a fundamental transformation? What went wrong with *laissezfaire* capitalism that operated in the 19th century? Before that question is operated, it would be worthwhile to note the achievements of capitalism briefly.

2. ACHIEVEMENTS OF CAPITALISM OR FREE ENTERPRISE ECONOMY

The following may be said to be the main achievements of capitalism:

1. *Powerful Incentive, most Efficient Use of Resources and Increase in Productivity.* As already noted, personal profit motive which is a fundamental feature of capitalism, is the most powerful incentive. Desire for maximising personal profit by succeeding makes men vigilant, calculating and ready to take risks for they know that slackness or misjudgment would mean their ruin. Naturally in capitalism everyone is keyed up to the highest possible pitch of efficiency.

Also, under capitalism, self-interest, economic freedom and competition result in the best utilisation of individual's and therefore community's resources.

Because of the above factors, under capitalism productive efficiency tended to continually rise.

According to Prof. J. A. Schumpeter, rate of increase in output in the USA was 2 per cent per year (compound rate) from 1870 to 1930. According to him, if capitalism repeats its past performance for another fifty years, starting from 1928, this would banish poverty even from the lowest strata of society. According to Prof. Schumpeter, in the USA, net output per man-hour (the national income divided by the total number of annual man-hours) was estimated at 17.3 cents per man-hour in 1850, 35.7 cents in 1900 and 74.0 cents in 1940.

2. *Rising Standard of Living for Masses.* If we take the case of the USA as a typical example of a capitalist country, one can very easily observe that people in the USA (as also in most European capitalist countries) have experienced since the advent of capitalism, rising material standard of living. In the USA (and also in the West European capitalist countries) productive system inspired by private profit motive has been operating at a high and rising level of efficiency, ensuring people continually rising per capita income, in spite of increasing population. What is to be noted is that in spite of great inequalities of income that persist in the USA, all sections of the community have had their share in rising income and material prosperity of the country.

It is observed that US economy with its capitalist system provides an annual flow of goods and services that is truly amazing, and majority of people have been sharing the increasing prosperity in the USA.

To give some instances, "Nine out of ten US families live in dwelling units with inside plumbing, hot and cold running water, electric lighting, and adequate heat — fundamentals still lacking for most of the world's population. Of 63 million households in 1970, 47 million were living in single-family houses, of which 40 million were owner-occupied. Eighty two per cent of all homes had telephones, and 95 per cent had refrigerators. The US stock of housing is so ample that old and badly located units are simply abandoned, whereas in other societies they would have been eagerly repaired."

It is found that US standard goes beyond this material achievements. Thus in 1973, of all persons of 25 years or above, 13 per cent had completed 4 years of college, 60 per cent had completed 12 years of grade school and high school; 76 per cent had completed 8 years of grade school. Only 4.5 per cent had received less than 5 years of schooling.

The US consumers have time and income to enjoy a diversity of recreation, entertainment and leisure-time activities. Thus of all US households, 98 per cent have TV sets; 82 per cent have at least one automobile, and nearly one-third households have two or more cars. The average US citizen travelled over 6,200 miles in 1972.

To give specific illustration from the USA, where capitalism prevails in its fundamental aspects to a greater extent than other countries, measured in terms of 1940 prices, the per capita income has gone up from about $ 200 in 1850 to about $ 600 in 1940. (Quoted by Loucks and Hoot in their 'Comparative Economic Systems' on page 69).

It was further claimed that even by 1940, 40 million homes were equipped with radios in the USA, 22 million homes with electric irons, 13 million with electric washing machines, 12 million with electric refrigerators and 11 million homes with electric vacuum sweepers. Since 1940, things in all these respects have further improved fantastically.

From the above description it is obvious that the fruits of increased productivity and rising living standards have not been confined to a small section of upper class; but the benefits appear to have got diffused fairly widely. In this connection J. A. Schumpeter writes: "It is the cheap cloth, the cheap cotton and rayon fabrics, boots, motor cars and so on that are the typical achievements of capitalist production, and not as a rule improvements that would mean much to the rich man. Queen Elizabeth owned silk stockings. The capitalist achievement does not typically consist in providing more silk stockings for queens but in bringing them within the reach of factory girls in return for steadily decreasing amounts of efforts ... The capitalist process, not by coincidence but by virtue of its mechanism, progressively raises the standard of life of the masses."[1]

While crediting capitalism with the above achievements, a number of aspects must be kept in mind. A number of questions arise: These improvements no doubt have taken place in capitalistic system; but have the improvements come about because of capitalist system in the USA ? Further, how much of the improvements in living standards are due to capitalism and how much due to abundant and varied resources of the USA ? All that we can say therefore is that such an improvement has taken place within capitalist system and it is not incompatible with capitalism. While capitalism may have ensured people under that system higher rising material standard of living than other systems such communism and mixed economy, whether that system also ensured greater happiness to people is a totally different question into which we need not go. And secondly as an author has pointed out, "capitalist institutions *per se* must not be given sole credit for raising our (*i.e.*, of citizens of the USA) standards of living. Scientific research outside the business system, for example, has played an important supplemental role in the development of technology and scientific knowledge."[2]

3. *Rising Opportunities for Individuals.* One of the most remarkable features of the US capitalism (as also generally of capitalism in Western European countries (and Japan) is that private profit motive, individual freedom, the institution of private property and individual freedom have all succeeded in generating massive ability and desire to mobilise various factors of production and direct them towards productive activities.

It may be said that the greatest strength of capitalism lies, in one sense, in its individualism which inspired by personal profit motive and personal freedom has come forward to take risk and organise productive efforts by mobilising resources of production. Individuals spurred by personal profit motive have sought to find out new commodities, new processes, new inventions all with a view to add to their reward or avoid losses. There is no doubt that US capitalism has provided horizontal and vertical mobility to millions of people as is evident from the success achieved by vast number of annual flow of immigrants into the USA. Public system of education, personal profit motives, institution of private property and individual freedom have made the USA a land of opportunities for millions.(The braindrain towards the USA of which we in India often complain can be explained in terms of increasing opportunities offered by the USA to people with different skills as compared with those offered by a mixed economic system in India.)

4. *Technological Progress.* Technological progress is one of the most remarkable achievements of the US capitalism. It would appear that generally the USA (and West European and also Japanese capitalism) is much ahead in respect of technological progress than other economic systems (though these days knowledge spreads quickly to all parts of the world so that the communist countries are trying to catch up as early as possible with the US technological advance).

One or two points need to be noted in this connection. Technological progress in the USA has been brought about by physicists, mathematicians, biochemists and other experts who are responsible for expansion of technological knowledge essential for industrial development. It would not be wholly correct to say that all these were actuated by private profit motive. But what needs to be noted however is that "The important point is that the capitalist setting in which technological progress has taken place provides motivation for cost-reducing technological developments. It also provides an institutional setting in which basic and applied research can be conducted."

5. *Flexibility.* It can be said about capitalism that "It has possessed a flexibility, an adaptability and resiliency which have permitted it to mould its forms and processes into innumerable changes in its environmental setting."

Thus one the greatest merits claimed on behalf of US capitalism is its great flexibility and adaptability. Since the emergence of capitalism by about the middle of the 18th century, innumerable changes have taken place in the US environment, for example, there were wars followed by peace times; there were changes in the technological field and basic shifts in consumer preferences and tastes, increasing urbanisation, industrialisation and increasing complexity of social and political conditions because of revolution in transport and communications and rapid travel which brought about shrinkage in the world.

The US capitalism has adapted itself to all these changes by devising suitable institutions to successfully face new challenges and new times; and what is more important, all these institutional changes came not by planning by the government but by decisions of millions of consumers and producers and within the broad framework of capitalism and without sacrificing the values and features of capitalism or free enterprise economy.

Only one or two instances would be adequate to illustrate flexibility or adaptability of US capitalism (and also of capitalism in other countries to more or less extent). One is the evolution of the corporate form of business organisation which got woven into the capitalist system to meet challenges posed by technological progress and possibility of large-scale production and economies of scale. (Of course large-scale production and big factories have come into existence in response to technological progress in the communist USSR also; but there everything has come out of planning by the State whereas in the USA, the initiative has come from independent decisions of innumerable entrepreneurs and not by any conscious planning by the State.)

Another notable instance of capitalism's flexibility and adaptability is the way the institution of private property went on evolving with changing environment. In the middle of the 18th century (*i.e.*, at the commencement of capitalism in the USA), the institution of private property included almost exclusively things like land, live-stock, and machinery; from that the concept went on expanding to include as time went on intangible possessions like copy and patent rights, contractual rights and obligations, goodwill of business and so on. These are all concepts (as part of the institution of private property) which are absolutely essential for smooth and efficient functioning of highly sophisticated industrial and business establishments in advanced capitalism.

What needs to be noted is that these and such institutional changes came about as a result of initiative taken by innumerable consumers, producers, savers, investors and entrepreneurs on their own to meet new challenges posed by changing environment and again inspired mostly by consideration of private profit.

After the end of World War II, the US society has become very complex necessitating innumerable governmental rules and regulations. It stands as a proof of its flexibility and adaptability that US capitalism has adapted itself to the new situation characterised by government rules and regulations, without however sacrificing its fundamental features.

6. *Liberty.* Capitalism has ensured not only economic freedom to consumers, producers, savers and investors, as we have already seen, but it is observed that wherever capitalism prospered, it has gone hand-in-hand with political democracy wherein people enjoyed not only economic but what is equally important, political equality and liberty. Improving standard of living ensured to people by capitalism aroused in their minds at a certain stage desire for political liberty so that during the 20th century monarchies after monarchies were swept away from capitalistic countries where they existed and in their place republic came to be established, or as in England, monarchy enjoyed only formal and ornamental position without any real power which came to be wielded by the people.

3. INADEQUACIES (*OR* SHORT OR COMINGS) OF CAPITALISM *OR* CRITIQUE OF CAPITALISM IN OPERATION

While capitalism in West European countries and especially in the USA has, as we have already seen, recorded many remarkable achievements which have either not been possible under other economic systems like socialism, fascism, communism and mixed economy, or have not been possible to the same extent, the fact remains that capitalism (laissez faire or old capitalism as well as modern form of capitalism) has been associated with some serious shortcomings, failures or evils. We shall therefore look here at 'critique of capitalism in operation'.

The following may be said to be the chief shortcomings or evils associated with capitalism or private enterprise economy.

1. *Inequality of Income and Wealth.* One of the greatest evils associated with capitalism is the great inequalities in income and wealth among people. In most capitalist countries and notably in the USA, distribution of income and wealth is most uneven, this economic inequality almost automatically leading to social and political inequality though in democracies that prevail in capitalist countries, socially and politically all are supposed to be equal. As Prof. E. H. Carr has remarked, "...the story of the industries errand boy who became the managing director and of the lazy son of the managing director who became an errand boy was soon an agreeable myth which took little or no account of the facts of life."[3]

As regards inequality of income, in 1948, it was observed in the USA that 74 per cent of American individuals earned only 44 per cent of the total income, which means that the remaining 26 per cent of the people enjoyed 56 per cent of the total income.

Prof. Colin Clark also found for the year 1936, that in the United Kingdom, some 12 per cent of income receivers took nearly 42 per cent of the total national income.[4]

TABLE 1

Present Share of US Households in Personal Income for Selected Years 1929 to 1972

	1929	1941	1947	1961	1971
Top 5 per cent	30.0	24.0	20.9	19.6	19.1
Next 15 per cent	24.4	24.8	25.1	25.9	25.6
Middle 60 per cent	42.1	47.1	49.0	49.9	50.5
Lowest 20 per cent	3.5	4.1	5.0	4.6	4.8

Source: Survey of Current Business, October 1974, page 27. D. B. Radner and J. C. Hinriches.

There is no doubt that inequalities at present are substantially smaller today than in the past. Thus while in 1929, the top 5 per cent received 30 per cent of total personal income, in 1971 their share came down to 19.1 per cent. The lowest 20 per cent of US families received only 3.5 per cent of all personal incomes in 1929; this was raised to 4.8 per cent in 1971.

But what needs to be noted is that most of the changes have taken place by mid-1940s, and since then share of the lowest 20 per cent or one-fifth of the total population has not increased at all. The relative gains have come to the middle 60 per cent of income group with incomes (after tax) running roughly between $ 7,500 to $ 19,000. What needs to be noted is that the botton fifth, though much better in real terms than 50 years ago, are far below national median now as they were then.

"Sixteen million out of 25 million US citizens with 1972 incomes below the officially determined poverty level were white. The other 9 million (36 per cent of the total) were made up of black, Chicano native Americans and Puerto Rican minorities... This over-representation of social minorities at the low end of the income structure represents among other things, a long era of systematic discrimination in education, housing, and jobs... In 1972, the median income of white families was $11,500; for other $ 7,100."

Thus, though compared to *laissez faire* capitalism, inequalities are comparatively less, still they are substantial. That even in 1971, the top 5 per cent should enjoy about one-fifth (19 per cent) of total personal incomes while bottom 20 per cent should get just less than 5 per cent shows the enormity of inequalities in income distribution in the USA.[5]

Inequality in income and wealth in capitalist countries arises mainly because of factors like the institution of private property (which itself was historically unequally distributed), law of inheritance and succession (which perpetuates inequalities), and free competition. Though under competition everybody is free to compete on equal terms, in actual fact, those with no or few assets find it very difficult or practically impossible to successfully compete with those with substantial assets. This results in rich becoming richer and poor, poorer. This inequality in income and wealth tends to get perpetuated because of the law of inheritance and succession. A rich man's son not only gets opportunities for better education and for acquiring specialised skills in best educational institutions but also inherits his father's wealth with which to command vast resources and in company with similar rich persons start and own business corporations run on a large scale. The poor have very little opportunities like this. And thus factory manager's son becomes a factory manager and a taxi-driver's son generally a taxi-driver.

The worst part of inequalities of income and wealth under capitalism is that inequality which arises on account of unearned income. A substantial section of people under capitalism are seen to live luxurious life on interest on saving left by their fathers or on rent from lands or buildings which they have inherited. That some should live luxuriously without contributing anything to national wealth while others who are able and willing to contribute or do contribute should be living rather lower or even poor standard of life is normally unjustifiable with corrupting influence.

In the case of the US "There is even greater inequality of unearned income. Most of the non-residential wealth in the United States is concentrated in the richest 5 per cent of population."[6]

Inequality of income and wealth has far-reaching moral, political and economic consequences in capitalist system. It is moral degradation that some should be living luxurious life without doing any worthwhile work while others should be anxious about their tomorrow's bread, in spite of hardwork which they are prepared to put in. The craze for acquiring still more income and property which come to determine the status of a family or person in society results in immoral practices such as tax evasion, speculation, corruption and so on resulting in lowering of moral standards of society. Even the highest in capitalist countries — presidents and prime ministers — are not above this.

Politically inequality gives great political control to the rich through control over powerful media, buying of votes and so on. It would be found that members of US Senate and Congress have mostly come from richer sections of the community and so have the US presidents. This is true of other democracies as also, as they alone can afford heavy election expenses.

What is equally dangerous is that existence of extreme inequalities of income and wealth is likely to split society into two classes of 'Haves' and 'Have-Nots' leading to class rivalry, conflict, violence and sometimes to revolution. On the other hand, cooperation among all these classes is absolutely essential if capitalism is to maintain its steady onward progress.

Economically also, inequalities of income and wealth produce many undesirable consequences. It breeds a class of people living, as we saw, on unearned income without contributing to national wealth and thus wasting their abilities and capacities. Also, able but poor do not get adequate opportunities to develop their abilities and contribute their best to society. Thus their abilities are also allowed to go waste.

Inequalities of income and wealth also come in the way of maximising welfare society as marginal utility of money in the case of rich is small and it is very large in the case of poorer sections of the community who however do not have adequate income. This would imply that more equal distribution of income and wealth would lead to increase in total social welfare.

The worst consequence of inequality of income and wealth is the recurrent economic crisis. The rich who constitute a small percentage of total population have enormous amount of purchasing power but have limited physical capacity to consume goods which because of technological progress are being produced on a vast scale, whereas the poor who constitute a large percentage of the total population have physical capacity to consume goods but lack adequate income to purchase them. The result is over-production, falling prices, rising employment and recurrent economic crisis.

2. *Emergence of Monopolies.* As we have seen, perfect competition is one of the corner-stones of capitalism. What however has taken place instead in practically all capitalistic countries is emergence of monopolies, duopolies and oligopolies. This emergence of monopolistic and semi-monopolistic industrial enterprise has been the result of competition itself (where each rival tries to outdo and destroy other rivals in the same line of production.) This was aided by technological progress and possibilities of large-scale production with economies of scale.

Under capitalism thus, "The individual businessman has been ousted by the company, the company by the cartel and the trust, the trust by the supertrust. In the process sky is the limit; nothing short of monopoly, first national, then in favoured cases, international, is the ultimate goal . . . The continuous and progressive replacement of the small by the larger unit has been the typical trend of the economic organisation of our time."[7]

In the USA, there are at present more than 100 million legally autonomous enterprises (most of them comparatively small, 99 per cent of them employing less than 100 employees).

But this large number of autonomous industrial enterprises is deceptive. It is noticed that bulk of US productive assets and income generated belong to a small group of giant industrial corporations whose reach extends to practically every sector of US economy.

Thus it is observed that out of 10 million legally autonomous industrial enterprises, "A mere 500 companies, including such well-known concerns as

General Motors, IBM, US Steel, and RCA, produce nearly 70 per cent of the nation's total industrial output."

It is also observed that the largest 50 of the 500 giant industrial establishments enjoy a combined sales revenue of $ 350 billion a year, "a sum that approaches one-fourth of America's gross national product."

General Motors alone employs 60,000 workers and its yearly sales revenue exceeds $ 35 billion-more than the GNP of such countries as the Union of South Africa, Denmark, Austria, Yugoslavia, Turkey, and Norway.[8]

These corporate giants enjoy great discretion in deciding what to produce, where, quality of produce and at what prices to sell. "The managers of the giant enterprises, in short, partially supplant the pricing mechanism in the allocation of resources in the United States and thus constitute centres of substantial economic power."[9]

But it ought not to be imagined that it is only capitalist employers who enjoy monopoly power.

If we consider the 'Labour Sector', through of the US total labour force only 24 million workers (roughly 27 per cent of US non-farm labour force) are organised, trade unionism is firmly established in most of the major manufacturing, transportation, and communications industries.

"Labour leaders in areas such as these have considerable power over workers, partially controlling their access to jobs and influencing their wages and working conditions. They have also substantial power over employers; by withholding the supply of labour, unions can raise wage rates or keep them from falling, change working conditions, and influence the level and composition of product demand. And unions have power over consumers, in that strikes reduce or cut off the supply of goods and services and union-caused increases in production and distribution costs often result in higher retail prices. In short, collective bargaining, especially when industrywise, can and often does distort the pricing mechanism as it affects society's resources and distribution of income."

The emergence of monopoly has produced a number of undesirable consequences. It has destroyed advantages claimed for competition, namely, maximisation of satisfaction of consumers and most efficient use of the community's resources. On the other hand, monopoly with control over market has tried to purposely create artificial scarcities by keeping resources idle to raise prices and make higher monopoly profits. This maximisation of consumer satisfaction as also most efficient use of community's resources have both come to be sacrificed under capitalism due to emergence of monopolies.

Further, these giant monopolies, national as well as international, have tried through bribes and other methods to influence national political policies in their favour. In this respect about 200 giant industrial monopolistic corporations have come to dominate US economic scene and control practically every phase of economic and political life of people in the USA.

3. *Failure to Provide Full Employment.* It was assumed that under competition, the level of full employment will be reached and the economy will automatically stabilise there. Unfortunately this has not been so and J. M. Keynes showed that due to various rigidities such as in respect of wage rates, etc., the capitalist economy may stabilise at lower than full employment level.

Failure to provide full employment or make full use of natural and human resources would mean so much wastage of natural and human resources which could have produced much needed wealth, especially by the poorer sections of the community. It also demoralises unemployed people who have to live on government doles euphemistically called unemployment allowances or insurance.

4. *Economic Instability.* Capitalist economy or private enterprise economy is a 'planless' economy where, as we saw, millions of consumers take their own decisions as to what commodities to consume and millions of producers take their own decisions as to what commodities to produce. In such an economy, it is rarely that appropriate balance between supply of thousands of goods and demand for them gets established. Often there is imbalance and capitalist economy therefore is repeatedly visited by trade-cyclical booms and depressions, recessions and frictional disturbances. It is inconceivable that a modern complex economy would work with a fair degree of stability without some sort of economic planning or broad plan framework. Thus economic instability which means anxious days for producers and workers and for every one who is taking part in the process of economic activity of the capitalist country has come to characterise capitalism or free enterprise economy.

A look at US economic history would be instructive in this regard.

"The panic of 1837 had lasted three or four years; that of 1873 had dragged on for five years; the dreadful depression of 1904, 1907 and 1921 were short-lived affairs. But the Great Depression of 1929 lasted almost a full decade. It was unprecedented in length and in the wholesale poverty and tragedy which is inflicted upon society."[11]

During the Great Depression of 1929-33, "Millions of investors lost their life savings . . . Business houses closed their doors, factories shut down, banks crashed and millions of unemployed walked the streets in a vain search of work. Hundreds or thousands of families lost their homes; tax collections dropped to the point where cities and countries were unable to pay school teachers; construction work all but ceased; foreign trade already badly hit declined to an unprecedented low."[12]

"By 1932 the number of unemployed had mounted to over twelve million; over five thousand banks had closed their doors; commercial failures totalled thirty-two thousands; farm prices had fallen to the lowest point in history; the middle class was in danger of being wiped out; national income had declined from over eighty billion in 1929 to forty billion. The whole economy of the nation seemed to be disintegrating and the people were in an ugly mood."[13]

All West European capitalist countries experienced similar developments during the Great Depression of 1929-33, may be on a smaller scale.

5. *Wastages of Capitalism.* Capitalism has come to be associated with wastages of resources and therefore sacrifice or neglect of social welfare.

As we saw, in the first place there are the trade-cyclical booms and depressions. During periods of depression vast amount of labour remains unemployed for days or months or even years which causes wastage of resources from the point of view of the community. The same is true during period of depression of the other factors of production which lie idle, instead of producing much needed goods especially by the poorer sections of the community who exist even in the USA (where one in every five lives below the national average even during 1970s).

Then, as we saw, there have emerged monopolies and that results in wastages of monopolies — keeping purposely certain factors idle, to create artificial scarcities, with a view to raise prices and make monopoly profits. This amounts to tremendous wastages of resources.

Then there are wastages of competition itself in those lines where instead of monopoly competition still prevails. Often in a particular line or in the case of a particular commodity or service, thousands of competing entrepreneurs are taking independent decisions of their own, based on their own independent estimates of demand. These decisions of thousands of producers are independent and not properly co-ordinated or planned. It is very likely that in the case of some commodities, estimates go wrong and there is overproduction in the case of some commodities and under-production in the case of some others. This is certainly a sort of wastage of resources.

In a competitive regime there is also wastage due to advertisement. There are hundreds of producers and each must spend a certain percentage of resources on advertisement. Since all rivals are advertising, it is possible that advertisement by each is neutralised by advertisement put up by the other rivals. Anyway from the community's point of view, it amounts to so much wastages of labour, paper, organisation, skill and so on which are utilised in the business of advertisement which at present in the USA and other capitalist countries of the West has become both an art and a science employing some of the best brains in the country.

Thus the claim which is made in the theoretical model of capitalism that there will be competition and that it will result in the most efficient allocation of resources is just not valid. The more capitalism departs from its theoretical model, greater has been the amount of wastages of all sorts. "Capitalism is anarchy."

6. *Disregard, and Indifference to Welfare of Society.* Under capitalism, production is for maximising private profit. Naturally those goods and services come to be produced for which there is demand and which would yield maximum profits. The richer sections of the community with great amount of purchasing power therefore determine what goods and services would be produced. That is how in capitalist countries production of luxury and semi-luxury goods which command higher prices and are always in great demand get higher preference, whereas production of goods needed by masses with little purchasing power come to be neglected. Thus in the words of John Strachey, there will be "a plethora of yachts and beauty parlours while men and women lack food and shelter."[14]

Thus, under capitalism making maximum profits by producing goods which are in greatest demand and command highest prices is the priority number one; welfare of consumers, workers and poorer sections of society comes to be sidetracked.

7. *Poverty in the Midst of Plenty.* Personal profit motive, craze to invent new commodities and new processes and to bring about technological progress all with a view to increase private profits have tremendously increased productive powers of capitalist system of economy. But, as we have seen, inequality of income and wealth due to institution of private property and law of inheritance and succession is also a consequences of capitalism so that vast number of people with nothing but labour to sell cannot have a share in increasing production that is possible under capitalism. "Amid the bounty that accompanies America's status as the richest nation in the world, it is an anomaly that approximately one out of every five citizens is too poor to be considered realistically as sharing in those riches."[15]

There is thus inner contradiction of 'Poverty Amidst Plenty' in capitalist system. It is this, as we saw, that causes trade cyclical fluctuations, unemployment and misery, while there is available all the knowledge and capital goods and labour with necessary skills to produce much needed goods. Capitalism which is a 'planless' economy has not been in a position as yet to fully resolve this inner contradiction. This means while capitalism has recorded tremendous success and achievements on the production front (as admitted even by Karl Marx, its severest critic), it has not been successful on the distributive front to the necessary extent.

8. *Undesirable Psychological, Social and Moral Effects.* Capitalist society, which places tremendous emphasis on personal profit-maximization (or in simple terms on money-making for self), naturally has to face some undesirable psychological, social and cultural consequences. In a capitalist society, money becomes the yardstick for measuring success in every field — art, music, and literature.

"The successful citizen is likely to be the man who is most successful financially; friendship may follow patterns of pecuniary success; art, music and literature may be threatened by pecuniary worth of their product."[16]

Emphasis on self-interest, private profit motive and on money-making under competitive conditions would arouse and nurture in men instincts of acquisitiveness, unscrupulousness, immorality, combativeness and suppress better attributes of human nature like love, co-operation and consideration for others. As Karl Marx pointed out capitalism "leaves no other nexus between man and man than naked self-interest."

9. *Exploitation of Underdeveloped Countries and Disturbances in International Sphere.* The giant private industrial concerns in capitalist countries are in virtual control of their governments and to a great extent influence and make their political and economic policies. These capitalist countries (*i.e.*, the giant industrial establishments) have formed groups of their own (*e.g.*, the Group of Seven) to protect their interests. Thus US armament factories (as also of France and the U.K.) would be seen selling arms to both the countries which are on enemical terms (*e.g.*, Arabs and Jews, India and Pakistan) and would be actually interested in provoking wars with a view to see that their armament factories are kept running and making maximum profits.

Also the rich capitalist countries are combining to take joint action (for example, encouraging trade among themselves than trading with developing countries) and thus forcing terms of trade against developing countries. The terms of trade have gone continually adverse against the Third World countries vis-a-vis Western industrialised capitalist countries, except in the case of OPEC countries which could succeed in raising price of oil by joint action since 1970s. Developed capitalist countries are taking joint action to see that the poor countries do not develop fast with the aid of assistance from capitalist countries and their dependence upon capitalist countries as in olden days when they were dependent colonies of the capitalist countries.

Also the giant industrial multinational concerns with the aid of governmental agencies like the CIA and through bribes and corruption often try to subvert governments which are not pro-Western or which are opposed to military blocks formed by capitalist countries. The case of Argentina is a classic example and it is not an exception.

Concluding Remarks. It would thus be observed that while capitalism or free enterprise economy has a number of virtues and accomplishments to its credit, the defects or evils associated with capitalism, especially as it existed in the form of *laissez faire* capitalism, became so grave as to be intolerable and out of tune with the modern ethos. Naturally these evils of capitalism in general and of *laissez faire* capitalism in particular, attracted a lot of criticism from various quarters. Communist critics like Marx and Lenin came to the conclusion that evils of capitalism and the inner contradiction with which it is riddled are so serious that survival of capitalism is impossible and it is only a question of time when it gets destroyed by itself.

There were and are other types of critics of capitalism. They were and are sympathetic critics who want to retain the virtues of capitalism and some of its institutions (like individual freedom, institution of private property — may be in a restricted form, competition and so on), while at the same time they want to get rid of serious evils of capitalism (like unemployment, monopoly extreme inequalities, wastages and so on). J. M. Keynes and his band of followers who were and are mostly from capitalist countries belong to this category.

Thus it is the socialist and communist criticism of capitalism, criticism of economists like J. M. Keynes and his band and above all the changed environment and changed set of values have brought about gradual transformation of orthodox or traditional form of capitalism into 'Managed', 'Guided' or 'Regulated' or 'Welfare' capitalism of the post World War II era.

REFERENCES

1. *Capitalism, Socialism and Democracy* — J. A. Schumpeter, page 67.
2. *Comparative Economic Systems* — Loucks and Whitney, page 41.
3. *The New Society* — E. H. Carr, page 23.
4. Prof. Colin Clark's "*The Economic Position of Great Britain*" (1936).
5. Economies of the World Today — Wilcox and Others, page 173.
6. *Comparative Economic Systems* — W. N. Loucks and W. G. Whitney, page 46.
7. *The New Society* — E. H. Carr, page 24.
8. Economies of the World Today — Wilcox, Weatherford, Hunter and Baratz, Third Edition (1976), page 159.
9. *Ibid*, page 160.
10. Economies of the World Today — Wilcox and Others, page 160.
11. The Pocket History of the United States — Allen Nevins and Henry Steele Commagar, page 469.
12. *Ibid*, page 468.
13. *Ibid*, page 470.
14. *Theory and Practice of Socialism* — John Strachey, page 42.
15. *Comparative Economic Systems* — W. N. Loucks and W. G. Whitney, page 45.
16. *Comparative Economic Systems* — Loucks and Hoot, page 83.

CHAPTER 11

TRANSFORMATION OF LAISSEZ-FAIRE CAPITALISM INTO A WELFARE STATE OR WELFARE CAPITALISM

1. INTRODUCTION

The dynamic and critical changes that took place in the US and capitalist countries of the Western Europe roughly during the period of two World Wars and especially after the end of World War II have transformed the *laissez faire* capitalism of pre-World War I period into welfare state.

The political and economic upheavals of World War I (1914-18) worsened the problems of chronic unemployment; it created the problem of inflation and fluctuating foreign exchange disturbing the pattern of international trade.

As already noted, the Great Depression of 1929-33 created in capitalist countries problems of unprecedented unemployment and economic upheavals inviting State intervention in an unprecedented way in economic affairs of the people in most of the capitalist countries.

The publication of *The General Theory* by J. M. Keynes in 1936 provided much needed theoretical rationale for the State intervention in the economic sphere which was already initiated on pragmatic grounds by President Roosevelt to fight the evil consequences of the Great Depression in the USA.

Then cane the World War II (1939-45) which created complexities and problems, made people accustomed to increasing State intervention and regulation of their economic activities changed altogether their value-system, and led to profound changes in economic structure of capitalism.

After the World War II, labour became much more politically organised in capitalist countries. In Great Britain the Labour Party came to power in 1945 immediately after the end of the World War II and initiated Welfare State programme which it was propagating since its establishment, and especially after the Great Depression.

"Welfare state Capitalism entails the use of old and new powers of central government in parliamentary democracies to make capitalism work differently from how it worked before the Second World War."[1]

The welfare State or welfare capitalism is still capitalism because it still retains the two basic organisational features of the 19th century capitalism, namely: (1) the institution of private property and private ownership of means of production with property incomes like rent, interest and profit, and (2) determination of output of commodities and services and incomes of the people by market forces of demand and supply.

But the welfare state or welfare capitalism, it may be noted, is 'governmentally regulated capitalism'. In welfare capitalism, government "assume responsibility to achieve and sustain full employment and income growth while providing an ever-widening range of health, educational, housing and other welfare services out of the ever-expanding gross national product. The policy techniques have permanently expanded governmental spending, taxing and control over labour resources and product markets. Markets remain basic to the system, but most are no longer autonomous or *laissez faire.* Government also contrives policy deliberately to affect income distribution, total investment outlay, the nation's balance of payments in international trade and the price level."[2]

It would be instructive to examine how the *laissez faire* capitalism got gradually transformed into welfare state or welfare capitalist system first during 1930s and 1940s and later after 1950s in the USA and other West European countries.

2. THE NEW DEAL IN THE USA

So far as the introduction of welfare measures in the USA, the main reason was the grave effects of the Great Depression and Roosevelt's pragmatic approach to the challenges raised and not any ideological or theoretical considerations.

The gravity of the situation created by the Great Depression (1929-33) and the problem of unemployment created in the USA by that unprecedented economic phenomenon can be gauged from the following Table No.1.

From the Table No.1, it would be clear that capitalism in the USA faced acute economic crisis between 1929-33. Nearly 5,000 banks failed; prices fell by more than 25 per cent and gross national product fell by nearly 50 per cent. It was observed that in 1932, in the USA net investment in new capital assets was close to zero; even depreciation of machinery was often not made good; one out of every four Americans became unemployed.[3] Literally thousand of business firms and farms went bankrupt. Practically all capitalist countries (with the possible exception of Japan) suffered economic decline during the years of Great Depression, though not all the capitalist countries suffered to the same extent as the USA.

It may also be noted that during the Great Depression of 1929-33, the USA and Germany experienced almost identical economic crisis. In the case of both the capitalist countries, the policy of State intervention was chosen."But the Germans chose Hitler and the Nazis, while the Americans chose Roosevelt and the New Deal."

TABLE 1

US GNP Federal Government Expenditure and Unemployment

Year	*GNP (Current Prices Billion $)*	*Federal Government Expenditure as % of GNP*	*Civilian Labour Force (In Millions)*	*Unemployment as Percentage of Civilian Labour*
1929	103	8	49	3
1930	91	10	50	9
1931	76	12	51	16
1932	59	14	51	24
1933	56	14	52	25
1936	83	14	53	17
1937	90	13	54	14
1938	85	15	55	19
1940	100	14	56	15
1944	210	46	55	1
1957	441	20	67	4
1968	864	23	79	4
1971	1050	22	84	6

Source: Samuelson (1973), page 203, quoted by George Dalton in his *Economic Systems and Society*, page 97.

It might also be noted that *The General Theory* of J. M. Keynes was not yet published (it was published only in 1936) and this meant policies of Roosevelt were "purely pragmatic, hastily improvised to cope with crisis". The New Deal legislation of Roosevelt passed during unprecedented depth of the Great Depression resulted in a mass of economic legislation affecting practically all the sectors of the US economy. The New Deal aimed at, "Relief, Recovery and Reform." It adopted policies to give immediate aid to the unemployed, the destitute and the bankrupt and to enlarge national income and output and achieve or get back to the level of full employment. The New Deal policies aimed at structural reforms in the sphere of banking, corporate finance and other sectors of the economy all aimed at preventing recurrence of a similar economic tragedy. "America's Welfare State was an infant born in crisis."

It would be observed that the New Deal legislation affected practically all sectors of the US national economy, namely agriculture, industries, banking, transportation and other public utilities, foreign trade, big business corporations as well as small business establishments.

The New Deal legislation substantially enlarged governmental taxing and expenditure and owning of assets and of course regulatory powers. As George Dalton has pointed out, the New Deal policies of President Roosevelt "were gross departures from *laissezfaire* in two principal ways. The nineteenth-century institutions of the gold standard, free trade and free labour markets were no more. The commandments of orthodox governmental finance were sinned against: You shall not spend more than you tax; shall not spend more than the absolute minimum necessary, you shall spend only to provide traditional services such as defence and justice, which then amounted to less than 10 per cent of gross national product."[4]

The orthodox financial tenets came to be replaced by what Aba Learner described as 'functional finance'. Under functional finance, government in any one year may spend more than the amount it collects through taxation; or it may tax more than it spends; or government may aim at establishing balance between its tax proceeds and its expenditure. What particular budgetary policy government will pursue out of the above alternatives (*i.e.,* deficit budget, surplus budget or balanced budget) should depend upon the condition of the national economy in any particular year.

For some time in the USA, the enlarged functions of the government adopted during the Great Depression were thought of as purely temporary affair and necessary as emergency measures. What however happened has been that these increased activities of the US Government (as also of governments in other capitalist countries) proved to be a permanent feature.[5]

In 1936 J. M. Keynes published his *General Theory.* The underlying idea or analytical conclusion of this revolutionary book is that capitalism is inherently unstable because it contains no automatic mechanism to assure that all the goods produced at the full employment level of the economy will all be bought by people at appropriate prices. This implies that J. B. Say's *Law of the Markets* stating that supply creates its own demand is not necessarily valid and therefore one cannot assume that under capitalism the level of full employment will automatically be attained and maintained. This would also imply that in order to attain and sustain the level of full employment the government will have to make intervention, the objective of such intervention being to take steps to see that the effective demand is maintained at the right level that would sustain the economy at the level of full employment.

The policy-implication of J. M. Keynes's analysis is that "government should use its formidable powers to tax, spend and change the quantity or money and rate of interest in such a fashion as to assure that total effective demand for currently produced goods and services is always sufficient to sustain the full employment level of output." The government can influence the level of spending of millions of households and business investments by varying tax rates upwards or downwards as needed, as also by changing the rate of interest, and it can influence the level of demand for various types of goods and services by its own spending on welfare services such as on social capital goods like roads and housing and on social welfare measures such as education and public health. Departing from the *laissez faire* principle and policy of which J. M. Keynes was very critical, he advocated for the purpose of always maintaining effective demand at a level that would ensure the level of full employment of resources in the economy, not only abandonment of the policy of *laissez faire* but government intervention as also establishment and maintenance of a public sector that would help manipulate effective demand at appropriate level as and when necessary.

J. M. Keynes also justified with a view to maintain effective demand at the appropriate level that government use its powers of taxation and of spending to reduce extreme inequalities of income distribution. "To redistribute income in favour of the poor is to assure a higher level of consumption spending — effective demand — Out of any level of national income."[6]

J. M. Keynes's *General Theory* provided the theoretical basis or foundation for the establishment of welfare state and various social and economic welfare programmes after the end of World War II. For example, it was agreed to Great Britain that during the post-World War II period, government should assume powers and responsibility to ensure full employment . The Beveridge Report of 1942 and the White Paper on Employment in Great Britain proposed a programme of social services and spending on social capital like roads, buildings, hospitals, etc., that would maintain effective demand at an appropriate level.

In the USA also the Employment Act of 1946 made the government responsible for maintaining full employment in the economy.

The Keynesian economics made an attempt to prove that the evils or inadequacies of capitalism, especially that of chronic unemployment, due to trade cyclical depressions, could be successfully tackled without wholesale nationalisation of the industrial sector of the economy or comprehensive economic planning of the Soviet type, and within the broad framework of the capitalist economic system itself. For example, the Beveridge Report of 1942 made it clear that "the government need only assure that total outlay be sufficient to employ all who sought work. To do so, government need not own factories. It could use its fiscal and monetary powers to increase private consumption and investment spending and to enlarge its own spending on social capital and social services."

Thus Keynes made a successful attempt to show that evils or inadequacies of capitalism such as chronic unemployment, instability and extreme inequalities of income and wealth could be removed by suitable governmental regulatory and promotional measures within the broad framework of capitalism and maintaining its broad fundamental features (such as incentive of private profit, institution of private property, competitive markets, individual freedom as consumers and producers and so on). Keynes made a successful attempt both to show inadequacies and necessity of abandoning *laissez faire* type of capitalism and also that socialism or communism was not the only alternative way of removing evils of capitalism. While doing all this J. M. Keynes played a vital role in transforming *laissez faire* capitalism into 'Regulated' or 'Managed' or 'Guided' or 'Welfare' capitalism.

3. WELFARE STATE IN GREAT BRITAIN

During the 1930s, the Labour Party of Great Britain put forward its programme in terms of abolition of primary poverty, achievement of full employment with socially guaranteed minimum of income to all, deliberate redistribution of national income by progressive taxation on income and inherited wealth, reduction of income from property and provision of welfare services from which people from lower-income groups would benefit to a greater extent. The Labour Party thus aimed at establishment of social equality, erosion of inherited wealth, class structure and unequal opportunities in the field of education.

The Labour Party in Great Britain also believed during the pre-World War II period that nationalisation of industries was the single most powerful instrument or means to remove income from property, reduce monopoly and concentration of economic power in the hands of a small section of the community and allow government to plan for policy for attaining full employment. But the Labour Party in those days did not specify how much of the industrial sector of the economy or which specific industries were to be nationalised.

The Labour Party in Great Britain came to power in 1945 at the end of the World War II. The Labour Government had the programme to nationalise some important industries, attain the goal of full employment, bring about redistribution of income with a view to reduce extreme inequalities of income and wealth and to provide social services, especially to people from lower income groups. The Labour Party was a part of the Coalition Government that was in power in Great Britain during the period of World War II and thus their members bad acquired considerable amount of experience in administration and running of national economy with all the war-time rules and regulations.

Broadly, it might be said that between 1945 and 1951 when the Labour Government was in power, it succeeded in achieving most of its objectives to a lesser or greater extent. During those years the Labour Government nationalised some selective industries after paying full compensation to former owners in terms of interest bearing bonds in return of shares of their formerly privately owned industrial establishments. Public utilities like civil aviation, telephone and telegraph, gas, railroads and coal mining were nationalised with little opposition from the former owners — all this taking place in England the birth-place and home of *laissez faire* capitalism propounded and helped to be established by Adam Smith, Malthus and Ricardo.

The Labour Government also extended welfare services: "The National Health Service, housing, old-age pensions and unemployment pay, family allowances, the provision of legal services and enlarged subsidization of higher education." Together with full employment, by progressive taxation, the Labour Government also brought about considerable reduction in extreme inequalities in incomes and wealth among people in Great Britain.

The Labour Government in Great Britain created a welfare state by bringing about the above mentioned reforms in the capitalist system of the national economy. In this connection, it might be noted that the British Labour Party was sympathetic to America's democracy and Russian socialism but hostile to America's capitalism and Russia's dictatorship.

It may be concluded that "chronic difficulties in the 1920s, the depression of the 1930s, followed by another World War plus Keynes radically reconstructed capitalism without revolution in Britain, America and West Europe by 1950s." The internal shock of Great Depression, external shocks of two World Wars and writings of J. M. Keynes finally brought about the transformation of *laissez faire* capitalism into 'Guided' or 'Managed' or 'Regulated' or 'Welfare' capitalism.

One more point needs to be stressed in this connection. As pointed out by George Dalton, "It was not only the crises of war and depression that killed the ideology and institutions of *laissez faire* capitalism. Affluence and intensified industrialisation and urbanisation also contributed. All these dynamic changes creating extremely complex social and economic problems of transport, housing, public health, pollution and so on necessitated the creation of welfare state as it would have been practically impossible for *laissez faire* capitalism (which was working fairly successfully under simple conditions existing in the 19th century) to solve these problems. Thus according to Myrdal, *laissez faire* capitalism in the USA and West European countries got transformed into welfare state or welfare capitalism more by pressure of events and circumstances and not so much on grounds of ideological considerations, though it must be admitted that criticism of capitalism by Marx and other socialist thinkers was also one of the factors in bringing about the above transformation.

4. RECENT DEVELOPMENTS IN CAPITALIST COUNTRIES

We have seen how *laissez-faire* capitalism gradually got transformed into 'managed' or 'regulated' or 'welfare' capitalism in the West European countries and in the United States.

Inspite of various direct and indirect measures that are being taken to get rid of the shortcomings of capitalism and with a view to maximise welfare of the community, 'welfare' capitalism appears to be experiencing certain serious difficulties in its operation during 1980s and especially during 1990s.

For example, West European countries and the United States have been experiencing since 1980 onward serious economic recession since the Great Depression of 1929-33. This recession has continued for fairly long time (*i.e.*, for a decade and more) in the United States and some West European countries including Great Britain.

In these capitalist countries there has been unemployment ranging between 7 to 10 per cent. In Great Britain, for example (in February 1993), the figure of unemployed was around 3 million and it was feared that the figure is likely to rise further.

There is also substantial unemployment in other West European capitalist countries like Germany and the Unites States. For example, in the United States even the IBM the largest corporation in the world has been experiencing losses amounting to 5000 million US dollars. The automobile industry in the United State and other West European countries is in deep trouble. The General Motors as also the Ford in the United States have shut down many of their factories. Many of the British industries, notably coal, are facing extremely difficult times never before experienced since the Great Depression of 1929-33. All this has been resulting in rising unemployment. This is also true of Germany which after the union of West Germany and East Germany is finding it very difficult to unite the two economies which had grown up differently since the end of World War II in 1945.

As a consequence of rising unemployment, there is great unrest especially among unemployed adults in capitalist countries seeking jobs but not getting them. In Germany this is resulting in racial riots and rise of Neo-Nazism. The same is true to a certain extent in the United States and England where restrictions are being imposed on migrants to those countries seeking better living conditions. In these countries peaceful life for citizens is disturbed and street violence, robbery and murder are becoming common things of life. For example, in the United States people are apprehensive to move about alone after 6 in the evening even in big cities like New York and Chicago.

Number of people living on state welfare funds has been rising rapidly. Consequently quality of social services provided by government agencies has been deteriorating gradually. This is especially so in the case of public health services.

Except Japan most of the capitalist countries are experiencing increasing deficits in their budgets and in their balance of payments position. This appears to be leading to a sort of trade-war among capitalist countries. For example, there is serious dispute regarding subsidy to agriculture by some West European countries, notably France which is resisting heavy pressure by the United States to withdraw the subsidy. Recently the United States has imposed heavy duties on import of steel from West European countries on the ground that they are 'dumping' steel in the United States. Promptly the West European countries have been threatening to take appropriate retaliatory action against the United States. The United States is facing huge deficit in its balance of payments is adopting almost protectionist trade policy against Japan which is one developed capitalist country enjoying trade surplus of billions of dollars. Trade rivalries among different developed countries of West Europe and the United States appear to be hotting up and Urugauy Rounds of talks appear to have reached the dead end. All this is reflected in growing number of unemployed in developed capitalist countries.

The fact of the matter explaining the growing economic prosperity of West European countries and of the United States till 1980s was the cold war climate existing between the United States and the West European countries on the one had and the Soviet Union and East European countries on the other. This political rivalry was giving tremendous boost to defence industries leading to rising level of employment in developed capitalist countries. Also it is now disclosed that during a decade of war between Iraq and Iran, the West European countries and the United States were supplying defence and armaments to both the warring parties at the same time and this had given tremendous boost not only to defence industries which occupied central place in the industrial structure of capitalist countries but to their entire economies. Before that those countries were supplying arms and various defence equipment to India and Pakistan which had fought three wars since their independence in 1947.

After the disintegration of the Soviet Union and end of cold war and agreements to slash down missiles and atomic and chemical weapons, the vast armament industries in West European countries and in the United States are finding it difficult to maintain the high production tempo in defence industries. It should also be noted that defence industries cannot be turned overnight into industries producing civilian consumer goods. Recession in defence industries has spread to other dependent or allied industries and to the economies as a whole with the consequence that developed capitalist countries are experiencing recession for more than a decade with rising unemployment with all its evil consequences. Economic prosperity of developed capitalist countries had come to be built on ever expanding defence industries. Once the international atmosphere started moving towards world peace, the changed atmosphere has given rise to recession during the last decade.

To successfully fight off economic recession, the United States is threatening application of 301 Super Act to India and other developing countries with a view to compel them to purchase more and more American goods and services.

To successfully fight off recession and increasing unemployment in the United States, which has control over the World Bank and the International Monetary Fund, is bringing pressure on India to liberally import American goods and give permission to American banks and industrial corporations to open branches in India as a condition for granting of loans which India urgently wants to avoid bankruptcy in the eyes of the world.

All this goes to show that foundations of not only laissez capitalism but even of 'managed' or 'regulated' or 'welfare' capitalism in developed capitalist countries and in the United States are not perfectly sound but are shaky.

REFERENCES

1. *Economic Systems and Society* — George Dalton, page 96.
2. *Ibid*, page 96.
3. In 1931, 1,00,000 Americans applied for 6,000 skilled jobs in the Soviet Union. (The Great Depression- D.A Shannon, page 12).
4. *Economic Systems and Society* — George Dalton, page 99.
5. Typical New Deal policies and legislation and the extent of increased State activities under the New Deal can be illustrated by giving the following illustrations:

   Under the New Deal, stringent legislative conditions were laid down for issuance of securities and operations of commercial and savings banks. Bank deposits came to be insured by the government which started auditing accounts of banks. The Federal Reserve Bank could lend money to commercial banks during emergencies. All this meant that *laissez faire* policy in the sphere of banking came to an end in the interest of and for safeguarding the welfare of society.

   The New Deal legislation affected other sectors of the economy also. Labour legislation favoured unionisation of labour and workers were given right to join unions as also right of collective bargaining. Government started giving loans to big and small business establishments, rail-roads and export industries.

   Minimum wage rates, hours and conditions of work all came to be regulated by factory legislation which also dealt with problems of child labour, conditions of safety in factories as, for example, in coal mines and other hazardous places of work.

In order to create increasing employment opportunities, the US Government started spending more on items like housing, roads, irrigational dams, generation of electricity in rural areas, etc.

The New Deal legislation also initiated a national programme of unemployment pay, old age pensions, aid to old and disabled persons and so on.

All this New Deal legislation introduced by President R. Roosevelt meant fundamental departure form the previous *laissez faire* capitalism. What was initiated as emergency measure some forty-five years ago has not only become permanent feature of modern capitalism but in fact in the USA and also other capitalist countries, governmental activities and regulations of economic affairs and activities of the people have continually gone on expanding.

6. The General Theory of Keynes explains a number of important economic developments such as why *laissez faire* capitalism produced wide and chronic fluctuations in national income, output and employment, why unemployment completely disappeared in capitalist countries like the USA during World War II (when the US Government was buying almost half of US gross national product; why Nazi Germany was in a position to come out of depression and unemployment that was effecting Germany due to Great Depression; and why no adverse affects of the Great Depression were felt at all in the planned economy of the Soviet Union.

CHAPTER 12

CAPITALISM AND TECHNOLOGICAL PROGRESS

1. INTRODUCTION

The English Classical School of Economists believed that capital was the most important factor of production. Thus Adam Smith wrote that 'Capital limits industry.' The early economists thus had a static concept of technology. They took a given technology for granted and did not anticipate any or much change in it.

It is only in the 20th century and especially during the last two or three decades that technological progress has come to assume increasing significance. It is now appreciated that it is the technological progress (rather than mere accumulation of capital which the Classical School emphasised as the most important factor of production) which would increase the per head productivity in every field of economic activity and ensure continual progress of the economy. Naturally during post-World War II period research and development which form the foundation or basis of technological progress have been assuming increasing significance.

2. THE CLASSICAL ECONOMISTS AND TECHNOLOGICAL PROGRESS

As stated already, the Classical School assumed technical knowledge as unchanging over time. And therefore according to them, it was the accumulation of capital that played a vital role in economic progress of a country.

Because the Classical School assumed that technological progress as a given constant, economists like Malthus and Ricardo arrived at pessimistic conclusions for the economy in the long run.

For example, Malthus while formulating his theory of population assumed that the existing agricultural technology will continue. And therefore he came to the pessimistic conclusion that population will increase in geometric progression whereas foodgrains will increase in only arithmetical progression. He therefore concluded that increase in population will overtake increase in foodgrains production and there will be repeated condition of over-population, the excess population being removed by positive checks like death, starvation, famines, wars, etc. The balance between population and foodgrains will be restored by removal by death of excess population; but again population will tend to grow faster than foodgrains production again bringing about the condition of over-population and operation of positive checks.

Malthus could not foresee rapid technological changes in agriculture bringing about rapid increase in per capita productivity and availability of foodgrains. That explains his pessimistic conclusion.

In fact rapid technological progress did take place in the agricultural sector; that resulted in increase in per capita productivity and availability of foodgrains and the fear of population explosion and operation of positive checks feared by Malthus have not come about in developed countries.

Thus in the United States there has been tremendous technological progress in the agricultural sector. Agricultural operations have all been mechanised. Use of tractors, threshers, combine harvests, artificial manure and pesticides have all become very common so that per head productivity as also per acre productivity have both been rising over years ensuring people continually higher availability of foodgrains. Thus an average American farmer is at present producing foodgrains sufficient for about 45 non-agricultural Americans. The United States now employes only about 5 per cent of its working population in the agricultural sector and those 5 per cent produce foodgrains not only adequate for the rest of the US citizens but a substantial portion is available for export to those countries where agricultural technological progress has not taken place to that extent.

Technological progress in the agricultural sector is further proceeding. Attempts are being made to find out more disease-resistant and quickly maturing and more productive seeds. Also attempts are being made to develop sea-food and so on. In fact there appears to be no limit on technological progress in the agricultural sector disproving pessimistic forecasts of the Classical School which assumed the prevailing technological knowledge as constant both in the short run and long run.

David Ricardo, a prominent member of the English Classical School and the real founder of *laissez faire* capitalism had similar views regarding technology. He took for granted the existing level of technology. Ricardo did not visualise that there will be technological progress.

The conclusions which Ricardo arrived at were therefore extremely pessimistic.

Because Ricardo assumed unchanging technology and also accepted Malthusian Theory of Population that population has the tendency to outstrip available foodgrains supply, Ricardo formulated on the above assumption the famous Law of Diminishing Returns in the agricultural sphere, antagonism between wages and profits (whatever increases wages will reduce profit and vice versa) and the concept of Stationary State.

As population increases, more and more foodgrains will be required and a community will either increasingly resort to intensive or extensive cultivation bringing more and more inferior lands under cultivation. Ricardo maintained that under both circumstances, Law of Diminishing Returns will operate. He could not or did not foresee the possibility of continual technological progress enabling mankind to continually increase productivity. Hence his pessimistic conclusion.

Also because of his assumption of constancy of prevailing technology, given output must be shared, according to Ricardo, between workers and capitalists. From this it follows that if the share of workers (*i.e.*, wages) rises from the given output, the share of capitalists (profits) is bound to decline, and vice versa.

Ricardo could not foresee the possibility of continual technological progress continually increasing the size of the output, so that wages and profits may both go on continually raising (though not in the same proportions). This is what, for example, is happening in the United States. Technological progress is pushing up the growth-rate of production rapidly so that rates of wages and profits are both rising thus proving Ricardo wrong that there is necessary antagonism between wages and profits. He arrived at his conclusion of antagonism between wages and profit (and therefore between workers and employers) because Ricardo assumed constancy of prevailing technology.

Ricardo's concept of Stationary State was also the result of his assumption regarding absence of technological progress.

According to Ricardo, with increase in population, more and more foodgrains will be needed. Consequently more and more inferior lands will be brought under cultivation. This would continually push up cost of production of foodgrains and therefore their prices. Since workers would and must get at least subsistence level of wages in real term, this would mean rise in wage rate (since prices of foodgrains are continually rising). And as we have already seen, whatever raises wages would reduce profits. Thus Ricardo concluded that continual rise in (money) wages will finally bring the rate of profit to such a level that entrepreneurs will not find it advantageous to invest any more and thus Stationary State where all further progress would be impossible would come into existence.

It will be seen that conclusion regarding Stationary State flows automatically from the assumption regarding constant state or condition of technology.

In fact, technological progress has been continual and countries which are bringing about technological progress have been moving to ever-rising levels of economic prosperity.

3. NATURE OF TECHNOLOGICAL PROGRESS

Broadly technological progress is of two kinds: 1. It is possible that new products may be introduced. In recent years this type of technological progress is taking place rapidly. For example, artificial fabrics, computers and calculators, TV and video tapes, plastic, transistors, etc., have come to occupy increasingly important role in the lives of even ordinary people. They are becoming an important part of common man's pattern of life. 2. Under the second kind, new processes of producing already known commodity or service may be found. For example, instead of handloom, weaving cloth by powerlooms and then by automatic looms; or car manufacture by assembly-line production, or computer-helped composing of types instead of hand or manual composing, or instead of ploughing by wooden plough drawn by a pair of bullocks, making use of tractors driven by motors run on diesel, etc.

While new production extends demand for them by entering consumption pattern of people and thus stimulating demand, new processes increase per head productivity, reduce cost of production and therefore lower prices of products. Because of lower prices markets for such goods get extended. It will thus be seen that under both types of technological progress, there is effect on the standard of living of the people which rises to a higher level than before.

4. DIFFERENCES BETWEEN INVENTIONS AND INNOVATIONS

Distinction is often made between 'invention' and 'innovation'.

Invention. Invention refers to finding or discovery of a new product or a new process of producing a commodity or service which was already existing.

Thus finding a first cycle, first tractor, and first plastic commodity is an illustration of inventions. Similarly replacing spinning of yarn by handloom in place of *charkha,* or by powerloom instead of by handloom, or by automatic looms instead of powerlooms — these findings of new processes of producing a commodity which was already existing, namely cloth, are all, illustrations of 'inventions'.

Innovation. Innovation, on the other hand, refers to the application or applied side of invention (either of a new commodity or a new process). When a new commodity like plastic first discovered in a laboratory (an invention) begins to be produced commercially, that process is referred to as 'innovation'. Similarly, when a new process of production begins to be made use of in factories or fields on a commercial basis that is innovation.

It follows from this that invention comes first, innovation comes next. That is to say invention proceeds innovation. It also means that without invention there cannot be innovation.

5. TYPES OR CLASSIFICATION OF INNOVATIONS

When, as we saw above, inventions are put to commercial application for practical purposes or use, we define it as innovation.

Innovations are of three types:

(*a*) Neutral, (*b*) Labour-saving, and (*c*) Capital-saving.

We shall briefly describe the characteristic of each type of innovation.

(a) Neutral Innovation. When an innovation results neither in the saving of labour nor of capital, such an innovation is defined as neutral innovation. If, for example production of a certain factor requires a particular combination of say two factors of production say labour and machines, if an innovation increases the marginal productivity of both those factors exactly in the same proportion, we say that the innovation is neutral. For example, to produce a commodity one unit of labour and one unit of capital were necessary and let us suppose that marginal productivity of labour and capital were in the ratio of 1:2. If after the introduction of an innovation, both those factors are still necessary for production ; but if the marginal productivity of labour and capital now is 2:4 (instead of former 1:2), we say that the innovation (commercial or practical application of an invention) is neutral.

(b) Labour-Saving Innovation. If due to a new invention, marginal productivity of capital rises more than marginal product of labour, it would mean that more capital will be used displacing (saving) labour. This would mean relative to capital less labour than before is being used to produce the same amount of a commodity.

(c) Capital Saving. When a commodity requires two factors of production, say labour and capital, and when a certain innovation results in raising the marginal productivity of labour relative to marginal product of capital, it would follow that more labour will be employed displacing (saving) certain amount of capital (*i.e.*, machinery).

6. EFFECTS OF TECHNOLOGICAL PROGRESS

Mankind has been right from the beginning facing numerous challenges. It has had to struggle against niggardly Nature. It has had to face problems created by ever-increasing population by making provision of ever-increasing quantities of food and other agricultural commodities, accommodation and innumerable other goods and services. Mankind has had to face problems faced by famines, wars, pestilence, disease, unemployment, inflation and mass poverty.

It is only the continuing technological progress that has been helping mankind to come successfully through all these problems and ensure ever-rising standard of living. If the ancient man living in an isolated den like a semi-savage always a victim of Natural forces has managed at present to attain the status of a superman, producing goods and services at almost breath-taking speed (imagine the fourth generation computer which can make a million complicated calculations per every single minute) and has managed to reach the Moon, has practically annihilated distance and has made nature yield incalculable quantities of material from her bowels which he has learned to fabricate into innumerable type of goods and services — at the bottom of it has been the continuing technological progress.

To be more specific technological progress has helped mankind in the following ways:

1. Developed countries with the aid of technological progress have been in a position to increase annual per capita productivity almost by 3 per cent. Though increasing accumulation of capital (more and more machines of the same type) has helped to a certain extent, it is basically continual technological progress that is helping man in general and people in developed countries in particular where technological progress is much rapid to attain and maintain this ever-increasing annual per head productivity.

2. Technological progress (along with increasing accumulation of capital which itself to a great extent is the consequence of technological progress) has made possible large-scale production of goods and services. This could bring down the cost of production and their prices. This could enable vast masses to enjoy increasing number of goods and services and raise their standard of living. Many of the goods which a common man (especially in developed countries) is enjoying today were a couple of centuries ago could be enjoyed only by the royalty and rich persons in society. As Schumpeter wrote : "...mass production means production for the masses." It does not mean providing more and more silk stockings to queens but to bring them within the reach of factory girls by producing them at steadily decreasing cost.

3. Technological progress has made possible production, distribution and consumption of new and ever-new products and also old products of better and ever-improving quality. Thus technological progress has been continually improving quality of life, in addition to, as we have already seen, continually raising standard of living.

4. In capitalist countries technological progress has resulted in continually raising real wages (wages in terms of goods and services) of workers who are in a position in developed countries to enjoy ever-rising standard of living.

Karl Marx had predicted that there is conflict between private profit of private industrialists and wages of workers; that industrialists would exploit workers by giving workers only subsistence level of wages in spite of increasing productivity of labour due to technological progress and go on accumulating private profits for themselves. This is proved wrong. Technological progress has made possible both rising rates of profit and continually rising rates of wages for workers. Labourers (for example, look at an average worker in the United

States) are allowed to enjoy a share in increasing productivity due to technological progress.

There is thus no doubt that on the material side technological progress has made possible ever-rising material prosperity not for a few but for the masses.

In case we want to know and appreciate the true impact of technological progress on people, just compare the way some of the tribal people are still living in African countries where modern technology has not penetrated with the life-style of an average American, or West European and one will come to appreciate what impact technological progress has created.

But technological progress has also created some grave adverse effects. While it has given mankind control over Nature, it has at the same time put at man's disposal incalculable destructive power. Think of the modern wars and compare them with old battles and one comes to know what damage atomic bombs and nuclear weapons can do. Nuclear weapons and chemical warfare, bombers and modern nuclear submarines and long-range missiles and so on are threatening the very existence of mankind. Technological progress has enabled some advanced countries to accumulate atomic and hydrogen bombs which are enough to kill entire mankind again and again nearly 200 times.

Thus while on the one hand technological progress has raised man from the state of a semi-savage to that of superman, at the same time, it has also put at his disposal weapons which either by accident or by design might annihilate entire humanity sending us all back to the Stone Age.

7. TECHNOLOGICAL PROGRESS AND OBSOLESCENCE

In the old days *i.e.,* till about the beginning of World War I or roughly first quarter of the 20th century, technological progress was by fits and starts. Occasionally a new product or a new process would emerge and gradually it came to be absorbed in the economic system. Thus when the new automatic machine, say automobile (*i.e.,* motor car) came to be invented in the beginning of the 20th century, only gradually did the motor car replace horse-drawn cars and other prevalent modes of transport and communications. The same was true of railways and aeroplanes. This would mean that till about the first quarter of the 20th century, the problem of obsolescence was not there or at any rate never assumed grave proportions.

But unlike in olden days, during post-World War II period technological progress is taking place in a regular stream and also at a fast speed. Thus it took very long to build first generation computer. But after that computers of the second, third and fourth generation have followed very quickly. Thus new and newer commodities, new and newer processes of production and new and newer and ever-more efficient machines have been flowing at a fast pace during present times. Naturally this has raised the problem of obsolescence.

Should an industralist replace a costly machine which he installed in his factory only 5 years ago, or 1 year ago or only last week by a new and more efficient and more productive machine which has quickly appeared on the scene? Should the third generation computer costing a lot and installed only last year and serviceable for many more years be scraped and the fourth generation computer costing a lot but many times more efficient be installed in its place?

In the face of extremely rapid technological changes and progress that is taking place in the world, the problem of obsolescence (scrapping of existing machines and installing new machines in their place) has become very acute and critical.

Various problems have arisen. Should I throw away the machine which I installed only last year and which is still serviceable for say ten years more ? Should I waste my resources invested in that machine by scrapping it? Should I continue with the same machine for, say another, 5 or 10 years though another brand and newly invented machine costing a considerable amount but many times more efficient and productive than the existing machine is available in the market? Should I continue with the old machine even though if I scrap it and install new machine, in the long-run I can make more profits than by continuing with the old machine though serviceable for another ten years?

The problem of obsolescence has become very difficult and very complex. It requires to be tackled in a practicable way.

In some cases old machines even though serviceable for another few years will have to be replaced by new machines because in the long run that is profitable. To continue with the old machine when new and more efficient substitute-machine is available would mean that taking long run into account total profits would be less in the long run. And therefore though replacing the existing machine by a new one, might mean substantial investment immediately, it wold still be more profitable to replace it by a new machine.

But it is also true that since technological progress is taking place at a regular and fast pace, an industrialist cannot go on every year, or every week or even every day replacing old machines no sooner substitute new machines become available in the market. It will be wasteful and also impracticable as new machines require new skills which are not immediately available in adequate quantity and of satisfactory quality.

And therefore an industrialist will have to take a pragmatic and practical view on the basis of his available resources in men and money, what machines should be scrapped and with what machines he should continue though new substitute machines are available.

But one thing is certain and it is that over a reasonable period of time he will have to phase out all old machines and replace them by new ones as and when it becomes practicable. Otherwise an industrialist will not be in a position to successfully compete with his rivals. The same would apply to a country. In the competitive world, only that country will survive which will systematically replace old technology when new technology becomes available. If it does not, it will lose in this highly competitive world. That will also explain why a small country like Japan with hardly any natural resources is in a position to successfully compete with a vast and rich country like the United States. The key to Japanese success lies in continually updating its technology in every field of its national economy. Failure to do that also explains why India of vast size, vast amount of human and natural resources happens to be one of the poorest countries of the world. The reason is we persist with old technology practically in every field though new technology is available and have thus failed to successfully tackle the problem of obsolescence.

8. TECHNOLOGICAL PROGRESS AND INSTABILITY

Does technological progress that is taking place cause instability in the economy?

There are different views in regard to this.

Karl Marx, for example, was of the opinion that private capitalists would go on accumulating more and more profit by exploiting labour (*i.e.*, paying workers much less than what they produce) and with a view to make still more personal profit and accumulate still more wealth which in their case is an obsession would try to invest new and newer machines.

According to Marx, these new machines would displace labour and the newly unemployed workers would go to swell the 'Industrial Reserve Army' (*i.e.*, the vast number of workers who are already unemployed). Thus new invention, machines and technological progress would go on causing more and more unemployment.

When there is increasing unemployment, wages would begin to fall and at lower wages than before, employers would find it profitable to employ more workers. Thus for the time being due to increasing employment of labour, waged rates would begin to rise. After wage costs and therefore cost of production have begun to rise, capitalists would begin to think of new machines that would displace workers who are now getting higher wage rates. These new machines would again mean displacement of labour and enlargement of the Industrial Reserve Army. Thus according to Marx, technological progress would cause instability.

According to Karl Marx, there is another way in which technological progress would cause instability.

As technological progress takes place, the productive powers of the community would increase enormously. But would all the goods and services produced be in demand and be purchased at appropriate prices? Would there be balance between supply and demand ?

Marx was of the opinion that in capitalism, this would not be possible. This is for two reasons. One reason is that the vast number of workers have the physical capacity to consume vast amount of goods that are being produced because of technological progress; but under competitive conditions, they would get only subsistence wages barely enough to purchase and consume goods just enough for self-sustenance.

On the other hand, the small section of rich people have enough amount of money to purchase vast amount of goods being regularly produced; but they do not have the physical capacity to consume them.

Thus according to Karl Marx, under competitive capitalism, there will scarcely be balance between supply and demand. This will repeatedly cause crisis of over-production, falling prices and rising unemployment. Recurring crisis, according to Marx, was like cancer which would ultimately destroy capitalism itself.

For some time, capitalist countries would try to dispose of surplus goods by conquering colonies. But Marx opined that there would be wars among capitalist countries to conquer colonies and that explains World War I and also World War II. Thus war becomes the only means of survival for competitive capitalism.

Schumpeter also was of the opinion that technological progress results in repeated instability.

His argument was as follows:

According to Schumpeter, technological progress takes place in ebbs and flows. For some time there is an outburst of inventions and innovations. Banks are in a mood to lend money and business activity in all sectors of the economy is on the upward move. Soon the ebb dies down; banks are reluctant to lend money; a sort of recession or depression develops and the economy is on the down swing with falling prices and rising unemployment. Again after some time there is an outburst of inventions and innovations with upswing of economic activities to be again followed by absence of new inventions and innovations and downswing in economic activities.

Thus according to Schumpeter inventions and innovations coming in ebbs and flows or in outburst will bring about regular booms and depressions in the economy. (For example, railway development, telegraph and telephones, steamships, automobiles, aeroplanes, etc., etc).

It is now observed in post-World War II years, that technological progress is not coming about in occasional outburst of inventions and innovations but that it is coming in a steady stream. This is causing less instability in the economy. And yet, new technology in a particular field may cause disturbance and instability in that particular industry or sector of the economy. But in recent years governments have developed policies and techniques of absorbing such temporary disturbances by measures such as social security, unemployment benefit, employment exchanges, by taking steps to increase geographical and occupational mobility of workers, and so on.

9. TECHNOLOGICAL PROGRESS AND UNEMPLOYMENT

Does technological progress cause unemployment? What exactly is the relationship between technological progress and level of employment in capitalist countries?

When we are discussing the relationship between technological progress and level of employment in a capitalist economy, we must take into consideration: 1. Short-term effects on level of employment, and 2. long-term effects on level of employment. We must also consider effects of technological progress: 1. on level of employment in a particular sector of the economy, and 2. level of employment in the economy as a whole.

If we consider effect of technological progress in the short term, there is no doubt that it is more likely to result in increase in the level of unemployment.

But in the long run, effect of technological progress on the level of employment will be favourable. This is because, technological progress reduces cost of production and price of the commodity affected by the new technology. At lower prices demand for that commodity will rise and more factories would be set up to produce additionally demanded amounts of that commodity. This will provide increasing employment opportunities to workers.

Also at a lower price of that commodity, though more is being now purchased, the total amount spent by the community on that commodity might be less than before. Thus the amount thus saved would be spent on some other commodities, now that there is some amount at hand for spending. Prices of those other commodities would began to rise. This would result in more factories being set up to produce additional quantities of those commodities. This would result in the long run in increase in the level of employment in the economy as a whole.

Thus though in the short run, it is likely that technological progress might result in increasing unemployment, in the long run, technological progress would be accompanied by increasing level of employment. This is also proved on the basis of empirical facts and figures observed from the developed capitalist countries.

The same type of argument holds good regarding effect of technological progress as regards employment in a particular sector of the economy and level of employment in the economy as a whole.

A particular invention affecting a particular sector (say textile industry where handlooms are being replaced by a new invention like powerlooms or automatic looms) would result in increase in unemployment in that particular sector (in our above illustration, textile industry).

But with technological progress, cloth would be cheaper; more cloth would be demanded; and if the demand for cloth is elastic, that very sector would soon provide increasing opportunities of employment for workers.

Failing that and if demand for that commodity (*i.e.,* textiles) is rigid, and no one purchases more of cloth though it is now cheaper, the amount saved by the community on cloth would be spent on other commodities the demand for which is income-elastic. In the face of increase in demand for these commodities and their rising prices, more factories would be set up to produce those commodities now in greater demand. There will thus be increase in employment in industries producing those commodities.

Thus if we consider the effect of technological progress on a particular sector of the economy or a particular industry, effect on level of employment might be unfavourable. But if we take the economy as a whole, there is no doubt that technological progress would mean rising employment level in the economy.

Technological Progress and Structural Unemployment

Technological progress causes a type of unemployment called 'structural unemployment' that needs comments.

This can be illustrated by taking an illustration. When, for example, handlooms were replaced by powerlooms, naturally the immediate impact was that there was a certain amount of unemployment among those who were engaged in handlooms. But as unemployment spread among handloom weavers because the structural change was taking place in the textile industry, the young, able and ambitious unemployed could learn new skills necessary to run powerlooms and were soon re-employed. Or they were dynamic enough and young enough to learn new skills required in some other expanding industries and got absorbed there.

But among handloom weavers there might be aged people for whom learning new trade was difficult or even impossible because of advanced age or lack of ability or some such reason. On handloom industry was concentrated in a particular locality and people in that locality were unwilling or unable to move to other places where jobs were available. Under such circumstances technological progress results in structural unemployment.

Thus a certain product suddenly goes out of fashion and the industry suffers a shock. Many old, aged or immobile people find it difficult to move out of that place or learn new trade. This would result in considerable amount of structural unemployment.

Thus rapid technological progress by often and quickly changing the structure of an industry or even of the economy is likely to result in structural unemployment.

In advanced capitalist countries attempts are being made to reduce such structural unemployment by providing training facilities, by establishing employment exchanges and by taking steps to improve geographical and occupational mobility. But with all this, rapid technological changes as at present are bound to result in certain amount of structural unemployment in capitalist countries.

10. SCHUMPETER'S THEORY OF CAPITALIST DEVELOPMENT: COMPARISON OF SCHUMPETER'S AND MARXIAN THEORIES OF CAPITALIST DEVELOPMENT

Joseph A. Schumpeter (1870-1950) was a towering economist among those of the first half of the 20th century. He was a sort of romantic admirer of capitalism and of its remarkable achievements. But by his observation and analysis he came to the conclusion that ultimately capitalism would perish and give place to socialism. Karl Marx also believed the same. But while according to Karl Marx capitalism was doomed because of its inherent internal contradictions, Schumpeter believed in the demise of capitalism out of its very success. A system may decay and perish as much because of its weakness and failures as by its over-reaching ambitions and outstanding achievements. Karl Marx believed in the former while Schumpeter believed in the latter.

In his famous book, 'Capitalism, Socialism and Democracy', Joseph Schumpeter has given an account of growth, development and decay of capitalism.

According to Schumpeter, entrepreneur is the key-figure in bringing about development of capitalism. If Karl Marx regards him as unproductive and a parasite, Schumpeter regards him as the main lever that pushes and prods capitalism to further attainment and success.

It is the entrepreneur who is inspired to find new products, new process of production, new forms of organisation and pulls the economy out of the rut into which it shows the tendency to get stuck up. It is entrepreneur who finds out new sources of raw materials, new products and process and new markets and ventures out into the unknown and untrodden path. Entrepreneurs by their energy, vaulting ambition and grand vision take capitalism to ever rising heights. It is this class which is the catalytic agent and brings about improvement in the standard and quality of life of the mass of people.

Entrepreneurs (like Henry Ford, Du Pont, Krupps or in the case of India, Jamshedji Tata and Laxmanrao Kirloskar) try to bring about new and better products and new processes. Thus for example, they think of mechanical tractor to destroy and replace ploughing b wooden tractor with a pair of bullocks ; or replacing handloom by powerloom and powerloom by automatic looms. Thus these entrepreneurs destroy old processes or methods of doing business or destroy old institutions and in their place introduce new goods, processes and organisations (like joint stock company form of organisation or Teller System in banking etc.,). Innovation thus is preceded by destruction of the old system. Schumpeter calls this 'Creative Destruction.'

These changes introduced by entrepreneurs or captains of industry bring about increase in per capital productivity and in total production. All this improves the standard of living as also quality of life. According to Schumpeter, benefits of capitalism have not been enjoyed only by a small class of rich persons but those benefits have gone to all sections of society in capitalist countries.

Material prosperity, according to Schumpeter, has brought in its wake social and cultural progress. Capitalism has ensured rising standard of living to common people.

According to Schumpeter, inventions and innovations do not occur at regular and stated or pre-determined period. They appear like swarms and in bursts. There is discontinuity in the process of inventions and innovations. They for some years come in bursts and this period is followed by lull which hardly experiences any new significant invention or innovation. During the period experiencing burst of inventions and innovations, there is great spurt of economic activities in all sectors of the economy because they are all interdependent. When the period of lull comes in inventions and innovations, there is dullness in economic activities until there is again burst of new inventions and innovations. Thus according to Schumpeter, competitive capitalism experiences regularly booms and depressions.

Why does not competitive capitalism continue indefinitely with booms and depressions, each boom taking capitalism to a level higher than before experiencing depression? Why according to Schumpeter, is competitive capitalism doomed and is bound to be in future replaced by socialism ? Why does he feel that competitive capitalism will die because of its remarkable achievements and attainments?

The following are the reasons or factors which according to Schumpeter would spell doom of competitive capitalism :

According to Schumpeter a stage is reached in the process of development of capitalism when the entrepreneur (the central figure in capitalism) becomes superfluous and unnecessary.

Entrepreneur, the distinctive feature of capitalism, becomes superfluous and unnecessary because of the following reasons :

1. As capitalism progresses, bureaucracy assumes increasingly important role in the corporate organisation under capitalism. A stage is reached when innovation and technological progress begin to be successfully undertaken by trained specialists making old time entrepreneur unnecessary. Capitalist progress turns entrepreneurs into a class of administrators working on salary basis. The response of consumers also becomes automatic and they begin to accept whatever products are given to them. All this development in capitalism makes entrepreneur superfluous.

2. As capitalism develops and reaches an advance stage, the basic competitive framework of capitalism undergoes a fundamental change. Capi-

talism comes to be dominated by big monopolistic business organisation leaving hardly any scope to small scale businessmen and entrepreneurs committed to the ideal of capitalism and emotionally attached to capitalism. Thus in the advanced stage of capitalism the very psychological base on which capitalism had come to be built is undermined so that hardly anybody feels any emotional attachment to competitive capitalism.

3. In the advanced stage of capitalism, the feudal lords, the rich landed gentry, the manor, craft guilds got all destroyed. Capitalism succeeded in the 19th century because there was a protective framework within which it was working. Historically capitalist class flourished when political power was wielded not by themselves but some other class that was sympathetic to capitalism, and when capitalists were free to pursue their business careers. When they were asked to govern or were required to govern the country, they could not do that well.

4. In its advanced prosperous stage capitalism was so prosperous that there emerged a class of people who could afford to live on accumulated wealth and without doing any work for their livelihood. These people took to intellectual criticism of capitalism and evils accompanying it. This naturally created hostile atmosphere against capitalism. According to Schumpeter this would lead eventually to decomposition and destruction of capitalism, its place being taken finally by socialism though his brand of socialism is different from that of Karl Marx.

This according to Schumpeter, the very success of capitalism paves way for its ultimate decomposition and destruction.

11. SCHUMPETER AND KARL MARX ON CAPITALISM

There is a fundamental difference between Schumpeter and Karl Marx in regard to their analysis and perception of capitalism, though both hold the same view that capitalism will eventually disappear giving place to socialism.

According to Schumpeter, capitalism is a progressive force which increases quantities of goods as also their quality. Schumpeter thinks that if this increasing prosperity made possible by efficient use of factors of production, all classes of people including the working class have a share. The quality of life of all people improves, according to Schumpeter, under competitive capitalism.

Karl Marx views things differently. According to him, competitive capitalism is characterised by inefficient use of factors of production, substantial portion of productive resources being allowed to lie unemployed during economic crisis which repeatedly visit capitalism because of imbalance between the rate of growth of productive powers and rate of growth of consumption of goods and services. Also according to Marx, not only is competitive capitalism inefficient, but it is also characterised by inequity and injustice. Prosperity of a few rich comes to be built on exploitation of vast working class of people who do not share in the increasing productive powers and production of competitive capitalism.

Both Schumpeter and Karl Marx think that eventually capitalism will disappear. But there is a difference between the two. According to Schumpeter, capitalism will die due to its extraordinary success which will create conditions leading to decomposition and decay of capitalism — such as entrepreneurs becoming superfluous, bureaucrats taking over functions of entrepreneurs such as research, development and management, emergence of a class of intellectual idlers who would only criticise capitalism, disappearance of the class of small entrepreneurs with emotional attachment to capitalism and so on.

Karl Marx, on the other hand, feels that capitalism will be ultimately destroyed because the capitalist structure has within itself some inherent contradictions giving rise to repeated and ever-more deepening economic crisis, unemployment and increasing misery of working class. These inherent contradictions would, according to Karl Marx, ultimately destroy capitalism.

While Schumpeter thinks that decay of capitalism would be a natural process of decomposition after it becomes mature, Karl Marx, on the other hand, though believing in ultimate destruction of capitalism, advocated forcible overthrow of capitalism by workers adopting violent revolutionary methods.

According to Schumpeter, the conflict under capitalism would arise between the employers or owners of the corporate sector intelligentia who supported by some sections of the working class would take to left wing causes undermining both theoretical and psychological base of competitive capitalism.

According to Karl Marx, the class conflict under capitalism would be between capitalist class of employers (the Haves) and the working class (the Have-nots).

Lastly, while Schumpeter admits that capitalism will die a natural death and will be replaced by socialism, he has no intellectual or psychological attachment to socialism.

On the other hand, for Karl Marx socialism is the ultimate ideal to be fervently hoped for and to strive after. With all factors of production nationalised, disappearance of the institution of private property, classless society without exploitation, socialism for Marx is the ultimate goal of all social development process.

12. FACTORS INFLUENCING TECHNOLOGICAL PROGRESS UNDER CAPITALISM

There is no doubt that remarkable technological progress has taken and has been taking place in capitalist countries. The United States and Western capitalist countries are technologically the most progressive countries in the world at present.

The technological progress commenced with-the end of Feudal Age and beginning of capitalism.

Since food is the priority number one and since adequacy of foodgrains can alone enable mankind to take up problems of industrial development and developments in services, naturally technological progress first made rapid strides in the agricultural sector.

Thus instead of open field system of agriculture with traditional pattern of cultivation with simple wooden instruments and natural manure, gradually new inventions took place and new machines to plough, sow, reap and harvest crops came to be introduced leading to agricultural revolution. Tractors, thrashers, harvest combines, artificial manure and pesticides, mechanical movement and storage of goods all meant mechanisation of agriculture.

Once food self-sufficiency was ensured, industrial revolution, took place. Inventions and innovations took place, as we saw, first in textiles and then in coal, steel and transport and various other industries.

This technological progress has been particularly rapid since the beginning of the 20th century and especially after World War II.

Next 25 years will see much rapid and revolutionary technological progress in developed capitalist countries.

The next quarter-century will see 'push-button' industry and economy. There will be computer-controlled machines. It will be super-industrial world.

It is expected that during the next 25 years in capitalist countries, there will be multiple applications of laser beams for measuring, cutting, heating welding and for several other uses. There will be nuclear power for excavation, mining and various other uses. Thermal and hydro-electricity will be replaced by nuclear power. There will be computers for practically every industrial activity. There will be communication through stationary satellites. Travel by super-sonic jets will be a common feature. There will be automated higherways, under-water travel, and such other technological progress in practically every field that cannot be imagined at present.

What are the factors or motivating forces that influence and bring about technological progress under capitalism?

In this connection following factors need to be noted :

1. Under competitive capitalism, private profit motive is the main spring of economic activities. If an entrepreneur invents a new product or new process by taking all the trouble and risk, he has the opportunity of making fortune for himself and his family and even for next generation. This goads private entrepreneurs to think of new things and processes.

2. Under capitalism, the law of a patents and copyrights and brand names gives an entrepreneur exclusive right of use to his invention, or new product, or a new process which others are forbidden to copy and therefore more and more people come forward to invest and find out new products and processes.

The same is true of private or public limited companies in capitalism. Many private and public limited companies have therefore established their own private research and development department (R & D) where day-to-day research goes on to find a new product or bring about improvement in the existing product, or a new process, and so on. This becomes the property of the company which is protected by the law of patents.

3. Under capitalism, people enjoy freedom of thought and action. They are not bound to conventions either by force or by customs. Universities have therefore become in capitalism centres of new ideas and inventions. Thus environment of personal freedom under capitalism encourages free thinking which leads to ever-fresh research and development which in turn leads to ever growing technological progress. There is also joy of new creation for individuals.

4. During post-war years problems of defence and security of a country are contributing substantially to technological progress. There is ideological rivalry between the United States and West European capitalist countries on the one hand and the Soviet Union and East European communist countries on the other. Each is trying to outbid the other in matters of defence technology and defence industries. But defence technology and defence industries form inseparable part of the general industrial structure of capitalist countries. And thus government for defence purposes encourages research in its defence department, in public and private industries, especially in those that contribute to the defence of the country. Thus research in nuclear energy, atomic fission, chemical warfare, space research, under-water travel, satellite tracking, have all been of significance from defence point of view and governments concentrated on them in their own laboratories and also encouraged private companies especially those connected with defence industries to undertake research and development.

5. Further as GNP grows, these rich capitalist countries are in a position to spend more and more on research and development and bring about further technological progress. Thus economic progress and technological progress have been acting and reacting upon each other, each stimulating and supporting the other.

Thus it is observed that in capitalist countries, nearly 4 to 5 per cent of their GNP is spent annually on research and development. In these countries, research and development have themselves become a sort of basic industry of vital importance.

Thus under capitalism, along with land, labour, capital and organisation, the traditional four factors of production, 'technology' and 'technological progress' have become possibly the most important factor of production resulting in increasing per head productivity and in total wealth of the country.

CHAPTER 13

SOCIETY AND ITS HISTORICAL EVOLUTION

1. INTRODUCTION

Marx's materialistic interpretation of history and evolution of different 'Modes of Production' help to understand the evolution of society through its various stages, namely, primitive communism, slavery, feudalism, capitalism, state socialism, and full communism. It is the changes in the mode of production due to dynamic changes taking place in the world that brought about, according to Karl Marx, evolution of society through different stages.

2. PRIMITIVE COMMUNISM

History of all civilised societies begins with what is described as 'Primitive Communism'.

Under primitive communism most means of production are owned by the community. All the members of the community have a right to use these means of production. In such a society there was no private ownership of the means of production.

Under primitive communism, land was the main and often the only means of production, along with some handicrafts. Land was owned and tilled by members of the community or tribe commonly. The produce from the land was divided among members of the tribe according to their needs and customs.

Each family supplied other needs of the members of the family by practising, in the family itself, simple crafts or occupations such as spinning, weaving and cattle-raising. Some degree of division of labour was practised within the family on the basis of sex, age and natural conditions.

According to Karl Marx these were "... communities of free individuals, carrying on their own work with the means of production in common in which the labour power of all the different individuals is consciously applied as the combined labour power of the community."

Under 'primitive communism' most production took place for direct consumption and not for exchanges which were extremely limited. It was use-value and not exchange-value that was the important determinant of production.

It is obvious that primitive communism could exist only under conditions where productivity of labour was extremely low making the use of combined labour of the community necessary for production. This would mean that with technological progress, primitive communism would break down or come to an end.

Causes of the Break-down of Primitive Communism

It was not Marx but Friedrich Engels who emphasised that it was the emergence of the institution of private property that spelled the downfall of primitive communism which subsequently gave place to slavery.

The following were the main causes that brought about the disappearance of primitive communism.

When means of production were owned by the community as a whole, productive relations under the system were such that production was not efficient. Under communal ownership there was not adequate incentive to individuals to increase production. Communal ownership of means of production thus meant inefficient production.

Inefficiency was also there because under the system there was no incentive for individuals to save and invest in means of production to increase still more production of goods. If people, could hunt in communally owned forests, or fish in communally owned ponds, or milk communally owned cows, there was no incentive to save and invest in these means of production. Thus, individual right to use communally owned means of production came in the way of individual's saving and investing with a view to increase the stock of communally owned means of production. This also meant inefficient production as quality and quantity of communally owned means of production was bound to suffer.

With the invention of better agricultural tools and rotation of crops, individuals or groups of individuals insisted on exclusive use of plots of land where they could invest their time, energy and knowledge to produce more foodgrains. Beneficiaries insisted on private ownership of land that they cultivated.

Similar result was produced by discovery of metals and evolution of better tools and implements. This was bound to increase efficiency of labour. If time and energy were to be invested in making these tools and implements, then not communal but their individual ownership was insisted upon. Gradually investment, preparation, maintenance and upkeep of tools and implements became individual or family responsibility. There was thus gradual decline of communal ownership of means of production and in its place arose private ownership (that of the individual or of the family) of various means of production. Under communal ownership of means of production economic relations became more and more strained leading to gradual evolution of the institution of private property which necessitated new mode of production in place of that under primitive communism.

With the invention of better tools and implements, an individual or a family could produce enough for its maintenance. Hereafter collective ownership of means of production once necessary (*e.g.*, common hunting, common cultivation, etc.) was no more necessary. Invention of better tools and implements thus enabled an individual or a family as a unit to produce enough for itself, instead of relying upon community for its subsistence. Thus evolution of the institution of private property spelled the doom of primitive communism.

With increasing diversification of occupations made possible by better tools, labour productivity went on increasing. There was a keen desire to own labour power to produce more, have a surplus and invest further. There was thus a keen desire not only to own land but also own workers. Those who were weak and dependent became slaves of the more powerful and efficient. Gradually thus along with private property, institution of slavery arose undermining communal ownership of means of production and communal production (and also distribution) which characterised primitive communism.

With dynamic forces working, with evolution of private property, with the emergence of institution of slavery and division of society into slaves and slave-owners, gradually primitive communism and the particular mode of production prevailing under that system gave place to 'slavery' and altogether new mode of production.

3. SLAVERY

Primitive communism gave place to the institution of slavery and a new mode of production.

With the evolution of the institution of private property and increase in productivity of labour, society gradually came to be divided into two classes—the rich slave-owners and slaves. Under the system of slavery not only tools and implements but even men (*i.e.*, slaves) became the property of slave-owners.

The system of slavery prevailed in ancient Egypt, Greece and Rome. Under this system the rich slave-owners were the masters who gave just enough for subsistence to slaves and made them work hard and appropriated the surplus for themselves. The rich slave-owners lived a life of luxury and abundance whereas slaves were made to toil hard on mere subsistence. The institution of slavery was so well-entrenched in ancient Greece that a philosopher like Aristotle wrote:

"Some are born masters and some are born slaves."

Under the system of slavery a new mode of production based on exploitation of salves by their masters came to be introduced.

Under slavery, greater specialisation and division of labour became possible. Thus the institution of slavery meant increasing division of labour and specialisation. This meant increasing number of exchanges and widening markets. This is turn led to invention and evolution of money and its increasing use for transactions and exchanges.

But for quite some time production under the system of slavery was mostly for personal consumption and not for exchange or market.

But with further increase in exchange, the lust for money and wealth of slave-owners went on increasing. Slave-masters started compelling slaves under them to work hard and harder so that slave-owners had more and more goods and made more money and wealth by selling produce in exchange. This resulted in increasing exploitation of slaves and luxurious life for slave-masters without themselves producing wealth.

Mode of production under the system of slavery was characterised by the following features:

Slavery made division of labour and increasing specialisation possible. This led to large-scale production of goods. To make more wealth, salve-masters went on exploiting slaves more and more. Masters owned slaves like other tools and implements. This resulted in increasing demand for slaves. Salve-masters obtained slaves by conquering foreign countries and converting defeated enemy into slaves. Salve-masters had complete control over slaves, including selling and purchasing them, or punishing them, including right to kill them. Thus rights of slave-owners over their slaves were practically absolute.

4. DISAPPEARANCE OF SLAVERY SYSTEM AND EMERGENCE OF FEUDALISM

Though compared to primitive communism, under slavery there was greater division of labour, specialisation, technological progress and increase in productivity of labour, progress under the system of slavery nonetheless remained slow. Slaves had no particular incentive to work hard and produce more as they were given only subsistence, however much they produced. Therefore there was no limit on surplus which slaves could produce. Also, slaves were mostly employed by masters for production of luxury goods.

System of slavery ultimately disappeared because of certain inherent contradictions in the mode of production prevailing under the system. These inherent contradictions became shackles on further production under the system of slavery.

Thus greater, the extent of exploitation of slaves by their masters, productive capacity of slaves got more and more weakened. Thus human resources in the form of slaves ceased to be more and more productive. There was weakening of human resource which formed the very foundation of the system of slavery.

Also, as slave-masters employed more and more slaves to increase production and surplus, the work of careful supervision necessary under the system of slavery became more and more difficult.

Further, masters owning slaves were not interested in increasing efficiency of tools and implements or in devising new tools, because they thought it easier to produce more by employing more slaves.

Further, slaves who got mere subsistence however hard they worked, were not interested in working harder or more. They worked out of fear of punishments. Often slaves destroyed tools or crops to avoid work. Thus under the system of slavery, mode of production or production relations were such that they acted as restraints on further production. Ultimately these inner contradictions and clash of interests between slave-masters and slaves brought about the destruction of the system of slavery.

Sharp contradictions that arose between the class of free peasants and artisans on the one hand, and masters owning slaves on the other, was another factor responsible for the ultimate disappearance of the system of slavery. It was the class of free peasants and artisans in the community that provided men for the army and also paid taxes needed to support the administrative machinery of the State.

The class of free peasants and artisans was adversely affected on the one hand by large-scale production undertaken by slave-owners who employed increasing number of slaves for the purpose, and on the other hand, mounting burden of taxes which they had to bear for financing military operations and to meet expenditure on administration. This reduced many free peasants and artisans to the status of slaves. This weakened the recruiting base for the army and thus the main source of adding to number of slaves by capturing prisoners in war gradually dried up. The number of slaves gradually began to decline and prices of slaves started mounting up. Cultivation of plantations and slave-based agriculture started giving place to tenant-cultivation. Masters tried to adapt to the new situation by dividing their vast landed estates into small patches of land which were let to free peasants for cultivation on the basis of share-cropping or even given to slaves for cultivation in return for part of the produce or some other conditions.

In addition, there was continued clash of interest and conflicts between slave-owners and slaves who because of extreme exploitations by their masters rebelled. This inner contradiction in the mode of production finally brought about the decline and disappearance of the system of slavery which came to be gradually replaced by the feudal system or feudalism in European countries.

5. FEUDALISM

Slave system and the mode of production under that system came to be gradually replaced by feudalism and feudal mode of production. It would be instructive to know the main features of feudalism and the feudal mode of production. This is for two reasons. Feudalism was established and continued its existence for about thousand years (roughly from 4th century A.D. to 14th century A.D.) in most of the European countries. Naturally one would be interested to know the details of the system that prevailed over such length of time. Second and more important reason is that it is out of the decay of feudalism that modern capitalism emerged. This means to know the historical background of modern capitalism, it is instructive to know feudalism and mode of production under it and why and how feudalism gave place to modern capitalism.

Feudalism and feudal mode of production prevailed for about one thousand years (*i.e.,* from the break-up of the Roman Empire in the 4th century A.D. to the beginning of the 14th or even 15th century A.D.) in most of the countries of Europe including Russia.

The essence of feudalism lay in this that society was divided into different strata or layers, each strata enjoying certain rights from and obligation to the strata above it, the supreme authority or apex being the king. Thus to take the typical example of England, the serf owed services to his lord; lord to his superior like a count, or a duke; and the duke owning his loyalty to the king.

Feudalism or the feudal system was the outgrowth of the decline and ultimate disappearance of the Roman empire. The feudal system was based around land as the main source of production of wealth and living.

The lord under whom the serfs worked gave them subsistence protection in return of various prescribed services and obligations from serfs.

To make these arrangements binding, one had to swear loyalty to one's superior. Society was thus bound together by an intricate system of contracts, the sanctity of which ensured and enforced by customs supported by force of upper classes to enforce those contracts. Since there was no powerful central government in Middle Ages to ensure people protection and maintenance, the whole social organisation under feudalism came to be based on a system of mutual obligations from top to bottom. Thus lord gave a piece of land for cultivation to a serf who sought his protection; in return the serf owed him some obligations such as sharing the produce, rendering manual service to lord for a specified number of days and so on. This was so for all layers of society, the lower layer claiming some rights from those above it and in return fulfilling some obligations.

Manor and Manorial System

Study of Middle Ages and of feudalism can begin with the study of manor. manor and manorial system were the characteristic features of medieval or feudal Europe.

Manor was a large landed estate. The land in the manor was owned by a manorial lord. People of the manor were attached to land in the manor where they had a right to work, whereas lord of the manor provided livery and maintenance to people who worked on the land in the manor, they in return owing many obligations to him. Though manors varied in size and in some details, broad features of the manorial system were generally the same.

Every manor had a lord during the feudal period. The lord of a manor was regarded as 'a tenant' and not 'owner' of his estate. Lord of a manor was a 'tenant' of another lord who was higher up in the social scale. Thus serf held the land from a lord, who in turn held it from a count, who in turn held it from a duke, who in turn held it from the king of the country. Only the king in theory was the absolute owner of all the land in his country. But the manorial lord who actually owned land in his manor could not be deprived of his land except when he committed treason against the king of the country.

Organisation of a typical manor was as follows :

In the centre of a manor was the manorial village dominated by the manorial castle, or manor-house which was well fortified. Manorial lord lived in this castle or visited it often, in case he had a many manors under him.

Around the manorial house were dwellings of serfs which were huts of wood and thatched roofs. Around the village was a stone wall for protection of the people.

Each manor aimed at self-sufficiency in respect of foodgrains and other essentials of life. Natural economy prevailed in a manor. Exchanges took the form of barter and little use was made of money.

Agriculture which was the main occupation, was of 'open field system'. All cultivable land was divided into two or three strips and one of the two or three strips was left fallow each year for recuperating its natural fertility. Only few crops like wheat, barley and rye were grown by rotation. After harvesting, all lands were left open for cattle to roam about and feed. All strip-holders were expected to conform to common pattern of agriculture — what crops to grow, time of sowing and reaping and leaving all lands for cattle for feeding once the harvest season was over.

It was only natural manure that was used. Consequently yield was poor, may be six to eight bushels per acre.

Inhabitants of a manor could be classified into two categories. There were free persons who included the lord of the manor, his bailiff, village priest and free men who were independent proprietors of land. They did not owe any obligations to higher-ups but only paid taxes to their overlord.

The other class which constituted the majority of people in a manor consisted of unfree persons who were tied to land that they cultivated.

The unfree cultivators could be classified into serfs, demesne serfs and villeins. While demesne serfs and villeins enjoyed certain additional rights and privileges from their overlord, the lot of the serfs who were at the bottom of unfree class of people was the worst.

The unfree classes in a manor were required to render various types of services either free of charge or in return of some petty reward to their overlord.

Conditions in which serfs, demesne serfs and villeins held and cultivated land and their obligations to overlord varied. But the different terms of these three categories of unfree people gradually merged into one another.

Manorial system based around land and rights and obligations was admirably suited to the Middle Ages (also known as Dark Ages). Though standard of life was low, especially of serfs (*i.e.,* unfree class of people in a manor), they enjoyed security and protection of their overlord in return for the duties which they had to perform for him. The question of unemployment or old age or sickness did not pose a serious problem for the people in a manor. Manorial system encouraged cooperation in those days when manual labour was the chief source of power with which to work and when individual labour was not efficient and by itself could produce little.

Not all lords of manors oppressed serfs in their manors. They were also bound by prevailing customs and conventions.

Under feudalism (*i.e.,* in manorial system) cattle and agricultural tools and implements were privately owned and operated. On this account many of the disadvantages or evils of primitive communism were avoided.

But feudalism also was associated with certain grave shortcomings or evils. Under feudalism, there was no incentive to accumulate and invest. Any capital equipment resulting from saving of a serf was at least partly subject to communal usage. Also, due to war, raids and plunder which were very common during the Middle Ages, there was hardly any incentive for people to save, invest and create costly capital equipment or productive assets.

Naturally under feudalism, due to low productivity social surplus was very low, so also rate of investment. Hence this period was characterised by economic stagnancy and hence also by lack of political, social, cultural and educational progress. That is why Middle Ages or feudal times are referred to as Dark Ages.

Also because of the open-field system of agriculture and necessity of adherence by all cultivators to common agricultural practices, there were land and boundary disputes, plundering of crops and stealing of cattle. No cultivator therefore was interested in saving more and investing his additional savings.

Practice of common cultivation thus prevented enterprising cultivators from innovating, saving more and investing, or improving livestock.

Mode of production under feudalism resulted in creating great inequalities of income and wealth. While manorial lord enjoyed life of luxury and affluence without any or much work, serfs who cultivated lands were living a very poor life. All this resulted in low productivity of agriculture.

Thus feudal relationship and feudal institutions became fetters on productive powers of land and people. That explains why feudalism (4th century to about 14th or 15th century) was characterised by economic stagnancy as also stagnancy in practically every field of human activity. That was the reason why this period came to be known as Dark Ages.

Reasons for the Decline of Feudalims and for Emergence of Capitalism

From 11th or 12th century A.D. onwards, technological progress started taking place in agriculture and industries (first in textiles, then in metallurgy, armament, printing, chemistry and so on). Primitive plough came to be improved and horse became a useful animal. In the industrial sector various machines were invented and introduced.

Gradually commercial revolution took place with technological progress in transport and communications. Agriculture and industry started producing surpluses. Trade instead of plunder became popular to earn a living and wealth.

Nation-state gradually emerged with monarch as a strong central power. People were now no longer required to take oath of loyalty to their immediate lord but to monarch of the country. Also, monarch raised standing armies so that feudal lords were no longer permitted to have private armies.

Also, monarch with strong army under him established law and order in the country. Gradually services like protection rendered by feudal lords to serfs and free people in the manor became less and less significant. Feudal lords also came to be deprived of their judicial powers and functions by the monarch. This reduced their status and influence in the community.

Another factor that brought about the decline of feudalism was that serfs who felt oppressed under manorial lord fled to nearby towns which had gradually sprung up due to rise of commerce and industry. The feudal lords facing scarcity of labour because of fleeing of serfs started gradually hiring agricultural workers on more favourable terms and conditions. Thus both in agriculture and industries hired or contractual labour started playing more and more important role.

With growth of commerce and industry, of towns and cities and replacement of money economy in place of barter economy, feudal lords also started specialising in production to earn money by selling their produce in nearby markets so that with money they could purchase whatever they wanted. They also started converting obligations of serfs to them into money payments after making which serfs were free of all their obligations to their lords (such as rendering personal services for specific number of days, giving part of crops or cattle, etc.).

Feudal lords also found that hired or contractual labour was more efficient and productive than serfs with conventional obligations.

Landlords observed that under money-exchanges which were gradually evolving, money served not only as a medium of exchange but also as a store of value. They therefore started producing more and more agricultural surplus, if necessary by encouraging serfs with initiative from whom they got their share in the additional produce, or by hiring more workers by paying money wages.

Thus many enterprising serfs became kulak peasants. Those who fled to towns or purchased their freedom from lords in return of monetary payments became artisans and small producers. By the end of the 14th century, serfs were found managing small landed estates of their own or their own small industrial workshops. Thus feudal relationship and exploitation were loosening.

Thus position of feudal lords in society gradually declined in importance due to factors like rise of commerce and industry, of towns, fleeing of serfs to towns to free themselves from obligations and exploitation of landlords, rising demand for labour from landlords and offering of better contractual terms to hired workers who also were found to be more efficient than serfs, uprisings by serfs against exploitation by manorial lords, increasing number of serfs fleeing to towns, and also due to Black Death in 1350 which killed nearly one-third of Europe's population.

Due to the above factors, feudal organisation and its mode of production were breaking down so that by the middle of the 15th century in most parts of Europe payment of money-rent by cultivators had become common in place of feudal system of personal rights and obligations. This meant serfs won complete freedom by the middle of the 15th century.

Thus, rise of commerce and trade, of towns, of money economy, emergence of national-state with strong central power represented by the monarch and several other factors referred to above, resulted in gradual decline of feudalism.

6. CAPITALISM : ITS EVOLUTION

It has been explained above how decline of feudalism and feudal mode of production gradually came about in Europe. We shall now examine how capitalism came to be established in place of feudalism in Western Europe from where it spread to America and other countries.

We have already seen that during the 12th to 15th century, in Western Europe, many freed serfs set themselves up as independent artisans or small farmers. These independent artisans often employed and worked with hired workers.

There were guild monopolies in respective crafts. Individual master-craftsman hired workers as apprentices who when they gained experience became journeymen (travelling from place to place selling goods of their guild-masters) and later, if a journeyman had accumulated sufficient means, set up himself as independent master-craftsman. Otherwise, these apprentices continued to work with master-craftsman. What is to be noted about the guild system in each craft is that the relationsip between master-craftsman and apprentices and journeymen was not like that of feudal landlords and serfs but that of equality. Each apprentice aspired to be an independent master-craftsman and many did attain that position.

Soon however this equality between master-craftsmen in different crafts and apprentices and journeymen gradually began to disappear. Rich master-craftsmen with substantial resources at their disposal began to hire more and more apprentices and journeymen and thus expand their business establishments. Thus gradually rich master-craftsmen in course of time emerged as industrial employers (*i.e.,* factory owners) hiring substantial number of workers by paying money-wages.

Thus rich master-craftsmen gradually moved up becoming capitalists who were hiring by paying money wages, increasing number of workers. This was the embryonic factory system that was to subsequently characterise capitalism. But as Karl Marx pointed out, initially the emergence or rise of bourgeoisie (people from middle class owning productive assets) was very slow. This was because they were hampered for quite some time by surviving feudal restrictions, traditions and conventions, by guild regulations, absence yet of the system of free contract, local legal provisions, privilege of nobility (which disappeared only gradually) and so on. There was in those days tendency to work for oneself as artisan or independent farmer with whatever means one possessed. The system of allowing oneself to be hired by others for money wages emerged only gradually and hence also the factory system.

Primitive Accumulation of Capital

The fundamental feature of capitalism is the existence of a class of employers and existence of labour power as a community (like any other commodity in the market) to be sold and bought for a price (*i.e.,* wages). Thus there must be class of labourers who want to sell their labour or labour-power, because these labourers are not in a position to make and sell goods on their own account under the prevailing circumstances (such as large scale production and existence of competition which gradually emerged under capitalism). On the other side there must exist a class of employers who are ready to hire labourers by paying money wages. Establishment of this type of production-relationship or mode of production in place of feudal relationship with mutual rights and obligations was the essence of capitalism and capitalist mode of production.

Roughly until the latter part of the 15th century, only the class of employers ready to hire labourers for money wages had emerged; the other half had not yet emerged, at any rate on a large scale. The emergence of a class of labourers ready to hire themselves for money wage arose as a result of Enclosure

Movement (*i.e.,* enclosing of farm with a view to large-scale machanised farming and cultivation) and expansion at about the same time of textile and woollen industry because of favourable circumstances due to factors like some inventions like Spinning Jenny, Crompton's Mule, etc.

As rich farmers began to enclose their fields and enlarging them and introduced machines and better methods of cultivation by evicting tenants or by purchasing small adjacent fields of independent small farmers or by purchasing common lands which were no longer available to small independent farmers to graze their cattle, a vast number of tenants and evicted small peasants were forced to seek jobs in textile factories which were gradually being established in towns and cities.

The process of emergence of the class of labourers ready to hire themselves for money-wages was accelerated by emergence of merchant-capitalist and the system of putting-out. Rich merchant capitalists purchased tools and raw materials on a large scale and gave them to craftsmen who could work with them at home. The merchant-capitalists then collected the finished products and sold them making profits for themselves. The craftsmen worked for money-wages, though at home (working in the factory set up by the merchant-capital was the next step which was to emerge gradually). Thus tools and raw materials owned by merchant capitalists were given to artisans who worked at home for wages. There were harsh conditions regarding hours of work, wages to be paid, and severe penalties for not delivering finished goods in time to merchant-capitalists.

Karl Marx calls this expropriation by merchant-capitalists of individual peasants or craftsmen 'Primitive Accumulation'. According to Karl Marx: ". . . primitive accumulation . . . is nothing else than the historical process of divorcing the producer from the means of production. It appears as primitive, because it forms the prehistoric stage of capital and mode of production corresponding with it."

Karl Marx viewed primitive accumulation as theft which gave capitalists their first major source of surplus value.

Once capitalists acquired means of production (like tools, etc.,) he could borrow money against them, hire more workers to do his work of production and pocket additional surplus value. Capitalists could thus expand their empires pushing ever-increasing number of workers into labour market from their independent status and thus increasing dependence of workers on themselves.

The second stage in primitive accumulation was characterised by increasing concentration of investible funds and wealth in the hands of smaller number of capitalists. This increasing concentration of investible funds and wealth during the second stage of primitive accumulation was brought about not by employing increasing number of workers and their exploitation but by plunder of colonies by imperial powers.

Two Phases of Capitalism

Karl Marx divided the era of *laissez faire* capitalism into two distinct phases on the basis of use of mechanical power and machinery.

The first phase of capitalism, according to Marx, lasted from the middle of the 16th century to the third quarter of the 18th century. This first phase of capitalism, broadly speaking, preceded the 'Industrial Revolution' which was dominated by use of steam power instead of manual or physical power and by increasing use of machinery.

The main characteristics of this first phase of capitalism were: increasing division of labour, increasingly larger scale of production and growing use of factory system of production. This phase was not characterised by increasing use of machinery.

The important aspect of development taking place in this first phase of capitalism was that an employer went on employing larger number of artisans who undertook to do all the processes of production, each worker doing all the successive operations or processes from beginning to the last stage of the final product. During this phase, as we saw, there was production on ever-increasing scale and expanding factory system.

The second phase was characterised by 'Industrial Revolution'. During this phase there took place increasing substitution of various types of machines for manual work predominating the first phase of capitalism. During this second phase, various machines were invented and introduced. The Industrial Revolution first took place in England and from there spread to other countries of Europe and to the United States.

New bourgeoisie (new middle class owning machines and factories) emerged in England and subsequently in other countries which experienced industrial revolution. This class also began to control political power in the state. This new capitalist class or bourgeoisie dominated the legislature and government. This resulted in gradual diminishing of the influence in government and society of the feudal landlords who at one time were enjoying highest social and political status and power.

It was during this second phase of capitalism that machines started making machines and machines were introduced increasingly making possible increasingly large-scale production of goods at decreasing cost. There was continual increase in efficiency and productivity of labour during this phase of capitalism.

It is essentially against this phase of capitalism that Karl Marx raised his voice of protest. It was during this Industrial Revolution phase that there was enslavement of man to machines, making of ever increasing surplus value to be pocketed by capitalists, increasing exploitation of workers, and increasing misery of working class.

Simple Commodity Production and Capitalist Commodity Production

According to Karl Marx, production of goods which are not meant for sale in a market (which was the case under feudalism or primitive communism when goods were produced for direct consumption or satisfying of one's wants), is called 'natural production.'

On or the other hand, Marx called production of goods for sale in a market 'commodity production.'

According to Marx, 'commodity production' is of two types:

(*a*) Simple Commodity Production, and (*b*) Capitalist Commodity Production.

Simple Commodity Production. Simple commodity production meant production of goods for sale in a market; but the production of such goods is done without the use of hired labour on wage basis. Also, under simple commodity production, means of production are owned by the producer himself. For example, under feudalism, when craftsmen owning their own tools and without hiring labour produced commodities which were sold in the market, that was 'simple commodity production.'

According to Karl Marx, 'simple commodity production' precedes capitalism. Even under capitalism, simple commodity production (as in the case of small farmers or artisans) is found side by side with the second type of production, namely *'Capitalist Commodity Production.'* Under 'capitalist commodity production', commodities are produced for sale in the market by hiring workers on wage basis.

Under 'simple commodity production' as well as 'capitalist commodity production' means of production are privately owned. But under 'capitalist commodity production', there is alienation of labour power. Thus under capitalist commodity production, labour itself becomes a commodity and is sold and purchased like any other commodity in a market. Lenin writes: "By capitalism is meant that stage of the development of commodity production at which not only production of human labour but human labour power itself becomes a commodity."

Thus under 'simple commodity production' goods produced by a worker belong to him and it is the worker who sells the goods produced by him in a market. On the other hand, under 'capitalist commodity production' goods produced by a worker are appropriated by the capitalist who sells those goods. This becomes possible because he owns factors of production as also employs workers by paying wages.

According to Karl Marx, the aim of 'simple commodity production' is satisfaction of wants (though process of exchange is involved in simple commodity production). In the case of 'capitalist commodity production' the aim of the capitalist owner of the means of production is to extract maximum surplus value or profit from worker's labour.

Fetishism of Commodities and the Concept of Alienation

The characteristic feature of capitalism is not just sale and purchase of various types of commodities but also sale and purchase of labourer's power to work or his ability to work. The peculiar feature of capitalism is that labour-power becomes a commodity, the purchaser is the capitalist and worker is the seller. Under capitalism, commodities (*i.e.,* use-values) are created. Labour power is thus the creater of use-values. Use-values are embodied in commodities which are produced by labour power. Thus commodities embody labour time or value. Thus labour power has also use-value of creating commodities with use-value. Labour power, the creater of use-value, is bought by capitalists. He then uses labour power to create commodities (with use-values). He then sells use-values as commodities. Capitalist purchases labour power by paying wages to workers. The capitalist thus controls the labourer and as also has the ownership of machines and tools with which a labourer works.

The commodities produced by labourers reflect social character of labour. When commodities produced by labour power are exchanged, that exchange in effect means that labour power is exchanged for labour power. The capitalists do not see the essence of exchange in this fashion. For them, this relationship between two workers or their labour power simply means that two commodities are exchanged, say one table in exchange of four yards of cloth. While capitalist production represents establishing social relationship between two workers, in effect to capitalist the exchange appears as relationship between two commodities —one table in exchange of four yards of cloth, and not as exchange of labour power of two workers. Karl Marx describes this perspective of capitalists, as 'Fetishism of Commodities.' This fetishism of commodities becomes very clear in modern capitalism where labour power is treated just like any other commodity.

Commodity fetishism which characterises capitalism becomes the basis of the 'Concept of Alienation'.

Concept of Alienation

What characterises capitalism is the 'alienation' of worker from his work and also from the commodity that he produces.

Alienation made its appearance quite long ago in the history of mankind. When the system of slavery succeeded primitive communism, 'alienation' appeared on the scene. The slave and the worker in capitalism produced goods not to express themselves or to satisfy their wants but out of necessity of earning a wage with which to live. The commodities produced by workers are not theirs but of the capitalist or employer. The capitalist or the employer of workers is not interested in use-value (with power to satisfy human wants) but in exchange-value (namely, in profit which he will make by selling the commodity). Alienation grows worse as we move from the system of slavery to modern *laissez faire* capitalism. Alienation becomes worse as division of labour grows more and more and any single worker just produces a small part of the final product and does not understand the significance of what he is producing. Long ago when a person was creating goods for satisfying his personal wants, his labour was of great significance to him. Today that labour has lost the significance and has become alienated from workers. Workers do not understand the significance of their own labour from which they are fully alienated. Workers feel alienated because they do not know the significance of what they are producing nor do they feel any joy of creation when producing goods. The worker has become alienated from his work.

CHAPTER 14

EVOLUTION AND GROWTH OF SOCIALISM

(UTOPIAN SOCIALISM)

1. INTRODUCTION

Growth of capitalism in the 19th century called forth three type of criticism : reactionary, nationalist and radical. The first is represented by Adam Muller who tried to fight "a rearguard action of feudalism" ; and second by Friedrich List. A new type of criticism that expressed itself by the beginning of the 19th century was of a different type. It was radical and revolutionary. All the above three schools had however one thing in common, namely, their opposition to the classical doctrine of natural economic harmony.

The radical or the socialist critics launched their attack against capitalism on two separate fronts. They began their career by attacking specific evils of fully developed capitalism. The story of the rise of the class of wage-labourers and their exploitation and oppression has often been told. To economic thinkers like Adam Smith and Ricardo who took a long-range view of economic happenings, capitalism meant "an undreamed of expansion of production, increase of wealth and economic intercourse between nations together with all the cultural benefits which those involved. It meant liberalism in politics and the destruction of oppressive regulations and obscurantist restrictions." The class of workers and the thinkers who sympathised with them, however, took a different view. They thought they were paying for this capitalistic revolution by their sweat and blood. To the working-class, 19th century capitalism meant pauperism, unemployment, or at any rate, hard labour in factories for themselves, their wives and young ones, coupled with long hours of work in insanitary conditions under most oppressive and inhuman supervision. The early socialist criticism aimed at the abolition of these evils of capitalism. This was one aspect of socialist criticism.

The second aspect of socialism was and is an ideological one. Here the socialists drew their inspiration from liberalism itself which was the philosophical basis of industrial capitalism. Was not capitalism more revolution in its own days than any other previous system of social organisation ? Had it not destroyed ruthlessly all the restraints and regulations of the feudal institutions, and this not in the name of this class or that, but in the name of humanity itself? Liberalism had its roots in ideas like freedom, equality, justice, rule of reason and the greatest happiness of the greatest number, and in its days had meant a new hope for mankind. And therefore, when the liberal capitalism failed completely in its attempts to take the people to the promised land of prosperity and happiness for all, the revolutionary attitude on which that system was based, turned against that very system. The critical attitude of mind developed by the writings of Machiavelli, Bacon, Hobbes and Locke had remained critical forever and now attacked the liberal capitalism itself. The socialists called industrial capitalism to account and agitated for reforms and better social order. These radical critics "gradually developed in Marxism a systematic philosophy and economic theory powerfully opposed to the doctrine of liberalism." The radical school was the only one to offer, in addition to the destructive criticism of industrial capitalism, an alternative positive programme in its place.

2. UTOPIAN SOCIALISM EARLY NINETEENTH CENTURY SOCIALISM : UTOPIAN, BOURGEOIS, HUMANITARIAN, ASSOCIATIONIST, EVOLUTIONARY

Industrial Revolution brought in its train many maladjustments so that economic crisis, poverty and misery of the working class became apparent. The critics were therefore inclined to blame and attack the capitalistic system as also the economic philosophy that attended it for the above evils.

In the 19th century, there emerged a group of thinkers who "while accepting the technical industrial progress of the time, with its large-scale production and division of labour, opposed some of the fundamental ideas and institutions of the existing social order, and censured the classical economists for postulating certain social institutions as though they were ultimate and merely to be taken for granted." Their criticism sprang out of those very theories which were the basis of the Industrial and the French Revolution. It was essentially economic in nature and insofar as it was not merely moral, their schemes differed from those of Sir Thomas More, Godwin and such other utopians.

The criticism of the early socialists represented the transitional condition of the time. These critics had imbibed the optimistic spirit of the French Revolution and were still under the influence of the idealistic Nature philosophy of the eighteenth century. Thus, they still had faith in Godwin's doctrine of the perfectibility of human nature. But at the same time, they were horrified by the excess of the French Revolution and considered the uneducated proletariat as still incapable of self-help.

Thus arose the class of the utopian socialists who thought of the idea of "bringing down aid to the poor from above, of regenerating mankind by educating them to live in an ideal social order guided by the wisest and best among them." These utopian socialists were speculative and started their reasoning from some ideal postulates. They were mainly humanitarian in their outlook and differed from the later revolutionary socialist in that, instead of seeking to organise labour and making them class-conscious, sought to improve their lot through educational experimentation. They appealed to the dominant capitalist classes for aid in their experiments, and were rather bourgeois in their ideas. They were certainly not revolutionary in their attitude. They were also called associationists in so far as they believed in reaching the goal of social and economic reconstruction through voluntary co-operation and association. Competition according to them meant inevitable monopoly and hence was looked down upon as an evil. Their watchword was co-operation. But though described as socialists, these critics were strongly opposed to "the passive acceptance of the compulsion which is a feature of collectivism."

3. SAINT-SIMON (1760-1826)

Saint-Simon was an economic liberalist. He departed but little from the basic teachings of the English Classical School.

Main feature of Saint-Simon's thought was his emphasis on 'association'. He emphasised 'exploitation of the globe by association'. He proposed the establishment of "a new social order, based upon progressive industry directed by experts." He aimed at abolition of class distinctions and establishment of industrial equality. He was not having in his mind so much the conflict between labour and capital as the conflict of a more general nature, namely, conflict between workers and idlers. Saint-Simon aimed at so organising society that all must work and in his scheme each person was to benefit in proportion to his potential capacity translated into productive performance. In his scheme even the State organisation was to be industrialised so that in his scheme power would be replaced by capacity and command by direction of experts. Politics would get completely merged into economics.

The heart of Saint-Simon's scheme was systematic direction of labour of a nation so that all achieve their physical and moral amelioration.

Saint-Simon wanted scientists and business executives to replace clergy and nobility in the new social order. He conceived the world as based on industry which was the one single cardinal feature of his scheme. He thus advocated broad industrialisation so that existing class structure would merge itself into a single class of workers who would all be working for their living.

According to Saint-Simon, prosperity of a society depended upon economic and professional classes. In his scheme all distinctions would disappear and all persons would be workers working as agriculturists, artisans, manufacturers, bankers, artists and a manual workers. Each would be drawing according to his contribution. The whole nation was to be organised like a vast industrial workshop. The only function of the government would be protection of workers from unproductive idlers and provision of security and freedom for workers.

Saint-Simon's Parable

Saint-Simon illustrated his point by the following parable : If France lost suddenly and at one stroke fifty first-class doctors, bankers, chemists, etc., the nation will degenerate into a mere soulless body and fall into a state of despicable weakness. But if France retains all its men of genius and in just one day loses all the royal family, officers of the crown, cardinals, bishops, government employees and cream of nobility, the loss would be only sentimental. But it would cause least inconvenience to society.

Saint-Simon's Contribution to Socialism

The following was Saint-Simon's contribution to socialism : Every man must labour for his living; society should pay respect to any individual according to his contribution to production; he emphasised opposition to all privileges and idlers. He was not opposed to the institution of private property; but he interpreted private property in terms of the right of controlling property in proportion to ability to use it for common good; his aim was industrial order to be directed by experts among whom bankers had most general capacity for planning ec8nomic affairs of the community. He had no notion of fundamental opposition between employers and employees. The constituted a single class with a common interest against all idlers.

Saint-Simon anticipated technocracy and important role of experts and financiers as against mere politicians. He emphasised that each had a duty to work and earn his living and it was the duty of society to plan and organise production by taking full advantage of all scientific and technical knowledge.

4. THE SAINT-SIMONIANS

Saint-Simonians were the followers of Saint-Simon. They aimed at leading humanity into a new era of peaceful industry and international cooperation.

Though Saint-Simonians called themselves disciples of Saint-Simon, there were sharp differences between Saint-Simon and Saint-Simonians.

Saint-Simonians were collectivist. They criticised the institution of private property on grounds of inefficiency in the sphere of production and injustice in the sphere of distribution. They saw exploitation of labour as inherent in the institution of private property. According to them efficient production and equitable distribution both required extinction of the institution of private property. They were also opposed to law of inheritance which is a recognised part of the institution of private property. According to them, the law perpetuated the evils of the institution of private property.

Saint-Simonians advocated a system where the State became the owner of all forms of wealth, at any rate of all factors of production. The government wold distribute all these factors of production through the agency of a central bank with branches spread all over the country. Direction of production was to be in the hands of experts so that it could rise to the maximum. This was to be equitably distributed. The motto of Saint-Simonians was: " From each according to his ability and to each according to his contribution."

Saint-Simonians' Contribution to Socialism

Saint-Simonians were socialists insofar as they exalted work and claims of all producers and denounced all idlers and inherited and unmerited wealth. They insisted on central planning and international harmony and cooperation.

But Saint-Simonians had no faith in democracy. They accepted great industrialists, bankers and other men of genius as natural leaders and were ready to work for realisation of their ideal through any type of government-monarchist, imperialist, bourgeois or any other type.

Thus significant contributions of Saint-Simonians to socialism were: Their conception of planned economy with an aim of achieving, full employment, wide diffusion of purchasing power, the idea that rewards should be strictly in accordance with service rendered to the community, abolition of the institution of private property and law of inheritance, and recognition of priority of economic over political forces operating in a community.

5. ROBERT OWEN (1771-1858)

Robert Owen was a British utopian socialist. To him goes the credit of being the founder of British socialism, of British co-operative movement, of movement for factory reforms, of trade union movement, and of many educational experiments.

Robert Owen made a name for himself by introducing in his factory at New Lanark technical improvements, construction of model dwellings, introduction of free educational system and elevation of moral standards of workers in his factory. He brought about better living conditions, habits of order, cleanliness, sobriety and thrift. He reduced hours of work and raised wages. A company store was opened.

Robert Owen was the first to introduce all these improvements in his factory in the early 19th century. What astounded the people was that in spite of all these unusual innovations, the factory became a commercial success. New Lanark became famous as a marvel among industries and a model community.

Robert Owen's methods were opposite of other factory owners. He abolished fines for damages; he did not employ children in his factory; they were sent to factory-school where free education was given to them. He provided recreation facilities to all workers ; he introduced system of insurance. To cap it all, when a depression came and his factory was closed for a period of four months, he paid wages to workers during those four months of closure of the factory.

Robert Owen came to believe that character of an individual could be properly moulded by suitable environment. He believed that mere patronage and legislation were ineffective as instrument of social progress.

In 1825 Robert Owen launched his plan for communal experiment by establishing colonies in America where he went to try his various experiments. New Harmony was an attempt to establish a full-scale Owenite community, free from old immoral world.

In 1832 Robert Owen (back in England) established the National Equitable Labour Exchange in London. This was primarily an experiment in cooperative marketing. Labour notes were given for commodities produced and deposited there, and with those labour notes produces were to purchase from that Exchange whatever commodities they wanted. Labour notes were given on the basis of hours of work put in to produce a commodity. But this experiment did not last long, the failure being attributed to " the inflow of much goods really unsaleable and the breakdown of the upon my honour valuation" process.

Robert Owen's two books, namely, '*The New Moral World*', and '*What is Socialism*' contain his major ideas. He was convinced that "given proper opportunities, all men are capable of goodness and excellence." He therefore protested against the inhuman working conditions prevailing in factories in early 19th century. He also opposed regime of unregulated competition as that compels employers to adopt inhuman practices in their factories. Thus Owenite socialism was " a form of cooperation that aimed at community living that was to come about through conversion of men's character (through improved environment), instead of through state legislation."

In spite of failure of most of Robert Owen's various experiments, to him is attributed "the beginning of factory legislation, the cooperative movement and socialism in Britain."

6. CHARLES FOURIER (1772-1837)

Charles Fourier was a French social theorist and reformer.

Fourier took into account an individual's likes and dislikes and his constant pursuit of happiness and being bored by monotony. He therefore wanted to make work attractive and pleasant and build an organisation on that basis. He believed that different varieties of labour would be made attractive by properly organising them and seeing that none worked at job except by his own free will. It was his theory that workers should not practice only one job or occupation but should work at many jobs so as to never feel the boredom of monotony. His organisation of Phalanx in 1841 was based on this principle.

The Phalanx organisation had agriculture and several industries. Each individual was free to do what he wanted. There was living accommodation of different types; there were also common rooms for dining, lectures, conferences and such other needs. There was to be a common kitchen and common dining room, meals being served at varying prices to suit to the needs of five classes into which some 1,600 members of the Phalanx were divided. But every member was assured support of a minimum level. This sort of living under common roof was meant to ensure maximum comfort at minimum cost.

Fourier wanted to convert all workers into productive cooperative partners because, according to him, private property has the greatest lure for mankind. That lure will not vanish because, according to Fourier, human nature throughout history has remained the same. He therefore wanted to build an organisation in tune with unchangeable traits of human nature. It was the environment that should suit human nature. In this he held views opposed to those of Robert Owen who held that it is environment that formed human nature and therefore by changing environment Owen believed that human nature can be altered.

Fourier's Contribution to Socialism

Fourier was a social thinker who made significant contribution to socialism and cooperative movement, to the solution of the entire problem of work and of incentives and human relations connected with it. His great contribution lay in his emphasis on the need to adapt social institutions to actual human instincts and desires. He uttered a great truth when he wrote that man can live happily only if he is given scope for satisfaction of his instincts and desires and is not forced to "live according to an artificial pattern of conduct devised by moralists in the name of reason." His works and experiments had great influence on social psychology, and problems of industrial relations.

7. LOUIS BLANC (1811-1882)

Louis Blanc was a French socialist thinker who condemned the existing individual and competitive rivalary and viewed society as a harmonious whole in which "each member contributed according to his ability and was recompensed according to his needs."

Louis Blanc believed that industry should be organised on cooperative basis. He was one of the earliest socialists to place the burden of reform on the State. He assigned to State an important position in economic planning and in the development of welfare services. He had deep faith in representative democracy and he was convinced that majority would arrive at right decisions on important issues. And though therefore he attacked capitalism and competition, he was at the same time opposed to the idea of class-war.

Blanc wanted the democratic state to take initiative in rebuilding society: He had also faith in association. He therefore wanted the State not to conduct or manage an industry but to help the establishment of self-governing agencies through which workers would conduct it themselves, electing their own leaders and sharing out the rewards on terms complying with a general set of rules designed to ensure fair distribution and proper provision for the maintenance of capital assets and for new investment. According to Blanc, function of the State was to pass laws necessary to create the proper environment in which the new system would work. That done the State was to stand aside. Blanc thus looked upon the State not as an instrument of the capitalist class for exploitation of labour (a view that was held by Karl Marx) but as an agent to be used by the working class for their benefit and ultimately for the benefit of all.

Louis Blanc's leading economic ideas were: 'association' and 'right to work'. His main proposal referred to cooperative producers' association which was his distinct contribution to socialist thought. He believed in social workshops engaged in cooperative production.

According to Louis Blanc who was an 'associationist', competition was the main cause of all economic evils — industrial crises, extreme poverty and misery of masses, and accompanying moral degradation.

Blanc was thus associationist. He advocated combination of members of the same trade. They were to be organised on democratic basis. Commodities produced were to be sold in the market in the ordinary way. Blanc's plan did not include socialisation of consumption. The principle of association was to be applied to large industries to serve as a beginning of building the whole society entirely on associationist basis. He also favoured application of the principle of association to agriculture which he thought could be organised along cooperative lines.

Blanc believed that State intervention or help was necessary to make a beginning of socialisation and to guide its development.

To the end Louis Blanc remained a reformist and a democratic socialist. He believed that socialism would be gradually introduced and it would be the only system that would appeal to intellectuals. He was therefore strongly opposed to the doctrine of class-war and use of violence.

Louis Blanc's Contribution to Socialism

Louis Blanc made significant contribution to socialism. He was an idealist; he was a reformist with a strong belief in democracy and democratic methods; he was interested in welfare of workers; he had faith in social solidarity.

Louis Blanc's slogan "From each according to his capacities: to each according to his needs" has an assured place in the history of socialism. His ideal was socialism based on public ownership of factories and industries that would be under the control of workers; and sharing of the product according to needs rather than capacities. Industrial democracy was to be the counterpart of political democracy. He was essentially a moderate and opposed to the use of violence to bring about reforms in society. Louis Blanc may appropriately be described as the forerunner of modern democratic socialism.

8. PROUDHON (1809—1865)

Pierre Joseph Proudhon was a French philosophical anarchist.

Proudhon put forward the idea of "the revolution in the minds of the people." He believed that all forms of government are essentially wrong, meant denial of human equality and set men in wrong relationship with one another. Proudhon aimed at getting rid of government and organising society on the basis of fullest mutual freedom. Though association cannot be avoided in large-scale industries, Proudhon believed that greater part of the work of society could be conducted on the basis of individual action without resorting to collective action.

Proudhon's main idea was liberty — liberty of an individual to do what he likes. His another passion was justice. He emphasised that justice involved reciprocity which was the only limiting condition of individual liberty. He wanted to organise society in such a manner that all men would enjoy liberty on reciprocal terms — which meant equal liberty to all. According to Proudhon society must be organised on the principles of liberty and justice.

But Proudhon believed that by the very nature of liberty and justice, they cannot be established by any authority set over men for the purpose of establishing such a social organisation. He believed that liberty is not the daughter but mother of order. Proudhon was the first to introduce the word 'anarchism' in political vocabulary.

Proudhon was opposed to the centralising principle of Saint-Simonians and on the other hand regarded associations as violating the principle of reciprocal liberty. He was not sure that majority rule would always lead to sound judgment. Proudhon was thus suspicious of all power — power element in the State as also in the associations.

Proudhon was attached the institution of family which was the most natural unit. He was opposed to the abolition of law of inheritance which was the foundation of family institution. Though Proudhon defined 'property as theft', he was not opposed to property as such but only to its perversion under wrong institutional arrangements.

Proudhon believed that property was extracted from the fruits of labour. He did not mean that all property was to be done away with. He objected to it only when property assumed the form of an absolute ownership denying the existence of social interest in it. He was in favour of ensuring every man private possession of such property as was needed for actual use in production.

Welfare of family provided, according to Proudhon, the greatest incentive to man to work and work hard. He therefore denounced communism as contrary to human nature. For the same reason he was opposed to economic equality. Unequal labour must get unequal rewards as it was in accordance with the principle of reciprocal justice. What was needed was not abolition of inequality but of injustice, not abolition of inequalities based on unequal labour but those based on privilege and monopoly. Every individual and family must receive full fruits of its labour.

Proudhon's Contribution to Socialism

Proudhon's idea of justice underlines the whole of his thought. By justice he meant reciprocity, equality and equilibrium. From that point of view he suggested reforms in the case of institution of private property.

Proudhon influenced considerably French cooperative movement and trade union movement. He gave considerable impetus to French socialism, though he also sowed the seeds of confusion there. Proudhon however is often referred to as the father of the anarchist movement.

9. CONCLUDING REMARKS

The English and French socialism up to 1848 was considered generally utopian and idealistic. The socialist movement up to 1848 was dominated by middle class intellectuals and it certainly was not a movement of workers.

These Utopian Socialists tried their various theories and experiments during the revolutions of 1830 and 1848.

But on the whole, most of their experiments collapsed because of impatience and akward execution.

The National Workshops (established to give effect to Fourier's formula of 'right to work'), the Workingmen's Associations and Consumers' Cooperatives based on the ideas of Robert Owen and Louis Blanc and various other socialist reformers tried during the revolutionary period of 1830 and 1840 fell into disrepute. Their failure was partly due to political reasons and partly due to lack of experience on the part of sponsors of new experiments.

In the face of this, there developed in contrast to utopian socialism, another brand of socialism known as scientific socialism the main proponent of which was Karl Marx.

But early socialist thought or utopian socialism did influence socialist thinking on competition, institution of private property, welfare of workers, justice and equality, right to work, reward according to contribution to production, opposition to unearned income and wealth, equitable distribution of income, organisation of society on the basis of equality and justice, and so on.

CHAPTER 15

MARXIAN SOCIALISM

1. THE IMPORTANCE OF MARXIAN ECONOMICS

Adam Smith, Karl Marx and J. M. Keynes may be said to be the three most important economic thinkers who have influenced not only economic thinking of people but also the course of human history. Until coming into existence of the Third World countries wedded to the doctrine of non-alignment, majority of the countries appeared to be divided into two groups — one headed by capitalist USA and the second headed by the communist USSR, whose policies have been greatly influenced by the theories of Karl Marx. The fact that more than half the population of the world lives in communist countries whose policies are based on the theories of Karl Marx should alone suffice to show the enormous importance of Marxian Economics.

The study of Marxian economics is important for the following reasons:

1. Marx was the fiercest critic of free enterprise economy or *laissez faire* capitalism. Though some earlier thinkers like Sismondi and utopian socialist thinkers have drawn attention to some of the defects of free enterprise economy, it was Karl Marx and Marxian Economics which in an integrated manner pointed out the evils of capitalism — exploitation of labour, concentration of economic power, deficiency of total demand, unemployment, inner contradictions of capitalism, economic crises and its ultimate but inevitable collapse. Criticism of capitalism was better integrated in Karl Marx than in the writing of any other previous critic of capitalism.

2. The above point would imply that study of Marxian economics helps even the proponents of capitalism understand capitalism and its functioning in a better way. Better understanding of capitalism would help the proponents of capitalism devise policies that would reduce or if possible eliminate defects of capitalism.

3. Practically half the population of the world seems to have accepted communism founded by Marxian economics as the best among all the economic

systems. For them it is the communist system of economy which has become a sort of religion "which promises paradise on this side of the grave."[1]

This alone is enough reason to compel students of economics to study and know what Marxian economics is and why it holds so much attraction to millions of people.

4. Understanding of economic history of Russia especially during the 20th century and of China after 1949 necessitates understanding of Marxian economics. The statements of economic historians and even the present policy-makers of those countries are couched in terminology used by Karl Marx. This makes study of Marxian economics necessary.

In fact the historical developments taking place in the world in the 20th century, division of the world into two power-blocs, the cold war climate, the armament race and so on necessitate understanding not only for capitalism but also of Marxian economics.

5. It is as much important for student of economic system to know the theories of Adam Smith, the founder of orthodox capitalism (with emphasis on harmony of individual and social interest, private profit motive, private property, individual freedom and *laissez faire*) as to know the theories of Marxian economics which while critical of capitalism offered the basis for alternative economic system, namely communism (with emphasis on social welfare, public ownership of all means of production, classless society and economic planning). One should not blindly accept any particular economic theory or system; he should examine alternative theories and systems also as that alone will broaden his understanding and make him more tolerant of other theories, viewpoints and systems.

6. Many countries in Asia, Africa and Latin America have won their independence after living as colonies of West European powers who had built their empires during the 18th and 19th centuries. Most of these newly independent countries like India have been in search for a model of economic system that would solve their major problems of unemployment, mass poverty and economic stagnation. Should they adopt capitalist system? Or communist system? Or a mixed economy as India is trying to do? In order to enable the leaders and governments of these countries to make an appropriate choice of a model, study of both capitalism as also of Marxian economics is necessary. For example, India is thinking in terms of a mixed economic system aiming to combine virtues or merits of both capitalism and communism, at the same time avoiding the defects of both the economic systems. This would necessitate study of both capitalism and Marxian economics.

7. Karl Marx was more than mere economist in the narrow or technical sense of the term. He was a historian, philosopher, sociologist and an economist. Marxian economic therefore represents a broad amalgam of all these social sciences. Marxian economics not only tries to look at and interpret past history

of mankind, its motives, actions, conflicts and their resolution but also tries to look into the future of human societies.

This would mean that Marxian economics represents a great contribution to the stream of human thought and flow of culture. The study of Marxian economics should therefore be of great importance — whether one agrees with and accepts all or part of Marxian tenets or not — as a mere intellectual exercise. From pure academic point of view, Marxian economics should make stimulating reading and study.

Thus both from the theoretical as well as from practical point of view, study of Marxian economics becomes very important. Blind adherence to one's own point of view and one's own economic system as sacrosanct and refusal to see and appreciate others' point of view and their economic systems will inevitably lead to intolerance, hatred, conflicts and wars. On the other hand, as another war would endanger or even wipe out the entire humanity, what is absolutely essential is not only peaceful co-existence but hearty cooperation between the two powerful blocs of countries as many of the world's problems such as poverty, population pressure, pollution, armament race, and so on can be solved only on the basis of international cooperation. This would come about only if each makes sincere efforts to understand the other's philosophy and economic system. This would imply that it is as much important for people in communist countries to study capitalism as it is for people in capitalist countries to study Marxian economics. Proper understanding alone can be the basis of hearty cooperation between the two.

2. MARXIAN ECONOMICS

THE ECONOMIC INTERPRETATION OF HISTORY

Marx's interpretation of history generally known as the materialistic interpretation of history constitutes an integral part of Marxian economics. It is therefore appropriate to begin the study of Marxian economics with the analysis of the Marxian interpretation of history.

The Hegelian Basis of Marx's Philosophy. Karl Marx was greatly influenced by Hegel and Hegel's dialecticism. Therefore before we try to understand economic or materialistic interpretation of history of Marx, it is essential to know the Hegelian dialecticism and Hegelian basis of Marx's philosophy.

It may be said that Hegel was the first thinker to look at and interpret human history in a comprehensive way and offer a theory of history.

To Hegel "the only immutable thing is the abstraction of movement." For Hegel not the exterior world but human mind and that which existed in human mind was the reality. All outward or exterior developments were mere manifestations of human ideas. For Hegel, human mind and ideas were the real thing and as stated above, exterior world and changes and developments therein were only the outward manifestation of human ideas which had independent existence without being formed or influenced by external surrounding.

Thus to Hegel it is the idea that is fundamental. But every idea has its opposite — the idea is beauty could not exist without the idea of ugliness; so also ideas like light and darkness, truth and falsity and so on. The original idea Hegel called thesis; and its opposite idea he called antithesis.

In the universe around us, continual struggle is going on between what Hegel called thesis and antithesis — conflict of ideas. Somehow the conflict between thesis and antithesis gets resolved and we get what Hegel calls 'synthesis'.

In turn this 'synthesis' becomes 'thesis' again producing its 'antithesis' and further clash between the two which again gets resolved in 'synthesis'. This process goes on endlessly.

All the outward phenomenon or outward developments are mere product resulting from thesis, antithesis and synthesis. Objective development or phenomena could not and cannot take place without these continual developments taking place in human mind or idea which is the only reality. It is an endless process. According to Hegel, all history is nothing but the outward manifestation of what is continually and perpetually going on in human mind — thesis, antithesis and synthesis.

Hegel was in a sense the first to offer unified causal explanation of what was happening in the outside world and what we call history.

What Marx Borrowed from Hegel and What he Rejected. Karl Marx accepted the Hegelian philosophy that fundamental changes occur in the world as a result of synthesis of opposing forces. Thus Marx was prepared to accept the idea of Hegelian dialecticism.

But Marx rejected the Hegelian proposition that idea is a fundamental phenomenon and what happens in the outside world is only the concretisation of ideas in human mind. Marx rejected the primacy of ideas. To him existence of the exterior world was the main thing and ideas were mere reflections of or formulated by external environment. Objective events in the universe were of fundamental importance and a reality and not ideas. Change the objective environment and human ideas will change. This, and not the reverse was true, according to Marx.

"The thesis and antithesis became to Marx actual opposing forces existing in the universe, with synthesis, the resulting objective phenomenon that becoming in its turn thesis with its antithesis, played its part in the creation of a new synthetical phenomenon." Thus Marx made use of what has come to be known as 'Marxian dialectit' as a useful tool of interpreting history and for understanding universe.

But Marxian dialectic has two limitations which Marx accepted. While Marx felt that Marxian dialectic would provide a universal explanation of all phenomena, he wanted to apply it only to the field of social institutions.

And secondly, among all social phenomena, economic phenomena were incomparably of greatest potential significance. According to Marx, "it was within the economic realm that the basic thesis, antithesis, and synthesis existed, and all the social institutions were the offshoots of economic forces."[2]

Marxian Interpretation of History. Before we try to understand the Marxian interpretation of history, it would be instructive to know how he dealt with other prevailing theories of history.

One interpretation of history held the view that all historical developments are pre-determined, and history is nothing more or less than unfolding of the will of God. It is the Providential Will that makes history.

Marx had utter contempt for this Providential Theory of history. Once this theory is accepted, it would be obvious that vast poor would have no escape from poverty since they are condemned to poverty by Providential Will against which individual or collective action would be futile. Thus Marx completely rejected this theory of history that "some providential persons or force ruled the universe creating historical events as mere extensions of its omnipotent will."[3]

Karl Marx also rejected the other theory of history, namely, the 'idealist' theory. The 'idealist' theory of history held the view that historical events were the products of human ideas; these human ideas were the original creative force which made or influenced the course of events in the universe which we call history. As already noted, Karl Marx contended that human ideas have no primacy, but on the contrary "the idea is nothing else than the material world reflected by the human mind, and translated into form of thought."

Against this background, it is now possible and easy to understand the Marxian interpretation of history or his materialistic interpretation of history. This may be summarised in a few well-known and lucid quotations of Marx and other authors.

In his critique of Political Economy, Marx wrote: "In the social production of their means of existence men enter into definite necessary relations which are independent of their own will, productive relationships which correspond to a definite stage of development of their material productive forces. The aggregate of these productive relationships constitutes the economic structure of society, the real basis on which juridical and political structure arises... The mode of production of the material means of existence, conditions the whole process of social, political, and intellectual life."

Marx's friend and collaborator Friedrich Engels describes the materialistic interpretation of history as follows: "According to this conception, the ultimate cause of all social changes and political revolutions is to be sought not in the minds of man, in their interesting insight into eternal truth and justice, but changes in the mode of production and exchange; they are to be sought not in the philosophy but in the economics of the epoch concerned."[4]

In his 'A History of Socialist Thought' H. W. Laidler summarises the materialistic interpretation of history as follows:

"The materialist or economic interpretation of history. . . means that in any given epoch, the economic relations of society, the means whereby men and women provide for the sustenance, produce, exchange, and distribute the thing they regard as necessary for the satisfaction of their needs exerts a preponderating influence in shaping the progress of society and in moulding political, social, intellectual and ethical relationships."

M. M. Bober explaining the materialistic interpretation of history of Marx wrote, "Production is the alpha and omega of history ... the mode of production is the prime cause of history, the sole cause."[5]

Did Karl Marx intend to make economic forces (man's search for bread and material comforts of life) the sole determinant of historical events or merely the most important among various factors moulding history? Karl Marx was clear on this point. Marx would not be satisfied with any causal explanation of history except it be a prime, original, or ultimate cause. It was in this sense that "the relations of production" or "mode of production" became the ultimate factors in determining the course of human history.

Marx and Engels made it clear that the causal relationship between the mode of production and social institutions need not be either immediate, direct as generally understood. Marx emphasised the essentially evolutionary nature of social and political institutions with the consequence that often the ultimate source of the evolutionary process is not observed or comes to be overlooked.

It should also be made clear that "There is nothing in this theory (*i.e.*, Marxian interpretation of history) to deny the contention that once non-economic institutions have crystallized from basic economic forces, they operate as independent forces modifying the mode of production and course of history." For example, Engels has pointed out how the idea of equality in the development of which economic forces played the prime role came to modify in the world. And yet, it will have to be admitted that in this case economic factor was still the primary factor or ultimate force working indirectly by creating ideas which in turn modify operation of economic force or mode of production and thus influencing or bringing into existence new social and political institutions.

Engels in this connection writes: "According to materialistic conception of history, the production and reproduction ... constitutes in the last instance the determining factor of history ... The economic situation is the basis ... The various factors of superstructure, the political forms of the class struggle and their results, *i.e.*, constitutions etc., established by victorious classes after hard won battles, legal forms — political, jural, philosophical theories, religious conceptions which have been developed into systematic dogmas — all these exercise an influence upon the course of historical struggle, and in most cases determine for the most part their form ... There is reciprocity between all these factors in which finally, through endless array of contingencies ... the economic movement asserts itself as necessary."

Thus Karl Marx attempted to do something neither historians nor economists had done before. Historians had recorded events and economists had explained causes of economic events in specific historical setting, analysing the creation of those settings.

Marx in the words of Lenin made an attempt to answer fundamental questions such as follows:

"People make their own history; but what determines their motives, that is the motives of people in the mass; what gives rise to clash of conflicting ideas and endeavours; what is the sum total of all these clashes among the whole mass of human societies; what are the objective conditions for the production of the material means of life that form the basis of all the historical activity of man; what is the law of the development of these conditions?"[6]

Coming to details, the Marxian interpretation of history means that the people's way of thinking is determined by their way of material living. If man's thinking is determined by the material conditions in which he lives, it follows that social classes are composed of all those individuals who live under similar economic conditions and therefore think alike. While not denying the relevance of classification of humanity on grounds of nationality religion etc., according to Marx, the most important division of society was into classes based on or determined by economic conditions. "It is thus the economic status that is the *differentia specifica* of a social class. Thus the chief classes of the ancient world were the masters and slaves; of the feudal age, landlords and serfs; and of the modern capitalist world, capitalists and workers.

According to the materialistic interpretation of history, the economic system or mode of production of a society at any given time determines the structure of social classes along with their ideologies, their manner of thinking and their relationship with one another. The essence of historical materialism is that the mode of production or economic system is the foundation of any society and that there is the definite structure of social classes corresponding to every mode of production or economic system. And the development of history is nothing but conflict and striving of these social classes.

"The history of all existing society is the history of class struggle."

Free man and slave, patrician and plebeian, lord and serf, guild-master and journeyman, in the world oppressor and oppressed, stood in constant opposition to one another, carried uninterrupted, now hidden, now open fight, a fight that each time ended, either in a revolutionary reconstruction of society at large, or in the common ruin of the contending classes.

The modern bourgeois society that has sprouted from the ruins of feudal society has not done away with class antagonisms. It has but established new classes, new conditions of oppression, new forms of struggle in the place of old ones.

Our epoch, the epoch of the bourgeoisie, possesses, however, this distinctive feature: it has simplified the class antagonisms. Society as a whole is more and more splitting up into great hostile camps into two great classes directly facing each other: "Bourgeoisie and Proletarial."[7]

Thus to summarise Marxian interpretation of history: Mode of production at any particular time brings about division of society into classes (based on common economic interests); there is clash of interests between the classes so brought into existence; clash of class interests results into class-war; and history is nothing but history of class-conflicts and class-wars.

Criticism of Marxian Interpretation of History. The Marxian interpretation or materialistic interpretation of history has come in for severe criticism. The main points of criticism may be pointed out as follows:

Marxian interpretation is extremely one-sided overemphasising as it does the economic factor as the ultimate determinant of the course of human history. According to critics, some non-economic factors also are independent and fundamental nature in determining establishment of social institutions and course of history. Not only economic but these non-economic factors are also among the ultimate determinants of the course of human history.

Prof. M. M. Bober is the severest critic of Marxian interpretation of history. He maintains that Marx has not given the recognition to non-economic forces that have continued and continue to influence the course of human history. Bober has made an attempt to demonstrate that the economic factor which according to Marx was the ultimate determinant of the course of history was comparatively less important in making or influencing the course of history than some non-economic factors — geographical environment and human intellect and other qualities of human nature — are the fundamental forces determining the course of history. According to Prof. Bober 'mode of production' is itself a derived function and as compared to the above-mentioned non-economic forces, is of minor importance in determining the course of history.

According to Bober, it is the geographical environment that gave rise to civilisation and cultures, to particular industries and mode of living and provided opportunities for economic development or created obstacles in its path. The non-economic effects of geographical factor are also equally important. People in mountainous region are independent minded and have protected their independence from foreign aggression. They are healthy and well-built and capable of bearing hardships. On the other hand people living of the plains with easy means of communications of rivers or roads have greater sense of unity among them. Geographical factor is a constant factor and the impact of a geographical factor like the English Channel can be seen throughout the course of English history. Bober is of the opinion that while emphasising the impact of mode of production, Marx neglected to assess the impact on history of an ultimate and independent factor like geographical environment.

Human intellect is another independent and ultimate factor governing the course of human history. Man is distinguished from other animals by his intellect. It is with the aid of intellect that man thinks of new ideas and builds a world of new ideas, one flowing from another. According to Bober, all these mental or intellectual exercises that distinguish man from other animals take place without being influenced by external world. If man were without this intellect he would have been like other animals, a slave to a given mode of production, responding in a mechanical way to given economic stimuli as animals do.

Also according to Bober, other characteristics of human nature like curiosity, aggressiveness or combativeness, feeling of enmity, of sympathy and love are factors the impact of which on the course of history has been neglected by Karl Marx.

Bober has emphasised two other independent and ultimate factors which are born out of relationship between man and environment — religion and science.

Even Marx and Engels admitted that origin of religion lies outside of economic world. But later they maintained that religion is nothing but mere manifestation of economic forces. Bober maintains that religion plays a vital role both in the life of individuals and along with economic and non-economic factors or even independently of them has a deep impact on the course of history. Religion is a powerful force; it is not the agent of economic factor or mode of production as Marx believed.

Science is another factor independently determining the course of history. According to Marx, science is nothing but the reflection or creation of a given mode of production — *i.e.,* it is purely the creation of economic forces. Bober does not accept this viewpoint of Marx regarding the origin and role of sciences. According to Bober, sciences may have their origin not only in economic factors but in other factors like geographical environment, religious inspiration or impulses, inventive genius, curiosity or some unexpected development or phenomenon.

Whatever the origin of sciences, once they are set on their course, they create and move about in a world of their own making. It would be incorrect to say that it is only the economic consideration that provides stimulus to scientific progress. People working in sciences like philosophy, philalogy, anthropology and astronomy cannot be said to be motivated by considerations of economic interests only. Scientists may be inspired by other considerations than purely economic. And therefore sciences which have a powerful impact on history cannot be said to be always having their origin in economic factors or mode of production.

Thus, according to Bober, geographical environment, various characteristics of human nature, religion, science and mental forces all act and react on one another and shape the course of history.

If we scrutinise history of past few centuries, it would be observed that along with economic factor, a number of other non-economic factors have moulded the course of human history and it must be admitted that Marx either did not pay much attention to the impact of those factors on history or completely neglected those factors.

With all the shortcomings, Marxian interpretation of history is of significance. Along with Hegel, Marx made the first comprehensive attempt to know the factors that mould the course of history and his interpretation is definitely better than previously held views of history, that history is lengthened shadow of a great man (say Alexander the Great, Fredrick the Great, Napoleon and Gandhiji) or that history is a mere conglomeration of happenings taking place accidentally, or that history is mere unfolding of the will of God or made along the course pre-determined by Providence. Marxian interpretation is definitely more satisfactory and hopeful than seeking explanation of history in supernatural or divine power. If there is general recognition of the fact that economic factor is an important (if not the only) factor influencing the course of human history, the credit for that goes to Karl Marx. Marx has given an interpretation of history which helps us to understand in a better way the development and course of human history.

3. MARX'S MODEL OF CAPITALISM

Karl Marx defined capitalism as an organisation of society in which production of commodities and services is mainly carried on in private enterprises operated by freely employed labour with a view to make maximum personal or private profit. It is possible that in such a capitalist organisation of society, there exist a number of classes like landlords, tenants, independent artisans and self-employed persons like small shop-keepers, tailors and so on. But in capitalism, the two leading classes are the capitalists who employ workers and the working class which having no productive means at their disposal, has to sell its labour to capitalists in return for wages on which workers live. The entire Marxian model of capitalism consists of analysis of relationship between these two classes, namely, capitalists and workers and the consequences following therefrom.

Emergence of Capitalism.

According to Karl Marx, circulation of commodities is the starting point of capitalism. Marx dates the modern history of capital from the 16th century when world commerce became possible. "As a matter of history, capital as opposed to landed property, invariably takes the form of money; the first form of appearance of capital is money. By purchasing labour power for less than its worth and retaining the surplus, money is converted into capital." "By turning his money into commodities that serve as a material elements of a new product and as factors in the labour-process, by incorporating living labour with their dead substance, the capitalist at the same time converts value *i.e.,* past materialised and dead labour into capital, into value with big value a live monster that is fruitful and multiples." Capital is thus a 'vampire' that sucks the blood of labour; it is wealth that is further employed to exploit labour.

Karl Marx explained the evolution of capitalism thus. In the earliest system of barter, commodities were exchanged for commodities. And these exchanges were mostly for satisfying one's wants. Marx has given C-C as the formula for barter exchange.

Due to inconveniences of barter-exchanges, during the next stage, exchanges began to be carried on with the aid of money. For the system of exchanges with the aid of money, Marx has given the formula of C-M-C. In this type of exchanges, commodities are exchanged for money which in turn is exchanged for commodities. In this type of exchanges also the objective is securing by exchange commodities for satisfying one's wants.

In the next stage further development of exchange takes place which Marx has represented by the formula M-C-M. Money is exchanged for commodities and commodities are again exchanged for money. In this type of exchange both at the beginning as also at the end the individual holds money and this means the purpose of exchange is not acquiring commodities for satisfying one's wants. The obvious end of exchange of the type M-C-M is obtaining more money. Two Ms represent different amounts and the second M in the equation is larger than the first M. The difference in these two Ms is the profit which now becomes the object of exchange. When a society reaches the stage of exchanges represented by M-C-M, that society may be said to have reached the capitalistic stage in the evolution of its economy.

From this Karl Marx draws some important conclusions and points out some specific characteristics of capitalism. Marx writes: "The circulation of money as capital . . . an end in itself, for the explanation of value takes place only within this constantly renewed movement (M-C-M). The circulation of capital has therefore no limits. Thus the conscious representative of this movement, the possessor of money, becomes a capitalist. His person, or rather his pocket, is the point from which the money starts and to which it returns. The expansion value . . . becomes his subjective aim, and it is only so far as the appropriation of ever more and more wealth in the abstract becomes the sole motive of his operations that he functions as a capitalist . . . use value must therefore never be looked upon as the real aim of the capitalist; neither must be the profit on any single transaction. The restless never-ending process of profit making alone is what he aims at."[8]

4. OUTLINE OF MARX'S MODEL OF CAPITALISM

Before a detailed analysis of Marxian economics which is mainly concerned with critical analysis of assumptions, functioning and future of capitalism, it would help our understanding if a broad outline is given of the Marx's model of capitalism.

1. *Materialistic Interpretation of History.* According to this, evolution of the history of mankind is made, not by the will of God or Providence, or by great men or by ideas by man's eternal search of bread and his efforts to satisfy physical or bodily necessities.

2. *Mode of Production and Emergence of Classes.* Man's search for bread and material pleasures of life inevitably leads to adoption of a particular mode of production, which results into division of society into two classes (a class being defined as a group of people sharing common mode of living under capitalism) namely, bourgeoisie and proletariat.

3. *The Theory of Class-war.* Since the interests of the two classes, namely bourgeoisie and proletariat are in continual conflict, capitalism contains within itself the seeds of class-war. In fact history of capitalism is in a sense history of class-war between the bourgeoisie (*i.e.,* the employers who own the factors of production) and workers who have nothing else to sell but their labour for wages on which they live.

4. *Labour Theory of Value and Surplus Value and Exploitation of Labour.* Since labour is unorganised and since a worker must earn his daily bread, employers are in a position to purchase labour-power of workers by paying them just the cost of production of labour power, *i.e.,* the subsistence wages, whereas the value of goods produced by that hired labour power is many times the wages paid. This surplus value is pocketed by employers as profit. This process goes on being repeated. With enormous profits made out of hired labour, employers employ still more labour which is followed by greater exploitation of labour and making of still greater profits by employers.

5. *Greater and Greater Concentration of Wealth and Enlarging Gulf Between the Classes of Employers and Workers.* In competitive capitalistic economy employers with rights of ownership of factors of production go on acquiring more and more wealth by exploitation of labour which thus results in greater and greater accumulation of wealth and enlarging gulf between the two classes of employers and workers.

6. *Theory of Economic Crisis.* In order to increase their profits, the employers go on saving and investing more and more. For some time this results in greater demand for workers and therefore for some time wages begin to rise.

But increasing investments and rising rates of wages begin to result in declining rate of profit. In order to ensure that rate of profit does not decline, the employers either reduce investments temporarily or begin to think of and introduce labour-saving devices. In either case there is displacement of labour. This displacement of labour results in enlarging already unemployed people, the Industrial Reserve Army.

The division of society into two classes of a few rich and vast poor also results in repeated economic crises. The vast investment made to increase profits results in production of enormous quantities of goods and services of all types. But it so happens that while the rich have the purchasing power to purchase vast quantities of goods, they do not however have the physical capacity to consume them; whereas the poor, who have the physical capacity to consume the vast quantities of goods and services produced, do not have adequate purchasing power to buy them as they get only the subsistence level of wages under the regime of competitive capitalism. Naturally this tends to result in overproduction of goods, falling prices, rising unemployment and economic crisis.

7. *Economic Theory of Imperialism.* With the emergence of capitalism in a number of West European countries, they tried to overcome these recurrent economic crises by turning their attention to economically backward regions of Asia and Africa which they conquered and built their empires, thus capitalist countries becoming imperial power and capitalism resulting in imperialism. The conquered colonies both supplied essential raw materials cheaply for the industries in West European capitalist countries as also provided captive markets where they could sell their goods to do which the imperial powers followed appropriate policies to destroy indigenous industries which were once flourishing in these colonies.

8. *Imperialism and Wars.* The desire to acquire more and more colonies on the part of industrialised capitalist countries of the West finally led to mutual conflicts among them as few backward countries were left to be conquered. Thus imperialism inevitably led to war. Thus war became the only means of survival of capitalism.

9. *Eventual Disappearance of Capitalism.* Thus competitive capitalism is ridden with a number of inner contradictions — division of society into a class of few rich and a class of vast poor, growing number of Industrial Reserve Army and recurring economic crises and imperial wars. Marx after analysing competitive capitalism accepts the doctrine of economic determinism that capitalism is doomed and is bound to perish one day. The inner contradiction is like economic cancer which one day is bound to destroy capitalism. It is only the question of time. (He therefore makes an appeal to workers to rise in revolt and hasten this process of destruction of capitalism because workers have nothing to lose but have everything to gain if they succeed as they did in Russia in October Revolution in 1917).

10. *Withering Away of the State and Coming of Socialism.* Once capitalism disappears, and all the factors of production are nationalised, the State, which is the creation of the bourgeoisie who use it as an instrument to keep their property intact, will wither away because with the disappearance of the institution of private property classless society will emerge with no class conflicts and therefore with no function for the State to perform.

11. *Dictatorship of the Proletariat.* Since workers have no experience of the running of administration and the economy of the nation, there would be for a temporary period dictatorship of the proletariat.

This in brief, outlines Marx's model of capitalism or functioning of capitalist system.

5. MARX'S THEORY OF VALUE AND SURPLUS VALUE

Karl Marx begins his analysis of the theory of value (as in the case of Adam Smith and Ricardo), with the distinction between 'use-value' of commodities, and their 'exchange-value', or in other terms, 'value' of commodities. Marx then proceeds to state that "if we abstract their use-value only the quality of value in exchange remains." Since, according to Karl Marx, it is labour that produces all value — capital, as we have already seen, being nothing but past stolen labour — it automatically follows that this abstract value quality in commodities exists "only because human labour in the abstract has been embodied in goods." In this sense, value is 'mere congelation of homogeneous human labour', or 'crystals of a social substance'.

Value of a commodity being thus abstracted from all relation to use-value of the commodity, it now remains to be seen how the value of a commodity is determined. Assuming the existing social order, Karl Marx maintains that the value of a commodity is determined by "the socially necessary labour" which is the time spent by the labourer with average skill under the existing social conditions or arrangements in the production of that commodity. If, for example, a piece of cotton cloth requires 'x' hours of labour and a table '$2x$' hours of labour, the table will have value twice that of the value of the piece of cloth.

Karl Marx was extremely critical of earlier political economists for not paying due attention to the quantitative and qualitative aspects of labour and for not making an attempt for reducing labour to "abstract social labour."

It is obvious that there are some inherent difficulties in making an attempt to reduce labour to an abstraction. Most of these difficulties spring from the fact that labour of one person compared to that of another differs in skill, intensity and character, and also because of the fact that goods produced by different workers have different utilities or use-value. Marx was conscious of these inherent difficulties; but he made an attempt to get around those difficulties, in the first place, by "conceiving of all labour power and all values as founded into homogeneous social aggregates, divisible into equal units"; and in the second place, by limiting his conclusions to "normal conditions of production" and "the average degree of skill and intensity prevalent at the time."

While advocating his labour theory of value, Karl Max drew upon the theories in this respect of Adam Smith and Ricardo but went beyond. For example, Adam Smith "explicitly regarded his labour theory of value as valid only under the special conditions imagined by Smith as having prevailed in a prehistoric, ultrasimple, primitive economy and recognised by him as not present in the kind of economy ... which Marx called 'capitalism'. (Under condition of capitalism Adam Smith instead presented his theory of value in terms of cost of production made up of wages, rent and profit).

"Ricardo tried to revive or reinstate Smith's 'Labour Theory' for application also to the existing capitalist economy; but Ricardo found that he would have to and he did qualify his labour theory considerably in its application and treated it as only approximatcly valid.

"In the Marxian theory, the 'value' of a commodity in effect means the amount of labour-time 'embodied in' the commodity or required to produce it." "There is simply a dogmatic, arbitrary, absolute equating of these two concepts with each other ... all of the value of all output is created entirely or solely by labour of (hired) workers."[9]

Marx's Theory of Surplus Value.

Thus Karl Marx based values of commodities on labour-time required to produce them. From that basis, Marx proceeds to formulate his theory of surplus value which is only an extension of his labour theory of value.

Marx maintains that in the competitive labour market, the capitalist buys labour-power at its value *i.e.,* paying the worker a wage which is equal to the value of worker's means of subsistence. Subsistence wage is the cost of production of the labour-power which the capitalist buys.

Assuming for the purpose of illustration that a worker is required to put out four hours of labour to produce this value of labour which means the subsistence wage. If the worker works only for that length of time (*i.e.,* four hours), he would be producing goods or services value of which would be equal to the subsistence wage rate which he is paid. But in a competitive labour market in capitalist countries (it should be noted that Karl Marx was analysing pure model of capitalism of Ricardo and when labour had not unionised), there is no reason why the working day should extend to only four hours and not to ten hours or even to twelve hours. (It should be noted that during the heydays of capitalism, working hours in factories in England often used to be twelve to fourteen hours per day). This is because the capitalist has brought the worker for a day by paying him the value of labour-power *i.e.,* subsistence wage-rate. Assuming that the worker is made to work eight hours per day, it would mean that during the last four hours, the worker would be creating value over and above the subsistence wage rate that he is receiving. This difference between the value that a worker produces and what he actually gets, according to Marx, constitutes the 'surplus' and it is in the creation and pocketing of the surplus value that the capitalist is interested.

It would thus mean that it is possible to divide the working day into two clear parts — that part or those hours of his work required to produce goods the value of which is equal to the wage rate that he is paid. Marx calls this part of work 'necessary labour'. And secondly, that part or hours of work in which the worker produces surplus value. Marx has designated this as 'surplus labour'. It is obvious that the rate of surplus value created by the worker and pocketed by the capitalist would depend upon the ratio of 'surplus labour' to 'necessary labour'. (In our above illustrations that ratio would be 4 : 4 *i.e.,* 1 : 1; but if the worker is made to work not eight hours but twelve hours per day as it happens in some of the unorganised industries even at present, then the ratio would be 12 : 4 *i.e.,* 3 : 1).

To summarise, according to Marx's theory of value and surplus value, all value is created by labour. Under the circumstances where labour receives less than the full value of the commodities produced by it, there appears 'surplus value' which is pocketed by capitalists either as rent, or interest or profit.

Criticism of Karl Marx's Theory of Value.

Marx's theory of value and surplus value has been subjected to very severe criticism by a number of economists, especially from capitalist countries. We shall consider here, in brief, some of the important points of criticism.

The critics have contended that Marx's theory of value is wrong in its complete rejection of utility or use-value as one of the factors determining exchange value or value of a commodity, thus making the Marxian theory extremely unsatisfactory for the purpose of providing a general explanation of the source of value. The whole trouble started with the distinction between value-in-use (utility) and value-in-exchange (value) by Adam Smith and the rejection of utility as determinant of value because of the unfortunate illustration of water and demand to which Adam Smith referred. That tradition was continued by both Ricardo and Marx. If a commodity has no utility, nobody will purchase it by paying any value and therefore existence of utility in all commodities was taken for granted and kept aside as a determinant of value of a commodity. With this assumption, Marx had no alternative but to come to the conclusion that commodities whatever their utility would be valued according to the abstract labour-time which the commodity embodies. This would imply that according to Marxian theory gifts of nature would have absolutely no value and this would also be the case in the case of all things which are not the product of labour. Marx tries to meet such a situation by a thoroughly illogical distinction between value and price. According to Marx such things or commodities would have price but not value.

But would all commodities produced by labour have value? Would for example, if some one spends hundreds of hours on manufacturing a wooden tyre, would it fetch any value simply because it has embodied hundreds of hours of work? Marx was compelled to admit that all commodities produced by labour may not necessarily have value. Marx gets around this situation by stating that labour embodied in a commodity must be "socially necessary" to acquire value. This would amount to stating that some commodities produced by labour would have value while other commodities produced by labour would not possess value. All this illogicality, contradiction and inconsistence in Marx's theory of value arise because of one simple fact, namely, rejection by Marx of utility or use-value as one of the major determinants of value of a commodity. All labour theories of value which keep aside utility as determinant of value of a commodity suffer from this serious defect. The labour theory of value of Marx overlooks the simple fact that utility (*i.e.,* demand factor) plays a vital role in the determination of value of a commodity. But once utility is accepted as a major determinant of value and not quantity of labour, then the whole theory of exploitation of labour would collapse.

Even granting for the time being that cost of production alone determines the value of a commodity, would there be justification for reducing all costs to only labour? What about claims of capital? Even in a communist country claims of capital will have to be incorporated in costs of production. Capital involves giving up of immediate consumption; it means waiting and that does mean a cost and therefore is entitled to some reward. It ought to be remembered that whether the ownership of capital is in private hands or whether there is collective ownership of capital is totally irrelevant fact in this connection. This would mean that return to capital does constitute an element of cost and returns to capital stand justified. It must be admitted that Marx's analysis of capital was far too inadequate and unsatisfactory.

Further, Marx's reasoning about abstract labour-power units, or 'homogeneous quantities of labour' or 'crystals of labour' faces unseparable difficulties. This is because of differences in the skills and qualities of labour. Analysis in terms of labour 'congelations' or 'crystals' of labour appears highly abstract and therefore thoroughly unrealistic. Is it possible to say that an hour's work of a surgeon is equal to forty hours' work of a carpenter, or fifty hours' work of a brick-layer and so on? It ought to be appreciated that labour is exerted in our above illustration on different planes and therefore any talk of 'crystals of labour' or 'congelation of labour' to say the least, appears both unrealistic and illogical. Ricardo while formulating his labour theory of value also faced this problem of comparing different types of qualities of labour. He tried to solve this problem by stating that such a comparison of different types of labour is already made in the market. When for example people are prepared to pay Rs. 500 for one's hour work of a surgeon and only Rs. 5 for an hour's work of a carpenter, this means that one hour's work of a surgeon is equal to 100 hours' work of a carpenter. It is obvious that a theory of value which aims at explaining what is happening in the market must not base itself on what actually is already happening in the market. Instead of squarely facing the problem, Marx like Ricardo evaded the problem in the same way and both of them appeared to argue in a circle.

As regards the reasoning of Karl Marx concerning 'surplus value', it met the same difficulty which compelled David Ricardo to qualify his labour-cost theory of value, namely, the time-element in capital.

Marx concluded that the rate of surplus value always equalled rate of profit. This assumption would be valid only under certain assumptions such as the composition of capital used in different industries is the same as regards the proportion of fixed and circulating or variable capital. Karl Marx admitted that only 'variable capital' by employing labour yielded surplus value. Thus while the absolute amount of 'surplus value' increases with the amount of variable (*i.e.*, circulating) capital, the rate of profit depends upon the total capital employed and must vary with the proportion of circulating to fixed capital. The chain of Marx's reasoning is broken because of the admission of the fact profits and 'surplus value' depend in part upon capital. For example, if a capitalist employs only a few workers but makes large profits by using much plant and equipment (*i.e.*, fixed capital), can it be said that all the profit has come out of exploitation of workers? Is it also always true that a capitalist who employs more workers (*i.e.*, substantial amount of circulating or variable capital) necessarily makes proportionately more profits? What actually we find is that there is the tendency of profits in different industries towards equality.

Karl Marx, in the face of all the above difficulties, almost admitted in the third volume of 'Das Capital' his failure to construct a satisfactory theory of value.

6. KARL MARX'S THEORY OF PROFIT

Marx on Variable Capital and Constant Capital.

According to Marx's analysis "the value of a commodity consists of three parts, namely, constant capital, variable capital and surplus value. Thus value of a commodity, *i.e.*, $V = C + V + S$.

In the case of constant capital the value of that part of the machinery that gets depreciated (*i.e.*, consumed in the process of production) comes to be included in the value of commodity. Constant capital also includes items such as value of raw materials used in the production of the commodity. Constant capital refers to or embodies past labour. It is called constant or fixed because "it does not undergo any quantitative alteration" and does not produce any surplus value for the capitalist; on the other hand the variable capital is called variable because "this part of capital is continually transformed from a constant into a variable magnitude." It is the variable capital which by employing labour produces surplus value.

Marx on Rate of Exploitation (Rate of Surplus Value).

Surplus value is explained by Karl Marx in the following manner: If a worker is employed for a certain number of hours per day, the labourer during one portion of his working day produces only the value of the means of subsistence on which the labourer and his family lives. Marx calls this part of working day, as we have already seen, 'necessary labour time'. During the second part of the working day, the worker creates 'surplus value' in which the capitalist is interested. Marx calls this part of the working day 'surplus labour time'.

Marx maintains that the rate of exploitation depends upon the length of the working day and the ratio of the necessary labour time required to produce subsistence wage to surplus labour time.

According to Karl Marx, machinery plays a vital role in increasing the rate of exploitation of labour. Machinery helps to increase the rate of exploitation in the following manner:

Increasing use of machinery results in cheapening commodities on which workers subsist; this results in reducing 'the necessary labour time' and increasing surplus labour time and therefore surplus value.

Machines result in employing women and children as they can attend to simpler processes of production of commodities by machines. This results both in the increased supply of labour force and competition among them to secure employment; also now the goods necessary for subsistence of the family come to be earned by combined labour of members of the family.

According to Marx, introduction of machinery lengthens the working day and production on an extended scale without any alteration in the amount of capital laid out (spent) on machinery and buildings. Not only is there, therefore, an increase of surplus-value, but the outlay necessary to obtain it diminishes.

According to Marx, introduction of more and more machines increases surplus value in another way. Machinery increases rapidity and intensity of work. Even when the government by legislation fixes the number of hours of work "machinery becomes in the hands of the capital . . . means systematically employed for squeezing out more labour in a given time."

Another way machines increase surplus value is that machines by displacing workers act as competitor of labour, thus reducing the wage rate.

Marx maintains that the capitalist must go on increasing his constant capital because of the pressure exerted on every capitalist by competition of other capitalists. The capitalist cannot hope to make increasing surplus value by employing more workers through old and out-dated machinery. According to Marx, therefore, there operates "a law of the progressive increase in constant capital, in proportion to the variable." A capitalist who fails to equip his factory with more and more machines (*i.e.*, increase constant capital) as required by continually progressing technology, will soon be unable to compete with other capitalists who are increasing constant capital and will soon be reduced to the rank of proletariat.

Thus according to Marx, there is continual change in 'the organic composition of capital'. There is a continual movement in favour of constant capital continually displacing labour. Thus surplus population is created which is the 'Industrial Reserve Army' which is always at the disposal of capitalist for exploitation.

Declining Rate of Profit:

According to Marx's analysis, the rate of profit is the ratio of surplus value to 'total' capital. Because of the fact that Marx views that there will be progressive increase in constant or fixed capital in proportion to circulating or variable capital, there will be a gradual fall in the average rate of profit, because, as already noted, it is only the variable capital that produces surplus value.

This raises a difficulty for Marx. "A higher organic composition of capital would tend to reduce the rate of profit only if the rate of exploitation stayed the same." It is possible that "an increasing rate of exploitation, however, tends to increase the rate of profit and, perhaps, to more than compensate the effect of the higher organic composition of capital." This however is in conflict with the gist of Marx's analysis. If there is constant rate of exploitation, that would result in higher real wages for workers with rising productivity of labour.

Tendency of the Rate of Profit to Equalise.

According to Marx's analysis, if the rate of exploitation were the same in different industries, in all the industries the rate of profit would be the same provided all those industries possessed the same organic composition of capital. What however is noticed is that different industries have different organic compositions of capital and yet the rates of profit tend to be equal in the long run.

Karl Marx tries to solve these contradictions by, for all practical purposes, abandoning the labour theory of value. It is the competition that makes rates of profit in different industries tend towards equality. According to Marx, "capital withdraws from spheres with low rates of profit and invades others which yield higher rate." The result is that there is "such a proportion of supply to demand that the average profit in various spheres of production becomes the same."

7. CRISIS AND BREAKDOWN (OF CAPITALISM) THESIS OF KARL MARX

Adam Smith and other members of the Classical School were of the opinion that an individual's economic behaviour is motivated solely by the desire to maximise his satisfaction from consumption of goods and services. Any saving or accumulation which meant postponement of immediate consumption would be undertaken by people only in return for a definite reward.

And thus we arrive at the classical position that higher the rate of interest, greater would be the amount saved by people from current consumption and lower the rate of interest, lower would be the rate of saving. Thus, according to the Classical School, under competitive conditions, demand for and supply of savings would be brought into equilibrium by changes in the rate of interest.

Karl Marx swept aside all this classical argument regarding savings being influenced by rate of interest which would also bring equilibrium between amount saved and demand for saving, as irrelevant. Marx on the other hand wrote : "The capitalist shares with the miser the passion for wealth as wealth. But that which is a miser is a mere idiosyncrasy, is, in the capitalist, the effect of the social mechanism of which he is but one of the wheels."[10]

The capitalist's very status in society depends upon the quantity of wealth he has accumulated. More the wealth accumulated higher will be his status in society; but on the other hand, if his wealth diminishes or he loses it, his status sinks down. Marx wrote: "... to accumulate is to conquer the world of social wealth, to increase the mass of human being exploited by him, and thus extend both the direct and indirect sway of the capitalist."[11]

There is an additional reason why the capitalist has to or is forced to accumulate or save more and more. Marx wrote in this connection: "... the development of capitalist production makes it constantly necessary to keep increasing the amount of capital laid out in a given industrial undertaking and competition makes the imminent laws of capitalist production to be felt by each individual capitalist as external coercive laws. It compels him to keep constantly extending his capital in order to preserve it, but extend it he cannot except by means of progressive accumulation."[12]

If the capitalist lags behind in the race to save and invest more and more in the latest and most up-to-date machinery, he will be crushed by competing capitalist producers and would soon be reduced to the rank of a proletariat. For Marx, unlike in the case of Classical School, saving and accumulation are basic to the structure of capitalist economic system.

The consequences of such accumulation by capitalists are disastrous for the workers. According to Marx, the process of accumulation begets an Industrial Reserve Army due to which competition for getting employment or jobs results in pushing down the wage-rate.

Of course, greater accumulation and greater investments means greater demand for machinery and raw materials on the one hand and for workers on the other. The initial impact of greater demand for workers results in pushing up the wage rate. When due to rising wage rate, employment of labour becomes costlier to capitalists, the latter try to introduce labour-saving devices which results in displacement of labour, the newly unemployed workers only going to swell the ranks of the Industrial Reserve Army, increasing competition among workers for jobs and consequent lowering down of the wage rate. If this is not enough to reduce wage level sufficiently, the capitalists would temporarily reduce investments under the impact of rising labour-costs. When investment is thus reduced or declines, this results in unemployment, depression and economic crisis. This process continues until due to competition among workers for jobs and consequent lowering down of the wage rate. If this is not enough to reduce wage level sufficiently, the capitalists would temporarily reduce investments under the impact of rising labour costs. When investments is thus reduced or declines, this results in unemployment, depression and economic crisis. This process continues until due to competition among workers wage rates are sufficiently reduced to make additional investments by capitalists worthwhile. This favours additional accumulation and investment and economy again begins to recover from depression. This process goes on repeating itself giving rise to periods of booms and depressions.

Thus in Marx's analysis of capitalism, depression and unemployment occupy a vital and almost a central position. The Classical School had not paid much attention to this phenomenon and dismissed it as merely accidental whereas J. B. Say spoke of logical impossibility of occurrence of general depression in the economy because of the principle that supply creates its own demand and competition would automatically establish full employment in the economy and the economy would stabilise automatically at the level of full employment. Marx on the other hand compared this inherent defect of capitalists structure to cancer which would go on worsening and would one day destroy capitalism itself.

There is according to Marx another tendency which goes on accentuating, resulting in economic crisis in capitalism — the tendency of over-production and under-consumption. It is logical to expect that if any economic system is to work smoothly, there ought to be proper relationship between rate of production of goods and services and rate of their consumption. Marx showed that under capitalist system due to the operation of several forces, such balance between rate of production of goods and services and rate of their consumption becomes practically impossible, resulting in crisis.

According to Marx, as capitalism develops further and becomes more and more wealthier, the tendency towards larger accumulation and investment get accentuated further and further, which means building up of continually increasing productive powers in the capitalist economy and continually rising flow of consumer goods and services.

But as already seen, at the same time capitalism develops the tendency to repress the growth of consumption from keeping pace with increasing production of consumption goods. This happens because of two factors. In the first place, not only the capitalists have limited physical capacity to consume goods and services but also because of their deliberate attempt to increase accumulation for further investment in the race with other capitalists and also to maximise profits; secondly, we have seen that under capitalist regime workers get only subsistence level of wages and therefore lack purchasing power to purchase all the goods that they need at the ruling prices. Increasing unemployment and increasing size of the Industrial Reserve Army only add fuel to the fire all of which results in underconsumption and thus lack of balance between rate of growth of production of consumption goods and services and rate of growth of consumption by society of those goods and services. Thus, according to Marx, there is "the fundamental contradiction between limitless striving for expansion of production which is the very essence of capitalism, and the restricted consumption of the masses."[13]

This inner contradiction in the capitalist system grows or becomes more and more severe as capitalism grows more and more wealthier, resulting in chronic depressions and crises of increasing intensity.

Capitalism makes desperate efforts to rescue itself from the growing menace of recurring economic crises of increasing intensity by the operation of outside factors like opening up of economically backward regions of the world and building colonies where in return for cheap raw materials it can dump its vast quantities of goods and make people purchase them at appropriate prices with the help of political power or new inventions requiring huge investments, or engaging in preparation of or even declaration of war which results in practically unlimited demand for all sorts of goods resulting in keeping the factories (especially armament factories) going, with the exploitation of labour and maximisation of profits of capitalists.

But there is limit to opening up of new colonies and new inventions cannot be brought into existence on order by capitalists. And therefore, according to Marx, resort to militarism and war becomes the only means of solving the problems of over-production created by inner contradiction of capitalism and of its survival.

After 1875 when capitalism developed in a number of West European countries, they tried, as stated above, to overcome the internal contradictions and recurrent crisis by occupation of backward countries in Asia and Africa where they invested their vast accumulations to develop cheap raw materials for their industries and where they could dump goods and thus solve the problem arising out of increasing production at home of all sorts of goods. But when soon these backward countries in different continents came to be fully occupied and there was no possibility of further occupation of colonies (— this happened especially in the case of Germany which was a late starter in the development of its capitalist system —) there inevitably was clash among the capitalist countries themselves which culminated in World War I.

Marx maintained that developments of capitalism in the direction of imperialism which is an inevitable step in the process of capitalist development brings out the supreme inner contradiction in the capitalist system "that death becomes the only means of life." But nobody knows where modern wars once started will end. But, according to Marx, it so happens that capitalistic system incapable of solving problems created by internal contradictions has no other choice but blindly to march the road to Armageddon.

Transition to Socialism

It is obvious that even if workers organise to hasten the process of destruction of capitalism, the capitalist class will not however easily give up the struggle.

Once the socialist revolution is brought about by workers, it would inevitably lead to transfer of state power from the bourgeois minority to the working class. As the workers are without experience in the art of running the government and national economy after all the means of production are nationalised and private property is abolished, according to Marx, in order to stabilise the communist revolution there should at least be for a temporary period dictatorship of the proletariat. This dictatorship of the proletariat is envisaged only for a transitional period. "The dictatorship of the working class is decisive for the socialist transformation of society. It heads the working masses, organises their struggle against the forces and traditions of old society. Crushing the resistance of the exploiters, defending the country against hostile actions from within, the dictatorship of the proletariat organises and heads the building of a new socialist economy. In the course of this economic upbuilding the old bourgeoise relations of production are destroyed and new, socialist relations of production are created. At the same time the new productive forces essential for building and developing the socialist mode of production are created."

"The building of socialist economy presupposes the introduction of fundamental socio-economic reforms, including the establishment of the social ownership of the basic means of production, the abolition of exploitation of man by man, the replacement of anarchical production conducted solely for the purpose of amassing capitalist profits, by planned production aimed at satisfying the requirements of society as a whole ..."[14]

Thus during the period of transition from capitalism to socialism the dictatorship of the proletariat has to take steps to crush all possible opposition from the capitalist class within and outside the country and make an attempt to lay firm foundation for building a socialist society.

8. MARX ON SOCIALISM AND COMMUNISM

Marxian economics is essentially an analysis of capitalism (as it was functioning when *Marx* was writing, *i.e., laissez faire* capitalism), its structures, its functioning and its future.

This being so, Karl Marx has very little to say on the future of alternative socialist economic system that would replace capitalism which is doomed to disappear sooner or later and for the earlier destruction of which Marx made an appeal to workers to accelerate the process of destruction of capitalism by violent revolution. Marx has little to say on the future economic system, namely, socialism or communism which is supposed to replace capitalism; and what little he says is definitely vague and in general terms which means he does not provide a blueprint either for socialist or communist economic system.

Marx writes: "The point of bourgeois society consists precisely in this, that a priori there is no conscious social regulation of production." This would imply that, according to Marx, the future economic system that would replace capitalism would be a planned economy. According to him, the socialist economy will have to take important decisions regarding not only how to allocate labour to its proper uses but also has to determine the most economical use of all scarce factors of production, namely, natural resources, capital goods and human labour. Naturally, according to Marx, in such a society book-keeping (national accounting and planning) will play a vital role.

According to Marx, between the two stages, namely, capitalism which is doomed to failure and communism which will eventually replace it, there lies a period of revolutionary transformation which is commonly referred to as socialism. This phase of socialism roughly corresponds to the period during which in the political sphere there would be dictatorship of the proletariat (which as we have already seen is to be only for a temporary period of time until the revolution is consolidated). Under socialism, in contradiction to communism, labour would be rewarded or would get a return in proportion to its contribution to social wealth; labour under socialism would cease to be exploited, but would be receiving a reward in proportion to work rendered. This also implies that since different workers contribute different quantities of socially necessary labour, (which in other terms means contribute quantities of product and of differing quality to social wealth), their rewards or incomes would differ.

Socialism is only a transitional phase and eventually it will give place to communism. Under communism, according to Marx, the principle of distribution would be "From each according to his capacity, to each according to his need."

In this connection Karl Marx writes: "In a higher phase of communist society, after a tyrannical subordination of individuals in the division of labour and thereby also the distinction between manual and intellectual work, have disappeared ... after productive forces have also increased and all springs of social welfare are flowing more freely along with the all-round development of the individual then and then only will the narrow bourgeois horizon of rights be left far behind and society will inscribe on its banner: "From each according to his capacity, to each according to his need."[15]

Marx has drawn almost a utopian picture of communism. According to him, once the bourgeois system of distribution of wealth is destroyed, there would be fantastic increase in productivity of labour to such an extent that even division of labour could be discontinued so also the task of allocation of labour through division of labour. "Then the time would come when the individual could hunt in the morning, fish in the afternoon, rear cattle in the evening and criticise after dinner, without specialising in any one of these occupations." The principle of division of labour with its distinction between manual and intellectual labour would have completely disappeared. Under the new system, namely, communism, productivity of labour would have increased so much that not only the narrow division of labour which cramps the development of human personality would be unnecessary but even the problem of 'economising' (by allocating labour to its best uses, etc., which was necessary during the transitional phase of socialism that lies between capitalism and communism) would be altogether eliminated. Naturally under such happy circumstances the 'State' as we know it would have hardly any functions of perform and would therefore 'wither away'.

9. CRITICAL APPRAISAL OF MARXIAN SOCIALISM

Having explained the main tenets of Marx's economics, his analysis of capitalism and its functioning and his views regarding the future of capitalism, it would be instructive to critically examine those views and also see to what extent his prophecy regarding future of capitalism has come true. We will critically examine the main tenets of Marxian economics one by one and later the Marxian economics as a whole.

As regards Marx's materialistic interpretation of history, we have already seen that it is considered as an extremely one-sided explanation of the evolution of history, over-emphasising economic factor. We have already noted that other factors such as national environment, religion, human intellect and sciences do greatly influence the course of human history.

In regard to his labour theory of value, surplus value and exploitation of labour by capitalists, it has already been noted that Marx himself was disillusioned with his labour theory of value and expressed his dissatisfaction about it in Volume III of *Das Capital.* Labour theory of value has for all practical purposes come to be rejected even in the USSR. Whether natural resources and capital are owned by private individuals or collectively by society, the fact remains that making use of all scarce factors of production will involve cost which will have to be taken into account while computing cost of production of a commodity. And this is what is being done in the USSR and communist countries today. Rent, interest and profit go to the State and instead of into the pockets of private individuals as under capitalism.

As regards Marx's theory of surplus value and increasing exploitation of labour, a number of points of criticism can be brought against the theory.

Marx was writing when labour was not unionised and competition prevailed in the labour market. Labour in capitalist countries has now been unionised with strong collective bargaining power with capitalists. And therefore we notice that wages have not remained at the subsistence level, but on the other hand real wages of workers in capitalist countries of the West, in the USA and Japan have shown tendency continually to rise.

The Marxian theory of exploitation of labour by capitalists had come to be based on Ricardian analysis regarding antagonism between profits and wages and Ricardo's proposition that whatever increases profits will lower wages and whatever raises wages will reduce profits. Marx could not envisage the possibility of both profits and wages rising at the same time. This is what the US experience has shown where profits as well as wages have both shown secular tendency to rise. Thus rising real wages increase labour productivity thus enabling capitalists to pay higher wages at the same time making higher profits. The proportions in which profits and wages rise in capitalist countries may be different, but the notion that there is fundamental antagonism between the two and one can rise only at the cost of the other has come to be rejected on empirical ground.

As regards Marx's views regarding increasing concentration of wealth and recurrence of deeper and deeper economic crises, it is surprising how a keen and penetrating analyst like Marx could not foresee the possibilities of joint-stock form of business organisation which was already in existence in capitalist countries during his times. Joint-stock form of business organisation has enabled vast number of middle class people to purchase shares in varying numbers of become joint owners of industrial enterprises. The small enterprises have also continued to remain in operation because of certain inherent advantages which they enjoy. This means concentration of wealth which Marx visualised has not taken place. Also may be because of Marxian criticism or due to the establishment of democratic form of government in capitalist countries with emphasis on equality, continual transfer of income from richer to poorer classes of people in capitalist countries is going on through fiscal measures (such as direct taxation, namely income tax and super tax, capital gains tax, succession duties, gift tax and also through indirect heavy taxation on luxury and semi-luxury goods consumed by the rich) and monetary measures. The consequence is that, as we have already seen in some other connection, there is in the USA (as also other capitalist countries) less inequalities at present in income distribution instead of increasing concentration of wealth which Marx predicted.

Due to increasing diffusion of purchasing power instead of concentration of wealth as anticipated by Marx, and also due to fiscal and monetary measures suggested by J. M. Keynes in his *'The General Theory'* published in 1936, capitalism seems to have acquired adequate knowledge and devised policy measures to overcome economic crisis. This is evident from the fact that though there have been occasionally mild recessions and certain amount of unemployment, deepening crises have not been visiting capitalist countries since the Great Depression of 1929-33. On the contrary, capitalist countries have devised various measures to attain the objective of full employment and stabilise the economy there as seen from developments in West Germany and Japan which attained during post-World War II period annual growth rates varying between 10 to 15 per cent and over-full employment.

And therefore the Marxian prophecy that the inner contradictions of capitalism resulting in deepening economic crises will ultimately destroy capitalism has been proved false. The evils associated with capitalism have been proved to be inherent but incidental evils with which it is possible to successfully deal. The collapse of capitalism anticipated by Karl Marx has not come about in industrialised countries of the West.

The State was interpreted by Marx as a political instrument devised by capitalists to protect their self-interest. This has also proved to be incorrect interpretation of the State. In capitalist countries workers' political parties often came to power and used the institution of State to bring about major changes is favour of the working classes.

Even in the USSR where Marxist envisaged revolution took place, the State has not withered away as anticipated by Marx, nor dictatorship of the proletariat proved to be only a temporary phenomenon.

Concluding Remarks.

Though practically every tenet or principle of Marxian economics can be and has come to be subjected to severe criticism and can be shown to be logically or empirically invalid, yet the amalgam of different tenets of Marxian economics seems to have certain amount of validity and continues to attract vast number of followers. Thus economic factor may not be the only factor influencing the course of human history; but the fact remains that it is one of the most potent (possibly the most important) factor. The labour theory of value and surplus value and exploitation may be proved logically wrong; and yet the fact remains that labour in most capitalist countries does not get its due and a small percentage of people seem to live luxurious life on unearned income without contributing anything to national product. Similarly concentration of wealth and economic crises in capitalism may have been avoided; but the fact of inherent instability of capitalism remains valid and attempts are made to overcome this by adopting certain of the devices suggested by Marxists, namely, nationalisation of certain sectors of the economy, increasing regulation of the economic activities of the people or even adoption of some sort of economic planning by capitalist countries.

Thus validity and attraction of Marxian economics do not appear to depend upon the analytical or logical validity of different tenets of Marxian economics which continues to attract increasing number of followers in various parts of the world.

REFERENCES

1. *The Theory of Capitalist Development* — Paul M. Sweezy (1942), page 5.
2. *Comparative Economic Systems* — W. N. Loucks and W. B. Whitney pages 63-64.
3. To make fun of or mock at the Providential Theory of History, Karl Marx gave the following illustration:

   "It is a fact that in Scotland landed property acquired a new value by the development of English industry. This industry opened up new outlets for wool. In order to produce wool on a large scale, arable land had to be transformed into pasturage. To effect this transformation, the estates had to be concentrated. To concentrate the estates small holdings had first to be abolished, thousands of tenants had to be driven from their native soil and a few shepherds in charge of millions of sheeps to be installed in their place. Thus, by successive transformation, landed property in Scotland has resulted in driving out of men by sheep. Now say that the providential aim of the institution of landed property in Scotland was to have men driven out by sheep, and you will have made providential history".

   (From '*the Poverty of Philosophy*' —— By Karl Marx, page 364).
4. Friedrich Engels in his '*Anti-Duhring*', in Handbook of Marxism, page 279.
5. Karl Marx's Interpretation of History — M. M. Bober (1948), page 274.
6. '*The Techniques of Karl Marx*', — V. I. Lenin in Handbook of Marxism, page 545.
7. Engel has explained the terms Bourgeoisie and Proletariat as follows: "By bourgeoisie is meant the class of modern capitalists, owners of the wage-labour; by proletariat, the class of modern wage-labourers who, having no means of production of their own, are reduced to selling their labour power in order to live."
8. Karl Marx — *Das Capital*, pages 169-170.
9. *A History of Economic Thought* — Overton H. Taylore, page 304.
10. *Das Capital*, Vol. III, page 649.
11. *Ibid.*
12. *Ibid.*
13. Lenins' Works, Vol. III, page 135.
14. '*Political Economy — A Condensed Course*', L. Leontyev, page 120-121.
15. Quoted by M. M. Bober in his Karl Marx, *Critique of Gotha Programme*, pages 352-53.

CHAPTER 16

SOCIALISM

(WITH SPECIAL REFERENCE TO THE U.S.S.R.)

1. SOCIALISM AND CENTRALISED PLANNING

Authoritarian socialism (or communism), as we have already seen, is characterised by social or collective ownership of all means or factors of production, and by centralised economic planning which is both autocratic and comprehensive determining the objectives, broad framework and all practicable detailed targets to be achieved by the economy within a specified time-limit. Though the Soviet economic planning today is not as autocratic as during the Stalinist regime and though consumers in that country have been now enjoying certain amount of consumer's freedom, still we use here for the purpose of analysis the prevailing Soviet model as an authoritarian model of socialism (or communism).

Paul M. Sweezy has made out a case that authoritarian socialism (or communism — the two words hereafter would be used interchangeably—) requires all-inclusive and comprehensive economic planning. Sweezy writes: "In an unplanned economy — whether capitalist or communist — investment decisions are made by many independent units ... It is this circumstance that accounts for the irritational behaviour of unplanned economy: the alternation of booms and depressions and slumps, the co-existence of gluts and shortages, the paradox of unemployed workers and unsatisfied wants..." On the basis of the above analysis, Sweezy emphasises the necessity of comprehensive economic planning under Soviet type socialism or communism. He writes: "It is scarcely conceivable that the socialist state will so decentralise the making of investment decisions as to recreate the blindness and uncertainty of unplanned capitalism. Moreover, it is not hard to see that the centralisation of investment decisions makes comprehensive economic planning inevitable. Assume, for example, that the government of a socialist society makes a basic policy decision to invest a certain percentage of the national income over a period of, say, five or ten years and lays down certain general goals such as building up of heavy industry, the housing for specified proportion of the population, and the development of hereto backward regions. The next step naturally would be to charge the Central Planning Board with the task of drawing up an investment plan for carrying out these decisions. The investment will begin by translating the general goals laid down by the government into quantitative terms; so many new factories, railroads, power plants, mines, apartment houses, schools, hospitals, theatres and so forth. The dates at which these construction projects are to be started and finished will have to be specified. From these data it will be possible to draw up schedules of the different kinds of materials and labour which will be required. At this point the investment plan may be said to be complete."[1]

It should thus be obvious that the essence or heart of centralised planning is planning of investment — how much of annual income is to be invested, and how much of total investment in each sector and sub-sector of the national economy. It is only through proper investment planning that the final targets of production of various types of goods and services can be attained.

Paul Sweezy further shows that the Central Planning Board in a socialist or communist country cannot logically stop with just investment planning. He has emphasised that as a consequence of above investment decision and as a logical next step, the Central Planning Board will find it "necessary to estimate consumer demand for all products which compete for resources" and "to draw up a second set of schedules showing the different kinds of materials and labour which will be required." This would make possible "consolidating the investment and consumption schedules ... and to work out a general plan for the development of the economy over the period in question." It is obvious that when such a comprehensive plan is formulated covering investment decisions and schedules of consumption goods and allocation of resources among various industries, "it cannot be left to the direction of individual industry and plant managers whether or not they confirm to it; rather it must be their first duty, imposed by law, to carry out their part of the plan to the best of their ability...."[2]

Thus under centrally planned economy in socialist or communist economic system, the freely fluctuating price-mechanism and consumer's free choice no longer decide (as under capitalism and to some extent under liberal or democratic socialism) what goods and services are to be produced and managers no longer have the power of acting independently on the basis of cost-price relationship as under capitalism. It is the Central Planning Board that controls everything and takes all important decisions regarding what goods and services are to be produced, in what quantities, how, where and how different productive resources all owned by the State are to be allocated among various alternatives open to it in consonance with the above decisions.

In the above model of centralised planning under socialism or communism, it is the Central Planning Board or Authority that makes all investment decisions according to scale of preferences of the government (and not of consumers as under capitalism); and the formulation and implementation of the plan is not based or influenced by freely fluctuating price-mechanism reflecting consumers' preferences. Production targets in various sectors and industries are fixed in kind and resources allocated for the realisation of those targets are also expressed in physical terms. In such a sort of comprehensive planning, money is used but it functions only as 'a unit of account' helping to express in uniform terms aggregates made up of dissimilar commodities. There would be markets for consumer goods and for labour and so on; and it would be the duty of the Central Planning Board or Authority to see that, for example, "the total supply of consumer goods times their sales prices equals the aggregate purchasing power of the consumers, or that the value of output equals the value of input plus planned profits in a given industry or enterprise."[3]

Maurice Dobb has also made a strong case for centralised planning in socialism or communism on the following grounds:

1. Consumer's sovereignty has been overemphasised by bourgeois writers; though consumer goods may be distributed through market, consumer's sovereignty need not direct production; consumer's sovereignty should be abolished.

2. It should be appreciated that choice among different methods of producing the same commodity, though theoretically limitless, in actual fact is fairly narrowly limited on account of social, historical and even technological considerations. Hence the Central Planning Authority should easily find the task of choosing the desirable technique of production manageable.

3. In long-term planning, since different sectors or even different industries are closely interdependent, such decisions regarding them therefore cannot be left to thousands of independent producers; it is only a Planning Authority that can take such decisions in a logically consistent way.

4. More important than merely reaching and maintaining static equilibrium is the question of achieving long-term economic development. This can be done only through a high-powered Central Planning Authority.

5. Economy and its different sections should have internal consistency which can be attained and maintained only through comprehensive economic planning.

6. Though the internal balances — sectoral and inter-industry-wise — are achieved under capitalism through price-mechanism, continual inconsistencies which are likely to occur because of rapid changes in technology and priorities can be more successfully tackled by only Central Planning Authority through comprehensive planning and not by crudely operating price-mechanism influenced by freely fluctuating forces of demand and supply.

Thus there appears to be inevitability of comprehensive centralised economic planning under authoritarian socialism or communism as in countries like the Soviet Union.

2. SOVIET EXPERIENCE IN CENTRALISED PLANNING

In the Soviet Union, all important decisions such as rate of saving and investment, expenditure on defence, rates of growth of different sectors, allocation of investment resources among capital goods and consumption goods are all made not by market forces of demand and supply as in capitalism but administratively *i.e.*, by the Communist Party of the Soviet Union. The Gosplan (which is a planning machinery of the Central Government) then draws up plans for all sectors of the economy.

The state planning body (Gosplan) has to perform five tasks:

"First, to determine the criteria of economic calculations underlying planning decisions.

Second, to determine and quantify the targets to be achieved in the planning period.

Third, to coordinate the targets so as to ensure the internal consistency of the plan.

Fourth, to determine appropriate methods of ensure plan fulfilment.

Fifth, to revise targets according to the changing conditions."[4]

The ultimate aim of economic planning in the USSR is to build a communist society. In order to achieve this objective the USSR has three types of planning, namely, long-term, medium-term and current (annual) plans.

The First Five-Year Plan in the USSR commenced from the year 1928 and covered the period 1928-32; the USSR is having at present the Eleventh Five-Year Plan which covers the period 1981-1985. The Eleventh Plan of the USSR is part of the long-term plan covering the period 1976 to 1990.

Necessity of long-term or perspective planning in the USSR arises because as the Soviet Union has achieved a fairly high degree of economic development, it has to further achieve new scientific, technological, economic and socio-political progress (commensurate with Western European countries and the USA). The perspective plan aims at provision of abundant consumer goods and services as well as to deal successfully with scientific and technological problems in a dynamic society such as development of nuclear power, "development of large production complexes southward diversion of waters from the great Siberian rivers to the Central Asian deserts, etc."

Before long-term or perspective plan of the USSR is drawn, intensive work is done on forecasting the country's development over a period of 15 to 20 years or even 30 years. Forecasts for the first fifteen years are fairly detailed and are in general terms for the latter period.

A perspective plan or long-term economic plan is based taking into account potential for economic growth and exploitable natural and other resources. This perspective plan includes "a forecast of the development of and application of science and technology, a forecast of social changes under mature socialism with its rising level of cultural and educational standards, expansion of health services, changes in working and living conditions and improvements in the management of the economy. It includes at present long-term development of power industry; electronics, chemicals, ferrous, non-ferrous and rare metals, land development and development of transport system."[5]

There is also, naturally, a demographic forecast estimating growth of population, changes in composition, size, structure, labour-force, etc., in USSR during the next 20 or 30 years. This aspect is basic to perspective planning as that determines the requirements of final consumption of goods and services.

A new aspect of Soviet perspective planning is the forecasting of economic ties with foreign countries for the next 15 to 20 years between the USSR and East European countries and with also capitalist countries like the USA and Japan and with developing countries like India with whom USSR trade contracts are increasing.

It should be noted that a perspective plan is not 'a definite plan' but only a long-range forecast broadly defining the trend and main growth parameters for the national economy and important particular sectors, establishment of major territorial and industrial complexes and laying down of broad trend of economic and social development and "approximate levels to be reached in each five-year period of the forecast as regards the growth of the social product, national income, major production items, investment and personal consumption."[6]

Five-Year Plans.

In the USSR, five-year plan is a basic type of economic planning. The long-term plan only outlines the broad developmental trends of different sectors and of the national economy. On the other hand, five-year plan (which is further broken down into annual plans) is essentially an operational plan. The basic Five-Year Plan sets "the main production targets for all the sectors, ministries and ministerial departments and Union Republics, determines the scale of investments and the main proportions of social production and principal assignments in the social and cultural fields and in raising the living standards of the people."[7]

In the five-year plan, every enterprise has its own five-year plan fixing the norms for the period. These plans of enterprises define what goods they are going to produce, at what prices, what funds they will have for payment of wages and what material incentives they propose to provide for increasing production.

Annual Plans. In the USSR, economic planning becomes still more detailed and specific when on the basis of five-year plan, annual plans are drawn.

While drawing long-term, five-year and also annual plans, the USSR planners keep two main considerations in mind — one, to ensure balanced development of the economy; and second, to raise efficiency of social production.

To increase efficiency of social production, since 1965 the Soviet Union has introduced some important reforms in its planning. A system of enterprise funds is introduced which include the material incentive funds for workers, the funds for social and cultural amenities and funds for housing for workers. This system of incentives brings forth the hidden potential of workers into operation. Under the 1965 system, if an enterprise exceeds the five-year plan targets, it is permitted to add to the material incentives fund.

"Thus the chief aim of planning in the Soviet Union is to raise the standard of living of the people by achieving maximum output with minimum input. The optimal economic plan aims at coordinating the various factors so as to ensure high and stable rate of growth of production, accumulation and consumption."[8]

Steps in Formulating a Plan in the USSR

The first step in the formulation of a five-year plan is that the Communist Party formulates priorities in the forthcoming plan, setting out desired rate of growth of some vital commodities.

The second step is to send these targets to the Gosplan which is busy gathering data on the performance during the previous five-year plan, the various bottlenecks faced and so on. On this basis, the Gosplan formulates some preliminary set of 'Control Figures' or targets for about 300 product-groups, keeping in view priorities fixed as the first step by the Communist Party.

As a third step, these 'Control Figures' are sent through ministerial organisations to individual enterprises, the control figures being disaggregated at every stage when they are passed on to various individual enterprises in every sector of the economy.

As the fourth step, information flows back from individual enterprises to the Gosplan. Each enterprise puts forward its input-requirements which in turn are aggregated for all enterprises in the ministry and thus are gathered by the Gosplan. "At every stage in the process the requested inputs are compared with earlier estimated input needs and the correlation principle is used to adjust differences between the two."

The fifth and final step is the finalisation of a five-year plan and the drawing up of the five-year plan.

Some Important Aspects of Planning in the USSR

(a) Material Balances. The consistency of 'Control Figures' which play such a vital role in economic planning in the USSR is attempted to be achieved

by the Gosplan by drawing up 'Material Balances' of important commodities, labour, finance and so on for the national economy as a whole. 'Material Balances' would be said to have been attained "when the supplies of each commodity equal its targeted material input requirements and final uses."

'Material Balances' are drawn for the country as a whole as well as for Union Republics. They are drawn for important commodities like iron, steel, fuel, timber, fertilisers and other important industrial items.

'Labour Balance' is also very important. It is this which makes possible allocation of manpower proportionately among different sectors of the USSR economy and helps fixing targets for training of skilled personnel.

'Inter-Sectoral Balance' (as between agriculture, industries, transport, energy etc., etc.) is also assuming increasing importance, and its attainment is a vital part of planning in the USSR.

Also attempts are made to work out balances between incomes and expenditures of people, between revenue and expenditure of the State and other value proportions of the national income. This very much helps ensure correlation in the distribution of the national product and national income.

(b) Balances in the Agricultural Sector. Material balances in the agricultural sector where nature plays a very vital role differs from working out of balances in the industries sector.

In the agricultural sector there are two types of balances: 1. Balance of total agricultural resources, and 2. Balance of the marketable share of resources which goes to the State.

Because of the seasonal nature of agriculture, plan targets for different crops and for the agricultural sector as a whole are worked out for each individual season by the organisation set up for the purpose.

It becomes necessary in the agricultural sector that a certain proportion of agricultural output is held back as means of production (*i.e.,* as seeds, etc.). Naturally these compulsory deduction from total agricultural output requires that very careful calculations are made of the volume of farm output at all stages of planning, namely, national and local levels, and particularly planning of State purchases of various agricultural commodities.

Over years the Soviet Planning Authority has developed an improved system of indicators for planning in the agricultural sector. The most important indicator is the volume of State purchases of the basic type of agricultural produce or different crops and of livestock farming. "The overall plan contains targets regarding the contribution of the Union Republics to the nationwide fund of specified quantities of meat, meat products, eggs, potatoes, vegetables, melons, fruits and berries, grapes, dried fruit, etc. Targets are also fixed for the delivery of breeder stock in general and of specific breeds of beat and dairy cattle, sheep, goats and pigs."

In the USSR, farm production is planned by the State Farms and Collective Farms themselves. "The volume of state purchases of agricultural product is the only targets set by the state." The state farms and collective farms themselves plan crop areas and livestock farming with a view to achieve a certain required level of production.

Besides the main indicator of State purchases, use is made in the agricultural sector of other indicators such as "crop areas and yields, the value of gross farm output in comparable and current prices in the Union Republics, utilisation of arable land and the allotment of land to specific crops, the use of local fertilisers, the head of cattle, the poultry count and the number of lives of bees, balance estimates of fodder and gross output of grain, oilseeds, potatoes, vegetables, fruits, grapes, meat, milk and eggs, etc."[9]

But of all these indicators, the State procurement target of agricultural produce is the most important indicator. State purchases at present cover about 85 per cent of total marketable farm produce and about 95 per cent of total output of grain, meat and milk. State procurement targets can stimulate or retard production of different crops in the agricultural sector.

Detailed planning of State purchases of different agricultural produce is necessary in the USSR because there it is the State responsibility to meet all requirements of foodgrains of people and raw materials for various industries as also for fulfilling export targets for agricultural produce. State procurement targets come to be fixed after taking into consideration factors like growth of population, especially of urban areas, changes in levels of income of people and its distribution, distribution of national income between consumption and saving, wage increases, export target, changes in dietary habits of people, size of reserves and requirements of industries of various agricultural raw materials.

(c) Manpower Resource Balance. In any comprehensive national planning in a communist country like the USSR, "the rational use of manpower resources is of the utmost importance in national economic planning..." Because it is on this planning of manpower resources that the rate of expansion of production of commodities and services and of the national economy depends as also standard of living of the people in the USSR.

An extremely important task of national economic planning in the USSR is "to provide all branches of the economy with adequate manpower resources of the required skills." The Planning Authority achieves this "by assessing the manpower requirements of the economy and checking them against the available manpower resources." After this is done the number of students to be enrolled in various technical and educational institutions for specialised training is determined. It is in this way that the most rational distribution of manpower resources or labour-force in the USSR economy is planned and ensured.

By way of conclusion it may be said that in the USSR, the balance method is used in practically every sector of the national economy—agriculture, industry, transport, fuel, manpowr, income and expenditure and so on.

The Soviet Union ushered in the era of economic planning with its First Five-Year Plan covering the period 1928-33 and is now having its Eleventh Five-Year Plan (1981-85).

During the 60 years of economic planning, Soviet Union has been transformed from an economically backward country into a mighty industrial power. The Soviet experiment has many lessons of which the following are important ones:

1. The Soviet experience showed that it is possible to transform from a backward economy into a developed economy without resorting to foreign aid or resorting to exploitation of colonies.

On the contrary most of the Western capitalist countries advanced either with the aid of foreign assistance or exploiting colonies or domestic labour.

2. The Soviet experience showed that through economic planning it is possible to mobilise domestic resources, control investments according to pre-determined priorities and deal successfully within a fairly short-time with the problems of mass poverty, hunger, illiteracy, and unemployment. The Soviet Union has provided an alternative route to growth, namely, growth through economic planning which most of the backward countries have been following.

3. The Soviet experience showed that there is no conflict between the objectives of rapid economic development and attainment of economic and social justice. For example, the Third World countries are being told that much of their funds used for welfare schemes for the poor are being wasted and should be used for investment purposes and for production of necessary goods and services. The Soviet experience has shown that it is possible to achieve a proper balance between objectives of development and economic justice which will automatically ensure higher efficiency of workers in various fields and increase national product making attainment of still faster economic growth, greater economic justice and equitable distribution of wealth possible.

All these lessons are of great significance for the developing countries of the Third World which are adopting economic planning to solve their problem of masss poverty.

4. The Soviet Union's experience has shown that even in advanced economies, it is possible to attain full employment with stability and without inflation. During the 1970s while all developed capitalist countries suffered from the evils of unemployment and inflation, the Soviet Union and China with their comprehensive and centralised economic planning were the two countries which were not afflicted by any of those evils.

The Soviet experience has shown that "the achievements of the homeland of the October Revolution over six decades convincingly show that socialism has created rates of progress in all areas of society's life never seen before."

The Soviet Union economy during the last 60 years has changed beyond recognition. Thus in 1976, the national income of the Soviet Union was 65 times greater than that before the October Revolution. "Today as many products are manufactured in two and a half days as were manufactured in all of 1913". Before the Revolution Russia accounted only for about 4 per cent of the world's industrial production; today, that is about one-fifth". The Soviet Union produces more cast iron, steel, oil, iron, manganese and chrome ore, coal and coking coal, cement, tractors (in aggregate engine capacity), diesel and electric locomotives, cotton, flax, mineral fertilisers and many different goods than any other country."[10]

With economic planning disparities in the levels of economic development of different regions in the Soviet Union have been levelled off, and fairly balanced regional development has been achieved.

Far-reaching structural developments in all spheres and sectors of the Soviet economy have been brought about (*e.g.*, collective and state farms in the agricultural sector) that have resulted in material and cultural development of rural workers along with that of urban population. This has helped lessen differences in the living conditions of rural and urban population.

The following Table compares how economies of the USSR and the USA developed during the period 1954 to 1974.

TABLE 1

Average Annual Growth Rate and Basic Indices in Economic Development of the USSR and the USA between 1954 to 1974

	Percentages	
	USSR	*USA*
National Income	8.2	3.4
Industrial Output	9.7	4.4
Agricultural Output	3.8	1.6
Investment in Fixed Assets	9.2	3.1
Social Labour Productivity	6.9	2.4

Source: USSR Economic Development, Moscow, (1976), page 12.

This Table shows how the economy of the Soviet Union maintained higher rates of growth compared to those in the USA, though it must be kept in mind while comparing the figures that by 1954 the USA had already achieved remarkable development in all sectors whereas the USSR was building on a comparatively narrow base.

By 1980, the Soviet experts expected that the USSR would be fairly close to the level of US industrial production, while in 1950 the USSR-US ratio was 1 : 3.

With all this progress since the Second World War, in per capita terms the Soviet Union is still lagging behind the six advanced capitalist countries, though the gap between them is getting narrower.

3. LIMITATIONS OF CENTRALISED PLANNING

The centralised planning in the USSR is being criticised on the following grounds: 1. Centralised planning of the USSR type cannot make rational or correct allocation of national resources; 2. Centralised planning leads to bureaucratic expansion and methods and therefore to inefficiency and waste of resources; 3. Centralised planning leads to a great amount of rigidity and inflexibility making proper adjustments in consonance with the dynamic forces in society and technological field difficult; and 4. Centralised planning leads to severe curtailment of individual economic freedom. A little detailed discussion of the above points would be instructive.

1. *Centralised Economic Planning and Allocation of National Resources.* Centralised planning of the USSR type involves abandonment of freely fluctuating price-mechanism. The critics therefore maintain that rational allocation of resources becomes impossible. In the free market economy, price-mechanism expresses the preferences of consumers and therefore leads to most efficient allocation of national resources.

Ludwig von Mises has put forward this point forcefully. He writes: "... as soon as one gives up the conception of freely established monetary price ... rational production becomes completely impossible. Every step that takes us away from private ownership of the means of production also takes us away from rational economics... where there is no free market, there is no pricing mechanism; without a pricing mechanism, there is no economic calculation."[11]

In simple terms, in the absence of freely fluctuating price-mechanism, producers will not be knowing what consumers, preferences are. Production of goods and services will come to be based on arbitrary decisions of a few members of the planning authority. This is unlikely to represent accurately consumers' preferences and hence such arbitrary decisions are likely to result in wasteful and therefore irrational allocation of national resources under the type of centralised economic planning adopted in the USSR.

The socialist writers answer to the above criticism in the following way. Freely fluctuating price-mechanism is an abstract model and it does not really function or is allowed to function in capitalist economies which inevitably come to be dominated by monopolies.

Secondly, people are often ignorant and their preferences are often guided by ignorance and prejudice and need to be properly guided. People often prefer harmful drugs and strong liquors the consumption of which is harmful to an individual and his family. It must therefore be curtailed.

Thirdly, a sort of price-mechanism has been adopted in the USSR whereby demand for and supply of consumer goods and services are brought into balance. Because of the equitable distribution of income and the various methods adopted by planners to ascertain consumers' preferences, it is wrong to say that in the USSR allocation of national resources takes place in an irrational way.

On the contrary claim is made that proper ascertainment of consumers' choices which are guided by expert knowledge, and assessment of community's needs and adoption of planning, which on the above basis allocates resources, can be said to be the truly rational allocation and the most efficient use of national resources which helps the community to realise the pre-determined goals.

2. *Expansion of Bureaucracy, Inefficiency and Wastage of Resources.* The critics of comprehensive planning in the USSR maintain that the system of comprehensive planning inevitably means taking of millions of decisions, bringing about their coordination, working out input-output tables and seeing that all these decisions are implemented at different levels — from the national to farm or factory level. This involves creation of a huge bureaucratic machinery involving vast number of experts in various fields doing this sort of work (instead of producing goods and services needed by the community) and brings in all the defects of bureaucracy, namely, plethora of rules and regulations, red-tape, delays, and difficulties of fixing responsibility on specific persons for wrong decisions, and inflexibility.

The proponents of the USSR system point out that since in all economic systems including capitalism, States have been compelled to undertake more and more functions, there has been considerable amount of expansion of bureaucracy under all economic systems and not only in the USSR economy.

Secondly, though initially, there had taken place very great expansion of bureaucratic machinery due to inexperience, many things have been now reduced to routine and bureaucratic expansion cannot be said to be excessive in the USSR.

Also as a consequence of experience, better techniques of planning have now evolved. Input-output techniques are evolved and kept up-to-date; proper methods of coordination are established. As a consequence of all this, the various defects of bureaucratic management mentioned above have been reduced considerably.

3. *Rigidity and Inflexibility of Centralised Planning.* The planning authority has to do more than setting broad development scheme. Comprehensive and centralised economic planning of the Soviet type means "the careful enumeration of hunderds of thousands of items which are needed in the life of a nation from rolling prices to hairpins, from nuclear reactors to school equipment and ballad performances." This task is formidable and yet centralised plan is required to work out all the hundreds and thousands of input-output tables and bring about allocation of resources accordingly to enable producing units to achieve the pre-determined targets.

In a static sense, it is possible to conceive the central planning authority achieving the required balance and equilibrium position. But technological changes are continually taking place in a dynamic situation that prevails in every country including the USSR. "Suppose that new chemical plants for fertiliser production are to be created. Since employment is full by definition, the allocation of factors must be changed and since all processes of production are interdependent, necessary adjustments will have to be brought about in all productive firms and in the economy as a whole. The factors needed in the new or expanded fertiliser production cannot be used any longer where they had been used before. But the reduction of other production processes means the reduction of inputs of still other industries and so on *ad infinitum.*"

In his "The Economics of the Soviet Bloc', Stanislaw Wellisz has given the following example:

If, for instance, more steel is needed to erect a new fertiliser plant, the following steps are involved in it:

"First it is important to find out how much more input will be directly needed by the steel industry in order to increase output by the desired amount. Let there be need, say, for X more steel, Y more iron and Z more transportation units. Now the balance for coal, iron and transport, have to be adjusted. To produce more coal, iron and transport one must increase the quantities of other inputs. If one of these inputs is steel, the steel balance must be rebalanced in order to take into account the secondary demand. The adjustment starts a second round or approximation, and a readjustment of the iron, coal, and transport balance. The process continues until the desired balance is achieved."

The above picture would help understand how very difficult it is to bring changes once the plan is formulated and why therefore centralised planning suffers from rigidity and inflexibility. Dynamic changes in the technological field or in the field of international trade or due to vagaries of nature in the agricultural sector readjustments become necessary. But often readjustment in respect of even one establishment or one sector necessitates readjustment in all other productive establishments and other sectors of the economy. These readjustments cannot be brought about easily and hence the rigidity or inflexibility of centralised or authoritarian planning. Naturally in the absence of such readjustment necessitated especially by technological advances, centrally planned economies tend to be inefficient compared to capitalist economies where fierce competition among producers makes absorption of latest technology not only necessary for maximising profit but also for survival.

4. *Economic Planning and Curtailment of Economic Freedoms.* Critics of centralised planning maintain that the State acquires complete control over all aspects of an individual's life and this leads to complete destruction of individual freedom (which is supposed to be ensured under capitalism). As Trotsky said: "In a country where the sole employer is the State, opposition means death by slow starvation and the old principle who shall not work shall not eat has been replaced by a new one: who does not obey shall not eat."[12]

The critics thus complain that under comprehensive planning as in the USSR, various freedoms such as political freedom, cultural freedom and economic freedom get curtailed or are altogether eliminated.

There is no doubt that centralised type of economic planning as in the USSR does curtail to a great extent political, civil, cultural and economic freedoms. Comprehensive planning must by logical implications imply some restrictions on all types of activities of the people.

The experience of the USSR (as also of communist countries in Eastern Europe) shows that political freedom in the sense in which it is enjoyed by people in capitalist countries does not and possibly cannot prevail under comprehensive planning. But it is observed since the 20th Congress in the USSR that there is allowed now greater criticism of economic and political policies of the government and voice of dissent is not ruthlessly suppressed as during the Stalinist days. The same can be said about cultural freedom.

In the case of economic freedom, planning under communist countries like the USSR involves nationalisation of all the factors of production and therefore there can hardly be producer's freedom as enjoyed by people in capitalist countries. But as noted elsewhere, farmers are being given small plots in the backyard where they are free to produce what they like and sell and make profit. Also in the industrial field, certain amount of decentralisation of authority is taking place and factory management is at present enjoying certain amount of freedom in the field of production. Such a thing was unheard of during the Stalinist period. Also, though there is and has to be manpower planning, individuals are offered certain amount of choice of occupations depending upon their potential, abilities which are objectively tested.

Consumer's freedom is enjoyed today in the USSR to a greater extent than before. In respect of many consumer goods they are free to exercise their choice and spend greater or smaller portion of their income on those consumer goods. It is wrong to suppose that under centralised planning in the USSR, all consumer goods are strictly rationed and consumers have absolutely no choice. The aim of perspective planning in the USSR is to see that people enjoy more and more freedom in respect of more and more consumer goods.

It is only in the case of really scarce goods that its distribution is rationed and consumers have hardly any choice except to accept such rationing.

4. ALLOCATION OF RESOURCES

Since money has come to be associated with capitalism, the impression is created that under communism, money has no role and that allocation of resources takes place in physical terms as under money-less economy.

In the first place this misconception about money must be removed. Any complex economy of modern times cannot function without money. The only thing that takes place under communism is that money acts only as a unit of account. Economic calculations without money would become impossible in any complex modern economic system. Thus under communism money will be there but will act only as a unit of account and allocation of resources will be worked out or calculated with the help of money as an accounting unit.

Another point needs to be noted. If Marxian labour theory of value is accepted, it would lead to inefficient use or allocation of both labour and other productive resources of the community. So long as other resources, land, capital and organisational skills are scarce and not free, socialist planners will have to give them a price or cost which alone will enable them to be properly allocated. Fixation of rent, interest and profit for non-labour resources may not mean that those shares will go to private individuals. They may be only accounting prices meant only for book-keepiung purposes rather than market prices as under capitalism. But a shadow price or accounting price must be put on every non-labour resource, if its allocation is to be brought about in the most efficient way.

The fact of public ownership of means of production does not by itself determine the system by which consumer goods are distributed among people and the way labour is allocated among different occupations.

One type of socialist economy that can be assumed is where there is freedom of choice in consumption goods and in choice of occupations. In such a case (*i.e.,* in market socialism), obviously consumer preferences expressed through prices happen to be the guiding criteria for the allocation of community's production resources.

There can be the second type of socialism, namely, authoritarian socialism or collectivism or command economy with centralised type of planning where people enjoy no freedom whatsoever either as regards consumer goods or choice of occupations. In this case free prices are not available to guide allocation of resources which takes place according to the dictates or preferences of policy-makers and administrators.

Another method, namely 'mathematical method' is suggested for the purpose of allocation of resources under socialism by economists like Lange and Dickinson, though they believe that though theoretically sound, in practice the mathematical method may not be of much practical use.

According to the mathematical method, allocation of resources is supposed to be done with the help of simultaneous equations which could be solved and would in one comprehensive calculation is supposed to determine prices of all consumer goods, intermediate goods and of the factors of production.

The mathematical method would require solving millions of simultaneous equations, one equation for each item the output of which the planners are trying to determine. This is going to be a stupendous task. In modern economy, output of any one good depends upon output of all other goods which means all outputs must have consistency among them.

Even if with the mathematical method and simultaneous equations the most efficient allocation of community's resources is attained at any given point of time, dynamic changes are continually taking place in the economy (such as appearance) of new commodities and new techniques of production and so on) so that mathematical method found satisfactory at one point of time would become practically useless with these dynamic changes. And therefore mathematical method for the most efficient allocation of resources in a socialist economy though theoretically sound would, as stated by Lange and Dickinson, be of very little practical use. They would be of use only in specific situations and for short time.

Trial and Error Method of Resource Allocation.

This method is suggested by writers like Lange, Taylor, Lerner and Dickinson.

According to Taylor and Lange, the most satisfactory way of allocating commodity's resources would be to distribute income among people in the form of money to be spent as in a free market on consumer goods and services. The Planning Authority should be guided by consumer's preferences in the sense that various consumer goods and services should be produced in such quantities (by allocating various resources for their production) as could be sold at prices equal to their cost of production. Naturally since all factors of production are owned by the State, while calculating cost of production, costs will have to be imputed to various factors of production, like land and capital. The planning authority would impute costs to various factors of production carefully on the basis of collected data and then proceed on the assumption that their imputed values are correct. There might be errors. Where values or prices are set unduly high, there would be undue reduction in their use or allocation and their surplus would appear in the economy; where the imputed price of a factor of production is set too low, there would be undue excess in the use of that factor and a deficit would appear in the case of that factor. Thus wrong valuation — imputed valuation — of factors of production or resources would result in their surplus or deficit. By suitably adjusting values imputed to different factors of production, it is possible to bring about proper balance when the demand for a particular factor and its supply would be in balance. Thus according to Taylor, socialist economy can solve the problem of allocation of resources by a process of trial and error, ensuring their most efficient use under the given circumstances.

In the USSR at present a sort of combination of all these methods of allocation of resources is used. Being a command economy with centralised type of economic planning, the State decides the schedule of preferences, though these days consumers' preferences are increasingly being taken into account while deciding what consumer commodities and in what quantities are to be produced and how much of resources are to be allotted for the production of those consumer goods. Also numerous mathematical tables and econometric models are worked out and kept up-to-date and refined expressing input-output ratios which play a vital role in the allocation of resources. The dynamic changes are taking place and often trial and error method has to be adopted to find out correct allocation. Thus in the USSR today there is established better correlation between various targets to be achieved in capital and consumer goods industries as per government's and consumers' preference and allocation of community's various types of resources.

5. EMPHASIS ON HEAVY INDUSTRIES

After the October Revolution of 1917, the Soviet Union had to face a number of problems such as repelling foreign aggression by capitalist countries and successfully dealing with internal resistance to communist revolution. The first five-year plan could therefore be introduced only in 1928.

As in the case of every backward country aiming at rapid economic development, the Soviet Union had to take a number of decisions in framing her five-year plans.

It is obvious that industrialisation of a country is absolutely necessary for its rapid economic development and for this purpose surplus funds necessary for investment in the industrial sector will necessarily have to come from the agricultural sector which happens to be the major or often the only sector in a backward economy.

Having given industrialisation an important place in development planning, two alternatives remain open to planners — 1. To give greater emphasis on capital goods, and heavy or basic industries and bring about development through heavy or capital goods industries, or 2. Bring about development through emphasis on and development of consumer goods industries and the agricultural sector.

The Soviet Union chose the first model, namely, rapid economic development through emphasis on and development of heavy or capital goods industries.

The arguments in favour of development through heavy industries (like iron and steel, other metallurgical industries, heavy machinery, electricity, heavy chemicals and so on) instead of development through consumer goods industries or through agricultural sector are as follows:

1. It would reduce dependence on foreign countries which may cause trouble by withholding at any time required machinery or spares. Also there is the difficulty of acquiring foreign exchange required for importing capital goods from foreign countries as also skilled personnel to manage them.

2. The main argument in the case of Soviet Union in emphasising heavy industries was that in the long run it would bring about more rapid economic development than if attempts were made to bring about development through

giving higher priority to consumer goods industries or to agriculture. Once heavy industries are developed, and once various types of machines begin to come out of factories, they would help rapid expansions of consumer goods industries as also advancement of agriculture through mechanisation.

But in the case of this method of development through heavy industries there is one danger, namely, since consumer goods industries and agriculture for sometimes come to be given lower priority and smaller investment funds, and since heavy and capital goods industries require very large investment resources or funds, there is likely to be scarcity of foodgrains and various consumer goods and that would mean not only no immediate rise in the standard of living but possibly reduction in that standard to attain rapid economic development and rapidly rising standard of living in future.

Having accepted the strategy of development through heavy industries, the Soviet Union tried to overcome the difficulties arising out of shortages of consumer goods and foodgrains through strict rationing of foodgrains and other consumer goods.

The adoption of this strategy of development through emphasis on heavy industries has meant for Soviet people tremendous immediate sacrifices and sufferings, and continuance of relatively backwardness of the agricultural sector necessitating import of foodgrains even as late as in 1980 from the USA. But there is no doubt that this strategy has turned the Soviet Union into a mighty industrial country.

Soviet Union's Five-Year Plans and Heavy Industries

The Soviet Union's emphasis on heavy industries and adoption of the strategy of rapid development of the national economy through development of heavy industries can be illustrated by detailed references to Soviet Union's five-year plans.

The First Five-Year Plan (1928-32). During the first five-year plan (1928-32), about three-quarters of capital investments came to be allotted to the production of capital goods to ensure priority to development of heavy industries. The emphasis was on development of electric power stations, both hydro and using peat and coal, metallurgical plants, tractor plants, farm machinery plants, chemical plants and many other heavy industrial enterprises. Thus the first five-year plan established a number of branches of heavy industries.

"During the first five-year plan period the USSR created or completely rebuilt ferrous metallurgy, machine-tool industry, car and tractor, chemical and aircraft industries and farm machinery industry. The Soviet heavy industry was set firmly on its feet, which created an independent base for the complete reconstruction of the national economy."[13]

Thus compared to production figures of 1928, in 1932 (*i.e.,* at the end of the first plan), production of pig iron increased by 188 per cent, of steel by 139 per cent; of coal by 181 per cent; of oil by 184 per cent; of electricity by 170 per cent; of metal-cutting lathes by 900 per cent; of tractors by 2,700 per cent and automobiles by 2,800 per cent.

Second Five-Year Plan (1933-37). The main task of the second five-year plan of the USSR was "to complete the technical re-equipment of the entire economy and to build a new technical base on heavy industry created in the first five-year plan period."

The second plan again focussed attention on machine-building, electrical engineering, metallurgy and other branches of heavy industries. It was proposed to increase output of engineering industry during the second plan period by 200 to 250 per cent. The engineering industry was to provide machinery for reconstruction of all branches of economy and introduce latest technology. During the second plan period, it was decided to create up-to-date power base to provide electricity to industry and transport and to gradually introduce electricity in the agricultural sector.

The following Table 2 illustrates the progress made by heavy and basic industries in the Soviet Union during the period of the second plan (1933-37).

TABLE 2

Production of Some Key Industries

	1932	*1937*
Pig Iron (million tons)	6.2	14.3
Steel (million tons)	5.9	17.7
Coal (million tons)	64.4	128.0
Oil (million tons)	21.4	28.5
Power (million kwh)	13,500	36,200
Mineral Fertilisers (thousand tons)	921	3,240
Metal Cutting Lathes (thousands)	19.7	48.5
Tractors (thousands)	48.9	51.0
Motor Vehicles (thousands)	32.9	199.9

It was observed that at the end of the second plan period, the Soviet Union had become a mighty industrial state. By 1936 Soviet Union, in respect of industrial output, occupied the first place in Europe and the second place in the world. By 1937, the Soviet economy was well stocked with machinery of various sorts and technical reconstruction was more or less complete making the Soviet Union an advanced and economically independent country. Also during this short period, Soviet railway transport system had become an advanced branch of the national economy.

Third Five-Year Plan (June 1938 to 1941 and War Years 1941-45). During the third plan also "The emphasis was once again on the development of the machine-building industry which was the only means of ensuring the introduction of advanced technology in all branches of the national economy......"[14]

During the third plan period industries that received special attention were: steam turbines, steam boilers, fuel industry, coal and oil, electricity, chemical industry, ferrous and non-ferrous metals, special steels, hard alloys, stainless steel, acid-and-heat resistant tools, ferro-alloys and locomotives.

In order to meet the situation created by the World War II, the third plan came to be replaced after 1941 by a military economic plan. Naturally the Second World War gave a shattering blow to the plan of industrialisation of the country. Thus to take a few examples, the territory occupied by the Germans accounted for 58 per cent of steel, 63 per cent of coal and more than 40 per cent of railways.

The Second World War caused stupendous damage to the Soviet Union's economy.

Fourth Five-Year Plan (1946-50). The objective of the fourth five-year plan naturally was "to restore the country's war ravaged areas, to attain the pre-war level of industry and agriculture and then to surpass the level considerably."

Again the focal point of reconstruction of the economy was industry, particularly heavy industry and transport system of the country. By the end of 1950 industrial production in general had surpassed substantially the pre-war level (1940).

The Fifth Five-Year Plan (1951-55). The fifth five-year plan again emphasised industries and especially heavy industries." The highest rate of growth of 120 per cent was achieved in the fifth-plan period in the engineering industry. Production of oil increased by 87 per cent, of pig iron by 74 per cent of coal by 50 per cent."[15]

The Sixth Five-Year Plan (1956-60). The sixth plan was interrupted after three years and was replaced by seventh five-year plan. The sixth plan therefore only covered the period of 1956 to 1960.

During this period (1956-60) obsolete plants came to be replaced by highly efficient and up-to-date machinery. During this period, the Soviet industry started "serial production of a thousand new types of machines, apparatuses and materials."

The Seventh Five-Year Plan (1959-1965). The seventh five-year-plan had as one of its objectives "all-round development of the productive forces in our country on the basis of the priority expansion of heavy industry..."

The remarkable achievements in the sphere of heavy industries during the Seventh Five-Year Plan period can be seen from the following Table 3.

TABLE 3

	1958	*1965*
Iron Ore (million tons)	88.8	153.4
Pig Iron (million tons)	39.6	66.2
Steel (million tons)	54.9	91.0
Coal (million tons)	493.0	578.0
Gas (million cubic metres)	29.9	129.3
Electricity (million kwh)	235.0	507.0
Mineral Fertilizers (million tons)	12.0	31.6
Machine Tools (thousands)	138.0	185.0
Tractors (thousands)	220.0	355.0

The Eighth Five-Year Plan (1966-70). In the eighth five-year plan, among other objectives aimed at, securing further considerable growth of industry was an important objective. In particular there was to be an improvement in the ratio between the production of capital goods industries (Group A) and the production of consumer goods industries (Group B). The rate of average annual increase of output in Group A industries was to be 8.3 to 8.7 per cent. (In the seventh five-year plan, Group A and Group B industries had increased their production by 58 per cent and 38 per cent respectively; but in the eighth five-year plan these Groups were to increase their production by 49-52 per cent and 43-46 per cent respectively).

"The engineering industry, particularly radio, electronics instrument-making industries and industries producing automation equipment and computers, the chemical and petro-chemical and power-engineering industries registered very high rates of growth. While the overall industrial output went up by 50 per cent, the output of chemical and petro-chemical industries registered an increase of 78 per cent, engineering and metal-working 74 per cent and power engineering 54 per cent. As a result, share of these industries in the total industrial production rose from 28 per cent in 1965 to 33 per cent in 1970."[16]

The production of highly efficient equipment of comprehensive mechanisation of coal-mining was launched. The output of farm machinery was quite impressive. Within the engineering industry itself, machine-tool building occupied an important place. The output of machine-tools increased by 65 per cent between 1966 and 1970. The eighth plan saw also major changes in chemical industry.

But the 24th Congress of the CPSU held in 1971 noted certain shortcomings. Thus the eighth plan target for electric power generation was 830-850 thousand million kwh; but the actual production in 1970 was only 740 thousand million kwh; similarly the production of coal was only 624 million tons as against the target of 665-675 million tons at the end of the eighth plan.

The eighth plan also witnessed measures at technical re-equipment of railway transport on the basis of electrification and wide use of diesel traction.

"Thus even before the ninth five-year plan, the Soviet Union was producing more pig iron, manganese and chromium ore, coal and coking coal, cement, potassium salts, tractors, diesel and electric locomotives ...... than any other country. Fertilizers were added to the list."[17]

"The share of the sector determining technological progress and efficiency of the national economy, as a whole, namely engineering, power, chemical and petro-chemical industries, in the total volume of industrial production went up from 31 per cent in 1965 to 36 per cent by 1970."

The Ninth Five-Year Plan (1971-75). The targets of the ninth plan for total output of heavy industries were surpassed. Thus in 1975, the Soviet Union produced 491 million tons of oil, 289,000 million cubic metres of gas, 701 million tons of coal and 1,038,000 million kwh of electric power. It was observed that swift growth of fuel and basic energy ensured in respect of those goods self-sufficiency, and also enabled the country to fulfil export commitments. The atomic power industry was further developed. The total of 141 million tons of steel was smelt in 1975; production of cement amounted to 122 million tons and 90 million tons of mineral fertilisers. The output of engineering industry increased by 1.7 times which helped further mechanisation, automation and technical level of production. All kinds of transport were further developed during the period of the ninth five-year plan.

The Tenth Five-Year Plan (1976-80). The tenth five-year plan again emphasised scientific and technological progress among other objectives.

It has been proposed that during the tenth plan, heavy industry should retain primacy. Thus it has been planned to increase generation of electricity to 1340-1380 thousand million kwh by 1980; the target for oil output including gas has been fixed at 620-640 million tons by 1980. The gas output is to be increased to 400-435 thousand million cubic meters by 1980, and output of coal production is fixed at 790-810 million tons by 1980.

The following Table 4 gives an idea of output targets of some of the heavy industries during the tenth plan.

TABLE 4

	1975 Actual Production	*1980 Targets*
Coal (million tons)	701	790-810
Oil including Gas (million tons)	491	620-640
Steel (million tons)	141	160-170
Rolled Ferrous Metals (million tons)	98.6	115-120
Mineral Fertilisers (million tons)	90.0	143

Thus the tenth five-year plan has fixed ambitious targets for power industry, oil, gas, coal, ferrous metals, non-ferrous metals, chemicals and petrochemicals, machine-building, power-machine building, heavy engineering and motor transport, vehicle manufacturing and agricultural machine-building industry.

Concluding Remarks. Thus during 1928 and 1979-80, the Soviet Union has transformed itself from backward economy into mighty industrial power. Thus as we have already seen, "The Soviet Union produces more cast iron, steel, oil, iron, manganese and chrome ores, coal and coking coal, cement, tractors (in aggregate engine capacity), diesel and electric locomotives ... mineral fertilisers ... than any other country."[18]

"In 1974 the Soviet Union occupied the first place in the world in the production of oil, including gas condensate, coal, pig iron, steel, iron ore, coke, mineral fertilisers, diesel and electric locomotion, tractors, cement, prefabricated ferroconcrete structures ..."

It should however be noted that while the strategy of rapid economic development through emphasis on heavy industries and capital goods industries (instead of emphasis on consumer goods industries and the agricultural sector of the economy) has brought the Soviet Union on par with the highly industrialised countries of the West, the USA and Japan or even surpass them in many respects (such as space technology), the Soviet Union had to pay a very heavy price for adopting such strategy for rapid economic development.

The above strategy has meant all these years comparative neglect of the Agricultural or primary sector which for long and even to this day continues to be a weak link in the various sectors of the Soviet economy. The agriculture in the Soviet Union is nowhere compared to agriculture in the USA. This has meant that to bring about rapid industrialisation and especially of heavy industries, the Soviet people have had to undergo for long tremendous sacrifices in terms of foodgrains intake, the situation in the agricultural sector often bordering on famine conditions. Even as late as 1974, the Soviet Union had to import foodgrains from the USA and Canada.

Emphasis on heavy industries and the strategy of rapid economic development through capital goods industries also has meant comparative neglect of consumer goods industries. For long the Soviet people have had to live on rations of some essential consumer goods and even at present though the Soviet Union happens to be one of the most highly industrialised countries of the world, the standard of living of the people is low compared to those in the Western European countries, not to speak of the USA.

6. ACHIEVEMENTS IN AGRICULTURE (IN THE USSR) AND ELEMENTS OF AGRICULTURAL PLANNING

In the USSR, agriculture is an important sector of production on which welfare of millions of people depends. It provides food to people in the USSR, various agricultural materials to industries in the country and market for manufactured goods. At present, the agricultural sector contribute about one-third of USSR's annual national income.

(A) Elements of Planning

In the Soviet Union, all land is national property which therefore cannot be bought or sold.

In the USSR agricultural production is organised on the basis of collective farms and state farms. Collective farms have at their disposal about half (223 million hectares) of the country's sown area and happens to be the most important form of organisation in the agricultural sector.

Apart from collective farms and state farms, there is a small 'private sector' in this field. Collective and state farms employees are provided with small household plots (of about half a hectare) on which peasants during their spare hours can raise cattle, vegetables, poultry or even crops, use it for family consumption or sell that in the market and keep such incomes to themselves. Of the total sown land in the USSR, such private plots accounts for about 3.5 per cent of the sown area.

Organisation of a Collective Farm. "A collective farm is a co-operative organisation of peasants who have united voluntarily for purposes of large-scale agricultural production on the basis of socialised means of production and collective labour."[19]

The collective farm which is made up of lands belonging to peasant households which are supposed to be given over to the State for perpetual use. In addition to State-owned land, there are on the collective farm, socially owned tractors, installations, transport facilities, livestock, irrigation installations and so on.

It is observed that each collective farm is guided in its activities by Rules which are based on Model Rules which are approved at the meeting of members on the collective farm. The Model Rules framed in 1969 aim at increasing labour productivity and efficiency of collective farms, increasing output and sales to the State, increasing mechanisation and electrification and widespread application of chemicalisation and land reclamation, working under the guidance of the Communist Party Organisation and to satisfy more fully material and cultural needs of farmers on collective farms and to improve their standard of living.

The Rules have laid down basic principles concerning all activities on collective farms. "The members themselves dispose of all the property of their farm, the output of the farm and money resources. Collective farm incomes earmarked for personal consumption are distributed among the members in accordance with the quantity and quality of work each one has invested in the common enterprise."[20]

All the work on a collective farm is performed by members according to Rules. Each is required to put in minimum labour-hours per year. If necessary, a collective farm can hire specialists.

According to Rules, each peasant household on a collective farm is allotted a patch of land (abour half a hectare) and can own some livestock. A part of the production on these personal plots is used for satisfying consumption needs of the peasant family, while surplus, if any, can be sold in the open market and income kept by the peasant household itself. It is maintained that "The socialised farming and personal plots are not in contradiction but combine the individual interest of the collective farmers with those of society's." (This in effect amounts to introduction of personal profit motive to a limited extent in the USSR agriculture to increase production.)

In 1965 there were in the USSR 36.9 thousand collective farms; in 1975 that number has come down to 29.1 thousand. This decline is due to the fact that collective farms are now much larger with mergers, with larger quantities of machinery and all types of equipment. Wage per man-day (in roubles) has risen from 2.68 in 1965 to 3.90 in 1970 and to 4.60 in 1975.

A typical collective farm today is a large mechanised unit covering, on an average, area of 6,500 hectares, 3,500 of which is under plough. Between 1965 and 1975, the average value of fixed and circulating assets on an average collective farm has increased nearly threefold.

In the USSR, these collective farms are the main producers and suppliers of agricultural produce. They sell bulk of their produce to the State at stable prices and according to stable plans of delivery. The State communicates several years in advance its agricultural requirements. This naturally helps collective farms to plan their production in advance, in the context of State requirements.

"A fixed purchasing plan can be regarded as a kind of an order to the collective farmers by the rest of the community."

The policy of the State is to encourage collective farms to produce more. With this end in view when procurement quotas were fixed in 1965, the State raised procurement prices of various agricultural produce; in 1970 this plan was extended to cover livestock products also. The State also provided additional incentive to collective farms to produce more and become more efficient by lowering the prices of machinery, spare parts and various other inputs required by collective farms.

Organisation of State Farms. The State farms are owned and operated by the State. Obviously all the means of production used on the farm as also the entire output belongs to the State. The workers on State farms are given fixed wages; but like peasant-workers on collective farms, they are also allotted small plots of lands for their personal use.

It is observed that State farms in the USSR are biggest and highly mechanised agricultural units. All the means of production (seeds, fertilisers, pesticides, machinery and so on) are provided by the State out of non-repayable investment funds provided in the annual State budgets. Profits of State farms go to State budgets which also provide for losses, if any.

State farms are operated on the basis of one-man management; there is participation of workers; their trade unions take decisions regarding production and other activities.

At the top of a State farm, there is a director who appoints heads of various departments like workshop, livestock and so on. The director of a State farm is assisted by agronomist, livestock expert, economist, engineer and so on.

Work on the State farm is done on the basis of division of labour. It has about five to six divisions each working under a divisional head.

Each State farm draws its own production plan on the basis of its potentialities. When approved by higher authorities such plans of State farms become part of the national plan.

During the last 10 to 15 years, there has been a steady increase in the number of State farms as also in their fixed and circulating assets. Thus the number of State farms has increased from 11,681 in 1965 to 18,064 in 1975; the number of agricultural workers has increased from 8,230 thousand to 10,320 thousand during the same period. If during 1965, the State farms had 59.7 million hectares under grain crops, by 1975 the figure has gone up to 67.4 million hectares. There is similar increase in the number of various types of machines used on State farms such as tractors, grain harvestors, lorries and so on.

In 1975, the average area in case of a State farm was around 19.1 thousand hectares of which 6.2 thousand hectares was arable land.

It is observed that the State farms are organised as specialised farms producing big marketable surpluses. Some State farms specialise in the production of cereals, others in fruit-growing, dairy and meat products, sheep-breeding, pig-breeding as also in the production of cotton, oil-seeds, tobacco and other crops. It is observed that these State farms account for about 36 per cent of agricultural marketable surplus in the USSR.

State farms usually sell their produce directly to the State through procurement agencies and depots owned by the State. The prices at which different products are delivered to the State are first approved by the government. Some State farms process part of their produce and the processed product is sold directly to the State.

Payment to workers on State farm is on the basis of job-cum-bonus system which takes into account quantity and quality of work of workers and production results.

Each State farm operates on the basis of a five-year and annual plan drafted by itself but approved by the higher authorities who see that they are in consonance with the overall national plan.

'Private Sector'. There is also 'private sector' in the agricultural sector of the USSR economy.

Each peasant household in allotted and permitted to work on a small plot (up to half a hectare) on which the peasant household during spare time can raise what crops or vegetable that it wishes to. It is also allowed to keep one milch cow. The produce on these tiny plots may be used for family consumption or is allowed to freely dispose of in the market, income being kept by the household. As cultivation of these plots is found quite profitable, they are taking much of the time and efforts of the peasant households often at the cost of work on collective farms or State farms where all these peasants are required to put in minimum nmber of hours of work. These garden plots of workers on collective farms and State farms and even of non-agricultural population constitute the 'private sector' in the USSR agricultural sector.

Although these 'private plots' account for only 3 per cent of total cultivated land in the USSR, they contribute about one-third of agricultural output and 12 per cent of marketable output, while claiming about 30 per cent labour-input. The higher efficiency of private sector agriculture in the USSR is due to various factors like private profit motive, and therefore more intensive cultivation of plots, consequent higher productivity of both man and land and concentration of production of high-value products like dairy products, fruits, vegetables, eggs and milk, etc.

(B) Achievements in Agriculture in the USSR

When Stalin prepared plans for rapid industrialisation, he realised that its successful execution would depend upon surplus provided by the agricultural sector both to feed urban population and for export in return for machinery and technology. Stalin therefore in 1929 launched a feverish programme of collectivisation drive. Practically all peasant households were compelled, sometimes with the use of force, to join collective farms, surrendering their lands and other assets. In the long-run these collective farms were to become highly mechanised and efficient units of production. Their main function was to deliver to State foodgrains fairly cheaply as a source for rapid industrialisation. Stalin also compelled peasants to work on collective farms and as they were paid fixed remuneration, they worked reluctantly and inefficiently as there was hardly any connection with quantity and quality of work and remuneration.

The result was not what was expected. The State could obtain large amount of foodgrains at little cost to itself and this helped to finance programme of industrialisation. But the compulsory collectivisation drive also resulted in steep drop in output of agricultural produce and slaughter of livestock. There was steep fall in the consumption level of peasants often leading to famines in the countryside.

The stagnation in the agricultural sector and low level of production with great suffering to peasant households continued until the death of Stalin in 1953.

It is only since 1950s that agricultural production has responded positively to various incentives provided by the State, and output started moving up. From mid-1950s higher prices and better remuneration to workers on collective and State farms have come to be provided to increase agricultural production. Since 1960s workers on collectives and also State farms are guaranteed not only minimum rates of pay but they are eligible for benefits of social security. There was still, until 1960s, considerable poverty among workers on collective farms, considerable inequalities of income, fairly low rates of remuneration, low morale and great amount of mismanagmeent especially by the higher authorities.

The agricultural sector has however risen to higher level of production and efficiency after the World War II, the especially after 1965 before which development of the agricultural sector was sluggish compared to industrial growth in the USSR.

Since 1965 a new strategy came to be adopted in the agricultural sector with emphasis on intensive cultivation, increased mechanisation and chemicalisation. There are still however wide fluctuations in agricultural output due to varying weather conditions. For example, if in 1973 grain output in the USSR was 222.5 million tons, in 1975 which was a drought year, it was only 137 million tons, while in 1976 there was record ouptut of 224 million tons. These wide fluctuations were not all due to faulty management as many Western critics allege, but mainly due to drought and frosts which are a recurrent phenomena in the USSR. The main problem today before the USSR policy-makers is to find varieties of seeds and other crops which can withstand frost and can mature early, and not so much that of organisation.

In spite of various difficulties, Soviet agriculture has made remarkable progress as is evident from the fact that if in 1960s the annual average production was 130 million tons, during 1970s, it is around 180 million tons. It is observed that the USSR has outstripped the USA in respect of butter and milk production within the pace of last 15 years.

However during drought years, the USSR is compelled to import foodgrains from the USA and Canada as it did in 1974 when it imported 7.1 million tons. But it should be noted that, 1974 was a drought year and foodgrains imported were mainly as feedstock for cattle and not for human consumption.

During 1960s agricultural output in the USSR rose at an annual rate of 3.5 per cent while population grew roughly at about 1 per cent per year. This means that foodgrains output is normally much more than required for human consumption and more and more foodgrains are available for human consumption. Import of foodgrains during certain years also becomes necessary because of the Soviet Union's export obligations to East European communist countries.

Thus, though Western critics are making criticism of organisational aspect of USSR agricultural sector because of occasional imports, it should be noted that such imports are only a temporary measure. Also Soviet Union planners through ever increasing investments in the agricultural sector are trying to further raise the efficiency and agricultural output to such a level that even weather conditions should have little impact on agricultural output.

7. BREAK-UP OF THE USSR (THAT IS SOVIET UNION)

The Union of the Soviet Socialist Republic (the USSR or the Soviet Union) underwent cataclysmic political and economic changes by the end of 1991. The architect of 'Glasnost' (*i.e.*, political liberalism) and 'Perestroika' (*i.e.*, economic liberalism) was Mikhil Gorbachev. It was Mikhil Gorbachev who introduced in the former USSR (*i.e.*, Soviet Union) 'glasnost' and 'perestroika'. Gorbachev made an attempt to free the Soviet Union from the ruthless and monolithic strangehold of the communist party on all aspects of lives of the people in all the constituent parts which were held together by the communist party since the October Revolution in 1917.

For three quarter of a century the communist party in the Soviet Union tried to build communist structure of economy as a superior economic system to the Western model of capitalism.

The communist system in the Soviet Union had failed to fulfill to any substantial extent economic aspirations of the people. People of the Soviet Union saw no alternative but to destroy the communist economic system with its highly centralised planning executed by vast bureaucratic machinery under the close supervision of the members of the communist party. As majority of people experienced continual hardships under the communist system of economy, they decided to move away from the communist system and towards free market private competitive system of economy. They had seen the enormous strides made by the free and competitive economy prevailing in West European countries and the United States of America. The West European countries rapidly rebuilt their economies after almost total devastation that was caused by the World War II (1939-45), while the masses in the Soviet Union were languishing in stunted economic growth and relatively unsatisfactory standard of living even four decades after the end of World War II. There was deep despondency among vast masses of people in the Soviet Union and East European communist countries. These people lost confidence in the dictatorial communist economic system. And therefore masses of people rose against the prevailing political and economic system. Thus, people rose against the communist system in Hungary, Poland, Czeckoslovika, Rumania, Bulgaria and even Albenia.

In the USSR (*i.e.* Soviet Union) the outburst of the people against their communist system of economy occurred a little later because the Soviet Union was still considered as one of the two superpowers in the world and also because the country was very large for bringing about sudden political and economic structural changes of fundamental nature. The glasnost (political liberalism) and perestroika (economic liberalism) gave to long oppressed people in the Soviet Union a chance to undo the enormous harm done to their political and economic life by the Communist Party and government which held all the reins of political and economic power in the vast country through extensive bureaucracy working under the direct supervision of members of the communist party. People wanted abolition of the communist party which was always watching people from behind their backs. They also wanted abolition of the communist system of economy.

At the same time people in the Soviet Union had seen that free private enterprise system had proved its efficiency and superiority providing people ever rising standard of living along with political freedom. Economic history of capitalist countries showed that it had adapted itself to changing times and changing demands of people and was getting more and more humanised.

Experience of West European countries and of the United States of America has demonstrated that free market private enterprise economy (*i.e.,* capitalism) can be well combined with political democracy where economic activities can be pursued by people efficiently and for the maximum good of the maximum number of people. It is felt that democratic control and guidance of economic activities under the system of free and competitive economy can provide a strong moral basis to the entire process of economic production and distribution, the end result being established of welfare state.

With the death of Lenin in 1924, Stalin assumed absolute power in the communist party as well as in the government of the Soviet Union. From 1929 to 1953 (*i.e.,* until his death), Stalin ruled over the USSR with an iron hand.

From 1953 to 1964 Nikita Khruschev became the first secretary of the communist party and he was the first to introduce fresh breeze in the Soviet Union by openly denouncing Stalin and Stalinist regime for its ruthlessness and autocracy. But Khruschev's liberalisation measures were spasmodic and peripheral and therefore with little effect on the Soviet economic system.

Khruschev was replaced by Brezhnev who was a hardliner and 18 long years of his rule saw intensification of the cold war between the USSR and the USA. When Brezhnev died in 1982, discontent within the Communist Party and the government was rife. People wanted change from hide-bound communist economic system. But they could not yet express their thoughts openly, having lived in fear for over seventy years. Gorbachev assumed power in 1985. He showed the courage to disband the Communist Party. He introduced in the Soviet Union 'glasnost' and 'perestroika'. He rose to the status of world class leader and was awarded Nobel Peace Prize in 1990 for putting an end to the long prevailing cold war.

In his July 1990 speech, Gorbachev defended his policies of political and economic liberalism which promised to the Soviet people for the first time (after 70 long years of autocratic rule with absolutely no trace of political and economic freedom) political and economic freedom.

Mikhail Gorbachev became the victim of his own liberal political and economic philosophy. When the hardliners from the communist party revolted against the liberal political and economic policies, it was Boris Yeltsin who came forward and with the support of vast masses of people succeeded in crushing the revolt by the reactionary elements in the Communist Party. This resulted in Boris Yeltsin replacing Gorbachev as the leader of the Soviet Union.

The USSR (The Union of Soviet Socialist Republic) or the Soviet Union was having within its boundaries various distinct ethnic, religious and linguistic groups which were held together by the Communist Party through ruthless methods employed by Stalin and Brezhnev. But with the introduction of 'glasnost' and 'perestroika' which represented a march from highly centralised and autocratic economic planning system to free and competitive market economy, the State playing minimum role in the economic activities of the people, the natural consequence was the break-up of the USSR or Soviet Union into autonomous republics numbering 15 (namely, Russia, Ukraine, Kazakhstan, Uzbekestan, Byelorussia, Azerbaijan, Georgia, Moldavia, Lithuania, Kirghizia, Tadzhikistan, Armenia, Latvia, Turkmania and Estonia).

Among the 15 republics into which the USSR or the Soviet Union got disintegrated, Russia is the largest republic occupying out of the total area of 22274500 square kilometres of the USSR, 17075000 square kilometres (*i.e.*, 76.6 per cent of the total area of the USSR), and accounting for 14.2 crore out of 28.7 crore people (which means around 50 per cent of the total population of the USSR). Thus among the 15 republics into which the USSR or the Soviet Union got disintegrated, Russia happens to be, both areawise and population-wise, the largest and most important republic.

Transition from Communism to Capitalism

We shall now concentrate on Russia the largest among the 15 republics into which the USSR got disintegrated. One more important reason for concentrating on Russia is that in his recent visit in January 1993, Boris Yeltsin has signed a treaty with India known as treaty of friendship and cooperation (excluding the security clause which the former treaty between India and the USSR contained). The security clause was excluded from the new treaty between India and Russia because after the end of cold war, the United States of America is the only superpower left in the world.

Transition from highly centralised, autocratic and bureaucracy-dominated communist planned economic system that prevailed in Russia for about 70 years to free and competitive private enterprise economy (*i.e.*, capitalism) is not going to be an easy task. The transition will be full of hazards and pitfalls.

It will necessarily be slow process. For example, Russian agricultural system until 1990 consisted of collective farms and state farms. The problem of distributing such huge farms among large number of individual farmers has no east solution. But land has got to be so distributed and private farmers will have to be provided with all the agricultural inputs at prices which farmers can afford. This will be an extremely complex task. Similarly, State-owned factories and all the factors of production will have to be handed to private individuals and private companies. This will pose enormously big problems which will have to be overcome.

Even as transition from communism to capitalism started from 1990 onwards, Russian economy has been facing severe problems of scarcity of essential commodities like foodgrains.

But the countries of the European Economic Community and the United States are bent on seeing that transition in Russia from communism to capitalism does take place smoothly and quickly and that due to sheer frustration in the case of failure of such transition, Russia does not go back to the old communist system. And therefore, the West European countries and the United States are rushing essential goods as also financial assistance to Russia with a view to make the transition from communism to capitalism as smooth as possible and as early as possible.

India is also eager to see Russia stabilise its new economic system because India very much depends upon Russia for its defence equipment as also because of India's substantial exports go to Russia.

Russia and the 15 autonomous republics into which the former Soviet Union got disintegrated are trying to work out a federal constitution that will hold all the autonomous republics together. As yet the attempt has not succeeded. What shape Russia and the 15 republics, if federated will take in future time alone will show.

REFERENCES

1. '*Socialism*' — Paul M. Sweezy (1949), pages 234-39.
2. *Ibid.*
3. '*Economic System*' — G. N. Halm (Third Edition), page 239.
4. '*Soviet Economic Development and Structure*' — Vinod Mehta, page 229.
5. '*Soviet Economic Development and Structure*' — Vinod Mehta, page 230.
6. *Ibid.*
7. *Ibid.*
8. *Ibid*, page 234.
9. *Ibid*, page 239.
10. '*Soviet Economic Development and Structure*' — Vinod Mehta, page 213.

11. Ludwig Von Mises, 'Economic Calculation in the Socialist Commonwealth' in 'Collectivist Economic Planning' (Edited by F.A. Hayek), pages 104 and 111.
12. Quoted by F. A. Hayek in his '*Road to Saerfdom*', page 89.
13. *Soviet Economic Development and Structure*, — Vinod Mehta, page 114.
14. *Ibid*, page 132.
15. *Ibid*, page 151.
16. *Ibid*, page 175.
17. *Ibid*, page 184.
18. *Ibid*, page 213.
19. '*Soviet Economic Development and Structure*', — Vinod Mehta, page 267.
20. 'The Basic Principles of the Organisation of Soviet Agriculture' — V. Abramov, page 22.

CHAPTER 17

LIBERMAN'S PLAN AND HIS PROPOSALS

1. INTRODUCTION

Experience of authoritarian planning in the Soviet Union showed some grave defects as planning proceeded, especially on the production front. Prof. Evsey G. Liberman made an attempt to analyse and point out these critical defects of the Soviet planned economy and in the Soviet economic structure and also put forward certain proposals to remove those defects with a view to improve the performance of the Soviet economy. These proposals are popularly known as 'Liberman Plan'.

2. LIBERMAN'S CRITICISM OF SOVIET ECONOMIC SYSTEM

Prof. Liberman accepts the Soviet type of planning as also the structure of authoritarian Soviet economy. His criticism is restricted to the production front, and especially to the bonus system of the Soviet economy.

According to Liberman, managers of public enterprises in the Soviet Union occupy the key figure on the production front. According to the bonus system that is prevailing, these managers who are in the know of technological aspects of establishments which they are heading, are forced to misinform the planning authorities about the true potential power of the establishment. They are more likely to understate the potential and overstate their requirements of various inputs and claim bonus for producing more than the target which has been fixed artificially low by the planning commission on the basis of knowledge supplied by the managers. Prof. Liberman wants to think of and introduce a bonus system that would be found to be profitable for managers of public establishments in the Soviet Union to take steps to reduce costs and improve output in the line with the potential capacity existing in the establishment and in line with the realistic targets fixed by the planning body. The idea is to bring about improvement on the production front of the Soviet economy.

According to Prof. Liberman the prevailing Soviet system of economic planning does not trust managers of public establishments. They are considered as people not to be trusted. They are therefore under constant supervision of the central planning authority.

Now it is practically impossible for the central planning authority to supervise all the activities of thousands of managers doing different types of jobs requiring different types of technical knowledge which is often not available with personnel of the supervisory staff of the central planning authority. Thus the work of supervision by the central planning authority is impossible both from physical point of view and also on technical ground. Prof. Liberman therefore pleaded that this type of "petty tutelage over enterprises" should be put an end to. The central planning authority should be freed from this petty job and managers of public enterprises should be freed from the ever-present fear of supervision and punitive action. Prof. Liberman wants such a bonus system that would inspire managers to put their best on their own.

3. PROPOSALS OF PROF. LIBERMAN

Prof. Liberman proposed introduction of an appropriate incentive system based on profits. He favoured retention of the basic levers of centralised planning and he wanted that attempts must be made to attain the centrally fixed targets.

But Prof. Liberman wanted that managers of public enterprises in the Soviet Union should be given more freedom of choice especially in matters of deciding how to produce a commodity, and how to invest portion of funds available to managers. He also favoured direct contact between suppliers and consumers and insisted that only goods sold should be counted for the purpose of attaining of targets. Management of public enterprises were to enjoy certain amount of freedom in devising their own plans on the basis of order received from customers. Once the central planning authority approved the output and delivery plan of an establishment, output and delivery plan was obligatory on the enterprises. Once the central plan approved output and delivery plan, management was to enjoy a certain amount of freedom in formulating their own labour and financial plans, except that the establishment, must conform to official wage-scales. It was not the job of the central planning authority to decide size of wage fund, cost and profit plan and productivity plan of an individual establishment. Prof. Liberman advocated this proposal because he was aware of the tendency of public enterprises to conceal and purposely understate production possibilities and prepare an easily attainable or realisable plan for the establishment. Prof. Liberman wanted that bonus rules should be such that full bonus be paid only taking into consideration planned output and planned profits. He wanted that any output beyond the planned output should be rewarded by bonus at only half-rate. He wanted that amount of retained profit and bonus should depend upon relationship between amount of capital invested in an establishment and profit percentage in relation to capital invested. Prof. Liberman envisaged different profit rates for different industries and different public establishments in view of different amounts of capital invested in them. He therefore envisaged different profit norms for different sectors of the Soviet economy. This was meant to offset 'unearned advantage' of modern equipment or locational advantage that might be available to some establishments. In such circumstances higher profit norms were to be prescribed to neutralise advantage accruing from more capital of locational advantage.

Under the Liberman plan managers of public enterprises could not afford to neglect cost and the revenue side of their enterprise as the enterprise would be penalised by lower rate of bonus. Under the prevailing system, the Soviet economy was ridden with separate incentive bonus payments related to various indices such as output, efficiency, etc. These systems of payment of bonus based on different criteria often overlapped one another. Prof. Liberman summarised all these and linked payment of bonus to an enterprise on the basis of profit which summarises under one heading all the above indices such as output, efficiency, lack of absenteeism, etc.

Prof. Liberman claimed that his proposals, if implemented could result in management making maximum use of productive potential because an enterprise is offered the opportunity of sharing profit. Also, if his proposals are implemented no enterprise would care to over-fulfil its target by first disguising and understating the potential capacity. This is because over-fulfilment would mean sharing of profit at lower rate. This would mean that to achieve high profitability to which bonus of an establishment is related, the establishment would make an effort to make full use of capacity, increase number of shifts, stop asking for additional capital goods, etc., Prof. Liberman's proposals are expected to do away with many of the malpractices in the Soviet economy — understating potential capacity, purposely fixing target at a lower figure, demanding extra units of capital goods, purposely make large inventories of spare parts, etc., and then cross the target overfilling the target. This was because under the prevailing system bonus was related to production exceeding the fixed target.

Prof. Liberman, with a view to encourage introduction of new processes and finding of new products, suggested that profitability norms might be fixed purposely at a lower scale in case of such priority industries.

Government of the Soviet Union accepted Prof. Liberman's proposals in September, 1965.

But not all of Prof. Liberman's proposals are implemented as yet. This is because of the desire of the vast bureaucracy to maintain vast powers of control which they will be losing, if managements of public enterprises are given greater freedom in carrying on their activities.

Also there is opposition on ideological ground to being given greater role to 'profit' which is considered a bourgeoisic concept. The implication of accepting important role of profit, it is feared, might have adverse implications going contrary to principles of socialism. It is feared that "neither the economic bureaucracy nor the local party apparatus is likely to accede gracefully to its own withering away."

But whether due to Prof. Liberman's analysis and above proposals, or due to realisation of defects on the basis of past experience or due to desire to catch up with capitalist countries where technological progress is faster and therefore annual growth rate is higher and material affluence is definitely greater, the Soviet Union as also other communist countries are introducing substantial reforms in their once highly centralised and authoritarian type of economic planning and socialism.

For example in the Soviet Union and also in other communist countries, greater freedom of decision-making and of action is being given to managements of public sector enterprises, though all must work broadly within the framework of the national plan; profit is being assigned more significant role, part of profit being shared by personnel in the establishment under certain circumstances; there is an attempt to provide more and more material incentives, instead of just relying on ideological inspiration; price mechanism is being given increasing role to assess demand of consumers and relate production to consumption; greater role is being assigned to finance and credit instead of condemning money as a capitalist device to exploit workers; closer link is being established between production and distribution through price mechanism in place of physical rationing; and there is now increasing role assigned to foreign trade instead of isolating communist regime from the outside world.

CHAPTER 18

MARKET SOCIALISM AND THE QUESTION OF DECENTRALISATION

1. INTRODUCTION

Two major defects of the centralised or authoritarian type of economic planning of the type adopted in the USSR were:

(1) In the absence of freely fluctuating price-mechanism expressing the preferences of consumers, allocation of the community's resources was arbitrary. This meant allocation of resources did not lead to maximum satisfaction of consumers which after all is and should be the end of all economic activities, whatever the form of the economic system adopted by a country. Thus absence of price or market mechanism led to misallocation of community's resources which meant they came to be utilised inefficiently.

(2) Centralised or authoritarian type of planning as in the USSR led to another serious defect, namely, extreme concentration of the power of decision-making in the hands of a small body which was called upon to take millions of decisions and bring about their co-ordination. In a modern complex economy, this is a super-human task. Such concentration of authority in regard to decision-making and also in regard to all other matters such as allocation of community's resources led to all sorts of difficulties — inordinate delays in decision-making, wrong or contradictionary decisions, absence of co-ordination among different decisions and so on. All this resulted in making working of an enterprise (which had no autonomy) rigid or inflexible and therefore inefficient. The two together made the working of the economy inefficient.

It is in response to the above two problems of centralised or authoritarian type of planning that prevailed in the USSR during 1950s and 1960s that problem or topics of 'Market Socialism' and 'Question of Decentralisation' in planned economies in communist countries assumed importance.

2. MARKET SOCIALISM AND DECENTRALISATION

Is it possible for centralised planning in a communist country to achieve the same type of allocation of resources that would be achieved under competitive capitalism ? If it can, then where is the need to change the economic system if only all that happens is that the Central Planning Authority takes the place of market in competitive capitalism?

According to Oscar Lange, the formal principles of allocation of resources under the socialist and capitalist economy are for all practical purposes the same.

Paul M. Sweezy however feels that Lange's Central Planning Board is not a planning agency in the true sense of the word (deciding the amount of investment out of national income within a given period of time, amounts to be invested in different sectors of the economy, drawing up detailed investment plans in terms of dwelling houses, school-buildings, hospitals, etc., deciding time schedules for commencement and completion of various projects, drawing up schedules of different inputs necessary for fulfilling targets assigned to various sectors and so on), but is only a price fixing agency. In Lange's model, what is to be notice is that various production decisions are left essentially to individual productive units each of which has its own forecasts and estimates. In Lange's model managers who are in charge of various units are however directed to make decisions according to certain rules or within the broad framework of the national plan. Also in the case of Lange's model individual managers make decisions while they are for all practical purposes ignorant of decisions of other managers. It is only through 'step-by-step procedure' that various decisions of different managers come to be woven into a consistent pattern.

Abraham Bergson is critical of Lange's model of market socialism and finds it deficient in a number of ways. According to Bergson, there might be errors concerning forecasts and estimates regarding future market conditions on the part of managers of individual enterprises (even though the Central Planning Authority may establish a channel to provide all possible information to them); secondly, the Planning Board may not be in a position to promptly adjust prices equating supply and demand for different commodities and services on account of dynamic forces affecting supply and demand factors; and thirdly, Lange's trial-and-error method (step-by-step method) is essentially static in nature and would not function effectively in a dynamic economy.

On 'trial-and-error method', Robbins writes: "On paper we can conceive this problem to be solved by a series of mathematical equations ... But in practice the solution would be quite unworkable. It would necessitate drawing up of millions of equations on the basis of millions of statistical data ... By the time the equations are solved, the information on which they are based would have become obsolete and they would need to be calculated anew. The suggestion that a practical solution of the problem of planning is possible on the basis of the Paretian equation simply indicates that those who put it forward have not grasped what these equations mean."

Jan Drewnowski who believes in market socialism and who is dissatisfied with the 'trial-and-error method' of Oscar Lange, has suggested what can be designated as 'dual preference system' in which individual preferences and State preferences working side-by-side can combine to guide the socialist economy.

Jan Drewnowski's 'dual preference system' may best be described in the words of Morris Bornstein:

"In socialism (and also in capitalism), two systems of preferences must be distinguished; the multiple system of individual preference functions of consumers, and the single State preference function. The latter embodies the State economic policy, as formulated by the government and as revealed by its economic activities. In contemporary centrally planned socialist economies, State preferences determine the distribution of resources among consumption, military programmes, and investment, as well as the composition of military and investment output. However, a dual preference exists in the sphere of goods production, where State and individual preferences jointly decide the allocation of resources and distribution of goods."

Drewnowski distinguishes three possible combinations of State (planners') and individual (consumers') preferences, with increasing degree of influence of the latter. In the "first-degree market economy", household possess only consumer choice in the purchase of consumer goods, the quantities of which are fixed by the planners. In the "second-degree market economy", consumer preferences also influence which goods are to be produced, with the resources allocated by planners, by the existing plants producing consumer goods. In the "third-degree markert economy", the pattern of new investments in plants producing consumer goods also responds to consumers' demand. Even in the last case, however, planners' preferences determine the overall magnitude of consumption (its share in national product) and the amount of investment devoted to consumer goods industries. As Drewnowski notes, most of the communist countries are now in transition from a "first-degree market economy" to the "second-degree market economy", extending the sphere of influence of individual preferences somewhat.

As stated above, Drewnowski thinks that there are two preferences, one of the individuals and second preferences of the State, in every type of economic system. While the theory of capitalism is based on one system, namely, preferences of individuals, in the case of the theory of socialism only the system of preferences of individuals cannot be thought of and preferences of the State are bound to play a vital role. The system of State preferences in a socialist State is not derived from preferences of individuals but is based on the national plan and the declared target announced by the State and by the policies implemented by the State.

The crucial problem for the State, according to Drewnowski, is the interaction of individual preferences and State preferences. According to him, there are broadly three zones: (*a*) a zone where the State preferences are supreme; (*b*) a zone where individual preferences are supreme; and (*c*) a zone where the State and individual preferences meet. It is only the third zone indicated above in (*c*) that is of significance to market socialism (the first being of relevance to absolute command economy where goods and services are strictly rationed; and the second is of relevance only to capitalism).

As already noted in the quotation by Morris Bornstein, broadly there are three classes or types of socialist economy. In the case of socialism which is the "first-degree market economy", goods are distributed through market; but quantities produced are not produced according to consumers' demand for them but by the Central Plan. In the case of second type of socialist system identified with "second-degree market economy", whereas the output of goods from the existing productive units is governed by the preferences of consumers as revealed in the market, it is the Central Plan that controls quantities of resources including capital equipment used in their production and the pattern of investment. In the case of a socialist economy which can be identified with the "third-degree market economy", current output of consumption goods as well as investment in plants required to produce consumption goods all come to be influenced by consumer's demand for consumer goods. It is only decisions regarding the aggregate quantity of consumer goods produced and aggregate investment that remain in the State zone.

According to Drewnowski, as a socialist system moves from lower degree of market economy to a higher degree of market economy, individual preferences begin to exert greater and greater influence on goods produced, whereas the place occupied by State preferences and national plan become of less and less significance.

According to Drewnowski, as a socialist system moves, consumers' preferences and State preferences — will be two independent set of prices — one set of prices for State preferences and second for consumer preferences. The 'State prices' will be applicable in the case of all dealings between State enterprises and will be used for the purpose of national accounting. The second set, namely, consumer prices will apply to sales of consumer goods by State enterprises to consumers. The two sets of prices have their own rationality; and the existence of these two sets of prices and their interaction upon each other is a characteristic feature of market socialism.

3. MARKET SOCIALISM AND DECENTRALISATION IN YUGOSLAVIA

Yugoslavia is the first country where 'market socialism' made its appearance. This development took place much before there was any theorising on the subject; it arose as a direct reaction to non-market socialism of the Soviet Union.

The end of the World War II saw the establishment of communist regime in Yugoslavia. But Marshal Tito was too independent minded and instead of acting as a mere satellite of the USSR as many other East European countries did, broke away from the Soviet Union in 1948.

This break from the communist regime in the Soviet Union enabled Yugoslavia to have an objective look at the centralised and authoritative system of planning then prevalent in the Soviet Union. They found it wanting on many scores: inefficient use of resources, neglect of consumer preferences, over-centralisation, over-bureaucratisation, lack of opportunity for workers to get involved in the work of productive units, and therefore feeling of alienation. If Marx's grouse against capitalism was this evil of alienation, it appeared illogical that communism should suffer from the same evil. Also, it came to be observed in Yugoslavia that collectivisation of agriculture based on the model adopted in the Soviet Union had become thoroughly unpopular among Yugoslav peasants and was coming in the way of increasing agricultural efficiency and production.

It was due to the above factors or to remove the above defects that during 1950s and 1960s Yugoslavia, after many trials and errors, introduced the system of 'marketising their command economy' and relatively higher degree of decentralisation to combat over-bureaucratisation and for affording greater opportunities for participation to management and workers, while at the same time preserving the socialist framework of the economy to speed up the economic development.[1]

In Yugoslavia, since 1953 peasants were given permission to leave collective farms if they wished; since then private sector in agriculture in Yugoslavia went on expanding covering nearly 90 per cent of arable land, though it declined to 85 per cent by 1970. Only 15 per cent of arable land is covered by collective farms and State farms. Private peasant farms are normally limited to 10 hectares; otherwise there are no other restrictions on operations of peasants.

Private sector operations are also allowed in non-agricultural sectors such as small-scale production and trading; the only restriction is that no more than five persons (excluding family members) should be employed in such private units.

With the above exceptions, all enterprises in Yugoslavia come within the 'socialist sector'. It is in the socialist sector that the most distinctive feature of the Yugoslav communist economy, namely, "Workers' Management" is found. "The basic idea is that the workers (including white-collar employees) of an enterprise, though not its legal owners, have the ultimate authority for its affairs as well as a financial stake in the results of its operation." Workers' management is an attempt to introduce industrial democracy, use potentialities of workers for their own and social good by increasing their efficiency, bring about decentralisation in decision-making and authority, and get workers involved in the enterprise, thus reducing or eliminating the feeling of alienation.

It is obvious that "workers' management" cannot be meaningful until enterprises enjoy certain amount of 'autonomy'. In Yugoslavia this is achieved by "relating the firm to the economy by means of the market mechanism rather than by the Soviet-type command hierarchy." The management board of an enterprise consists of elected representatives of its own employees and is responsible to workers' council, itself elected by all the workers of the enterprise. The day-to-day management is in charge of a manager or a director. He looks after the day-to-day management and he submits his reports to the management board and has the power to overrule in the event of conflict with law.

Workers' earnings are fixed by workers' council of each enterprise and come from net income of the enterprise itself, though the State has fixed minimum earnings for workers.

In the case of establishment of a few enterprise, it may just be a 'spin off' by an existing enterprise; or the initiative may come from the State government which may make necessary funds available to the new enterprise; or the initiative may come from the commune (*i.e.*, local government) since profits of an enterprise is a major source of revenue for local government, or the idea of the local government may provide increasing employment opportunities to people in the commune or to increase supply of certain goods to people in the commune or merely for the sake of increasing prestige. In such enterprises sponsored by a commune or local government, investment funds come from resources of the commune as also from various investment banks and from the State government.

In Yugoslavia people enjoy freedom as consumers and also in regard to choice of jobs, and there is considerable amount of household freedom. In these spheres market mechanism operates on the whole along familiar lines. Individual enterprises are guided by market signals, primarily prices which help their determining output, inputs, amount to be invested, choice of technique of production, etc. Activities of all enterprises also come to be co-ordinated essentially by market mechanism. All this is in sharp contrast with the principles of command economy of the USSR. It is interesting to note that in Yugoslavia during the last 20 years, market mechanism is being allowed increasing role in the economy in place of administrative directives and controls. There is increasing belief that 'marketisation' of the economy leads to increasing efficiency; and therefore this belief is leading to increasing autonomy to individual enterprises, especially in the matter of retaining proportions of their income for purposes of internal investment. There are however some restrictions on capital flows as the State does not want to replicate 'capitalism'.

With wider marketisation, the Yugoslav economy is subject to various evils such as monopoly, excessive earnings of workers of monopolistic enterprises, higher prices and misallocation of resources. But Yugoslav government has not been taking determined steps to combat these evils and put restriction on competition.

Another evil that has made its appearance in Yugoslavia is inflation which is the concomitant of development. In such cases the State resorts to price controls which naturally distorts balance between demand and supply of goods and services, distorts investment pattern and hampers autonomous working of enterprises. But unlike in the USSR where price control is a permanent feature, in Yugoslavia, it is regarded only as an emergency measure.

It is observed that labour market in Yugoslavia exhibits some distinct features. There are no nominal wages for workers who however are paid shares of the net income of their respective enterprises instead of wages and salaries. This implies that workers employed in similar establishments may be remunerated unequally depending upon the net income position of individual enterprises. This may be in accord with the principle of workers' management and provide incentives to workers to increase their efficiency but such an arrangement of remuneration has resulted in inequalities in earnings of labour which are often thought of as not equitable.

Trade unions do exist in Yugoslavia in spite of worker's management. But their main job is not collective bargaining but removal of worker's grievances. On the national level trade unions sometimes press claims for increasing the proportion of national income for consumption.

Role of Planning. As market economy started taking place of command economy in Yugoslavia, the role of economic planning has got changed considerably. The one-year plans giving detailed directions and targets to each individual enterprises as in the USSR have disappeared. Five-year plans has remained; but it has become 'indicative' planning, combining government programmes and forecasts for the rest of the economy. "Thus, planning in Yugoslavia is much more similar to that in France than to that in the USSR, although in the relative extent of its publicly owned sector it is much closer to the latter than to France"[2].

Concluding Remarks. Thus since 1950s ownward, communist Yugoslavia has developed what may be called 'market socialism' with decentralisation and workers' management within the broad framework of national planning. The Yugoslav experiment of market socialism with workers' management and decentralisation has clearly shown that the market socialism is workable and possess some marked advantages over the centralised type of command economy in the USSR. Some of the important advantages of the market socialism of Yugoslavia as compared with the command economy of the USSR are as follows:

1. On account of the operation of market mechanism, there is faster and better co-ordination or adjustment between demand and supply of consumer

goods and services and greater attention to consumer preferences within the limits allotted to the production of consumer goods.

2. This implies that consumers under Yugoslav market socialism enjoy greater freedom of choice.

3. There is greater initiative on the part of both consumers and productive enterprises because of the system of workers' participation in management.

4. Though there is still authoritarian political control over all the facets of life in the society, market socialism in Yugoslavia has resulted in less administrative pressures by the State and therefore much more relaxed atmosphere, both among consumers and among employees in enterprises.

5. Yugoslav system has resulted in avoidance of wastes arising out of collective farming of the USSR type and greater provision of incentives of farmers to produce more agricultural commodities.

6. There is also significant measure of democratic management or industrial democracy not only in private sector enterprises but even in public sector industrial enterprises and greater welfare measures for workers.

But the Yugoslav experiment has had to face certain problems. It has not always been possible to reconcile national objectives with decentralised management. This has meant frequent revision of some institutions and policies and also maintenance of some strong central controls over vital matters.

It is observed that Yugoslav economy has not been too doctrinaire compared to other communist countries. The country has managed to achieve a growth rate which is one of the fastest in the world. Thus during 1950 and 1970, the average annual growth rate has been 5.6 per cent and about 4.5 per cent per capita. The Yugoslav market socialism has functioned reasonably well bringing both rapid growth and also technological and organisation innovations, greater satisfaction of consumer demand, and flexible adaptation of the economy to export requirements. It is claimed in the above three respects (consumer satisfaction, growth with technological innovations and meeting export requirements) that Yugoslav economy appears to have functioned better than command economies of other communist countries. And of course, the institution of "workers' management" occupies a pride of place in the Yugoslav economic system.

Thus Yugoslavia, through its market socialism and decentralisation, provides an alternative working model of socialism in place of command economy of other communist countries.

REFERENCES

1. In 1967 Czechoslovakia and in 1968 Hungary adopted the system of market socialism. But Soviet invasion of the former hardly gave any scope for the reform there, while in Hungary market socialism is very much a going concern, in spite of Soviet Union's opposition.
2. '*Economic Systems*' — Gregory Grossman (Second Edition), page 157.

CHAPTER 19

MIXED ECONOMIES AND THEIR PROBLEMS

Why Mixed Economy?

Many countries have accepted in recent years what may be called a mixed economic system. Before examining the characteristics of a mixed economic system, it would be instructive to know why many countries have come to accept this model of economic system.

It has been observed that generally up to the beginning of World War I many countries had come to accept what roughly may be called *laissez faire* capitalism. No doubt capitalism has certain inherent merits such as provision of powerful incentive of personal or private profit, competition and therefore efficient use of resources, increasing opportunities for individuals and rising standards of living, creation of environment leading to technological progress in the community, flexibility and adaptability to changing circumstances and above all enjoyment of personal freedom as consumers and as producers.

But as noted already, it had become obvious that capitalism (and especially *laissez faire* capitalism) resulted in certain grave evils such as great inequalities of income and wealth, emergence of monopolies, wastes of monopolies and competition, failure to provide full employment, great instability, general disregard and indifference to social welfare, and increase in inequalities of income and wealth leading to division of society into two classes of 'Haves' and 'Have nots,' and mutual tensions and conflicts between the two, leading to social and political instability.

Thus as Kenneth K. Kurihara has observed:

"On the one side, there is a policy of *laissez faire* designed to leave individual economic decisions and activities entirely unchecked even when these activities lead to general instability, insecurity and inequity. Here economic man is assumed to be so rational, economic calculus so precise, economic machinery so efficient and private property so sacrosanct that inferentially almost nothing and nobody should be subjected to public control. Here is the one extreme case of statecraft where individual liberty is misconstrued as individual licence, where political democracy is undermined by economic anarchy, where private virtues are mistaken for public good, and where private initiative is misinterpreted as a sufficient as well as necessary condition for economic and social progress."[1]

J. M. Keynes who contributed substantially to the emergence of mixed economy wrote: "The world is not so governed from above that private and social interests always coincide. . . It is not a correct deduction from the principles of economics that enlightened self-interest always operates in the public interest; nor is it true that self interest is generally enlightened. More often individuals acting separately to promote their own ends are too ignorant or weak to attain even these."

The alternative to capitalism came to be advocated in the form of socialism or communism which evoked great response in the beginning. Some of the features such as public ownership of means of production, concern for social welfare instead of personal or private profit, economic planning providing for full employment, equitable distribution of income and wealth, economic stability and creation of classless society greatly attracted the attention both of the intellectuals and of the masses.

But in course of time, evils of socialism or communism came to the surface. For example, as already seen, it meant complete suppression of individual freedom both as consumer and producer under authoritarian planning, preponderance of bureaucratic regime with all the evils of bureaucracy (namely, complicated rules and regulations, red-tape, delay, difficulty of fixing responsibility in case of failure), lack of proper incentives and therefore general inefficiency in the use of resources.

Thus as K. K. Kurihara has observed: ". . . There is a policy of authoritarian planning aimed at organising individual economic units into classes for central control at the calculated risk of class wars, partisan strife, personal or individual hatred. Here central authority is assumed to be so anti-social and public ownership so indispensable that, by implication, almost everything and everybody should be subjected to public control. Here is the other extreme case of statecraft where economic planning is abused by political totalitarianism, where national interest is misrepresented by class interest, and where public policy is misinterpreted as self-sufficing."[2]

"It was as offering a better alternative to those extreme types (namely *laissez-faire* capitalism and communism) that Keynes conceived his mixed statecraft."[3]

Thus 'Mixed Economy' is an economic system, which combines some of the features of capitalism and of socialism or communism. Mixed economic system is a system which tries to combine the virtues of capitalism and communism and at the same time tries to avoid evils associated with both those economic systems.

1. CHARACTERISTICS OF MIXED ECONOMY

Mixed economy may be said to be a 'Compromise System' lying between the two extreme systems of organising society, namely, *laissez-faire* capitalism (emphasising individual freedom, institution of private property, personal profit motive, competition and *laissez-faire* or non-interference) on the part of the State in the economic affairs of the people with the belief that if each individual is left to himself, he would strive to realise his maximum satisfaction and when each individual does that, maximum satisfaction or welfare of society would be automatically realised, and socialism or communism (emphasising collective ownership of the means of production, emphasis that the State or society is the best judge of individual and social welfare and not the individual who requires guidance from the State, possibility of conflict between individual interest and social welfare and therefore centralised economic planning with a view to make the best use of community's resources on a pre-determined basis to realise the well-thought out and planned objectives and targets with a view to maximise social welfare).

Thus while mixed economy appreciates the role of self-interest and private profit, of the institutions of private property and competition in bringing about rapid economic development, efficient use of resources and rising standard of living of the masses as evidenced in West European countries, mixed economy also recognises that self-interest may run counter to social welfare, that competition may be disadvantageous to those without productive assets, specialieed skills and the poor, that competition may lead to private monopoly with all the evils associated with monopoly and that *laissez faire* policy may result in neglect of welfare of society.

Mixed economy while providing scope for private enterprise also stipulates that self-interest should reconcile itself to social welfare; while competition is permitted to some extent, it should not lead to monopoly; while personal freedom is ensured, care is taken to see that it does not degenerate into irresponsible personal licence to do what one wishes irrepective of its effects on social welfare.

Mixed economy may be said to have emerged out of the disenchantment with *laissez-faire* capitalism (and especially the shock in capitalist countries of the Great Depression of 1929-33) on the one hand, and on the other hand, disenchantment with communism which was tried in the USSR during the Stalinist regime with its most authoritarian planning, administrative control and ruthless suppression of individual freedom in the economic sphere reducing individual to the status of just a clog in the huge State's economic administrative machinery.

Keeping the above background in mind, it would now be easy to analyse the characteristics of a mixed economy.

The following are the important characteristics of a mixed economy or a mixed economic system:

1. *Co-existence of both Private Sector and Public Sector in the National Economy.* The most important feature of a mixed economy is the co-existence in the national economy of both private and public sector. Existence of a small private sector and substantial public sector does not cannote a mixed economy. Both sectors should be substantial and should be functioning vigorously. It should be noted that private sector in a mixed economy does not exist by sufferance or inability of the State to run business units in that sector. Private sector in some spheres come to be accepted because of its inherent strength. Psychologically people and the State come to accept the co-existence of substantial private sector and substantial public sector. The State clearly demarcates fields open to the two sectors. Generally in a mixed economy agriculture, large-scale industries, producing consumer goods, small-scale and cottage industries, retail trade etc., are left in the private sector, whereas basic and heavy industries, and other strategic sectors of the economy such as banking, transport, energy, etc., happen to be in the public sector. The idea behind the co-existence of these two sectors is to enable the mixed economy to enjoy the fruits of private sector as also of public sector through which attempt is made by the State to have general and strategic control over the national economy.

2. *Existence of Economic Planning.* Concept of a mixed economy does not merely mean that the State gives up the policy of *laissez faire*; it also does not mean that the Government tries to regulate the economic activities only through means such as monetary, fiscal and international trade policies involving various controls. If in a mixed economy private sector and public sector are allowed to go their own way, the two sectors might function in contrary ways and that might result in economic chaos. Mixed economy (where both sectors exist) automatically implies that both the sectors would be required to function in properly co-ordinated manner. This means mixed economy is characterised by economic planning which is not of the authoritarian and comprehensive type as in the USSR but which nonetheless lays down the broad framework within which the economy as a whole is expected to function to realise specific goals of which social welfare is one of the most important one.

3. *Combining Some Features of Capitalism with Some Features of Socialism.* In a mixed economy freely fluctuating price-mechanism is allowed scope in the case of most of the consumer goods industries; but in the case of their unusual scarcities, their prices are controlled and their distribution may also be rationed. Also along with freely fluctuating price-mechanism, in the case of goods and services produced and distributed by public sector industries and enterprises, prices are generally regulated or are administered prices. Thus mixed economy is characterised by both freely fluctuating price-mechanism and a system of administered prices.

Similarly while industries and industrial establishments in the private sector are allowed freedom to operate, the Government puts restrictions on their functioning as regards rates of wages, conditions of work, rates of dividend to be paid to shareholders, their anti-social activities and so on. Thus in a mixed economy while private sector is allowed to operate, it has to operate within the broad framework fixed by the State in the general interest of the society.

Also, while mixed economy accepts public sector, care is taken to see that it is not the only sector and that it does not encroach on the field reserved for the private sector unless under extraordinary circumstances.

Though a mixed economy accepts economic planning, care is taken to see that the planning is not authoritarian and comprehensive type of planning destroying all personal initiative, private property and personal freedom as consumers and producers.

The underlying idea is to retain useful features of capitalism and those of socialism and bring about their happy marriage.

4. *Government's Positive Role.* Mixed economy definitely means abandonment of the policy of *laissez faire* on the part of the State. But that does not mean that the State interference in the economic affairs and activities of the people is casual or occasional or intermittent. The State makes conscious effort by using various positive and negative instruments at its disposal to direct the economic activities of the people and thus the national economy towards predetermined goals. But though there is State interference in the economic sphere, in a mixed economy, this State interference is not all comprehensive and total so as to completely crush individual initiative, their competitive spirit, their innovative abilities and personal freedom. The State policy in this regard is to combine in a balanced way State interference and individual freedom.

From the above characteristics of mixed economy, it should be obvious that mixed economy is the 'Middle Way' lying between *laissez-faire* capitalism and socialism or communism, aiming at combining the best features of both and at the same time avoiding the defects of both those economic systems.

2. ROLE OF THE PUBLIC SECTOR

After the publication of the *General Theory* of J. M. Keynes, and especially after the end of World War II, public sector appears to be assuming increasing importance. Thus in England, coal, iron and steel industries were all nationalised; and the same is true in respect of France where the public sector happens to be contributing about 20 to 25 per cent annually of the national product.

Most of the Third World countries which became independent after the Second World War and which have all been suffering from unemployment, underdevelopment and mass poverty have all started to develop their economies by adopting economic planning wherein expanding public sector has been expected to play a more and more prominent role. Thus in the case of India public sector has expanded considerably. For example, if in 1951, there were only 5 public sector enterprises (apart from railways, post and telegraph, etc.) involving only an investment of Rs. 29 crores; at present there are more than 200 public sector enterprises involving total investment of more than Rs. 1 lakh crores. Thus by the Industrial Policy Resolution of 1956 heavy and basic industries such as iron and steel, heavy chemicals, metallurgical industries, heavy engineering industries, generation and distribution of electricity, atomic energy have all been reserved for the public sector. Not only that but the Government of India has also entered the field of consumer goods industries like bread and hotelling (*e.g.* Asoka Hotel at Delhi).

The following is the role which the public sector is expected to play in developing countries.

1. *Rapid Economic Development.* Rapid development of backward countries, it is felt, can be brought about only by rapid expansion of the public sector. Reliance on private sector or private enterprise for the establishment and development of heavy industries would not be appropriate because private enterprise may not be in a position to raise huge investments needed to start heavy and basic industries which also require long gestation period before they begin to yield profits. In backward countries State alone is in a position to mobilise required funds and wait for long period for profits to arise.

The State by starting heavy and basic industries is in a position to provide infrastructure facilities needed for the development not only of public sector enterprises but also for industries in the private sector.

Public sector (banks for example) is in a position to mobilise resources and invest them in priority or neglected sectors development of which is necessary both to provide increasing employment opportunities and accelerate economic growth. Private sector financial institutions may not be forthcoming to invest in such field for feat of initial loss or lower rate of profit which they might expect to make.

2. *Reduction of Extreme Inequalities in Income and Wealth.* By nationalising heavy and basic industries, it is possible to prevent profits from such industries going into the pockets of a small rich section of the community who happen to hold large proportion of shares of such industries. Also nationalisation of such industries would mean that their huge profits would go to public exchequer and those funds can be used for the betterment of the lives of poor masses. Thus public sector can be effective instrument of reducing extreme inequalities of income and wealth.

3. *Controlling Level of Economic Activities.* Nationalisation of basic and heavy industries gives government control over strategic heights of the economy through which it becomes possible for the government to control the level of activities in the economy.

Thus during period of slump when private enterprise is unwilling to invest and take risks because of falling prices, government may be unable to persuade private enterprise to increase their investments through appropriate fiscal and monetary policies by offering concessions. Under such circumstances when the level of activities is low or sagging, government which is not much concerned with profit or losses can afford to come forward and push up the rate of investment (if necessary by deficit financing) in nationalised industries. This by multiplier effect will raise the level of economic activities in the economy.

If on the other hand there are inflationary pressures operating in the economy and the economy is overheated and there is hoarding and speculation, the government under such circumstances can reduce its investment in nationalised industries and with multiplier now operating in the reverse manner, the government may be in a position to contain inflationary pressures. Thus through nationalised industries, the government will be in a position to control or influence the level of economic activities in the economy.

4. *Developing those Sectors where Private Enterprise may not Enter.* There are certain industrial enterprises which are very important for the general economic development of a country. But such ventures like large irrigational projects, iron, steel and heavy metallurgical industries, heavy engineering works or heavy chemical establishments, oil exploration, fertilisers, mineral exploration, etc., require huge investment funds and also have long gestation period; often the element of risk is also great. The private enterprise guided by the consideration of making maximum profit in as quick a time as possible, is not likely to take initiative and enter these fields which therefore may remain underdeveloped hampering the development of the entire economy.

Under such circumstances State has to come forward, take initiative and undertake investment, in these industries, if necessary by creation of more money and importing skilled experts. The State is in a position to do this because it is not concerned mainly with short-term consideration of making profits or suffering losses. It has to and can take long-term perspective. Public sector has thus a vital role to play especially in backward countries in the above fields from which private enterprise either because of lack of enterprise, or skilled workers, or inability to raise funds or take risks, is likely to shy away.

5. *Rendering Assistance to Private Sector Enterprises*. Public sector (*i.e.*, the State) is in a position to play active role in assisting private enterprise which otherwise is likely to work under severe handicaps. Thus by providing cheap electricity, fertilisers, seeds, the public sector can help private enterprise in the agricultural sector. Similarly by importing necessary machinery and providing raw materials purchased in bulk by public sector enterprises, small-scale industries and cottage industries can be helped and be enabled to stand on their own feet; otherwise they may not be in a position to do this. As the State is the guardian of the nation's economy, it is in a position to undertake this work which if left to private enterprise may not be done equally satisfactory. We have in

India instances where private enterprise dealing with fertilisers and seeds provided adulterated stuff with adverse effect on agricultural growth in some regions.

6. *Public Enterprise as Source of Funds.* Public sector enterprises can be an important source of funds to the government. Not all public sector enterprises may yield profits especially in the short term and some even in the long run. But by carefully evolving and implementing suitable pricing policies in the case of some public sector enterprises, they can be made to yield substantial funds to the government which can be used for reinvestment or for other public welfare measures. This would be welcome instead of such profits going into the pockets of private individuals.

7. *Mobilising and Diverting Funds in Proper Channels.* Another objective or role of public sector financial institutions such as the IDBI, the Industrial Finance Corporation, the State Financial Corporations, the L.I.C. and the 20 nationalised commercial banks is to help mobilise financial resources in the community and to regulate and control flow of investment funds in different sectors of the economy according to plan priorities and in such a manner as would help development of industries needed for acceleration of the growth rate of the economy, or industries as would fill the gap in the existing structure of the economy or as would help promote export of goods enabling the country to earn much-needed foreign exchange.

8. *Public Sector and Anti-Monopoly Measures.* There are certain industries where if private enterprise is allowed, the result might be a monopoly which might purposely curtail production, raise prices and exploit consumers thus making enormous monopoly profits. This is possible in the case of those industries the demand for whose products is inelastic *(e.g.,* transport and communications, electricity, medical drugs and so on). Mere putting restrictions on such monopolies by the government to curtail the evil practice of these private monopolies is not likely to succeed as the experience of anti-monopoly legislation in the USA during the last half of the century (since the days of Sherman Anti Monopoly Act) has shown. The only answer to the emergence of such monopolies in vital industries is to nationalise such concerns. It is possible that nationalisation of such industrial establishments may not result in higher efficiency; or in fact efficiency may be reduced. But anyway the exploitation of consumers and monopoly profits going into the pockets of a few individuals would be stopped. By preventing growth of private monopolies, expanding public sector would prevent the growth of concentration of economic power in a few hands with all its social and political evil consequences.

9. *Public Sector as an Instrument of bringing Balanced Regional Development.* In the case of private sector, industries tend to move to those centres or regions which are already well developed and therefore where finance, transport and other infrastructure facilities are already available. At such developed centres, new industries will find that unit cost of production is

lower than in backward regions where various infrastructure facilities are not available. Due to this factor and also because of external economies, there is always tendency towards industrial and commercial concentration on the part of private enterprise. This will only increase regional imbalances, the backward regions remaining backward or in fact becoming more backward as savings and young and energetic youth from those areas are likely to move away to centres which are well developed as they offer increasing employment opportunities.

Public sector can act as an important instrument of removing regional imbalances. Government not obsessed by profit motive can establish giant industrial establishments in backwards regions, using local raw materials and workers and if necessary by providing rationing opportunities for them. Establishment of a giant industrial unit in a backward region will result in establishment of various ancillary industries and thus there will be forward and backward linkage-effects which would help raise the region from its economic backwardness. For example, the Government of India has been trying this policy in economically backward States of Bihar, Orissa, Assam and Rajasthan.

10. *Promoting Self-Reliance.* Another role expected of the public sector is to promote and achieve self-reliance in various modern technologies for designing and development of skills so as to enable the country to lessen and eventually eliminate dependence on foreign countries in such vital matters because such dependence is likely to harm the economic and political interests of the country in case of certain eventualities.

11. *Public Sector and Conservation of Natural Resources.* Public sector or nationalisation may by following suitable policy help conservation of natural resources such as minerals and oils the stock of which is exhaustible. If private enterprise is allowed in these spheres, with a view to make maximum profit in as short a time as possible, it will exploit these exhaustible resources in a ruthless manner without caring as to whether they will get exhausted sooner or later and for possible consequences of their exhaustion for the future. If government steps in and if public sector enterprises are put in charge of such exhaustible natural resources, they will plan their rational use on long-term basis, avoiding all possible misuse and wastages. Such a perspective planning in the use of valuable and exhaustible natural resources like rare metals and petroleum oil will be possible only by nationalising establishments in such fields.

12. *Public Sector and Strategy for Planned Rapid Economic Development.* Developing countries like India have adopted economic planning as an important means to attain as quickly as possible various socio-economic objectives like accelerating the rate of economic development, reduction of inequalities of income and wealth, attaining self-reliance or even self-sufficiency in respect of certain essential industries or goods, bringing about balanced regional development, helping upliftment of tribals, providing increasing employment opportunities and so on. Now the government will not be in a

position to realise these socio-economic objectives by merely relying on the private sector. This would mean that existence of expanding public sector becomes an important part of the planning strategy of backward economies. Without this strategy (*i.e.*, bringing into existence expanding public sector in a systematic way), planning process will not succeed in attaining the various objectives mentioned above.

13. *Public Sector as a Model Employer.* All backward countries have come to realise that rapid industrialisation is essential to enable those countries to make the best use of their potential, natural and human resources, to provide increasing employment opportunities, to produce more wealth and bring about increase in the standard of living of the people. Along with the development of agricultural sector, development of industries is deemed essential to lift backward countries from their centuries-old economic stagnation.

Rapid industrialisation requires training facilities for workers, development of various modern technical skills, research and above all maintaining good industrial relationship and industrial peace in the country without which industrialisation will be hampered at every stage.

Government enterprises which are not over-obsessed with profit consideration and with pretty abundant funds and other resources can create ideal working conditions for workers and set a model of a good employer — a model which is bound to influence conditions in private establishments, all this leading to good and healthy industrial relations and rapid industrialisation and economic development. Public enterprises can afford to start research wings and help advancement of industrialisation which private establishment with limited funds and objective of maximising profit in the briefest possible time generally do not undertake.

Concluding Remarks. From the above analysis it is clear that public sector has a vital role to play in developing economies.

Thus in brief the role of public sector in developing economies is: (*a*) to promote rapid economic development by effectively mobilising resources, (*b*) to fill-up gaps in the industrial structure of the economy and thus remove the possible bottlenecks likely to obstruct industrial and economic growth, (*c*) to initiate, undertake and manage economic activities which are of strategic importance to the growth of the national economy, (*d*) to ensure balanced regional development by bringing about decentralisation of industries, (*e*) to bring about reduction of inequalities of income and wealth, (*f*) to reduce concentration of economic power in a few hands with disastrous social, economic and political consequences, (*g*) to effectively mobilise and channelise investible funds through public sector financial institutions, as per the plan priorities, (*h*) to achieve self-reliance in such vital matters as technology, designing, technological knowhow, apart from heavy machinery essential for rapid economic development, (*i*) to create increasing employment-multiplier effect, and (*j*) to establish and promote such industries as could promote exports enabling the country to earn much-needed foreign exchange.

Role of Public Sector in Developed Countries. But it should also be noted that public sector is also expanding in developed economies of the West. There public sector plays vital role by helping to overcome cyclical booms and depressions, by helping to stabilise the economy at the level of full or near-full employment, in reducing inequalities of income and wealth, in bringing about development of backward region (as in the case of Tennessee Valley Project in the USA) and for mobilising resources for pushing up the rate of investment and thus of growth.

This should make clear the fact the public sector is called upon to play and is playing a vital role both in developing as also in developed countries.

Criticism against the Public Sector (or Arguments against Nationalisation)

Introduction. Though in the first flush of enthusiasm many developed countries (with the notable exception of the USA) and almost all developing countries came to adopt expanding public sector as an important or even vital part of plan or economic strategy to achieve various socio-economic goals, in course of time experience has brought out certain evils or defects or deficiencies that have got associated with nationalisation (*i.e.*, public sector) with the consequence that the process of nationalisation (*i.e.*, expansion of public sector) has in most countries appears to have slowed down. Anyway, public sector has come to stay, and if it is to be made to work efficiently and to enable it to realise the various goals set before it, it is essential to know the defects or evils that have come to be associated with it so that steps can be taken to remove them.

Public sector has come to be associated with the following defects:

1. *Inefficient Management.* It is a common experience that public enterprises are not efficient as similar enterprises in the private sector. There are various reasons for that. Even when the management of a public enterprise is entrusted to an autonomous body, the conduct of officials and other employees is governed by complex set of rules and regulations so that it is not easy to remove (as in a private sector establishment) any official or employee, even if found inefficient. Detailed rules and regulations bring in bureaucratic management with all the defects of delay, red-tape and difficulty of fixing responsibility and of taking action against any individual for any default.

Inefficiency of a public sector enterprise is also due to lack of personal profit motive. The rules govern salary, bonus and other emoluments to which every employee is entitled, even if he puts in just minimum work. There is hardly any incentive in the form of more remuneration for more work in the public sector enterprises or recognition and reward for merit.

Another reason for inefficiency is political interference in the management and working of public enterprises. There is often too much of political interference from the members of the party in power. Also, appointments are made on political grounds, so are promotions. Then often management is elected on political grounds and employees happen to be the voters. Managing bodies are therefore influenced by political considerations rather than economic and technological in managing the public enterprise. No wonder public enterprise does not show as much efficiency as private enterprise.

2. *Inability or Unwillingness to Take Risks.* Public enterprises are run by management personnel who are paid according to fixed scales. They are therefore unlikely to take any risk which must be taken in any business, if it is to prosper. Their attitude is that of indifference. If the risk is successfully borne and the public enterprise makes extraordinary profit, the person concerned or management is not going to get any extra remuneration; if on the other hand the risk results in a loss, the person or management will certainly be blamed for such a failure. So the attitude is to play safe. For the same reason, no worthwhile research and development efforts take place in public sector enterprises as that involves undue risk, which the management is loath to take.

3. *Political Interference.* The accountability of public sector management is ultimately to political authority. This implies that the management cannot afford to displease their political bosses. This opens a floodgate of political interference not only in matters of appointment of higher officials but even of employees of lower grade and interference even in day-to-day affairs of the public enterprises with the cumulative result of increasing inefficiency.

4. *Wastages and Corruption.* Availability of plentiful funds from the government at concessional rates, political interference, maze of complex rules and regulations, difficulty in regard to taking quick action against defaulters, limited power of management in matters of promotion, demotions and punishments — all result in over capitalisation of public enterprise, longer gestation period than in the case of similar private sector enterprise, huge inventory stocks to play safe, wasteful use of resources, tremendous amount of bribery and corruption, labour indiscipline, nepotism in respect appointments and promotions, corruption while purchasing various inputs required or while giving subcontracts and so on. All this amounts to waste of nation's resources which goes on in a very large way in most public sector enterprises.

5. *Lack of Competent Personnel.* Most of the developing countries have launched ambitious programme of expanding public sector by establishing more and more units in various basic and heavy industries. But most of these developing countries lack top level or even middle level managerial and technical personnel with the consequence that in India very often for months on end, dozens of large public sector enterprises were functioning without top managing executives, which posts could not be filled for want of competent personnel.

Often attempt is made to solve this problem by entrusting the administration of public enterprises to civil servants. But these civil servants on account of their background, training and mental attitude are incapable of running public enterprise where risk-taking, quick decisions and business attitude are necessary.

6. *Wrong Impressions About Profitability of Public Sector Enterprises.* Even when some public enterprises show some or substantial profits, often such profits are not indicative of or index of true efficiency but only happen to conceal inefficiency of those enterprises. Such profits are often the result not of hard, sustained and efficient efforts of management and workers but arise due to concessional finance provided by the government and other concessions such as cheap land, water, electricity, tax rebate, relaxation of rules etc., which are not enjoyed by similar enterprises in the private sector. Such profits are therefore only superficial and do not reflect the efficiency of the public sector enterprises.

Measures to Make the Role of Public Enterprises Efficient

With all the defects associated with the public sector, it must be appreciated that for backward countries which have adopted economic planning to achieve various socio-economic goals, there is no alternative to acceptance of expanding public sector because reliance on mere private enterprise will not enable them to attain their pre-determined goals. If it is so, it follows that since there is no alternative to expanding public sector, the only course left open is to take steps to remove the defects and deficiencies associated with the public sector. Also it should be noted that the defects mentioned earlier are not inherent oı built-in or irremovable defects of public enterprises. This means with conscious and sustained efforts those defects can be removed and public sector can be made to play its role more effectively.

The following steps are generally advocated to remove the defects or deficiencies of public enterprises:

1. Almost as a rule commercial and industrial enterprises in the public sector should not be run departmentally as that arrangement involves red-tape, delay, political pressures and interference in day-to-day activities of the enterprise which in fact must be run on commercial and business principles where quick decisions are required to be taken and business principles required to be strictly adhered to.

The suggestion is that such public enterprises should be entrusted to autonomous public corporations or should adopt public limited company form of business organisation. These business forms enjoy autonomous status and adequate powers the use of which must be encouraged in the interest of public enterprises.

2. Political parties by common agreement among themselves should decided to desist from interfering in the working of public sector undertakings. Once the policy is determined by the political authority concerned, its execution and implementation should be left in the hands of the management.

3. For purposes of recruitment, promotion, demotion, etc., there should be a body of the nature of Public Service Commission. This would result in less or elimination of nepotism and corruption and wrongful recruitment and promotions.

4. Higher executives of public enterprises should not be recruited from among senor civil servants from the administrative cadres as they are generally found unsuitable for the job. The persons recruited for such jobs should receive adequate training and experience. They should be encouraged to take quick decisions, undertake research and if their efforts are honest, in such cases failures must not be met by punishment.

5. The present system of promotion by seniority comes in the way of increasing efficiency especially among people in the lower cadre. Attempt should be made to build up a proper system of incentives which would encourage both top management as well as workers from all cadres to put forward their best efforts with the belief that their extra efforts or efficiency will be appropriately rewarded.

6. Government must set forth definite goals and targets for each public sector enterprise to be attained in prescribed time, instead of leaving things vague or setting vague objectives like increasing welfare of the masses. Also appropriate price policy should be prepared for each public sector enterprise taking into consideration the nature of the commodity supplied and the specific objectives in view. It must be kept in mind that in capital-scarce backward countries, as far as possible the price policy followed should ensure adequate returns on capital invested in the public sector, though in some service sector public enterprises for some time there might be losses (as for example when the objective is to electrify all or most of the villages or reach remote villages by S.T. buses to open up the interior and so on).

7. The most important step called for is creation among workers a sense of involvement with the public sector establishment. The worker should not consider himself as a mere employee of the enterprise. The present labour troubles adversely affecting efficiency of many public sector undertakings in India are due to wrong attitude of management towards workers. Public enterprises belong to society and workers are as much citizen of the country as top management people. By establishing works committees, joint management councils consisting of all parties concerned and by recruiting worker-directors, it is possible to create a deep sense of involvement among workers. Among all reforms, this reform of bringing about change in the attitude of workers towards the public enterprise happens to be the most important as that would result in workers taking greater interest in their jobs and thus working as efficiently as possible.

As stated already, the defects of public enterprises mentioned earlier are not inherent defects. By steps suggested above it is possible to minimise or even to eliminate many or even all the defects, so that public sector can play its allotted role most effectively and attain the socio-economic goals set before it.

3. CO-ORDINATION BETWEEN PUBLIC AND PRIVATE SECTORS

We have seen that while in capitalism private sector predominates and public sector plays only a minor role, under socialism or communism, it is the public sector that predominates, private sector playing only a minor role. On the other hand, we have seen that in the case of a mixed economy, both private sector as well as public sector come to be accepted as essential part of the economy and both play substantial role in the national economy. Since both the sectors co-exist and function side-by-side in a mixed economy, the problem of co-ordination between the two sectors becomes a matter of great importance.

Importance of Co-ordination between the Two Sectors

Before we examine how the co-ordination between the two sectors is or should be brought about, let us first understand the importance or significance of such co-ordination.

National economy has to work in a co-ordinated and integrated manner, if it is to function smoothly. Different sectors of the economy (namely, agriculture, industry, trade, transport, banking etc.,) are all closely inter-related. If these sectors do not function in a co-ordinated way, there will be several bottlenecks and efficiency of the economy will suffer. It is immaterial whether some of those sectors are in the private sector or in the public sector, smooth and efficient functioning of the nation's economy requires that all the sectors move in step. If any sector gets far ahead and any other sector lags far behind, there will be difficulties in the smooth operation or functioning of the economy.

Also the national economy is an integrated whole in the sense that output of one industry or enterprise serves as input of another sector or enterprise. Thus to take an example, proper industrial development in a country will require adequate raw materials, transport and banking facilities, adequate supply of energy, marketing facilities and so on. Even if one of them lags behind, there will be adverse effects on the functioning of the economy as a whole. It should again be emphasised that the above analysis is irrespective of whether a particular enterprise or industry is in the public sector or private sector, or whether all are in the private sector or in public sector.

Co-ordination between the Two Sectors in Mixed Economy

In a mixed economy there are both public and private sectors. In some fields private enterprise and management rules, whereas in certain other enterprises and industries ownership and management rests with the government. Naturally since there has to be co-ordination among all industries and enterprises, the problem of co-ordination between the two sectors assumes great significance in a mixed economy.

Generally co-ordination between the private sector and public sector in a mixed economy is or should be achieved in the following manner:

1. *Proper Demarcation of Fields or Sectors.* Ideological the two sectors must come to be accepted as essential parts of the economy each having a distinct role to play. This means there should be no bias in favour of or against one or the other sector.

There is or has to be proper and clear-cut demarcation as to which activities, enterprises and industries will be in the private sector and which will be in the public sector. It is necessary that this demarcation is clear, based on certain definite principles and is not frequently changed. This will create confidence in the private sector enterprises and enable them to embark on long-term planning. If there is continual threat of nationalisation, private sector enterprises would be working in a nervous atmosphere and in an indecisive manner as regards investment, expansion, planning etc.

Also the clear-cut demarcation will help to avoid overlapping and duplication.

2. If due to historical or any other reason, enterprises in one and the same industry are operating both in the private sector and public sector (as for example, Tata Iron and Steel Works in the private sector and Bhilai, Durgapur and Rurkela Steel Works in the public sector in India) government generally sees or should see that there is perfect co-ordination between the two in matters of investment, target-fixation, wage-rates, pricing policy and so on. If there are big differences in these matters in different units in the two sectors, that is bound to lead to comparison and unfavourable effects upon their working.

3. The two sectors in a mixed economy must work within the broad national plan-framework. Mixed economy, as we have already seen, generally is associated with planning. Naturally private sector or enterprise has to operate within the broad plan framework as also the public sector. Since, as we have seen, output of one enterprise is the input of another enterprise and since all industries are closely inter-linked and inter-dependent, co-ordination between the two sectors is achieved or should be achieved by properly fixing priorities, amount of investment in each industry, targeted output to be achieved within the prescribed time limit and so on.

4. Since enterprises and industries both in the private sector and public sector will require long-term and short-term finance for working smoothly and realising the planned targets, flow of funds and bank credit will have to be properly controlled so that each enterprise or industry gets necessary finance. There should be no favouritism in favour of public sector industries or enterprises at the cost of those in the private sector.

5. There will have to be proper co-ordination between price policies to be followed by enterprises and industries in the two sector. This co-ordination between price policies of the two is essential for smooth functioning of the economy.

As we have seen, generally basic and heavy industries like iron and steel, electricity, fertilisers, chemicals, and transport services are in the public sector. Their output forms important inputs for enterprises and industries in the private sector. If for example, agriculture which is in the private sector in India has to pay controlled prices for fertilisers and hybrid seeds and electricity produced and distributed by the public sector, naturally prices which agriculture has to pay form their cost of production and therefore these prices must be taken into account when procurement prices or guaranteed prices for agricultural commodities are announced by the government. Price of all commodities and services are inter-connected because they are related as inputs and outputs and therefore when government does try to influence or guide or formulate pricing policies for goods and service in the private sector instead of entirely leaving them to the market forces, prices of government supplied goods and services must be taken into account while formulating pricing policies for goods and services produced in and supplied by the private sector. If these prices are fixed too low so as not to cover even costs of government supplied inputs and leaving satisfactory margin of profit, private sector enterprise and industries will not function satisfactorily And therefore, proper co-ordination, formal or informal, between the pricing policies of the two sectors is absolutely essential.

6. There should not be great or striking differentiation between the wage-structures and conditions of working or system of incentives in similar enterprises or industries in the two sectors. Differences, if any, should be based on rational considerations; otherwise there will be flow of personnel from one sector to the other causing difficulties in their smooth working. (For example, in India, private enterprise is supposed to pay more by way of remuneration and perks than comparable enterprises in the public sector, with the consequences that public sector enterprises often find it difficult to get the requisite personnel for top management.)

7. In order to bring about appropriate co-ordination between the public and private sectors, there should be frequent meeting of the representatives of the two sectors or bodies where both the sectors are represented. The idea is that common problems should be thrashed out, mutual experience and data should be exchanged and common strategy in respect of export should be evolved so that each sector plays a supportive role to the other sector.

Once a system of mixed economy is accepted on ideological or pragmatic grounds and once private sector and public sector are allowed to co-exist and function side-by-side, the above steps are generally taken or should be taken to bring about proper co-ordination between the two sectors so that the mixed economy of which they constitute important parts and have come to be accepted as such works smoothly and efficiently.

4. PRICING POLICIES AND EFFICIENCY OF PUBLIC ENTERPRISES

Introduction

Price-mechanism in the private enterprise economy reflects buyers' preferences and helps bring about allocation of community's resources in the most efficient way, ensuring at the same time maximisation of satisfaction of consumers. In private enterprise economy no machinery is needed to formulate or regulate prices which come to be formed by the changing forces of demand and supply.

But in the case of public sector enterprises, the position is different. The Government invests huge funds in such enterprises. Though all public sector enterprises are not expected to make maximum profit or profit consideration may be minor, the fact remains that in capital-scarce developing countries public sector enterprises cannot go on making losses year after year. Though the funds are provided by the government, formally interest on such investments will have to be earned and credited to government; also depreciation funds will have to be set aside; and in the case of many; if not all public enterprises, adequate net return on capital invested will have to be earned. It may go to public exchequer, or be used for expanding existing enterprises or for starting new ones. But the fact remains that on the whole, adequate rate of return or profit must be earned, both because capital is scarce and also because rate of profit would be an index of efficiency of a public sector enterprise.

Different Pricing Policies in Public Sector Enterprises

While every private enterprise unit always aims at maximising profit, in the case of public sector enterprises often they are expected to help attain various socio-economic objectives. This means their pricing is not always governed by the consideration of maximising profits. Depending upon the socio-political and economic objectives, different pricing policies are recommended for public enterprises. Some of the important pricing policies recommended for public enterprises are as follows:

1. No Profit, No Loss Policy.
2. Marginal Cost Pricing Principle.
3. Principle of Average Cost Pricing.
4. Principle or Policy of Making Maximum Profits.
5. Policy of Charging Discriminating Prices.
6. Cost Plus Pricing.
7. Import-based Pricing.

It would be instructive to analyse in detail the above principles or policies adopted by different public sector undertakings as also to know the reasons as to why a particular pricing policy is adopted by a particular public sector undertaking.

1. *No Profit, No Loss Policy.* The policy of 'no profit no loss' implies that the public sector enterprise following this principle should neither make profit after meeting all charges on capital and current account, nor suffer any losses. The idea behind this principle is that some public enterprises are not meant to make maximum profit but are meant to serve public interest or public welfare without at the same time subsiding the commodity or service in question. As W. A. Lewis has stated, "If the corporation makes a profit or loss, it should be required so to adjust its prices as to eliminate the profit or loss."[4]

Lewis supports this principle on the ground that "it prevents over-expansion and under-expansion of the industrial unit and thus helps to avoid inflationary or deflationary trends in the economy.

'No profit no loss' principle of pricing cannot be followed as a general rule by all public sector undertakings. Backward countries are capital-scarce countries and they must push up the rate of capital accumulation and investment. This rules out the possibility of general adoption of this principle. But the principle of 'no profit no loss' is followed or should be followed in certain specific cases like important life-saving drugs supplied especially in backward areas of the country, or provision of transport and electricity to poorer sections of the community whose level of income is such that their capacity to bear burden of higher prices is limited.

2. *Marginal Cost Pricing Principle.* Hotelling in 1938 and later on Mead, Lange and Lerner advocated the theory of marginal cost pricing. They advocate that public sector enterprises should determine the prices of their products on the principle that the price equals marginal cost of the commodity in question. The argument in favour of this principle is that it ensures the optimum output and at the same time ensures maximum welfare under given conditions.

But the principle of marginal cost pricing for public enterprises is criticised on the following grounds: Which marginal cost pricing principle is to be followed? Long term or short-term ? If it is the long-term, marginal cost will be equal to average cost; if on the other hand it is the short-term marginal cost, that would result in frequent changes in price of a commodity causing frequent fluctuations in conditions of supply and demand.

Another difficulty is that ". . . if prices are fixed equal to short-term marginal costs and fixed costs are neglected, then the public enterprises which work under conditions of increasing returns would run into huge losses. The decreasing cost industry will not be able to cover their full costs, if they follow the marginal cost pricing principle. It means that all the factors used in the enterprise will earn less than what they could have earned somewhere else. As a result there will be misallocation of resources, or in other words, they will not be used in the optimum manner."[5]

An important and almost insurmountable difficulty in respect of this principle is that due to indivisibility of certain factors of production, it is difficult to calculate marginal cost in case of some commodities.

But theoretically the marginal cost pricing principle is sound and wherever it is possible to fairly accurately calculate marginal cost, this principle may be adopted in public enterprises.

In public enterprises like Bharat Heavy Electricals and electricity generator undertakings where under-utilization has been an inhibiting factor, the application of marginal cost pricing principle has enabled them to cover a portion of total costs. In multiproduct public enterprises, the subsidy on account of marginal cost being lower than average cost in some products are offset by average cost being lower than marginal cost in the case of some other products.

3. *Principle of Average Cost Pricing*. In many public sector enterprises the principle of average cost pricing is widely followed. There are two main arguments in favour of this principle. In the first place it is easy to administer. And secondly, full costs (fixed as well as circulating costs) are covered under the principle of average cost pricing so that the community is spared the burden of additional taxation to support the industry as would be the case if the principle of marginal cost pricing is adopted. Also nobody is required to pay more than the cost of production under this principle and therefore there is no exploitation of consumers or discrimination. Another advantage is that average cost pricing by covering all costs of production would ensure economic viability of a public enterprise and because it has not to beg for subsidy from the government, it might also ensure its autonomous status. Above all it provides simplicity in calculation and administration.

But there are some difficulties in following this principle. The main difficulty arises due to accurately calculating depreciation charges in respect of machines which last for pretty long period. This means we have to go only by rule of thumb and the cost calculated may not truly represent average cost of production.

Though average cost pricing principle may not be followed by all public sector undertakings as they have to fulfil some social objectives which transcend cost consideration, as a starting point for most public sector undertakings the opinion is that this principle would be quite satisfactory.

4. *Policy of Making Maximum Profit*. In developing countries capital is scarce and therefore it is reasonable to expect that investment in public enterprises earns maximum profit so that additional funds would be available for investment or expansion of the existing units and that would mean acceleration of the growth rate of the economy.

Thus the Taxation Enquiry Committee (1952-53) was of the view that the no profit, no loss policy has no place especially in the long-run in a developing economy and the Ooty Committee also concluded that public enterprises "should be so conducted as to yield planned profits and thus add to revenues, available to the public sector." Hanson also opined that, "In most cases. . . a public enterprise should aim at a normal rate of profit, on a basis of a price policy reflecting real costs."

In a developing economy funds for investment are scarce; naturally huge investments in public sector enterprises should aim at earning at least a rate of profit which a similar enterprise in the private sector would be earning. Profit also would serve as an index of efficiency of public enterprises. No doubt, making maximum profit may not be the sole consideration of all public enterprises as it is in the case of a private enterprise and in some cases (such as provision of cheap electricity for the development of backward areas, or provision of cheap seeds and credit for drought affected areas) even incurring losses may appear justified. But on the whole and in the long run public enterprises will have to earn normal profits as that would mean that they will have to work efficiently and earn funds for their expansion or for investment in other public enterprises the funds for which otherwise will have to come out of additional taxation or from budgetary sources.

5. *Policy of Discriminatory Prices*. Since public enterprises have to fulfil certain socio-cultrual and political objectives, in case of certain public enterprises policy of charging discriminatory prices is advocated and is also followed. For example, to stimulate agricultural growth in backward areas, charging lower rate for electricity than what is charged for urban industries appears quite reasonable. Also charging lower rate for agricultural inputs in the case of small and marginal farmers compared to big farmers would appear justified due to their differing capacity to bear burden. The public sector banks and financial institutions in India have been following policy of charging lower rate of interest (about 4 per cent) in the case of producers from poorer sections of the community while charging anywhere up to 15 per cent in the case of big farmers and industrialists. Sometimes even free loans or free distribution of seeds may have to be undertaken in case of flood-affected poor sections of the community.

Discriminating prices are also used by the State Electricity Boards, Indian railways, Indian Airlines and the State Trading Corporation of India.

Charging discriminatory prices keeping in mind what the different sections of the society can bear appears quite a sound principle in view of the fact that the aim of some public sector enterprises is not just to make maximum profits possible but also help achieve other social and cultural objectives to increase welfare of masses.

6. *Cost Plus Pricing*. In the case of the principle of 'cost plus pricing', the objective is to cover whatever costs are incurred, plus (*i.e.*, to which is added)

a certain percentage by way of reasonable return on investment in the project. It is observed that 'cost plus pricing' formula is utilised in India in the case of Indian Telephone Industry, Hindustan Cables and Hindustan Aeronautics in which cases Government is the major buyer.

The advantage in the case of this principle is that reasonable return on investment is assured and that helps additional capital formation which might be used for further expansion of industry or for starting new industrial units in the public sector.

But the great disadvantage of this principle is that since there is a guarantee that whatever the costs, they are bound to be covered (plus some return on investment), there is no incentive whatsoever on the part of the management and employees to make efforts to reduce cost of production. Naturally this principle is likely not only not to increase efficiency of the industrial unit but in fact may have adverse effect on efficiency.

7. *Import-based Pricing.* The principle or formula of import-based pricing is adopted in the case of those public sector enterprises which have not to face competition in the home market, but prices of which goods are likely to be higher than similar goods imported from abroad. Under such circumstances in order to safeguard the interest of domestic consumer, the import-based price formula is accepted as the basis for price fixation. In India, this principle is adopted in the case of public enterprises such as Heavy Engineering, Bhopal, Bharat Heavy Electricals, Hindustan Shipyards, Hindustan Photofilms, etc.

The advantage of this principle is that as some public enterprises are the only producers in a particular line of production and since there is no competition from any domestic producers, left to themselves in the absence of competition at home, their inefficiency is likely to increase. If their prices are however linked to prices of similar imported goods, that would bring in an element of competition with international producers. Naturally this is likely to result in increasing efficiency of such public sector enterprises which will always be comparing their cost of production with those of foreign producers of similar goods.

Concluding Remarks. From the above analysis of various principles or pricing policies to be followed by different public sector enterprises, it follows that there is not just one pricing principle or policy that is applicable to all public enterprises. Not all public enterprises can follow just one of the above principles rigidly. Each principle has its merits and defects. For each public enterprise, it is necessary that its aims and objectives should be considered and with that view a suitable pricing policy adopted. While certain public enterprises may be permitted (at least for some time) to suffer losses, others may be required to follow the principle of 'no profit, no loss', while still others may be expected to generate surpluses.

And yet with all these provisions, it should be emphasised that in capital-scarce developing countries, public enterprises taken as a whole will have to earn adequate returns and generate reasonable surpluses required for further expansion of those enterprises or for establishing new ones for accelerating the rate of growth of the economy. This means that a planned economy should have a planned price policy for each public sector enterprise setting out clearly its objectives and the pricing policy to be adopted and possible losses to be suffered or surpluses to be generated as also fixing the overall returns and surplus which public sector investments as a whole must annually earn.

Pricing Policies and Efficiency of Public Enterprises

Pricing policies adopted by public sector enterprises have great influence in their efficiency.

In the case of private enterprise, we have already seen, how under competitive conditions, every producer tries to do his best, make most efficient use of various productive resources at his command, cut down costs to the minimum all with a view to successfully compete with the rivals and make maximum profits. Thus under competitive conditions under capitalism, freely fluctuating price mechanism ensures the most efficient use of productive resources so that every enterprise tends towards moving to a size which ensures optimal use of all the resources employed. (Of course, when competition, as we have seen, gives rise to monopolistic conditions, all sorts of wastes result).

It would be instructive to see how a principle or policy of pricing adopted by a public sector enterprise influences its efficiency.

If a public sector enterprise adopts 'no profit, no loss' principle of pricing, since the management's efficiency is not going to be judged by the amount of profits made or rate of return on capital invested, there is no incentive to improve efficiency of the enterprise. Since the price charged ensures neither profit, nor loss, the enterprise is likely to remain stagnant.

In the case of marginal cost pricing as well as average cost pricing, there will hardly be any incentive to increase efficiency on the part of management. Even if there is under-utilisation of installed capacity, over-staffing and heavy inventories involving excessive storing costs, etc., since either marginal cost is covered or average cost is covered, respectively, there is no incentive on the part of the management of a public sector enterprise following the above of the either principles to remove those deficiencies and increase efficiency by making the maximum use of various resources at its disposal.

Principle of profit-making is a principle which will stimulate management of a public enterprise to increase efficiency and produce surplus or increase profit which is going to be the index of its performance. This principle or policy will stimulate management to reduce unutilised installed capacity, avoid over-staffing and excessive inventories and make maximum use of all available inputs. This principle thus will have direct influence on efficiency of a public enterprise (though it has been already made clear that it would not be correct for all public sector enterprises to adopt this principle because of the social and cultural objectives which they are expected to attain).

In respect of the principle of discriminating prices, while prices charged for some sections of the community may be lower than marginal cost or average cost of production, since the public enterprise is allowed to charge higher than marginal cost or average cost of production to richer sections of society and thus make good losses incurred by the charging lower prices, the enterprise with powers to charge discriminating prices may not have adequate incentives to increase its efficiency.

The principle of 'cost plus pricing' is likely to have adverse impact on the efficiency of a public sector enterprise. Since the enterprise is ensured (whether there is under-utilisation of capacity, over-staffing, excessive inventories or wasteful use of resources) that not only will it be allowed to cover all the costs incurred, but will also be allowed to charge a certain additional percentage over and above the costs incurred and thus earn certain return on investment, there will be absolutely no incentive for the management to make efforts to reduce costs (by reducing unutilised capacity, appropriate staffing, avoiding wastes of resources and so on).

The principle of 'import-based pricing' will stimulate efficiency on the part of management of public sector enterprises. Foreign firms are generally more efficient that Indian firms, and since the prices to be charged for goods of certain public sector enterprises in India are to be compared and fixed in relation to prices of similar goods imported or similar goods in foreign countries, management will be compelled to make maximum efforts to bring the level of efficiency of their enterprises on par with similar enterprises in foreign countries. This principle will therefore have favourable impact on the efficiency of public sector enterprises.

Concluding Remarks. Public sector enterprises have to attain not only maximum profit but various other social objectives such as regional balanced development, opening up of backward regions, taking banking into the interior and among people still following the system of barter-economy, distribution of fertilisers, water and seeds among drought affected areas and so on. It is therefore possible that for some time public enterprises (*e.g.*, public sector banks in backward areas or state transport buses in isolated areas with *kaccha* roads) may not be in a position to work in the most efficient manner. It will be too much to expect that they must make profits from the beginning. But when conditions are different as in the case of public sector banks in urban areas or public sector industrial establishments in Bombay or Delhi or Calcutta, they will have to show maximum efficiency. And therefore whether a public sector enterprise makes profits or incurs loss is not always the proper criteria as different objectives have to be attained by different public sector enterprises. But the fact remains that whatever the objectives and circumstances under which public sector enterprises are working, they must aim at making the best use of their resources and show maximum efficiency.

5. PUBLIC SECTOR IN INDIA-RADICAL CHANGE IN APPROACH

After the passing of the Industrial Policy Resolution of 1948 and especially of 1956, Government of India made concerted efforts to expand public sector in the industrial sphere with a view to make it the dominant sector in the Indian economy.

The rapid expansion of the Central Government's public sector enterprises becomes clear from the fact that in 1950-51 there were only 5 central Government public sector enterprises (apart from railways, post and telegraph and armament factories) with investment of only about Rs. 29 crores. By 1990 their number went beyond 225 with total investment of Rs.113234 crores. There are also state government public sector enterprises like Maharashtra State Electricity Board, Road Transport Corporation and so on.

It was said in favour of the public sector in India that those enterprises will help check private monopolies, help expand employment opportunities, earn profit for the government which otherwise would have gone into the pockets of private individuals, help rapid economic development of backward areas in the country, and help government in influencing level of economic activities in the country.

But experience of the Central Government public sector enterprises (as also of the state governments') showed the following defects: There was excessive investment in many public sector undertakings because money was easily available from the government; there was generally longer gestation period with cost mounting manyfold of the original figure; there was generally excessive manpower recruitment due to political pressures; there was generally inefficient management because of political appointments of head of the public sector units; there was hardly any autonomy for the management which was almost bureaucratic with all its defects — all these defects resulting in heavy annual losses. Also as many of the public sector units were in infrastructure industries, their inefficiency resulted not only in hampering development of public sector industries but also of those in the private sector and therefore of the Indian economy as a whole. Public sector in India had in fact become the private sector of the Indian politicians.

And therefore, reappraisal of the industrial policy and of the public sector undertakings started after late Rajiv Gandhi became the prime minister in 1980.

Reappraisal of the Policy of Expanding Public Sector

After Shri Rajiv Gandhi became the prime minister with his liberal views and emphasis on updating technology in different sectors of the Indian economy, and especially after Shri Narasimha Rao became the prime minister of India in 1991, there is taking place almost radical reversal of the policy of expanding public sector followed since 1956.

A number of factors have combined to bring about the new approach and reversal of the policy of expanding public sector in India.

As we have already seen, there was for long severe criticism of the ways in which public sector industrial undertaking were functioning especially in vital industrial sectors like oil, coal, steel, power, mining and metals, civil aviation, communications, banking and finance. Their working was characterised by inefficiency, bureaucratic management with all its defects; and the recurring deficits were being made good year after year by additional taxation or deficit financing with adverse effects on the whole economy.

Extreme scarcity of infrastructural facilities in which field public sector enterprises had almost monopolistic position was adversely affecting growth rate of the Indian economy. Public sector in India was hanging like a millstone around Indian economy.

A number of developments were taking place in the world at large which also were responsible for the reversal of India's policy in respect of public sector industries.

When Mikhail Gorbachev came to power in the former Soviet Union, he had the courage to admit that State ownership of all productive factors of production and management of all productive sectors of the Soviet economy by the State had resulted in overall inefficiency and scarcity of all types of goods because of complete domination of the extensive bureaucracy over the entire economy of the nation. He showed the courage of introducing perestroika which finally resulted in switching over from communist economy to free market or competitive (*i.e.,* capitalist) economy. The liberal economic policy of Gorbachev also ultimately resulted in breaking up of the Soviet Union into 15 more or less independent or autonomous republics all of which started introducing market and competitive economy which meant less and less role of the State and of the public sector in the nation's economy.

This trend of march from communist economy to competitive market economy (which meant less and less emphasis of the role of the public sector) spread to practically all of East European countries. In Russia every citizen is given equity shares pertaining to public sector industrial enterprises. Thus it is the disenchantment with the performance of the public sector enterprises and better performance of free market economy in West European countries and in the United States that forced Government of India to reappraise its policy of laying emphasis on the role of public sector and nationalisation of all important industries in the Indian economy as direct by the Industrial Policy Resolution of 1956.

Even in communist China there has been gradual movement towards free market economy. There is increasing privatisation of many sectors of the Chinese economy. Foreign capital has begun to be freely admitted and share and stock markets have begun their functioning. The Chinese leaders call this system 'Socialist Free Market Economy.' Clearly the communist China has been moving away from the traditional 'Maoist Path.'

Another adverse development in India that was developing since mid-1980s and soon reached the crisis point was the foreign exchange crisis and increasing deficit in India's balance of trade and balance of payments position. There was a time in 1990-91 when there was not adequate reserves of foreign currencies even to pay the servicing charges on foreign debt and India was near bankruptcy in the eyes of foreign creditor countries. Under such circumstances India was forced to apply to the International Monetary Fund and the World Bank for a massive loan of 5 billion US dollars. These two international financial institutions are dominated by the United States. Naturally, conditionalities were imposed upon India before granting the loan which were urgently required to save India from bankruptcy. Their conditionalities included clauses such as curtailing the role of the public sector and to liberalise the Indian economy from various restrictions such as licensing system and the MRTP and the FERA Acts, etc. And therefore, India was forced to de-emphasis the role of the public sector as that was one of the conditions for granting of the loan by the IMF and the World Bank directly under the dominance of the United States which is the only super power left after the disintegration of the former Soviet Union.

But right since early 1980s because of the problems of scarcity and inefficiency raised by the public sector units (PSUs) in India, gradual steps were being taken to de-emphasis the role of the PSUs.

MAIN FEATURES OF GOVERNMENT OF INDIA'S POLICY IN RESPECT OF PUBLIC SECTOR AFTER THE ANNOUNCEMENT OF THE NEW ECONOMIC (INDUSTRIAL) POLICY OF JULY 1991

The main features of government's policy in regard to public sector are as follows:

(1) There is to be no further expansion of public sector in Indian industrial sphere.

(2) There is to be allowed privatisation in certain industries which since 1956 were reserved for the public sector. For example, private enterprise is to be allowed in energy sector such as electricity, road transport, civil aviation and so on.

(3) There are about 58 chronically sick or unviable public sector units under the jurisdiction of the Central Government. If workers of those sick PSUs are ready to manage and run them on co-operative basis, Central Government is prepared to write off their past liabilities and losses incurred so far.

(4) PSUs are to be allowed to float equity and debentures to be sold in share and stock markets. This means private participation is to be allowed in the administration of the PSUs.

(5) Foreign equity to the extent of 49 per cent is to be allowed in some Central Government PSUs.

(6) In the case of many PSUs which are as yet not financially viable, their cases are to be referred to the Board of Industrial Finance and Reconstruction and further action is to be takén on the recommendation of the Board.

(7) In those cases of Central Government PSUs which are financially viable and manageable and which for strategic reasons cannot be handed over to private sector, more decision-making administrative and financial authority and autonomy are to be given to them to encourage their efficiency and profitability. This means there will be less political and bureaucratic interference in their day-to-day working and management.

(8) Out of 225 and odd Central Government PSUs, around half of them are to be handed over to State Government's for management with funds meant for them.

(9) In the cases of closure of any Central Government PSUs, with a view to minimise hardships of affected workers losing their jobs in such PSUs, attempts will be made to lessen their hardships by retraining them for other jobs for which increasing employment opportunities are or will be available in future. For this programme there has been made provision of Rs.200 crores.

Along with curtailing the role of the PSUs attempts are at the same time being made to encourage rapid growth of private sector industrial units. With the aim of encouraging more rapid growth of private sector industrial units, for all practical purposes private sector is being allowed entry into some of those industries so far reserved only for the public sector; licensing policy so far in operation in respect of private sector industrial units has been for all purpose is been withdrawn; also, for all practical purposes the MRTP and FERA Acts are cancelled and cease to be in operation.

Chapter 20

ECONOMIC PLANNING

Since the end of World War II economic planning has been assuming great significance both in developed and developing countries. This is especially so in developing countries of Asia, Africa and Latin America.

Before we examine the role of planning in developed and developing countries and also in order to understand the role of planning in a satisfactory way, it would be instructive to understand the concept of planning and its characteristics and why planning came to be accepted at all in developed and developing countries.

1. MEANING OF PLANNING AND ITS CHARACTERISTICS

Definition and Meaning of Economic Planning

In his well-known definition, A. D. Dickinson has defined economic planning in the following way: "Economic planning is the making of major economic decisions — what and how much is to be produced, how, when and where it is to be produced, and to whom it is to be allocated by the conscious decision of a determinate authority on the basis of a comprehensive survey of the system as a whole."[1]

Mrs Barbara Woottan writes: "Planning may be defined as the conscious and deliberate choice of economic priorities by some public authority."

Thus, economic planning is "conceiving, initiating, regulating and controlling economic activity by the State according to set priorities with a view to achieving, well defined objectives within a given time."

Lorwin defines economic planning as "a scheme of economic organisation in which individual and separate plants, enterprises and industries are treated as coordinate unit of one single system for the purpose of utilising available resources to achieve maximum satisfaction of the people's needs within a given interval of time."

The Indian Planning Commission writes: "Planning is essentially a way of organising and utilising resources to maximum advantage in terms of defined social ends."

Main Characteristics of Economic Planning

By studying the above definitions of economic planning it would be observed that economic planning has the following characteristics:

1. Economic planning implies, a 'conscious' and 'deliberate' process which aims at attaining certain specific objectives and targets (such as, say 5 per cent annual growth-rate, pushing up the rate of saving and investment by a certain percentage, bringing about balanced regional development, reduction of inequalities of income and wealth, full employment, etc., etc.) within specified time limit.

2. Planning implies existence within the national economy of a single and undivided authority (may be, it is the Government itself, or a specially created Planning Authority or Board) invested with the power of taking all the important economic decisions (such as what to produce, where, how and how resources are to be allocated among various sectors of the economy) on the basis of comprehensive survey of existing and potential resources in the country.

3. Economic planning implies that planning is comprehensive covering in an integrated manner all the important sectors of the national economy (and not just this or that sector like agriculture or industry, transport and communications or energy and so on). Economic planning implies comprehensive planning and not just sectoral planning.

4. Economic planning is characterised by the use of limited resources on the basis of pre-determined priorities with a view to attain maximum welfare of the community. Economic planning is not planning just to attain welfare of one section or another of the community, but welfare of the community as a whole.

5. Economic planning covers not only planning of production of goods and services but also covers pattern of distribution of income and wealth as conceived by the planning authority or the Government.

6. Economic planning implies that there is a definite time span within which fixed targets (such as 5 per cent growth-rate of the economy, or 10 per cent growth-rate of the industrial sector, or provision of employment opportunities for a million persons, or construction of an irrigational project) are to be attained. Unless the time limit is set, economic planning would cease to be planning in the strict sense of the term.

The above study of definitions of planning and its characteristics would help in understanding the role of planning.

Why Planning Came to be Accepted?

As already noted, *laissez-faire* capitalism and even capitalism with a certain amount of State regulations came to be associated with many serious shortcomings. Large number of protagonists of capitalism also came to lose faith in capitalism after the Great Depression of 1929-33.

Laissez-faire capitalism (as also capitalism with certain amount of State regulations) came to be associated with defects or deficiencies such as recurrent economic crises, increasing inequalities of income and wealth, wastages of various types of community's resources due to competition, emergence of monopoly and monopoly abuses, concentration of economic power leading to undue influence of the rich class on the political and economic policies of the government which came to be manipulated in their favour, uncertainty, instability, division of society into rich and poor classes, class rivalries and class antagonisms leading to social and political tensions, neglect of social welfare and international rivalries and conflicts.

The free enterprise system did not function as expected. It achieved neither the most efficient use of community's resources nor maximisation of welfare of the community. In this connection J. M. Keynes wrote: "The world is not so governed from above that private and social interests always coincide. It is not a correct deduction from the principles of economics that enlightened self-interest always operates in the public interest. Nor is it true that self-interest generally is enlightened, more often individuals when they make as social unit." Keynes showed how under unplanned or free enterprise system there may be no identity of individuals interest and social interests and how monopolies which came to dominate capitalism in the West European countries and the USA exploited consumers and almost held society to rànsom.

With the Great Depression of 1929-33 people lost faith in the Say's Law of Markets that supply creates its own demand and that under competitive conditions economy will automatically reach the level of full employment and stabilise there. Keynes showed convincingly that free enterprise capitalist system may stabilise at lower than full employment level.

1. ROLE OF PLANNING

Role of Planning in Developed Countries

The role of planning assumed increasing importance in developed countries with a view to prevent recurrent economic crises, to stabilise economy at the level of full employment, to reduce extreme disparities of income and wealth, to develop backward regions or pockets (which exist even in highly developed capitalist countries like the USA, not to speak of Great Britain and France), to bring about balanced growth of the economy, and above all with the prevailing climate of cold war and mutual rivalry between two blocs led by the USA and the USSR, to bring about acceleration of the rate of growth of the economy on which military strength of States depends.

Thinkers like Schumpeter predicted decline and ultimate collapse of free enterprise system. It thus came to be realised that if capitalism with many of its virtues is to be saved, some sort of economic planning must be adopted by capitalist countries.

In developed countries some sort of planning became necessary also to combat enormous powers of monopolies and to ensure smooth working of the economy. In this connection Sir William Beveridge wrote:

"It is no more likely that individualistic growth of many small separate business will produce an industry laid out on lines of maximum overall efficiency, than it is likely that the disorderly uncontrolled activities of innumerable small property owners will produce a planned town without needless corners, duplicate streets and traffic congestion."

After the Second World War, complexities of modern life have so much increased and so many variable factors working within and outside the country influence the economy and lives of people, that unless some sort of economic planning is adopted even by developed capitalist countries, modern capitalist society will find it extremely difficult to adjust itself to rapidly changing times and to meet the ever new challenges created by varied dynamic forces. To entertain belief that free enterprise system without any sort of economic planning would work smoothly in the second half of the 20th century because it operated fairly smoothly in the 19th century would be foolish and such an attitude is frought with danger. As one writer stated: ". . . the old paternalistic system of private capitalism and uncontrolled capitalism are out of date, and everyone has to adjust his outlook and ideal to the new outlook."

Another role has been thrust on economic planning after the end of World War II. It was observed that USSR and China achieved remarkable progress in a short period by adopting economic planning. Naturally because of the mutual rivalry on ideological grounds which gave rise to cold war problem, this development posed a military challenge to capitalist countries. These countries realised that military preparation requires strong economic base and relative economic positions between the two sets of countries must be maintained if necessary by abandoning free enterprise system and adopting some sort of economic planning. In view of rapidly accelerated rate of growth of communist countries with their planned economies, the capitalist countries, though highly developed and much ahead of communist countries, want to accelerate rate of growth of their economies to maintain the same relative positions of economic strength. This they thought could be done only by adopting economic planning and not by reliance on free enterprise system.

Thus economic planning has come to be accepted in most of the developed capitalist countries and is expected to play a varied role — accelerate growth-rate, attain full employment and economic stability (which in other terms means help avoiding recurrent economic crises), reduce extreme income and wealth disparities, help develop backward regions and help smooth working of the economy in constantly changing and dynamic circumstances which have been constantly posing new challenges. It is believed that free enterprise system would not be in a position to play the above role effectively and hence the acceptance of some sort of economic planning even by developed countries of the West.

Role of Planning in Developing Countries

It is observed that almost all newly independent countries in Asia, Africa and Latin America have adopted economic planning as the chief instrument to realise as early as possible their socio-economic and cultural objectives. It would be instructive to know why these countries have accepted planning and what role economic planning has been playing or is expected to play in developing countries.

Characteristics of a Backward (Developing) Economy

The role of planning in developing countries will be better appreciated, if the characteristics of developing *i.e.*, backward countries are kept in mind. It is observed that developing or backward countries like India suffer from various socio-economic evils such as excessive and rapidly increasing population (annual growth rate of population varying between 2 and 3 per cent), predominance of agricultural or primary sector, excessive pressure of population on land, extremely low agricultural productivity, low degree or absence of industrialisation (or existence of only some consumer goods industries with predominance of small-scale and domestic industries), absence or inadequate infrastructure facilities (like roads, railways and other means of communications, electricity, banking and so on), primitive techniques of production both in the agricultural and industrial sectors, inadequately developed tertiary or service sector (which means absence of various types of modern skills and technical know-how), illiteracy and ignorance, predominance of feudal social institutions and old-world values and value-system, low productivity in practically every field of economic activity, hence low level of annual national income, and hence extremely low level of per capita income resulting in extremely low standard or level of living for the vast majority of people in the country. The backward countries are thus caught in the vicious circle of poverty, namely, low level of income, low rate of saving, hence low rate of investment and consequently low level of national and per capita income which means poor standard of living.

The West European countries which were also poor in the 16th and the 17th centuries brought about their economic development through not planning but through private enterprise economy. But circumstances in those countries then were different and especially population in those countries was comparatively small. The backward countries at present will find it practically impossible to bring about their rapid economic development and solve many other socio-economic problems through private enterprise economy; and even if an attempt is made in that direction, it would take enormously long period to attain the objectives and also it would entail enormous sacrifice on the part of people, especially poorer sections of the community. With rising expectations, people may not be ready to wait so long. This would mean that only economic planning would help developing or backward countries to attain the various socio-economic goals within reasonable period of time.

Why Planning in Developing Countries?

Or

Role of Planning in Developing Countries

Economic planning plays or will have to play the following role in developing countries:

1. Planning will have to make an effort at effectively mobilising community's resources for investment purposes. Through fiscal, monetary and other measures, planning will have to aim, at accelerating the annual rate of saving up to at least 15 to 20 per cent of national income as that much saving and investment is considered as essential for initiating and promoting self-sustained economic development.

2. Planning will have to play the role not only of mobilising savings but push up the annual rate of investment and see that there is appropriate pattern of investment. This means planning in backward countries will have to fix priorities and direct the flow of investment funds in particular channels (*e.g.*, in agriculture and essential industries instead of in luxury or semi-luxury goods producing industries as so on.

3. Planning will have to play the role of bringing about rapid industrial development of the country. Economic progress of a country generally requires industrialisation without which various industrial raw materials and minerals of the country will remain unutilised.

Planning will have to aim at diversified type of industrialisation (*i.e.*, capital goods industries as also consumer goods industries). This will reduce reliance of backward countries on foreign countries for machinery and spares and the process of industrialisation will also provide increasing employment opportunities for increasing population of the country.

4. Planning will have to play the role of introducing modern techniques in the agricultural sector to increase productivity of that sector. A certain amount of surplus of foodgrains is absolutely essential for the purpose of accelerating the process of industrialisation as industrial workers do not produce foodgrains but need foodgrains for sustenance. Planning by modernising agriculture must increase agricultural productivity per man and per hectare and see that not only the country becomes self-sufficient in agriculture but enough foodgrains surplus is created. If agriculture is modernised that would also help export of agricultural commodities enabling the country to earn foreign

exchange with which to purchase essential machinery, spares and technical know-how which the backward country may take some time to produce.

5. Planning will have to play and effective role in developing tertiary sector, namely, social and economic overheads such as schools and technical institutions to train people and help them acquire necessary modern skills, roads, railways, and other means of communications, banking, electricity, water, research and data collection, extension services to train people in modern methods of production and so on. Planning will have to take steps to develop scientific attitude among people in place of fatalistic outlook of people in backward countries and change their value-system and create faith in themselves that not providence or God but they can by proper and hard work remove their poverty.

6. There is an additional role which planning in backward countries is called upon to play. Most of these backward countries were for two hundred years or more colonies of West European imperial powers like England, France, Holland, Germany, Italy, etc. Those imperial powers went on for hundreds of years exploiting their colonies, made them produce raw materials and minerals necessary for industries at home, took steps to destroy their domestic industries, built railways that helped them defend their empires, neglected development of indigenous industries, shipping and banking. The consequence of this foreign rule over centuries has been that the economies of these former colonial countries have developed a sort of extremely lop-sided economic system with extreme dependence on foreign countries for vital goods and services and with a number of loopholes and gaps in the economy creating bottlenecks for the rapid economic development. Planning will have to see that this lop-sided development is removed and that various sectors of the economy as also various geographical regions of the country develop in a balanced way, on the basis of the existing and potential resources available in those parts.

7. All this amounts to saying that planning in backward countries will have to take steps necessary for breaking the vicious circle of poverty and age-old stagnation and to bring about all round rapid economic development enabling people in these countries to get adequate opportunities of employment in various fields and help them to earn adequate real income to enable them to live satisfactorily material and cultural standard of living, instead of the miserable and sub-human standard of living which majority of people are living in these countries for centuries. Role of planning would thus be to provide opportunities for all to develop their personality.

Concluding Remarks

From the above analysis it would be clear that more than in developed countries, it is in backward countries like India that economic planning assumes greater significance and is called upon to play comprehensive and effective role. It is when resource position is very unsatisfactory, saving rate low and so is the rate of investment, and various skills are lacking, when agricultural sector has become stagnant, and infrastructure position is extremely unsatisfactory, when due to long foreign rule and age-old poverty people's faith in themselves as also their enthusiasm, initiative and enterprise have all got stifled, when acceptance of democracy has raised high hopes regarding increasing employment opportunities and earning rising incomes and raising standard of living, when failure to achieve quick improvement in the material and cultural standards of living by solving problems of mass unemployment and poverty would threaten the country with social and political tensions and result in conflicts and possibly violent revolution it is then that role of planning not only assumes great significance but becomes a matter of great urgency. The various economic and other problems besetting the backward countries in Asia, Africa and Latin America are so baffling and their dimensions so vast and solutions so urgent that there appears no alternative before these countries to acceptance of economic planning as an instrument to solve these problems in as short a period of time as possible.[2]

2. TYPES OF ECONOMIC PLANNING

Economic planning or types of planning can be classified as follows:

The following are important basis of classification:

1. On the basis of 'Economic System', we get the following types of planning:

(A) Capitalist Planning and Socialist Planning.

(B) Totalitarian Planning and Democratic Planning.

(C) Centralised Planning and Decentralised Planning.

(D) Functional Planning and Structural Planning.

2. Economic planning can be classified on the basis of 'Time' element. On this basis, we get the following types of planning:

(A) Perspective Planning, Medium-Term Planning and Short Term Planning.

(B) Permanent Planning and Emergency Planning.

3. Planning can be classified on the basis of 'Region'. On this basis of classification, we get the following types of planning:

(A) Regional Planning.

(B) National Planning.

(C) International Planning.

4. Planning can also be classified on the basis of 'Finance' or 'Real Output.' On this basis, we get the following types of planning:

(A) Physical Planning.

(B) Financial Planning.

We shall now analyse various types of economic planning in detail — their features, advantages and disadvantages and so on.

1. Classification of Planning on the Basis of 'Economic System'

(A) Capitalist Planning and Socialist Planning

Capitalist Planning. In the case of capitalist planning, capitlism is associated with some sort of planning, instead of there being *laissez-faire* type of capitalism of the 19th century when capitalism was totally 'unplanned.'

Under capitalist planning, though *laissez-faire* principle is abandoned and some sort of planning comes to be associated with capitalism, it should be noted that at the same time most of the fundamental features of capitalism (such as institution of private property, profit motive, competition, price-mechanism, etc.) are maintained or modified only to a limited extent. Under capitalism, the planning authority prepares a broad framework of the plan. The plan broadly indicates the objectives and targets of different sectors, and the annual growth-rate to be attained within specified time. Whatever the extent of planning under capitalism, it is implemented through the price-mechanism which is manipulated through subsidies, tax-concessions, etc., in such a manner that the price-manipulation helps attainment of the objectives and targets. In this connection Prof. W. A. Lewis writes: "The State can plan as much as it wants but it should plan not by direction but by manipulating the market."

Thus under planning in capitalism, the State offers various types of fiscal and monetary, positive and negative incentives to private enterprise units to induce them to take up some particular line of production and refrain from taking certain other lines, the idea being to induce production of those commodities which are conducive to welfare of society. Planning under capitalism is thus planning not by command or direction but by inducements. It mainly aims at removal of various evil of capitalism (already mentioned elsewhere) and to attain pre-determined objectives. Planning under capitalism is planning within the broad capitalist framework. The implementation of the plan is not by command or order or force but by offering various inducements like cheap loans, tax concessions and so on to persuade private enterprise establishments to move along lines broadly indicated in the plan so that pre-determined objectives and targets can be realised.

There are critics who maintain that capitalism is incompatible with planning. This is because planning to be effective does require some degree of compulsion and direction. It is also possible that private enterprise may not adequately respond to various positive and negative inducements offered and therefore the plan objectives and targets may not be realised. Anyway more and more sophisticated monetary, fiscal and other policies and instruments are being evolved to make planning under capitalism successful. The experience also shows that planning under capitalism can be successful. The experience also shows that planning under capitalism has helped to remove certain of the grave defects of capitalism and help capitalism attain desirable goals and objectives.

Socialist Planning. As we have seen, under socialism (or communism), all factors of production are owned by the State. All productive economic activities are carried on by the enterprises which are established, owned and managed by the State. Under such circumstances, planning becomes easy. Under socialist planning, government formulates the plan and also implements it. This implies that socialist planning is essentially planning by direction and not by merely offering inducements.

In socialist planning, all the economic activities are centrally planned and the economy is directed towards the attainment of certain specific goals and targets.

The fact that under socialism, all factors of production are owned by the State and there is only public sector (or only insignificant private sector) very much helps planning authority to formulate and implement a plan. A socialist economy, where there is absence of the institution to private property, private profit-motive, competition and freely fluctuating price-mechanism and where there is public ownership of all factors of production and complete control of the State over all the economic activities of the people, is in the best position to successfully formulate and implement a plan. As an author has put it, "No country can have much planning with little socialism or much socialism with little planning."

The merits of socialist planning are that under socialism, planning can be comprehensive and its implementation effective. But the defects of socialist planning are that consumers and producers enjoy hardly and personal freedom and they just become tools in the hands of the State acting under its command.

But experience has shown that socialism and planning not only are compatible but go hand-in-hand and that planning has greater chances of success than under capitalism.

(B) Totalitarian Planning and Democratic Planning

Totalitarian Planning. 'Totalitarian planning' may be defined as economic planning under totalitarian regime of the right (as in the case of fascist dictatorship of Stalin in the USSR). Under totalitarian planning, all authority comes to be concentrated in the hands of one or a small coterie who take all important and even minor economic decisions in respect of formulation and implementation of the country's economic plan. If found necessary, these totalitarian regimes while implementing a plan will not hesitate to use repressive and punitive measures as for example heavy punishment in case of failure of a manner of an enterprise to realise a specific target within specified time. It is the concentration of authority that is the fundamental feature of totalitarian economic planning and not whether it is dictatorship of the right or of the left. For example, under Hitler in Germany of 1930s, all the outward features of capitalism were more or less maintained and yet plans were formulated and implemented ruthlessly, while during the Stalinist regime in the USSR, totalitarian planning came to be resorted to under socialist regime.

Democratic Planning.'Democratic planning' may be defined as an economic plan formulated and implemented in a democratic way. In the case of a democratic country adopting economic planning, it will be observed that there are planning cells, or boards or commissions at different levels (as for example in the case of India at district, State and National levels) which formulate plans for their respective areas, taking into consideration views of or consulting elected representative bodies in respect of all important economic matters or decisions before formulating a plan. At each stage, the draft plan is debated in elected bodies where opposition parties are free to criticise the plan and suggest amendments or modifications or even an alternative plan. The central planning authority will then try to co-ordinate all the tentative plans coming from lower levels and the final draft of the plan is thrown open for debate in the parliament where elected representatives of all people in the country debate the plan, opposition parties suggesting changes or even fundamental modifications. It is only after the parliament approves and finalises the draft plan that the plan is supposed to be rendy and its implementation commences. (Thus in the case of India practically each village panchayat prepares a tentative plan for the village; these village-plans in a particular district come to be co-ordinated, debated and approved by zilla parishad; then in the similar manner different district plans in a State are co-ordinatcd at the State level by the State Planning Board and debated and approved by the State legislature; subsequently all the State plans come to be co-ordinated after necessary pruning or additions with the approval of States concerned and then debated and approved by the Indian Parliament. It is then that the implementation of India's Five-Year Plans commences).

Even in the process of implementation of a democratic plan, there is no use of force or repressive measures. Democratic planning comes to be implemented with the help of monetary and fiscal instruments and various controls (such as, in the case of India, control over investments, on location of industries, on production, controls such as compulsory procurement of foodgrains, fixation of prices, rationed distribution of scarce commodities and so on).

Comparing totalitarian planning with democratic planning, we notice the following merits and defects in each of them:

In the case of totalitarian planning, since a small coterie formulates the plan, plan formulation is easy and expeditiously done; its implementation, because of the use of repressive measures if need arises, is more effective as the experiences in the USSR, China and East European countries would show.

But the demerit of totalitarian planning is that too much power comes to be concentrated in a few hands; any mistake on their part which is very likely will have disastrous effects. Also, since people are not consulted while formulating the plan, the plan priorities may not represent the wishes, aspirations and needs of the people and therefore people will not feel that it is their own plan and hence their co-operation in its implementation may not be hearty or willing co-operation. Use of force or repressive measures has its limitations and therefore totalitarian planning may come to be riddled with inefficiency and therefore it may fail to realise the targets (as it repeatedly happened in its agricultural sector in the USSR).

The merit of democratic planning is that since people or their representatives at different levels are consulted before a plan is formulated, they would feel that it is their own plan representing their priorities and aspirations. They are therefore likely to offer their hearty co-operation in its implementation and that is likely to ensure its effective implementation.

But the defects of democratic planning are that since the draft plans or a plan has to be debated and approved at different levels, plan formulation may not be done expeditiously. Also all sorts of compromises and give and take takes place and hence democratically prepared plan may represent not a closely knit plan but a loose assemblage of various State Plans. Also since much reliance is placed on the willing co-operation of people and favourable response by the people to different policies adopted, people left to themselves may become indifferent with the consequences that the democratic plan may fail to realise the pre-determined objectives and targets.

(C) Centralised Planning and Decentralised Planning

Centralised Planning. On the basis of mechanism the planning may be classified into two types, namely: (*a*) Centralised planning, and (*b*) Decentralised planning.

In the case of centralised planning, one centralised planning authority, or board or commission is entrusted with all the powers of taking all the important economic decisions such as decisions regarding rate of saving and amount and pattern of investment, rate of growth of the economy, sectoral allocation of resources, fixation of targets in different industries and so on. The central planning authority further splits these resources and targets which each region or enterprise is asked to fulfil. Regional planning authorities may be existing and may be consulted; but all the final and vital decisions are taken by the central planning authority.

The central planning authority may ask the regional bodies to implement their part of the national plan; but all the implementation will be done under the direct supervision of the central planning authority. Thus, in the case of centralised planning which is also known as 'planning from above,' all the powers of taking vital decisions regarding formulation, adoption and supervision over implementation are entrusted to the central planning authority.

It need to be noted that though communist countries are generally associated with centralised type of planning and capitalist countries and mixed economies like India with decentralised type of planning, there is no logical connection between the two. Yugoslavia, a communist country, had adopted decentralised type of planning, whereas India with its mixed economy and democratic form of government, adopted, at least initially, centralised type of planning.

Since a single and all powerful planning authority enjoys all powers in respect of formulation and implementation of a plan, centralised planning possesses certain advantages such as expeditious decision-making in regard to planning, logical consistency, effective and efficient implementations or execution of the plan all leading to substantial results as regards achievements of predetermined objectives and targets.

But centralised planning also suffers from grave defects such as predominance of subjective considerations or even whims and fancies of prominent members of the central planning authority, lack of flexibility, non-involvement of people in plan formulation and therefore failure of the plan to represent needs, wishes and aspirations of the people in general, lack or absence of hearty co-operation of the people in the implementation of the plan, and because of the vastness of the task of evolution and implementation involved, inefficiency and therefore failure to attain objectives and targets within specific time limit.

Decentralised Planning. As regards decentralised planning, there is not just one all-powerful central planning authority; there are several regional and even lower level planning bodies. These bodies enjoy the power of formulating plans for their own regions taking into consideration local needs, cultural background, priorities and so on. But these regional planning boards are required to formulate their regional plans within the broad framework of the national plan previously discussed and agreed upon by all parties concerned. This sort of planning is known as 'planning from below.'

In the case of decentralised planning the advantages are that there is no concentration of authority in the hands of a single person or a small body of persons; hence there is little scope for domination over planning of such a person or body; since people are involved and consideration is given to different regional and local needs and resources, planning from below or decentralised planning becomes more representative of people's needs, aspirations and priorities. And since people feel involved in planning directly or through their elected representatives, decentralised planning is more likely to enlist voluntary co-operation of people.

But decentralised planning has certain defects. Each region may make excessive demand without reference to nation's resource position. This would make pruning and chopping of regional plans necessary and here political pressures may exert undue influence with the consequence that some regional plans may suffer unjustifiable cutting down while those with political pulls may have bigger regional plans not justifiable on any logical grounds.

This means co-ordination of different regional plans poses serious problem so that final shape of the plan may be a sort of compromise. This would mean that there is no proper co-ordination which might make implementation of the national plan difficult.

When the country is vast with varigated resources and cultural backgrounds, the best method of planning would be to combine in a proper way both 'planning from above' and 'planning from below.' The central planning authority should draw broad framework of national plan, fixing general objective and broad targets and ask regional planning bodies to prepare regional plans in such a way that they fit into the national plan which may have to be modified here and there only to some extent. This combination of both type of planning will ensure the merits of both, avoiding the defects of either at the same time.

(D) Functional Planning and Structural Planning

Functional Planning. Functional planning is that type of economic planning which aims at improving the functioning of the economy. It aims at improving the efficiency and performance in the economy by pushing up the rate of saving and investment, or improving efficiency of labour or by such other innovations like rationalisation of industry, etc. What is to be noted is that functional planning aims at bringing about all these improvements without fundamentally altering the structure of the economy or without introducing fundamental changes in the institutional pattern or structure of the society. At the most, only minor structural or institutional changes or adjustments necessary to enable the economy to function more efficiently and attain specified targets and objectives within the prescribed time limit, would be brought about. Thus Prof. S. Zeweig writes: "Functional planning will only repair, not build anew; it will only improve the work of existing order, but not supersede it. Functional planning is conservative or rather evolutionary type of planning which will not overturn the existing structure and moves only within its narrow borders."

Structural Planning. By structural planning is meant a type of economic planning which aims at achieving the objectives and targets within specified time limit by improving the functioning of the economy, by bringing about some fundamental structural and institutional changes in the economy. These structural and institutional changes in the existing socio-economic and political institutional pattern are deemed essential because it is felt that with the existing institutional system or pattern it would be very difficult or practically impossible to improve the functioning of the economy and attain the aims and targets of planning within the specified time limit. This structural planning is planning which aims at improving the functioning of the economy by bringing about radical or fundamental change in the existing socio-economic and political institutions which are to be replaced by more suitable socio-economic and political institutions conducive to better functioning of economy.

The concept of structural planning (and by implication, that of functional planning) can best be illustrated by taking the illustration of planning in India.

Like other developing countries when India adopted economic planning, it had many feudal socio-economic and political institutions, attitudes and the value system. Planning in India had therefore to be both functional and structural. Thus planning in India aims at improving the functioning of the economy and its efficiency which is very low, by bringing about several radical or fundamental alternations in its social, cultural, economic and even political institutions prevailing in the country. These structural changes aim at or include radical changes like abolition of the Zamindari system and absentee landlordism, substituting institutional credit like credit by co-operative societies and commercial banks in place of traditional moneylenders, abolishing barter-system of economy prevailing in many backward parts of the country and monetising that economy, abolishing the managing agency system and substituting it by professional management, restrictions on activities of private sector and bringing basic and heavy industries in the public sector which is to be made dominant, nationalising commercial banking and other financial institutions, changing the pattern of education by substituting technical and professional education in place of old type of learning so that modern skills can be acquired by people, changing the attitude of people (by replacing fatalistic attitude by scientific attitude) and making necessary changes in the value system of the society. These fundamental structural changes are being brought about because of the belief that without such fundamental structural changes (and not just marginal institutional changes) economic stagnancy in which the country has got submerged for centuries cannot be removed and the functioning of the economy cannot be appreciably improved. It should thus be noted that structural planning does not just emphasise negative aspect of destroying old institutions, but also is constructive as it aims at introducing new and more suitable institutions in place of old ones to be removed. It should be noted that structural planning aims not only at changing radically economic institutions but also socio-cultural, political and administrative institutions in the country, if need be, as also attitudes and value system prevailing in the country.

This should make clear why developing countries in Asia, Africa and Latin America need not only functional planning but along with that structural planning also. In fact in the case of these countries one wonders whether without structural planning, there can be much of functional planning.

2. Classification of Planning on the Basis of 'Time-Element'

(A) Perspective Planning, Medium-Term Planning and Short Term Planning

Perspective Planning. 'Perspective planning' refers to long-term planning covering a period of 20 to 25 years or even longer period. Perspective plan only lays down the broad direction in which the economy and different sectors of the economy are expected to or should move and the broad objectives which the economy aims at or should aim at attaining in the long run.

From the concept of perspective planning, it follows that such a plan, can be drawn only in broad terms and not in detail. It also follows that longer the span of time of a perspective plan, more broader and vague will be the direction and objectives and less detailed the programmes and projects. It should be clear that as in the modern complex world, many dynamic changes are continually taking place, drawing a perspective plan today for the country for the next 25 or 30 years is going to be based on a number of assumptions which may prove invalid and the perspective plan may prove unrealistic and therefore require drastic modifications.

The concept of 'perspective planning' may be illustrated by taking Indian illustration. When planning came to be adopted in India in 1950, there was drawn a broad perspective plan for the next 25 years. It was broadly aimed that during the next 25 years, per capita income should be doubled, that there should be rapid industrialisation of the country, that the country should become self-sufficient in foodgrains and for that purpose agriculture should be modernised, that all children should get primary education which should be compulsory and free and so on. The perspective was in broad terms; but it was necessary, as it showed the direction in which the country should move. It is to realise these long-term aims and objectives that medium-term and short-term plans come to be drawn in concrete terms.

To give another illustration, India by the turn of the century will have a population of about 100 crores. With this assumption in view, the perspective plan will have to be drawn calculating the amount of foodgrains, clothing and other necessaries that would be required at the end of the century as also the number of houses, schools, teachers, doctors and technicians and so on and so forth by the year 2000. On the basis of this rough calculation, the perspective plan for the next 25 years would indicate the broad targets which different sectors of the economy like agriculture, industry, transport, banking, energy should attempt to attain, and the direction in which and the speed at which these sectors should move right from now onwards. It is possible that the assumptions on which the perspective plan is drawn may prove invalid. A major war may completely upset the calculations or new inventions (such as quickly maturing crops making possible three or four crops per year instead of just one or two) may take place making nonsense of the perspective. And yet with all these hazards, there will have to be a perspective plan, because without these broad objectives, goals, direction and targets to be attained at the end of 20 to 25 years, the country will be just drifting aimlessly.

Medium-Term Plan. The perspective plan of 20 or 25 years, for operational purposes, comes to be split into several medium-term plans. The medium term plan generally covers a period of five years and is called a Five-Year Plan. (But sometimes, the period of a medium-term plan may be 4 years as it happened in the case of India's Fifth Plan or seven years which the USSR adopted once).

The medium-term plan enables the planning authority to lay down specific targets in specific sectors and formulate specific policies and projects to be followed or completed to attain the targets. Thus India's Five-Year Plans lay down specific targets in respect of foodgrains and other crops, output of different industries, specific projects (like irrigational projects or factories) to be completed and so on. Naturally there is more definiteness in these medium-term plans.

Since planning is a continuing process, each Five-Year Plan is succeeded by the next Five-Year Plan again with specific targets and projects. The idea behind is that these successive Five-Year Plans should enable the country to move towards the broad objectives and targets conceived in the Perspective Plan of the country.

Short-term Plan. The medium-term plan (of 4, 5, 6 or 7 years) is further split into several one-year plans laying down targets in still more specific terms which the economy should achieve at the end of each year. The rationale behind the formulation of one-year plan has been that experience in India showed that in the case of a Five-Year Plan very little was generally done during the first two or three years of a Five-Year Plan and then execution of projects and expenditure over several projects used to be rushed through during the last two or three years of the Five-Year Plan to show that targets were attained in time. This often resulted in wasteful expenditure and inferior quality of work done or goods produced. In order to avoid this sort of concentration of work and expenditure during the latter part of a Five-Year Plan, it was found that it would be desirable to break up a Five-Year Plan into several one-year plans. This resulted in spreading the work to be done in a proper way so that implementation of different projects had to be done at reasonable speed from the beginning of a Five-Year Plan to the end of it. It would be observed that the relation between annual plans and a Five-Year Plan is much the same as between several Five-Year Plans and the Perspective Plan.

It needs to be emphasised that the Perspective Plan, Five Year Plans and Annual Plans all need to be properly coordinated and integrated, if the country's economy is to move smoothly and efficiently towards the fixed goals in an orderly manner.

(B) Permanent Planning and Emergency Planning

Permanent Planning. By 'Permanent Planning' is meant economic planning which has been accepted by a country on ideological grounds as in the case of the USSR and other communist countries, or even some of the democratic countries where all political parties appear to have agreed on acceptance of some sort of economic planning to attain certain socio-economic objectives. In the case of permanent planning, planning comes to be accepted as the most satisfactory way of managing the nation's economy so that economic planning becomes a permanent way of managing the economy sales and part and parcel of philosophy and way of life of the community.

Emergency Planning. 'Emergency Planning' on the other hand, means planning which comes to be adopted for a temporary or short period because of the force of circumstances like war, or continual drought or depression creating an emergency situation in a country. It is possible that the country has no faith in planning or in fact is opposed to economic planning on ideological grounds; but the force of circumstances is such that for a temporary period of emergency the country is forced to adopt some sort of planning.

Thus the USA which is opposed to the acceptance of the concept of planning adopted 'New Deal' which in fact was a sort of planning during the Great Depression of 1929-33. Similarly several capitalist and democratic countries adopted planning during the period of World War II to meet the emergency situation created by war, and during post-World War II period to solve post-war problems and rehabilitate national economies.

3. Planning Classified on the Basis of 'Region'

(A) Regional Planning

In countries like India and the USSR which are vast, different regions of the country have different economic and cultural characteristics, different types of resources and different priorities and needs. In the case of India, for example, compare regions like Assam with Rajasthan or Konkan region with Marathwada, or Punjab with Tamil Nadu. It logically follows that under such circumstances one centralised plan drawn on a uniform basis for the entire country and covering all the regions would not be a suitable type of planning to realise rapid economic development of the country and for attaining other socio-economic objectives.

Under such circumstances, decentralised type of planning is adopted wherein each region prepares its own plan and implements it. But it should be noted that these various regional plans are not drawn by different regions independently of each other, nor are they implemented like that. It should be noted that regional plans are drawn within the broad framework of the national plan of which regional plans form inseparable parts. Regional plans come to be coordinated by the Central Planning Authority pruning some parts of some regional plans and adding something to some other regional plans, taking into consideration regional as also national resources, priorities and needs. It also needs to be noted that while different regional plans may have before them some special objectives which are relevant to particular regions, these objectives of regional plans must be in consonance with the broad objectives of the national plan. There need therefore be no conflict between regional plans and the national plan of which they form parts. S. Zeweig writes: "Planning of this kind (*i.e.,* regional planning) is carried out within the framework of a national scheme and the wants of its population. Regional authorities are endowed with certain powers in regard to the regional area, *viz.*, as to the constitution, execution and supervision of plans. Every country whose area is large needs a high degree of regional decentralisation."

Thus, the objective of regional plan is to ensure that existing and political resources of each region are fully utilised and social, economic and cultural differences are taken into account while framing regional plans. But all this is to be done within the broad framework of the national plan, and objectives of different regional plans must be in broad consonance with the objectives of the national plan. This means regional plans are not formulated independently of each other, nor do regional plans seek regional self-sufficiency; nor is a regional plan rival or alternative to the national plans. There is bound to be certain amount of rivalry and excessive demands by regional planning authorities on national resources when different regional plans are formulated. But the Central Planning Authority takes steps to harmonies these differences and rivalries and to see that different regional plans fit approximately together into a national plan.

In recent years regional planning has been assuming increasing significance. The reason is that in big countries like India, a national plan, while resulting in the economic development of the nation as a whole, yet left certain regions backward denying people in those regions fruits of national economic development in the shape of increasing employment opportunities, rising incomes and standard of living. Thus in the case of India, while the national economy went on developing at an average rate of 3.5 per cent per year since the era of planning commenced in the country, certain regions in the country advanced fairly rapidly (*e.g.*, Punjab, Maharashtra, Gujarat and Tamil Nadu), certain other regions (*e.g.*, Assam, Bihar, Orissa, Rajasthan etc.,) did not progress at the same rate, whereas some sub-regions like Konkan and Marathwada hardly recorded any economic progress.

It has also come to be realised that unequal development of different regions might lead to regional rivalries encouraging disruptive tendencies which would have adverse effects on development of the national economy.

Also, regional planning would lead to checking current trend towards concentration of industries in certain regions or areas leading to over-growth of urban centres creating complex socio-economic and political problems.

Regional planning would thus lead to more balanced growth of different regions which is desirable both on social and political grounds. Even from the strategic point of view, balanced growth of different regions is desirable and dispersal of industries instead of their concentration in certain areas would be welcome.

In the case of India, regional planning would be welcome due to the following factors: våst area of the country which is equal practically to the whole of Europe minus the USSR, varied resources position of different regions, existence of social and cultural differences, differences in levels of economic development already achieved, existence of pockets of extremely backward areas in certain regions, concentration of industries at certain centres like Bombay, Calcutta, Ahmedabad, Kanpur and Delhi while industrial and human resources are lying unutilised or underutilised in various regions, differing per capita income and standards of living in different regions, and therefore existence of regional rivalries and sometimes demand for formation of independent States.

(B) National Planning

In the case of national plan, the area covered by the national plan is identical with the national boundaries. In the case of a national plan, planning comes to be accepted and adopted by the people as a whole and in the interest of the people of the country. National plan is naturally backed by the central or national government; it has the national objectives before it such as rapid economic development of the country, rapid industrialisation, food-self-sufficiency, equitable distribution of income, balanced regional development in the country, full employment, and so on.

National plan to be successful requires certain conditions. If it is a democracy all the major political parties must accept economic planning on ideological grounds which means that there should be no fundamental opposition to the acceptance of the concept of planning among different political parties as such and therefore planning would be a continual process; the national plan must be backed by national will behind it; people must be convinced that benefits of progress due to planning would be equitably distributed among people and therefore ready to offer willing co-operation for its implementation. The national plan envisaged must be practicable and backed by adequate resources of the nation which means the plan must not be over-ambitious. If a country has varigated resources, formulations and implementation of a plan becomes easier. On the other hand, as in the case of very small countries like England and Japan which also depend to a very great extent on foreign trade which happens to be their life-line, national planning in such countries is likely to encounter a number of difficulties arising on account of different agricultural, industrial and international trade policies adopted in different countries with which the above countries are trading. It is difficult for the governments of these countries to control developments in other countries and therefore the direction and quantum of their own international trade. Naturally formulation and implementation of a national plan in such countries will have to face many unexpected hazards and uncertainties. But it is possible to argue that it is precisely because these countries face such stupendous problems arising out of developments with their trading partners that there is all the greater need for planning which thinks of and provides for various alternatives should circumstances compel them to abandon a particular course (*e.g.*, if country A prohibits imports from England, the latter must anticipate and build relations with countries B and C as possible substitutes and so on).

(C) International Planning

The concept of international planning refers strictly to pooling together of resources of two or more independent countries or of the world as a whole having a broad plan to make maximum use of the resources concerned with a view to attain certain objectives. Thus international planning involves pooling part or major portion of resources of two or more independent countries to attain certain common objectives which would benefit all the countries involved in such international planning.

International planning may be interpreted in a narrow sense where two or more countries voluntarily cooperate for attaining a specific objective or objectives such as two countries coming together for establishing a giant steel factory, or for water-management and control of floods (as for example, India and Pakistan coming together in the case of the Indus River Treaty or India and Bangladesh coming together for controlling of floods and water management with reference to rivers flowing through both the countries, or a number of countries coming together for the construction of Asian Highway, or the tea-producing countries like India, Ceylon and East Africa coming together for controlling production and prices of tea).

International planning is becoming popular since the end of World War II since then a number of countries are coming together to attain certain common objectives. The Anglo-American Loan Agreement, General Agreement on Trade and Tariff (GATT), the Marshall Aid Plan, the International Bank for Reconstruction and Development (IBRD), the International Monetary Fund (IMF), the Asian Development Bank (ADB), the Colombo Plan all indicate how the way was being prepared after the end of World War II for international co-operation and planning. The European Economic Community and similar bodies involving countries in Africa and Latin America are also cases in point.

The concept of international planning is assuming increasing significance in recent years, because it is realised that there are certain problems which the world as a whole is facing — rapidly increasing population of the world, problem of pollution and environmental imbalance, sharing sea-bed, control of contagious diseases, armament race, energy problem, and so on. These problems, it has come to be realised, cannot be solved on national basis, but that they will have to be solved only on the basis of international co-operation and planning. There is increasing realisation that poverty and ignorance in any part of the world are directly or indirectly a threat to the peace of the world. Thus circumstances are compelling countries of different continents in the world to come together and co-operate on an increasing scale for attaining some specific or general objectives.

It is obvious that there are a number of difficulties in formulating and successfully implementing international planning. Some of the difficulties are: cultural and linguistic differences, differences in levels of economic development, in per capita income and levels of living, historical and religious rivalries and different value-system in different countries. As Prof. Lionel Robbins has pointed out: "When it is a matter of pooling the total resources of of different national units, the obstacles are likely to be so great as to be totally insurmountable — at any rate by peaceful methods. There is no vested interest more intractable than the vested interest of national group."[3]

Difficulties in respect of international planning can easily be appreciated by considering how though a number of mutual problems can be satisfactorily solved to the benefit of both India and Pakistan, how such co-operation and planning has become practically impossible till today because of religious differences, historial conflicts and rivalries, conflicts of economic interests in the short-term and political game played by big powers, setting one against the other.

But one feels hopeful by taking the fact into account that France and Germany who were mortal foes for over a century have now realised the folly of mutual conflicts and have joined hands in mutual co-operation by forming the European Economic Community and thus in international planning after the disastrous World War II.

International planning, as things stand at present, is likely to succeed if the following considerations are kept in mind:

1. For the time being, international planning should be proceeded within a narrow sense — construction of a joint steel factory, joint railway system, a common river valley project, or atomic power stations, etc., the benefits of which would be obvious to all and can be equitably shared between or among the participating countries.

This implies that it is no use beginning with over-ambitious international plans and facing certain disappointment with a setback to international co-operation and planning.

2. As a principle, there should be no interference in the internal affairs of participating countries by the joint planning authority constituted for formulating and executing an international project.

---

3. The developing countries should forget the past rivalries fostered by their old imperial masters for their benefit and look at problems of international co-operation objectively and scientifically. Also big powers should encourage such international co-operation among developing countries instead of playing old power-game dividing them for their selfish economic and other benefits.

4. There should be willing co-operation in the formulation and implementation of a joint project by participating countries and this can be ensured if they are convinced that the joint project would benefit the participating countries and that costs and benefits are equitably shared.

If international planning is begun in this small way between two or a few countries (as it has already begun), the way will be paved for international planning in the broader sense to solve many of the complex problems which the world as a whole is facing and which can be successfully solved only at the international level.

4. Classification of Planning on the Basis of 'Physical Output' and 'Finance'

(A) Physical Planning

Distinction is made between 'Physical Planning' and 'Financial Planning'.

When economic planning is formulated and executed in physical or real terms, we have what is called 'Physical Planning'. Thus to give an illustration, if a Five-Year Plan aims at the target of increasing foodgrains production, let us suppose by 20 million tonnes during the next five years of the plan, then the government will have to work out the amount of additional land that will have to be brought under cultivation, additional irrigational facilities, fertilisers, seeds and various agricultural as also non-agricultural inputs that will have be made available to the agricultural sector, if that target is to be reached within the specified time, and steps will have to be planned to see that the required inputs are made available in appropriate quantities, at right time, and at reasonable prices. Similarly, if the Five-Year Plan aims at increasing during the next five years steel output by one million tonnes, the planners will have to calculate and plan steps to provide various required inputs like coal, furnaces and technical personnel to train which additional technical institutions may have to be planned and established. Physical planning is a very complicated process as various physical input-output tables will have to be worked out and kept up-to-date taking into consideration continual technical progress that is taking place in methods of production. Physical planning will thus have to take stock of real or physical resources in terms of natural and human resources, input-output tables and then fix targets in physical terms in consonance with the above considerations. Physical planning requires that the physical targets planned are consistent among themselves because of the close interdependence between different sectors of the economy and among different commodities because output of one industry becomes the input of another industry. Thus one wrong calculation of a physical output will produce its repercussions throughout the economy. If the target fixed for production of coal turns out to be an under-estimate, then the output target of steel cannot be reached, so also targets of tractors, machinery for fertiliser production and hence of fertiliser and hence foodgrains target. Thus planning in physical or real terms is called 'Physical Planning' which happens to be an essential part of economic planning. In a sense, physical planning is the heart of economic planning.

It should be obvious that in a developing country like India mere manipulation of the quantity of money, rate of interest and flow of funds will not create real resources if they are not existing. The essence of economic planning therefore in developing countries is to create and mobilise real resources available in the country. While formulating overall plan and sectoral plans, the planning authority will have to ensure that there takes place adequate mobilisation of resources like land, water, labour, different skills, import some of these items if need be in return for export of surplus of some goods. Planners will have to supervise how the different sectors and projects are progressing and that the progress is as per the schedule fixed. Again when the plan or particular project is completed, the planners will have to calculate the benefits accruing from the plan or project in real terms, *i.e.*, additional land brought under cultivation, fertilisers and foodgrains produced, level of improvement in the standard of living effected and so on. For convenience all the above calculations are generally done in terms of money and planning and sectoral allocation or allocation for a particular project comes to be expressed in terms of money. But it should be noted that what really matters is the attainment of planned targets in real terms — additional amounts of foodgrains, of clothing, fertilisers, steel and tractors, oil and so on. For convenience all the above calculations are generally done in terms of money and planning and sectoral allocation or allocation for a particular project comes to be expressed in terms of money. But it should be noted that what really matters is the attainment of planned targets in real terms-additional amounts of foodgrains, of clothing, fertilisers, steel and tractors, oil and so on produced within the stipulated time-limit.

(B) Financial Planning

'Financial Planning' is planning that is made in financial or monetary terms. Modern economy is necessarily money economy and values of all commodities and services are expressed in terms of money and are called prices. All of them thus have prices which facilitate calculations.

Financial planning consists of planning regarding how much total investment in monetary terms would be needed to realise the targeted growth-rate, how that amount is to be raised: how much is to be raised by taxation, how much by changing rates such as electricity and railway rates, how much through profits of public sector enterprises and how much by deficit financing. Financial planning also involves allocation of required amounts of investment funds in different sectors to enable them to realise targeted real output. Financial planning also involves calculations in terms of money costs and benefits accruing from a project and from the execution of the plan as a whole.

It should thus be clear that while physical planning involves calculations in terms of real factors of production and real output, financial planning involves their calculation in monetary terms which is facilitated because all commodities and services have prices. It should be obvious that while expressing a plan in physical terms would be very difficult or practically impossible, its expression in financial or monetary terms is comparatively easy. Thus to take an illustration, in physical terms we will have to say that to attain a target of 20 additional million tonnes of foodgrains, 'a' quantity of additional land, 'b' quantity of additional water, 'c' quantity of additional fertilisers, 'd' quantity of additional seeds and so on and so forth will be required. This would be extremely clumsy way of expression, though necessary. Instead since all the above have prices, to multiply the various required inputs by their prices and simply to say that to produce targeted agricultural output during the plan period, additional investment of say Rs. 1000 crores would be necessary would be easy way of expression. Of course, if prices of required inputs change, suitable adjustments will have to be made and the amount of investment expressed in monetary terms will have to be suitably adjusted. But this is a comparatively simple matter.

The relationship between the physical plan and the financial plan should now be clear. The two are closely connected and in fact represent two ways of expressing the same plan.

Since finance or money represents command over resources the amount of money that is going to be mobilised for investment purposes and is going to be allocated among different sectors must be in consonance with the real resources available for investment. There has to be an equilibrium between physical plan and financial plan in so far as money is supposed to represent real resources. And therefore money flows must be properly controlled. Failure of financial planning — either in the mobilisation of necessary finance, or in maintaining equilibrium in demands and supply of funds — will definitely result in failure of physical planning. It is thus conceivable that there might be available real resources for investment and economic progress, but because of the failure of financial planning *i.e.*, failure to mobilise financial resources and invest them appropriately, the country's progress may not take place. This necessitates proper integration between physical planning and financial planning. As the Planning Commission wrote: "... whether one thinks in terms of physical or financial planning — the two are complementary — the object is to secure the various balances in the economy at continually higher level."

3. SWEDEN'S 'MIDDLE WAY'

The most satisfactory way of understanding the system of a mixed economy is to analyse the working of some of the successfully functioning economies of countries which have adopted that type of economy. In this respect it may be said that Sweden provides a classic illustration of how a mixed economy in an European country has been successfully functioning. It would therefore be instructive to analyse and understand the functioning of Sweden's economy.

The phrase the 'Middle Way' has been supposed to be coined by Harold Macmillan, a prominent member of the British Conservative Party and one-time Prime Minister of Great Britain. He used the phrase the 'Middle Way' to denote an economic system that combined some of the features of the *laissez-faire* capitalist economic system that prevailed in most of the West European countries during the 19th century, and the socialist economic system advocated by the British Labour Party. Thus the 'Middle Way' lies between *laissez faire* capitalism and socialism. It is an attempt to combine features of both the systems so that certain broad socio-economic objectives can be attained. Allen Gruchy in his 'Comparative Economic System' describes the Middle Way or a mixed economic system as follows: "While attention is paid to meeting certain minimum welfare needs of the general population, the main emphasis is upon securing high levels of consumer and occupational freedom in an efficient economic system. And the main reliance is upon the free market mechanism as an allocator of economic resources and a distributor of goods and services in accordance with individual consumer preference."[4]

In this sense, Sweden provides a classic example of the 'Middle Way.'

The 'Middle Way' of Sweden

In Sweden, we observe successful functioning of a mixed economy. Sweden has made a fairly successful attempt at combing economic planning with private sector and price-mechanism and government intervention in economic activities of the people with freedom of private enterprise, competition and price mechanism.

Sweden has adopted economic planning which takes the form of long-term forecasting of the direction and objectives to be reached. This long-term planning provides for the functioning of the private enterprise in the country. By successfully combining economic planning with the features of capitalism, Sweden has managed to attain the objectives of high level of growth rate, full employment, economic prosperity with fair amount of stability and a high standard of living for the people of the country which is the highest among the European countries and next only to that of the U.S.A. The Swedish economy is often described as 'Welfare Capitalism' and illustrates how economic planning with successful use or reliance on fiscal and monetary measures can be combined with free enterprise economy.

Features of Sweden's Mixed Economy

In Sweden, there is dominance of the private sector. Nearly 91 per cent of industrial enterprises are privately owned and operated, employing about 85 per cent of the labour force in the country. Government-owned industrial enterprises account for only about 4 per cent of the industrial enterprises in the country, while the rest (namely, about 5 per cent) are accounted for by the co-operatives.

It should be noted that public sector or public enterprises are mainly confined to railways, telegraph and telephone system and provision of other public utilities. The Government provides various incentives to the private enterprise through provision of liberal depreciation allowance while computing income tax and helping industrial corporations in the private sector to build investment reserve fund which allows a corporation to make a tax-free deduction of 40 per cent of pre-tax income.

In the Swedish economy production and distribution of capital and consumer goods are mostly in private hands (the Government as we have already noted mostly providing only public utilities). Basic decisions regarding allocation of community's resources are also the responsibility of the private enterprise. Co-operative sector also plays a fairly important role in manufacturing and retail distribution of consumer goods.

But it should be noted that in Sweden's Middle Way or mixed economy, Government also plays a prominent role. In the first place it draws as we have seen a long-term plan the objectives of which have been: (*a*) Economic growth with stability; (*b*) Maintenance of high level of employment; (*c*) Improvement in the standard of living of the people; and (*d*) Promotion of labour welfare.

As we have already seen, the Government owns and provides public utilities, as also certain ownership or part-ownership of certain basic industries through which private enterprise can be helped and made to proceed in a way that would help attain the objectives of economic planning.

But the main control in the hands of the Government is in the form of fiscal and monetary policies. It is through progressive taxation and public expenditure policy that the Government has sought to bring about redistribution of national income and help raise living standard of masses. Also the Government relies heavily on fiscal and monetary measures to influence allocation of community's resources by the private-sector in a manner that would help realise the objectives of growth with stability, full employment and rising standard of living of the people. What distinguishes the Swedish economy and why it truly deserves the title of a mixed economy is that the Government, while playing a significant role through planning and by influencing allocation of the community's resources through fiscal and monetary measures, mainly aims at coordinating the activities of the Government sector, private sector and the cooperative sector. The Government seeks the cooperation of all, namely private enterprise, co-operatives and trade unions and attempts to follow a co-ordinated approach. It therefore can be truly described as the middle way.

4. SWEDISH LABOURISTIC ECONOMY

Labouristic economy may be defined as an economy where labour or workers in a country are assigned and play and important role and where welfare of workers forms an important objective of the economic policy or planning of the country.

In Sweden labour movement and its influence play a dominant role in the economy and in fulfilling the objectives before the Swedish economy. It so happened that during the post-World War II period, the Swedish Social Democratic Labour Party came to power and remained in that position for considerable time. It naturally accepted labour-oriented policies. The programme accepted by the Party has been labour-oriented. It aims at providing full employment of workers as also increasing the share of income going to workers out of the total annual income. Thus specifically the labour-oriented programme has the following objectives: (*a*) Attaining full employment; (*b*) Increasing the share of income going to workers out of the annual national income; (*c*) Bringing about fair distribution of national income among people majority to whom constitute the working class; (*d*) Ensuring rising standard of living to workers; (*e*) To take steps to increase productivity of labour; and (*f*) To introduce industrial democracy.

From the above objectives, it should be clear that one of the main aims of Swedish economy and planning is to attain welfare of workers. That is why the Swedish economy is called 'Labouristic Economy'. Allen Gruchy in this connection writes: ". . . the programme emphasises that a principle objective of the Swedish labour movement's post-war economic policy was to be full employment. Monetary, fiscal and wage policies were to be combined at all times to ensure the full use of labour and material resources."

The objectives of full employment and welfare of workers are to be achieved not by authoritarian type of planning as in the USSR, China and East European countries, but mainly with the aid of fiscal and monetary policies and by providing all types of incentives to increase productivity of agricultural and industrial workers.

In the labouristic economy, trade unions and labour movement play an important role. Trade unions recognise the importance of increasing productivity of workers in all the sectors of the economy; they therefore also recognise the importance in this regard of education of workers and of industrial and technical research which have direct bearing on labour productivity and through that on share of income going to workers and their standard of living.

Trade unions in Sweden play an important role in helping to attain the objective of full employment with stability (*i.e.* without inflation). Swedish trade unions are all organised in a centralised confederation. The confederation of trade unions in the country enjoys the power of collectively bargaining for the economy as a whole. What is remarkable about trade union movement in Sweden is that trade unions do not work in an atmosphere of confrontation with private enterprises; on the other hand, the confederation of trade unions, when collectively bargaining take into consideration the effects of wage increases on the objectives of full employment and price stability. Unlike in many West European capitalist countries, trade unions as well as the confederation of trade unions in Sweden show a sense of self-discipline and co-operation and recognition of the importance of co-ordinated action (with private enterprise and Government) for achieving various objectives of economic policy and of long term planning.

The objectives of full employment and of increasing the share of workers in the national income are achieved by adopting various measures and policies. Government exercises control over the total amount of investment in the economy, through 'Investment Reserve System' (more of it below) which is used to avoid both depression and over full employment and attain the goal of full-employment with stability. Private enterprise is also allowed various tax and monetary concessions when needed in such a manner that problem of unemployment is not allowed to arise.

Also, Government takes steps to influence supply and demand for labour through proper development of labour market. The Government and private enterprise take steps to impart technical training so that workers are well-equipped for jobs created by new technological and dynamic changes continually taking place in society. Continual steps are taken by Government, private enterprises and trade unions to increase labour productivity. Government takes steps to increase geographical mobility of labour with a view to bring about appropriate regional distribution of labour force in the country. This not only helps to avoid concentration of labour but also promotion of labour welfare. Thus it would be seen that the Swedish government ensures full employment not by expanding the public sector but by helping development of labour market by improving productivity of labour and helping private enterprise to attain the objective of full employment.

As regards redistribution of increasing share of national income in favour of the working class, along with full employment, the instrument of steeply progressive taxation on richest sections of the community is used by the government. The tax proceeds are spent on ensuring that minimum needs of all workers are satisfied and for increasing the welfare of workers. This should make clear why the Swedish economy is called the 'Labouristic Economy.'

5. SWEDISH PLANNING

The Swedish Social Democratic Party which came to power prepared in 1947 the first of a series of annual economic plans. In 1948, the first long-term economic plan for the country was prepared. The Swedish Labour Government found economic planning a useful tool to solve the various economic problems during the post-World War II period, and for achieving various other economic objectives.

The following description will enable the reader to know how economic planning function in Sweden.

It is the Swedish Cabinet which is mainly responsible for drawing up the annual plans and five-year plans for the nation. But the Cabinet only lays down the general guidelines along which the national annual plans and five-year plans are to be formulated.

It is however the Economic Division of the Ministry of Finance which prepares a detailed plan. In this task of construction of the national plan, the Ministry is assisted by the National Institute of Economic Research a government agency. The work of this Institute is to analyse past economic developments, collect and analyse the data, anticipate on the empirical basis the future requirements and trends in demand for various commodities and services and thus provide much of the statistical data and basic information necessary for preparing the annual and five-year plans to the Ministry. The Research Council is made up of representatives of the National Institute of Economic Research and other government agencies, representatives of private agricultural, commercial, trade and industrial research groups and advises the Ministry of Finance in respect of preparation of annual budgets.

The Bank of Sweden and other financial institutions like commercial banks also play a significant role in the process of planning.

It is observed that in Sweden national economic planning has come to be based essentially on a sort of informal relationship between governmental bodies like the Cabinet and Ministry of Finance and Institute of Economic Research and various private economic groups and agencies representing agriculture, industry, trade, transport, etc. The institutional arrangements for formulating and implementing planning in Sweden are mostly informal. It would thus be observed that there is no fanatical attachment to economic planning nor is planning shunned. Planning in Sweden is carried on in an informal way and in the spirit of give and take between various Government bodies and private bodies with a view to achieve some commonly agreed national objectives. That is why it may truly be said that Sweden's way is the 'Middle Way' or that Swedish economy truly represents a mixed economic system.

Planning Policies and Methods in Sweden

As regards the various instruments and methods used in Sweden to attain various plan objectives such as economic growth, full employment, rising level of income and standard of living for the working class, etc., the Swedish Government has come to rely upon not direct physical controls like compulsory procurement, price control and rationing but on fiscal and monetary measures.

Great emphasis is placed on fiscal measures, that is, Government taxation and expenditure policies, with a view to direct the activities of the private sector in the desired direction and for bringing about redistribution of national income as envisaged in the plan. Thus is Sweden, budgetary policy has become an important tool to equate demand for and supply of goods by controlling purchasing power in the hands of the people through taxation, for stabilising capitalist economy, and by progressive taxation to increase the share of working class in the national income with a view to increase welfare of society. Policies based on Keynesian analysis are made full use of to stabilise the Swedish economy at the level of full employment.

Similarly, in Sweden the Government provides direction as to how private financial institutions should invest their funds. If necessary, Government may ask private financial institutions like banks to invest part of their funds in buying Government bonds and securities that would make funds available to the Government for investment in public utilities owned and managed by the State or may direct commercial banks to invest their funds in priority sector or export industries instead of non-priority sector industries.

It is observed that in Sweden fiscal policy and monetary policy work hand-in-hand and in a closely co-ordinated way. Sweden has one of the most highly developed tax systems in Europe where direct taxes provide about three-quarters and indirect taxes only about one-quarter of the total tax revenue of the central and local governments.

Thus it is observed that in Sweden fiscal and monetary policies have come to be used fairly effectively to avoid fluctuations in the level of economic activities by establishing a fairly close balance between flow of real goods and services and flow of funds.

One of the important reasons of unemployment is lack of mobility of labour. In order to encourage mobility of labour, Government provides a variety of incentives such as travel grants and subsidised housing facilities. To promote occupational mobility of labour, various training facilities are provided. Thus to solve the problem of unemployment, the Government instead of depending upon nationalisation, encourages private industrial establishments by providing incentives to employ more workers.

Investment Reserve System

Along with monetary and budgetary policies (surplus and deficit budgets to control flow of funds), public works and stand-by public works programme, provision of loans for house-construction (providing as high as 90 per cent of credit for private housing by the Government), we find in Sweden a distinctive institution known as the 'Investment Reserve System'.

The Investment Reserve System is an important organisation that plays a major role in the National Labour Market Board (NLMB). This NLMB is not a government institution but is a tripartite organisation consisting of representatives of government, private employers and of workers. This National Labour Market Board with about 25 Local Labour Markets and many regional officers is mainly responsible for full employment programme. One of its functions in this connection is to collect necessary information and keep it up-to-date, prepare forecasts of supply and demand for labour, encourage regional mobility of labour and advise local firms in regard to employment situation and availability of labour of different types.

. The National Labour Market Board also plays another vital role in relation to the Investment Reserve System.

Private enterprises in Sweden receive tax incentives for the purpose to setting aside up to 40 per cent of their pre-tax annual profits in any year as an investment reserve. Of the amount set aside by any firm or industrial establishment, 46 per cent is deposited with the Central Bank of the country where it remains frozen until such time as the fund is officially released. Of the reserve fund, the remaining portion (*i.e.*, 54 per cent) is retained by the firm or industrial establishment with itself.

This Investment Reserve System plays an important role in Sweden's economy. When business conditions begin to show signs of sluggishness and decline, to counteract such tendencies increasing investment in the economy becomes necessary. The Ministry of Finance decides how much of investment reserves built over years may be released and used for investment purposes and the Ministry informs the National Labour Market Board accordingly. The NLMB informs and gives permission to individual industrial firms to increase investment. The industrial firms or establishments must use funds from the reserves partly with the Central Bank and partly with themselves in the same proportions, namely 46:54. The Central Bank on its part releases the required investment funds to the credit of firms with itself. Under such conditions, to increase investment, the Government also provides additional incentives as accelerated depreciation write-offs and tax-reliefs to stimulate use of investment funds from the Investment Reserve System.

The Investment Reserve System thus becomes an important instrument to counteract trade cyclical fluctuations in the Swedish economy. The NLMB takes care to regulate private investments in such a way that the cyclical fluctuations are not allowed to affect the economy. This means while during the period of depression increasing amounts are released for investment, during period of boom, rising prosperity and rising prices, bigger reserves are built out of deductions from rising profits of industrial establishments.

Since 1963, the Investment Reserve System is also being utilisied to bring about economic development of depressed areas by promoting private business activities there. What is to be noted is that the working of the Investment Reserve System is flexible, timely and efficient as regards the time and investment amount to be released or the region where investment from the reserve funds should be encouraged. It is seen that bigger reserves are built out of deductions from rising profits of industrial establishments.

Concluding Remarks on Sweden's Middle Way

It is observed that Sweden through the 'Middle Way' or a system of mixed economy has achieved remarkable results. The middle way has enabled Sweden to achieve satisfactory growth rate that is comparable to any in the European countries and that has ensured the Swedish people possibly the highest standard of living among the European countries. The Swedish economy has for all practical purposes accomplished the objectives of full employment, the rate of unemployment during 1970 being just around 1 per cent of the labour force and never exceeding 3 per cent. Swedish economy has also attained the objective of equitable distribution of income, thus maximising welfare of society.

But the critics of the Swedish economy are not prepared to give full credit for the achievements of the above objectives to the middle way or its system of mixed economy. There are three things pointed out in this connection. The critics point out that all the success which Sweden has achieved so far cannot be attributed to her middle-way. Sweden's economy was not disrupted due to the World War II as throughout the war the country remained neutral and was not involved in the world conflict. The country thus got a flying start as compared with most other European countries.

Secondly, it has been pointed out that inflationary pressures are emerging in recent years, especially due to shortage of labour force and the middle-way has not succeeded in fully containing inflationary pressures.

Another point that is made out is the booming conditions that characterised the Swedish economy are slowing down in recent years and one is not sure that the rate of growth and prosperity would continue as they did since 1947-48.

Also Sweden's economy is mainly export-oriented economy and therefore the future of the Swedish economy will depend to a great extent on international competitive conditions in export markets of the world and international trade policies adopted by other countries.

With all these criticisms and limitations, the fact remains that Sweden has built a fairly sophisticated economic system designated as a mixed system or the middle way by combining economic planning with *laissez faire* capitalistic economy and it has achieved remarkable results in the field of employment, equitable distribution of incomes, rate of growth and welfare of the community.

6. CO-OPERATION BETWEEN DIFFERENT SYSTEMS

One remarkable feature of the 20th century as compared to the earlier centuries including the 19th century, is the existence of different types of economic systems people in different countries have built up with a view to solving satisfactorily their economic problems. In building these different economic systems, different countries have been influenced by various factors such as their natural resources, their histories and traditions, religious and cultural factors, their different value systems and so on and so forth. As circumstances changed and countries had to face new problems or new challenges, they suitably modified their economic systems so as to make them subserve the ends people cherished as desirable and worth attaining.

Certain illustrations will make the point explicit.

In the 19th century there was only one brand of capitalism, namely, *laissez faire* capitalism. But we find today in the 20th century different brands of capitalistic system or various subtypes of capitalism. We have, for example, as yet relatively unregulated and unplanned capitalism in the U.S.A. and on the other hand we have capitalism in France which goes with economic planning by inducements. Between these two types, we have different brands of capitalism in countries like the U.K., Netherlands and Belgium which have moved far away from the U.S. brand of capitalism but have not gone to the extent of accepting planning as in France.

The same is true in respect of socialism. Socialism as preached and practised in the 19th century has come to be considerably modified and we have at present different brands of democratic socialism as practised in India, Sweden, Norway and a number of other countries.

The same is true of communism which is also exhibiting different types. We have the authoritarian type of communism as practised in China, and decentralised and more humanised type of communistic system as adopted in Yugoslavia and a number of East European countries.

And we have already noted that a number of developed and especially developing countries have adopted what may be called mixed economies in which elements of capitalism and communism are mixed in different degrees or proportions.

Thus the different economic systems in different countries of the world cannot be classified into just one or two broad categories like capitalism and socialism or capitalism and communism, but there is a regular spectrum of different economic systems ranging all the way from unregulated and unplanned capitalism to authoritarian communism.

As we have already noted, different nations have adopted economic systems influenced by factors like their history, geography, culture, environment which surround them and the challenges which had to be met, the type of leadership that emenged and the character of the people.

Initially capitalism claimed that it was the most rational and efficient economic system and that it was only under capitalism (especially *laissez faire* capitalism) that a community's resources came to be allocated in the most efficient manner and maximum satisfaction of consumers was realised.

When as a reaction to the various evils of capitalism (which we have already analysed in great detail elsewhere), Marx and others advocated socialism or communism and consequently when communism came to be established in the USSR in 1917, there was inevitable confrontation between the two economic systems. Communism also claimed that it was only under the planned type of communist economy that the community's resources come to be allocated in the best manner possible and maximum welfare of the community is realised.

Till about the beginning of World War II, there was thus confrontation between the two economic systems each claiming superiority over the other. Naturally each system tried to destroy overtly or covertly the other system. The capitalist countries thus tried to invade the USSR after the October Revolution (1917) and destroy the communist regime there with the help of some Russian elements that were in support of capitalist economic system. Similarly, the USSR through the communist International and by openly or clandestinely helping to establish and sustain communist parties in capitalist countries tried to undermine capitalism, holding the Marxist view that capitalism was doomed and it was only a question of time when it would collapse and vanish from the world. This mortal confrontation between the two economic systems reached a high watermark during the 1950's when the views of Joseph Macarthy and John Foster Dulles prevailed in the U.S.A. and when Stalin ruled over USSR.

Conditions, however, started gradually changing after the collaboration between the capitalist and communist countries during the World War II against their common foe, namely, Herr Hitler. Also the possession of atomic and hydrogen bomb by the USSR in early 1950's changed the situation. Intellectually also there was better understanding among both the capitalist and communist countries about the working of different economic systems in different countries. It may therefore be said that the days of original confrontation are over and the era of peaceful co-existence or detente between capitalism and communism has dawned. And yet there is a sort of tacit competition as yet going on between the capitalist and communist countries each trying to show how under its system only the maximum rate of growth, full employment and maximum social welfare can be attained.

But things have changed almost fundamentally in recent years and there is a sort of healthy competition between the capitalist bloc led by the U.S.A. and the communist bloc led by the USSR in the economic, political, technological, cultural and sports fields. What is more striking is the increasing cooperation between different economic systems that have come to be adopted in different countries of the world at the present.

This increasing cooperation in economic, technological and other fields is mainly due to the following factors:

1. There is now greater intellectual understanding and comprehension among peoples in different countries of the world and especially among their

intellectual, political and social leaders that no economic system by itself is sacrosanct. There is now greater understanding that the economic system of each country is influenced and determined by geographical, historical and cultural factors and therefore it would be a folly to suppose that only one's economic system is the best in the world and try to foist it upon other countries. And thus it is that we find capitalism with its various sub-types, socialism with its sub-types and communism with its various sub-types, have come to be accepted as germane to their respective countries and have come to coexist. As a matter of fact even tribal organisations and cultures are allowed to exist in their isolated pockets and no attempt is made to purposely destroy their systems and socio-cultural patterns still existing in isolated areas of even advanced countries of the world.

2. The second important factor that has enforced co-existence and co-operation among different economic systems in different countries of the world is the fear that any confrontation and attempt to impose one's economic system upon others by destroying their systems would result in conflict and war and the fear that any out break of atomic war which appears inevitable in the event of any open and direct confrontation between major powers will pose a threat to the very existence of entire humanity. Thus it may be said that it is the common fear arising out of nuclear war and of annihilation of mankind that is forcing co-operation among different nations with their different economic systems.

3. There is now greater understanding that the world as a whole is facing certain problems such as population explosion (which at present is around 500 crores but is expected to cross the figure of 600 crores by the end of the century), world food shortage and mass poverty, energy crisis, armament race, protection of natural environment and maintenance of ecological balance, control of pollution, etc., can be tackled successfully only willing co-operation among different nations of the world and not in isolation by any countries. Thus it is realised that starvation or disease in any part of the world and therefore threat of disturbance there directly or indirectly poses a threat to the peace and stability in the neighbouring countries and of world. This realisation that most world problems referred to above can be solved only co-operation among different countries, whatever the economic systems which they may have accepted, has been bringing about increasing co-operation among different countries of the world.

Forms of Co-operations Among Different Countries

Co-operation in various fields among different nations of the world with their different economic systems has been taking the following forms:

First there are international organisations established since World War II which are trying to solve possible mutual conflicts among nations and thus fostering co-operation.

Thus there is the United Nations Organisation where more than 170 countries of the world are represented. They debate mutual problems and try to find out mutually satisfactory solutions for them.

There are then the International Bank for Reconstruction and Development (the World Bank) and the International Monetary Fund founded by countries which are also the members of the UNO These financial institutions help countries through monetary and financial assistance and mutual financial adjustments. Thus the World Bank has been helping many developing countries of the world through loans and technical assistance to bring about rapid economic development by modernising agriculture and rapid industrialisation.

There are other international affiliates of the UNO such as World Health Organisation (WHO), UNESCO, FAO and so on which have specialised in rendering assistance to different countries of the world in specific fields such as combating of diseases, agricultural development, technological and cultural advancement and so on.

Another manner in which different nations with different economic systems are co-operating is through formation of regional organisations like the European Economic Community (EEC), the OPEC, Council of Mutual Economic Assistance (CMEA), Free Trade Association (EFTA), the East African Community (EAC), the Central American Common Market (CACM), the Asian Development Bank and so on. Through these bodies different nations with different economic systems are co-operating among themselves by providing financial, technological and other assistance to the mutual advantage of cooperating countries.

Another method adopted for mutual co-operation is through bilateral agreements between two or more countries. Through such bilateral agreements attempts are being made to promote trade, undertake projects to exploit internationally flowing rivers, have international highways (such as Asian Highway) or joint steel or other metal projects (such as, for example, Kudremukh Project wherein Iran and India had been co-operating for mutual advantage).

Developing countries of the Third World are also trying to co-operate among themselves on bilateral or multilateral basis (*e.g.*, the Indus River Water Treaty between India and Pakistan), and agreement between India, Ceylon and East Africa, the three tea-producing countries to protect the price of tea in the international marketing).

But unfortunately because of factors like recurrent economic crises or instability, religion and cultural differences, historical rivalries, different levels of economic development in different countries etc., the extent of co-operation among developing countries is not all that it needs to be. Anyway circumstances are forcing them to mutually co-operate among themselves for common benefit, forgetting their differing economic systems.

REFERENCES

1. '*Economics of Socialism*': A. D. Dickinson, page 4.
2. The role of planning in developing countries can be well appreciated if we observe the various objectives which India's Five-Year Plans have had in view.

   Thus, some of the important objectives of India's Five-Year Plan were or have been as follows:

   1. To bring about increase in national income roughly at an annual rate of about 5 per cent.

   2. To achieve self-sufficiency in foodgrains and to increase agricultural production to meet requirements of industry and export.

   3. To bring about rapid industrialisation of the country with special emphasis on heavy and basic industries.

   4. To expand basic industries like steel, chemical industries, fuel and power and establish machine building capacity so that the requirements of further industrialisation of the country can be met within a specified period of time.

   5. To bring about large expansion in employment opportunities for the people.

   6. To establish progressively greater equalities of opportunities and to bring about reduction in disparities of income and wealth and a more even distribution of economic power.

   7. To lay firm foundation of further economic progress in subsequent Five-Year Plans.

   8. To build administrative structure and other organisations necessary to carry out the various programmes envisaged in Five -Year Plans.

   8. To build administrative structure and other organisations necessary to carry out the various programmes envisaged in Five Year Plans.

   9. To check inflationary pressures likely to be generated during the process of development.

   10. To attain economic stability.

   11. To attain economic self-reliance.

   12. To bring about balanced regional development.

   13. To bring about expansion of the public sector and make its role more effective.

   14. To successfully implement a National Programme of Minimum Needs for the poorer sections of the community by providing facilities like elementary education, drinking water, medical facilities, house-sites, rural electrification, improvement of landless agricultural workers, backward classes, tribals and the poorest sections of the community.

   15. To adopt a programme of adequate procurement and public distribution system for assured supply of essential commodities at reasonable prices to the poorer sections of society in urban and rural areas.

16. To bring about promotion of exports and to encourage import substitution.

17. To establish equitable price-wage-income policy.

18. To attain social and economic justice and establish socialist pattern of society.

The above objectives stated in different Five-Year Plans of India should provide broad idea regarding the role which planning is expected to play in developing countries like India.

3. *Economic Planning and International Order*—Prof. Lionel Robbins, page 66.
4. *Comparative Economic Systems* — Allen Gruchy, page 157,
5. Jan Prybla: *Comparative Economic Systems.*

CHAPTER 21

BROAD FEATURES OF INDIA'S SOCIALIST PATTERN

BACKGROUND OF INDIAN ECONOMIC THINKING

Serious and sustained economic thinking along modern lines commenced in India only after India came in contact with England.

The establishment of the British Rule in India (which was wholly occupied by 1818) and introduction of English system of Education naturally introduced in India some of the British economic institutions and political and economic thinking.

Attempts were made to introduce *laissez faire* type of capitalism in the traditional Indian society. The ideas of Adam Smith, Malthus, Ricardo and J. S. Mill were taught in Indian universities and had their influence on Indian economic thinking, especially liberal thought of J. S. Mill.

As a reaction to the liberal thinking of the English Classical School, there was reaction to classical thinking by about the end of the 19th century. As a result of the impact of the nationalist thought of Friedrich List of Germany, Dadabhai Nowrojee, M. G. Ranade and others advocated that instead of following *laissez-faire* policy, the Government should actively intervene to protect Indian industries and agriculture from the severe and unequal competition which the country was forced to face with industrialised countries of the West.

After the emergence of Gandhiji on the political scene of India after 1920, m any of his economic ideas, as we shall see, influenced economic thinking and institutions of the country. Gandhiji emphasised Swarajya, self-sufficiency of villages, decentralisation of industries, small-scale and cottage industries, khadi,upliftment of masses, and so on. As is obvious many of Gandhiji's ideas have had their impact on the thinking of policy-makers and people of India.

But in the formation of thinking of Indians, Jawaharlal Nehru played a crucial role. He was greatly under the influence of English thought. His belief in democratic form of government and in Fabian socialism ultimately resulted in his preaching of democratic socialism. Nehru's visit to the USSR greatly convinced him of the utility of economic planning as an instrument to solve many of the complex and pressing economic problems faced by the country. Thus for Jawaharlal Nehru, democracy, socialism and economic planning became the watchwords.

These ideas of Nehru were in the formative stage for a considerable length of time and as and when they evolved he introduced those ideas in the Congress pledges and programme envisaged during the days of struggle for independence.

When the country became independent and Jawaharlal Nehru became the Prime Minister of India which post he continued to hold uninterruptedly for about 17 years, he tried to shape economic institutions and policies of the country along the above lines, namely, on the basis of modern scientific approach instead of old traditional approach, democratic socialism and economic planning. These economic ideas have broadly come to be accepted by the enlightened Indian public opinion.

1. BROAD FEATURES OF INDIA'S SOCIALIST PATTERN

After India attained its independence in 1947, till 1950, the country was busy dealing with the immediate problems created by the partition and independence of the country. There was the refugee problem, problem of law and order, of princely states, of framing the constitution for the country, and there was war with Pakistan on the issue of Kashmir.

It was therefore only in 1951 that India could think of adopting economic planning to solve her various socio-economic problems on long-term basis. The First-Five Year Plan (1951-1956) was not a plan in the true and strict sense of the term but a device to solve some of the immediate and pressing problems created by World War II and the partition of the country, namely, scarcity of foodgrains and of raw cotton and jute for the cotton textile and jute mills in India. It also aimed at completing some of the projects already commenced in the country.

The era of true economic planning might be said to have commenced only with the Second Five-Year Plan in 1956. It was the Second Five-Year Plan which clearly accepted the goal of establishing in the country the socialist pattern of society.

Though it is difficult to define in clear and concrete terms the concept of socialist pattern of society, the draft of the Second Five-Year Plan gives us a broad idea of the socialist pattern of society which has come to be accepted as the ultimate goal of economic planning and policy in India. The Second Five-

Year Plan, clarifying the concept of socialist pattern of society, says: "The socialist pattern of society means that the basic criterion for determining the lines of advance must not be private profit, but social gain, and that the pattern of development and the structure of socio-economic relations should be so planned that they result not only in appreciable increases in national income and employment, but also in greater equality in income and wealth. The benefits of economic development must accrue more and more to the relatively less and less privileged classes of society and there should be progressive reduction of concentration of incomes, wealth and economic power. The accent of socialist pattern of society is on the attainment of positive goals, the raising of living standards, the enlargement of opportunities for all, the promotion of enterprise among the disadvantaged classes and the creation of a sense of partnership among all sections of the community."[1]

Broad Features of India's Socialist Pattern of Society

Though so far no policy-maker of India has given a clear definition of the concept of socialist pattern of society or made a successful attempt to give its contents in specific and concrete terms, the nature of the socialist pattern of society which Jawaharlal Nehru and other leaders had in mind may be inferred by taking into account the broad features that characterise economic policy and the socialist pattern of society envisaged in India.

The following broad features may be said to characterise the socialist pattern of society in India:

(*a*) *Rapid Economic Development.* If India happens to be one of the poorest countries in the world with about half her vast population of more than 87 crores living below the poverty line, the most important reason for it is the underdeveloped state of her economy. Mass poverty can be removed only by accelerating the growth rate of the economy by utilising the vast unutilised and under-utilised natural and human resources. It is certain that mass poverty cannot be removed by only redistributing what is being already annually produced in the country. The socialist pattern of society envisages removal of mass poverty by ensuring satisfactory standard of living for all. This would be possible only if the growth rate of her economy is substantial and much ahead of the annual rate at which the country's population is growing. India's Five Year Plans therefore have been aiming at an annual growth rate of 5 to 6 per cent.

(*b*) *Equitable Distribution of Income and Wealth.* It is not enough to increase annual rate of production of goods and services for removing mass poverty. What is equally necessary is their equitable distribution. Care has to be taken to see that increased wealth produced does not get concentrated in a few hands or only a small section of society.

Attempts are therefore being made in India to bring about equitable distribution of income and wealth. For this purpose minimum wage legislation is passed and various direct taxes such as income tax, wealth tax, capital gains tax are being imposed in a progressive way on the richer sections of society. Often ceilings on income of richer sections of society (such as executives of private industrial establishments, etc.) are imposed. Thus along with increased production of wealth, the socialist pattern of society also aims at equitable distribution of income and wealth.

(c) *Raising the Standards of Living of Masses of People.* The socialist pattern of society aims at raising the standard of living of masses of people who are very poor by trying to guarantee them minimum necessaries of life. Various schemes are being formulated and implemented to help the weaker sections of the community such as the scheduled castes and tribes, landless agricultural labour and bonded labour, small and marginal farmers and rural artisans and to ensure them a minimum standard of living.

(d) *Employment Guarantee.* The most important reason of mass poverty is mass unemployment . People are poor because they have no regular income as they do not have regular and adequate employment opportunities. This would mean that first step in fighting mass poverty is to ensure job-opportunities for all and ensure that all get regularly at least minimum income.

From this point of view the Government of Maharashtra has adopted the Rural Employment Guarantee Scheme which other states in India are also thinking of adopting . Nearly 70 per cent of people in India live in rural areas and it is here that unemplcyment and mass poverty prevail in their most virulent form. And therefore Rural Employment Guarantee Scheme on lines adopted in Maharashtra ensuring employment to all able bodied and willing workers in rural areas at stated minimum level of wages is supposed to go a long way in relieving mass poverty in rural areas.

(e) *Bringing about Fundamental Changes in Socio-Political and Economic Structure of Indian Society.* It has been realised that establishment of socialist pattern of society would involve fundamental changes in the socio-political and economic structure of the country. Without such basic structural changes, mass poverty cannot be removed. With that end in view attempts are being made to abolish Zamindari system, absentee landlordism institution of money-lenders, the Managing Agency System, untouchability, bonded labour and so on. All this aims at establishing classless society without violent revolution where every individual personality carries equal value irrespective of the person's status and wealth. Attempts are also being made to establish modern progressive institutions like co-operative credit societies, professional management, peasant proprietorship and so on as part of establishing socialist pattern of society.

(f) *Increasingly Dominant Role of the Public Sector.* Expanding public sector has become an important feature of the socialist pattern of society in India. If in 1951 there were only 5 public sector commercial and industrial enterprises (apart from Railways, Post & Telegraph, etc.,) involving investment of Rs. 29 crores only, at present there are about 225 public sector enterprises involving investment of about Rs.1.3 lakh crores.

Most of the basic and heavy industries are in the public sector. For example, iron and steel, other heavy metals, heavy chemicals, heavy engineering machinery, electricals, aircraft, metal fabrication, etc., are in the public sector. The State controls these commanding heights through which it is in a position to control private sector industries and level of economic activities in the country.

The profits of these public sector enterprises go to the State instead of into private pockets and thus help reduce inequalities of income and wealth. These profits become available for expenditure on welfare activities for the masses. Often the State establishes these enterprises in backward areas thus providing employment opportunities to weaker sections of the community and help develop backward areas.

(*g*) *Regulation of the Private Sector.* India has accepted a mixed type of economy and therefore along with the public sector there is also substantial private sector. At present the ratio of annual investment in the private and public sector is in the proportions of 60:40.

The State tries to regulate the functioning of private sector industrial establishments in the public interests. For example, there is regulation of investment through capital issue controls; wages and conditions are regulated; salaries and remuneration of higher executives are regulated. Workers are provided certain rights in matters of trade unions and by way of collective bargaining and in regard to participation in management. There is also limit on the rate of dividend to be given to shareholders whereas workers guaranteed minimum wages and also bonus. Thus in the socialistic pattern of society, private industries in India are coming under greater and greater regulations by the State, these regulations being imposed in the interest of workers and for the welfare of society.

(*h*) *Land Reforms.* India is essentially an agricultural country where four out every five people live on land. Before independence ownership of land was concentrated in a section of a community and vast masses of people in rural areas either had no land or only small pieces of land. Consequently poverty in its most virulent form is observed in the agricultural sector which as yet greatly depends upon monsoon rains.

The Government to overcome poverty in rural areas has undertaken land reforms. The main features of these land reforms are: fixing of reasonable rent, fixing of tenure, ceilings on ownership of land, abolition of Zamindari and absentee landlordism, and establishment of peasant proprietorship, stopping of sub-division and fragmentation of land, if necessary and possible by co-operative farming. It is by these measures that attempts are being are being made to fight vast poverty in the agricultural sector of India.

(*i*) *Emphasis on the Co-operative Sector.* India has a mixed economy composed of public sector, private sector and co-operative sector. Since the vast poor cannot stand on their own legs while carrying on their economic activities, they are being organised on the basis of co-operation among themselves. They are being taught to come together and adopt the principle of co-operation for meeting their various needs such as credit, agricultural marketing, establishment and running of agro-industries as for example co-operative sugar mills, weaving factories, dairies, banking, housing and so on. The Government tries to help these co-operative organisations both in the rural and urban areas by various means such as provision of concessional finance, technical advice, tax and other concessions and so on. Thus a characteristic feature of the socialist pattern of society in India is the predominant role which is assigned to the co-operative sector with a view to help poor and middle sections of the Indian community to help themselves.

(*j*) *Development of Backward Areas.* While all parts and regions of India are poor, some are relatively poorer than others. Naturally people in these extremely backward regions are the poorest sections of Indian community.

Attempts are being made to develop these areas and relive to some extent at least extreme poverty of the people there. Community Development Projects are an attempt in this direction to help some of the backward areas in the country. Also, attempts are being made to see that industrial units are established in these backward parts, with their forward and backward linkage-effects. For this purpose various State governments have been offering concessions — cheap land, water, electricity, concessional loans and various socio-economic infrastructure facilities — for bringing about development of these backward regions. Establishment of industrial estates is also an attempt in this direction.

(*k*) *Upliftment of Scheduled Castes and Scheduled Tribes and Other Backward People.* Schedules Castes and Scheduled Tribes which number about 15 crores of people in India happen to be the poorest section of the Indian community living for hundreds of years almost sub-human life. Socialist pattern of society will have no meaning, if the lot of these people is not appreciably improved as early as possible.

Attempts are therefore being made to improve their living conditions by measures such as free gift of cultivable lands and housing sites, cheap loans, free educations, reservation of jobs in government and semi-government establishments, scholarships for educational purposes and so on.

(*l*) *Development of Small-scale and Cottage Industries.* Provision of employment opportunities to the unemployed especially in rural areas and guarantee of steady minimum income is the first condition for removal of mass poverty. There is great pressure of population on land and it is obvious that agriculture cannot provide increasing opportunities of employment to increasing population. Also large-scale industries requiring huge amount of investment cannot also provide vast employment opportunities to increasing population. The socialist pattern of society in India therefore envisages development of small-scale and cottage industries, especially of agro-based rural industries, as a solution to the problem of rural unemployment and poverty. The industries can be developed by using local natural resources, local labour and their skills and to meet local demands. They have been therefore given an important place in the socialist pattern of society. The government is helping their development by various steps such as cheap loans, provisions of training facilities, and various infrastructure facilities, by suitable government purchasing policy, by promoting their marketing and export and, as we have already seen, through establishment of Industrial Estates and District Industrial Centres.

(*m*) *Acceptance of the Concept of Industrial Democracy.* The socialist pattern of society in India is characterised by acceptance of the concept of industrial democracy. It is accepted that industrial establishments, whether in the public or private sector, are a joint venture wherein workers play an important role and therefore must have a voice in their management.

From this point of view, steps are being taken to promote industrial establishments both in the public as well as private sector, Works Committees, Joint Management Councils and such other worker's bodies which enjoy a right in the management of industrial establishments. Practice of appointing directors from among workers has been accepted by public sector industrial establishments. Workers are given the right of organising trade unions which enjoy several rights including the right of collective bargaining. The ultimate objective is to make industrial workers part and parcel of industrial establishments in the country, and thus establish industrial democracy in the country.

(*n*) *Acceptance of Economic Planning.* In order to deal with the vast and complex agricultural and industrial problems and problems of mass poverty and unemployment, the socialist pattern of India has accepted economic planning. The planning adopted however is not authoritarian and centralised type of planning but planning that is compatible with a mixed type of economy and with democratic socialism. Planning in India combines both planning from above and planning from below for which there are planning bodies at the district and state levels wherein people participate in the process of formulation and execution of plans. Acceptance of economic planning has thus become an important feature of the socialist pattern of society.

(*o*) *Panchayati Raj Institutions.* Planning to be successful requires certain conditions. Planning must truly represent the needs and aspirations of the mass of people. It must not be imposed upon them. People must feel involved in the formulation and execution of economic plans.

As a result of the experience gained, attempts are being made to create a sense involvement among people in respect of planning the socialist pattern in India by establishing Panchayati Raj Institutions. It has three layers-Gram Panchayat , Panchayat Samiti and Zilla Parishad. These are elected bodies with voice in the formulation and implementation of local activities and plans for their respective areas. The idea behind these Panchyati Raj Institutions is to encourage local initiative, create opportunities of exploiting vast unutilised or under utilitsed local potential and create among people in all regions a deep sense of involvement with the affairs of the country and in plan formulation and execution.

(p) *Free and Compulsory Primary Education.* It is realised that there cannot be establishment of socialist pattern of society where people are ignorant and illiterate and where lives of people are governed by traditions and superstitions. Education is the best antidote to arouse people and help them to wield their destiny. From this point of view, the constitution of India rightly laid down that there will be free and compulsory primary education in India. This alone would arouse people from their age-old slumber and make them active and participating members in the process of socio-political and economic development of the country marching towards the goal of socialist pattern of society.

Concluding Remarks

Above are the broad features of the socialist pattern of society which leaders like Jawaharlal Nehru, planners and policy-makers have in view. It is the goal which the nation is striving for and wants to attain in the long run.

There is criticism that we have been marching towards the goal of socialist pattern of society very slowly and that in some respects the country is moving in the opposite direction. For example, the percentage and the absolute number of people living below the poverty line in 1971 appears to be higher than that in 1961. There appears to be increasing unemployment and the economic condition of the weaker sections of the people in many regions and pockets appears to be deteriorating. It is said that inequalities of income and wealth are increasing.

All this may be true and steps will have to be taken to halt the retrograde march and move towards the goal of socialist pattern of society to which goal there appears to be no alternative.

2. SYSTEMIC (OR STRUCTURAL) CHANGES IN INDIAN ECONOMY

Introduction

During the 1980s and especially after the announcement of the New Economic Policy in July 1991, a number of radical changes are being introduced in the Indian economic structure or system.

There are a number of factors, domestic and international, that are responsible for these structural changes that are being brought about in the Indian economic system.

Some of the important factors responsible for these structural or systemic changes in the Indian economy may be stated as follows.

All these years (*i.e.*, from 1948 and especially after the Industrial Policy Resolution of 1956) Indian economic system was characterised by very detailed and time-consuming licensing system which was being managed by bureaucracy characterised by delays, corruption and all other defects of bureaucratic management. This was resulting in holding up rapid industrial development notably in the private sector to its full potential.

The Indian economic system or structure was characterised by a cobweb of rules, regulations and restrictions (which according to one senior industrialist numbered around 4,000) which were so many hurdles in the way of rapid development of private sector industries.

Then there were in operation the MRTP and the FERA Acts which had proved to be the biggest hurdle in expansion of private sector industrial units with adverse effects not only on industrial development but also on India's exports which accounted for less than one percentage of the total world exports.

Since 1956 there was emphasis on expansion of public sector which had become the main pillar of government's industrial policy as also of economic policy — the policy of controlling commanding heights of the Indian economy and through that retaining control over the entire Indian economy.

But as we have already seen, public sector industrial units were characterised by various serious defects which were hampering not only development of industrial units in the public sector but also of industries in the private sector as public sector units were in charge of infrastructural facilities like oil, coal, steel and other metals, railways, civil aviation, finance and banking and so on. Inefficiency in these sectors was producing extremely adverse effects on the growth of the entire Indian economy.

For long India was following a protectionist industrial policy, and industrial development in the country was sought of be achieved by heavy import duties and export subsidies — policy of rapid industrialisation through import substitutions. This policy had resulted in Indian industrial structure characterised by high cost and low quality.

All these factors had resulted in increasing deficits in India's balance of payments position which had become chronic forcing India to borrow heavily from abroad. Naturally foreign debt was mounting and so also servicing charges on foreign debt.

When India went in for huge loan of 5 billion US dollars from the IMF and the World Bank, naturally those international financial institutions imposed severe conditionalities regarding systemic or structural changes which India was required to bring about, if she was to get loan from those international financial institutions.

International changes of radical nature were taking place which also influenced structural changes in the Indian economy especially after 1985.

The Soviet Union got disintegrated into 15 more or less autonomous republics after the introduction of perestroika in late 1980s by Gorbachev. The former Soviet Union and the East European countries had lost faith in State-owned, managed and controlled communist economy and they were all thinking in terms of free and competitive market economy, thus de-emphasising role of the State, of the public sector and highly centralised bureaucracy-managed national economy. This disillusionment with communism (with its authoritarian and highly centralised planning and all pervasive role of the State in the nation's economy) had its deep impact on Indian policy-makers.

It is because of these domestic and international developments that India was forced to bring about structural changes in her economy since 1980s onwards.

Structural (or Systemic) Changes — India's Perestroika

According to the July 1991 New Economic (Industrial) Policy, the following structural changes are being introduced and implemented.

The structural change aims at unshackling Indian private sector industries from the complex cobwebs of bureaucratic controls and regulations and in their place to introduce policy of liberalisation.

To achieve the above objective 'Industrial Licensing' is to be abolished for all industries, except in the cases of a few specified industries of strategic significance. This applies to industrial units irrespective of the amount of investment. (Licensing will continue in respect of industries related to security of the country and industries manufacturing goods of hazardous nature and those likely to pollute environment.)

As regards foreign investments, it has been decided to provide automatic approval up to 51 per cent of foreign equity in the case of high priority industries requiring investment.

Government has decided to provide automatic approval for technology agreements between Indian industrial units and foreign industrial units. The idea behind this provision is to introduce high and latest technology in Indian industries.

The most important structural change that is taking place is in the sphere of public sector industries. There is reversal of the policy of expanding public sector followed since 1956.

Government will not hereafter take over ownership, control and management of sick industrial units as was done in the case of about 100 sick textile mills which were taken over by the government for management which was entrusted to National Textile Corporation which is incurring heavy annual losses in managing them).

Chronically sick public sector units (about 58) are to be closed down. In the case of many existing public sector units, there is to be part privatisation by selling their equity shares to public financial institutions and to private companies and even to individuals.

In the case of such public sector units which are viable, greater autonomy is to be given to them in respect of management with a view to promote their efficiency and productivity as also profitability.

(Only the following industries will be hereafter reserved for the public sector: Arms and ammunition and defence equipment, atomic energy, coal and lignite, mineral oils, mining of important metals and railway transport, etc).

The compulsory licensing will not be required in the case of small-scale industrial units. In their case limit of capital investment has been raised to Rs. 60 lakhs.

The reversal of the policy of expanding public sector and increasing privatisation of public sector industrial units mean that in the industrial sphere private sector is being given increasing scope for expansion by removing licensing hurdles and by practically abolising the MRTP and the FERA Acts.

In this government appears to have been influenced by the collapse of the communist regimes in the former Soviet Union and most of the East European countries which appear to be moving away from their hereto communist type of economy towards free market competitive economy (*i.e.*, capitalism). This trend appears to have influenced Indian policy-makers also, apart from the sad experience and disillusionment with the functioning of many public sector units in the country with adverse effects on the growth of industrial sphere and in fact on the Indian economy as a whole.

An important structural change that is taking place in Indian economy is that almost every big private sector industrial unit is entering into collaboration agreement with well-known foreign multinational industrial corporation. In years to come multinational industrial corporations would be playing increasing role in the Indian industrial sphere and in Indian economy as a whole.

Another important systemic or structural change is the decision by the government to cut down and gradually eliminate direct and indirect subsidies (amounting to Rs.15000 crores annually) to the Indian agricultural sector. The subsidy is being reduced on fertilisers and electricity. The idea is to make Indian agriculture increase its efficiency and self-reliance, instead of depending upon government support for an indefinite period of time.

This will also help reduce deficit in Central Government budget which has gone on increasing all these years resulting in creating more and more money by resorting to deficit financing which has become a source of easy money to the government but with extremely adverse effects on Indian economy through generation of inflationary pressures.

Along with fairly free entry to foreign capital after winding up of most of the FERA Act provisions, government would freely allow foreign banks to open their branches in India with a view to attract foreign capital into the country.

Adverse balance of trade and balance of payments in the case of India have become a recurring feature of the Indian economy. To overcome this Indian rupee which for long was over-valued has been allowed to float to a substantial extent and find its own level in freely fluctuating foreign exchange market, instead the rate of exchange between Indian rupee and foreign currencies being determined and regulated by the Reserve Bank of India. This structural change allowing part-floating of the Indian rupee is expected to boost Indian exports, cut down her imports and thus help restore some sort of balance in India's balance of payments position.

The above structural changes which are being brought about, especially after July 1992, mean that the high protective walls erected by the government to protect Indian economy from foreign competition are being gradually demolished and Indian economy is being made to function in international competitive environment and join and move along with the main stream of world economy, instead of functioning in isolation behind the protective walls erected by the government since the commencement of the Planning Era in India in 1951-52.

Appraisal of the New Structural Changes

We have already seen that fundamental structural changes are taking place in the Indian economy since 1980s and especially after July 1992.

Arguments are put forward both in favour and against those structural changes in the Indian economy.

Arguments in Favour

It is maintained that for long Indian economy (especially the industrial sector) was protected by the government from foreign competition. This had resulted in characterising Indian economy (especially the industrial structure) by rising costs and lower efficiency and low quality goods.

Now that Indian economy will be functioning with great amount of freedom, it will have to make efforts to increase its efficiency, productivity and profitability. The international competitive atmosphere in which Indian industries will have to work may make Indian economy more efficient and competitive. This may help curb inflationary pressures in the Indian economy.

Free entry of foreign equity capital will help both to raise rate of investment in the industrial sector and in the Indian economy as a whole and also help bring about technological upgradation. This would help push up both growth rate of industrial sector and also of the Indian economy as a whole.

Collaboration agreements between Indian industrial companies and foreign companies will help bring about technological upgradation in the industrial sphere.

It is expected that marketing collaboration agreements with foreign companies will help push up India's exports. This would help India earn more foreign exchange which is likely to reduce pressure on India's balance of payments position.

All these structural changes are likely to make industrial sector rapidly growing and vital sector of the Indian economy which itself would therefore grow at a faster rate in future.

Arguments Against

Fear is expressed on the following grounds about the possible adverse effects of the structural changes in the Indian industrial sector consequent on the July 1992 New Economic Policy.

The critics point out that since India was forced to go in for a big loan to the International Monetary Fund and the World Bank which are under the influence of the United States, these international financial institutions have imposed upon India the structural changes which are now being introduced by the Government of India. The critics point out that this means India is sacrificing her economic sovereignty and is being dictated by the United States what policy India should adopt and follow. The critics point out that the United States will naturally suggest structural changes in the Indian economy that would be in the interest of the United States and not in favour of Indian economy.

The critics draw attention to the following points against the structural changes in the Indian economy.

Would Indian industries, without government protection enjoyed heretofore be in a position to successfully compete with vastly superior and highly developed industrial corporations in developed countries and especially with those in the United States ? The critics maintain that this is very unlikely at least for many years to come.

According to the critics, free entry of foreign capital and of multinational industrial corporations into India would raise some important problems for India. Would not the big foreign industrial corporations entering India through collaboration agreements with Indian companies be dominant partners, their Indian collaborating companies only acting at the behest of foreign companies and as their mere passive appendages ? Would not the big foreign collaborators be dominant in the management of such joint ventures ? Would not free flow if foreign equity capital bring with it secondhand and outdated technology and not the latest technology ? Would not the high profits to be sent abroad to mother countries by the foreign collaborating corporations result in huge outflow of foreign currencies thus making worse India's position in respect of her balance of payments ?

Would not new technology which is likely to be introduced by multinational corporations in India lead to increasing unemployment in the country worsening the already miserable condition of the poorer sections of the Indian community ? Is it not surprising that much vaunted phrase for long, namely 'the socialist pattern of society' is no more heard for quite some years ?

Industrial licensing policy has been for all practical purposes abolished. Would not abolition of industrial licensing policy result in following undesirable consequences? Would not new industrial units be established at places where infrastructural facilities are already available ? Would this not lead to industrial concentration? Would not industrially backward areas remain backward for years to come? Would this not deprive people in industrially backward areas of employment opportunities thus resulting in increasing inequalities of income and wealth leading to social and political unrest ? Would industrial planning be possible without industrial licensing policy of some sort ?

By way of conclusion it may be pointed out that conditions being what they are, both in domestic and international spheres, India should boldly face and try in a determined manner to solve the various problems raised by structural changes by the July 1992 New Economic Policy. This is because Indian economy cannot afford to function in isolation and it will have to move and function along lines of the world economy.

REFERENCE

1. Draft of the Second Five Year Plan (1956-1961).

CHAPTER 22

GANDHIAN ECONOMICS

1. GANDHIAN IDEAS ON ECONOMIC SYSTEM

Gandhiji was perhaps the most original among the Indian thinkers and made an attempt to base his economic and other ideas on the sound foundations of Indian culture, traditions and environment. It also needs to be noted that his thoughts on economic activities and system were not viewed in isolation but were an integral part of his general philosophy of life which he tried to evolve out of his own personal experience and various practical experiments that he undertook from time to time to deal with the manifold problems including that of mass poverty faced by India.

Though Gandhiji was an original thinker, his mind in its youthful days appears to have been influenced by ideas in Indian scriptures and especially Bhagavad Gita, by John Ruskin's 'Unto the Last' (which taught him the importance of the concept of 'dignity of labour' and conducting economic affairs in such a manner that they lead to maximisation of social welfare), and teachings of Leo Tolstoy who, it appears, made him a firm believer in the doctrine of Ahimsa (non-violence).

Since some of the main economic ideas of Gandhiji are to be analysed in greater detail in the following pages, here only a brief outline of those ideas and their general appraisal is attempted.

Gandhiji based his economic system on the fundamental foundation that happens to be totally different from the accepted foundation of the modern Western economics. As we shall see in greater detail later on, he was firmly of the opinion that unlimited pursuit of material pleasures by man would result in all sorts of injustices and evils in the economic system. Attempts by everyone to satisfy their unlimited and ever-increasing material wants would thus result in exploitation of one man by another, economically stronger exploiting the economically weaker sections of the community, class conflict and violence, ruthless exploitation of natural and human resources, erection of an economic structure that would ever be unsteady because of its weak moral foundations. Gandhiji therefore wanted that everyone limit their material wants. By that he did not mean that all of us live a life of an ascetic. All he meant was that there should be some ceiling or limit on the material wants of man, if he desires to attain satisfaction and peaceful and contented life.

Once the above fundamental basis of Gandhiji's economic system is understood, all his other ideas automatically fall in their proper places and their implications become clear.

Gandhiji advocated self-sufficient villages, instead of the modern crowded towns and cities resulting from unlimited pursuit of human beings after material pleasures. He favoured simple division of labour and decentralised industries and economy. This would help develop natural and human resources in every village and provide employment to villagers. The economic system adopted, according to Gandhiji, should lead to welfare of the community. That economy was best which attained maximum satisfaction of all the people.

As we saw, Gandhiji was in favour of decentralised type of economy. He favoured decentralised industrial structure. This naturally meant that Gandhiji placed great emphasis on the development of small-scale and cottage industries which can be practised in every village or even every home where people can work in a congenial atmosphere even during their spare time.

Naturally in the Gandhian system of thought, 'Khadi' occupied the central place. Next to food, man's requirement is cloth. Khadi would provide not only employment to a vast number of people but would also provide an important necessity to the community at large.

This implied two further things. Gandhiji was not opposed to modern machinery as such. But he was opposed to that type of machinery that would displace human labour and create unemployment. On the other hand, he favoured that machinery like electricity and simple tools and instruments that would relieve pressure on man and help him improve his productivity and help him live a decent life. Thus it is wrong to suppose that Gandhiji was opposed to all types of machinery.

The above thoughts also implies that Gandhiji laid great emphasis on dignity of labour. He made no distinction between one type of work and another as is clear from the fact that he himself for quite some time cleaned latrines. He insisted that all men undertake some physical work every day and treat all types of work as carrying the same dignity.

Gandhiji's objective of self-sufficient and regenerated villages where decentralised industries prospered along with agriculture and where everyone was fully employed and made no distinction between one type of work and another further involved another important doctrine, namely, the Doctrine of Trusteeship. He firmly believed (as we shall see later when we analyse his Doctrine of Trusteeship) that private property beyond a certain limit was to be held as trust on behalf of the society of which we are all members. Without social sanction, there cannot exist the institution of private property. This implies that the rich with vast amount of land at their disposal or other forms of productive assets should not use them to exploit the poorer sections of the society. Private property beyond what is required to satisfy one's needs should be utilised for the welfare of society. Gandhiji was of the opinion that the Trusteeship Doctrine would avoid division of society into classes of 'haves' and 'have-nots' and avoid class conflict and violence.

Gandhiji was aware of the dangers of ever-increasing population to human and family welfare. He therefore advocated strict limit on size of the family which was to be limited by moral self-restraint and continence and not by using methods like sterilisation and contraceptives. In every field Gandhiji insisted on moral basis and moral force and was opposed to the use of external force. This is because he felt that any improvement and self-reform, if it is to be enduring and ever-lasting, must come from within and must not be forced from above or outside.

Gandhiji for moral and social reform advocated complete prohibition which would have salutary effect on human welfare which afterall is the end of any economic system. He believed in abolition of untouchability and a comprehensive programme of constructive activities in every village where all would live like brothers and children of God.

Through the above means Gandhiji aimed at bringing about Sarvodaya wherein all people would participate in the common joys and moral and material well-being of the community.

It would thus be observed that Gandhian economic system touched every aspect of human life (and not just economic aspect) and aimed at welfare of society.

2. APPRAISAL OF GANDHIAN IDEAS OF ECONOMIC SYSTEM

Though later on some of the important concepts and practical programmes suggested by Gandhiji will be critically examined in greater detail, here a general appraisal of Gandhian ideas may be undertaken.

There are two approaches from which Gandhiji's ideas are appraised.

There is a school of thought which maintains that Gandhiji's ideas and the entire programme or economic system suggested by him is reactionary, against the modern, current and international trends and tendencies, against scientific and technological progress and therefore one which would take the country back to medieval times. His ideas regarding limiting human wants are criticised as impracticable for most persons. His ideas regarding self-sufficient villages, opposition to large-scale industries, broad opposition to machinery, to emergence of big towns and cities all appear to go against the modern powerfull currents of history. It is feared that a country with institutions suggested by

Gandhiji would not be in a position to successfully compete with technologically and industrially highly advanced countries of the world and in international competition and inevitable conflicts would not be in a position to stand up against them and would easily go under. Also his Trusteeship Doctrine, however sound on moral grounds, is criticised as impracticable. Thus some of his critics maintain that however sound morally and on idealistic grounds, in a modern competitive world full of rivalries and conflicts, Gandhiji's ideas would prove impracticable and take the country back to olden times.

There are others who believe that Gandhiji's ideas and programmes have sound moral and economic basis, and are of great practical significance.

They maintain that ever-increasing wants of man would only result in misery. For example, population of the world at present is around 500 crores and would be around 600 crores by the end of the century. In the case of India the present population of about 87 crores would be around 100 crores by the end of the century. Would it be possible to go on increasing production of all types of goods and services to meet ever-growing demands of such rapidly increasing population, especially when we know that certain natural resources like oil and minerals are exhaustible? Recent discussions regarding 'Limits to Growth' is an indication of the Gandhian thesis that man must put a limit somewhere to his wants. Their indefinite multiplication would sooner or later result in disaster. There is also the argument that attempts to satisfy ever-increasing wants are not going to make man happy and contented.

In a country like India where 70 per cent of the people live in villages with vast and varied resources but with great amount of unemployment, decentralised economy, emphasis on small-scale and cottage industries, use of only those machines which normally will not displace labour, emphasis on dignity of labour all assume practical significance.

Emphasis on capital-intensive large-scale industries which get concentrated in a few centres has only resulted in increasing unemployment and increasing poverty of the masses. And therefore we do notice that there is at present greater emphasis on village reconstruction (so that rural migration towards towns and cities would be stopped) and development of small-scale and cottage industries making use of local raw materials and local personnel and skills and thus providing employment opportunities to a vast number of people. Gandhiji was opposed to concentration of power in the hands of the State and therefore he was opposed to the nationalisation of the institution of private property which gives enormous powers to the State. This would mean that Gandhiji's Doctrine of Trusteeship is the only alternative left to mankind to avoid the evils of exploitation, class conflicts and violence. Gandhiji's ideas are being reappraised and are finding increasingly important place in our Five-Year Plans and increasing acceptance in the world at large. There is no doubt that Gandhian economic system based on the Indian culture, values and traditions and Indian environment has sound basis.

According to J.C. Kumarappa, Gandhism is Marxism without violence.

3. CONTAINMENT OF MATERIAL WANTS AND ACCENT ON PHYSICAL LABOUR

It may be said that the foundation on which the Gandhian economics or Gandhian economic system is based on his ideas regarding containment of material wants by man.

This idea regarding containment of material wants is based on the Indian tradition and cultural values that human happiness does not depend upon the satisfaction of more and more material wants or pleasures but that it is a condition of mind depending upon mental contentment.

According to Gandhiji, once man is after satisfying more and more of the material wants, there is no end where he would stop. It is this craving after more and more material wants of pleasures by man that is the root cause of most of the troubles that man, the country and the world is experiencing.

In the first place, man's craving for satisfying more and more material wants is not going to make him more and more happy but only more and more discontented and unhappy. This would imply that happiness of human beings would be in satisfying his minimum and necessary needs and put a limit on his material wants after his minimum needs are satisfied.

Further, human craving for satisfying more and more material wants leads to a number of undesirable consequences. When men crave for more and more material pleasures, it leads to accumulation of more and more wealth by those who are in a position to do that at the cost of impoverishment of those who cannot do that. Thus according to Gandhiji:

"The rich have a surplus share of things which they do not need and which are, therefore, neglected and wasted, while millions are starved to death for want of sustenance. If man retained possessions of only what he needed, no one would be in want, and all would live in contentment."

The pursuit after satisfying more and more material wants leads directly to exploitation of poor by the economically strong. This leads to division of society into the rich and the poor and into class conflict and violence. Thus, human pursuit after material wants or pleasures leads to exploitation of one man by another, by one section of society of another section and by one country of another (in the form of colonialism and imperialism). All this leads to violence and undermine the sound basis or foundations of human society and world order. The most unsatisfactory aspect of the whole thing is that even when one gets all the material pleasures one seeks, his material wants would still go on multiplying and he will ever be dissatisfied, possible more dissatisfied than before.

There are some points that need elaboration. It ought to be noted that when reaching the doctrine of limiting one's materials wants, Gandhiji was not preaching asceticism or renunciation of worldly life. In a sense Gandhiji was too much of a worldly man and absorbed in worldly affairs. All he wanted was that after satisfying minimum material wants necessary for good living, everyone must put a limit to his wants as otherwise those wants will go on ever-multiplying to which there will be no end. Satisfying more and more material wants does not necessarily mean that a man is deriving more and more happiness therefrom. Quite the contrary.

There is another aspect to the problem which is more important and which has been attracting the attention these days of even Western economists.

The population of the world is increasing rapidly. Thus the population of India which was about, 85 crores in 1991 would be around 95 to 100 crores by the turn of the century and the population of the world which is at present around 500 crores would be more than 600 crores at the turn of the century. Thus with a big base the population of different countries and of the world is increasing very fast.

If in the face of such rapidly increasing population, each person is also going to multiply his material wants indefinitely would the production of the world keep pace with the needs of increasing population? There appear to be two clear limits to increasing goods and services indefinitely. The final limitation arises because certain essential resource vital to modern material civilisation are limited and exhaustible. For example, this is so in the case of petroleum and a number of vital metals. These cannot be replaced, and it may or may not be possible to find satisfactory substitutes for them. Thus relative scarcity of petrol has already been resulting in citizens of the USA limiting the number of motor cars in possession of each family and on the milleage they are to make every day, week and month.

Secondly, and more importantly satisfying material requirements of this ever-increasing population aiming at continually multiplying their material wants would require ever-increasing industrialisation and mechanisation of agriculture which would require ever-increasing quantities of chemical fertilisers, tractors, pesticides and so on which again would mean more and ever more factories to produce both industrial goods and various agricultural inputs. It has now been recognised that greater the industrialisation, greater the amount of atmospheric pollution — pollution of air and water and noise explosion, apart from the stresses and tensions created by industrial civilizations and new diseases consequent of such stresses and mental strains. If a man's possession of more and more material goods and wealth is going to be accompanied by ever-increasing mental and physical stresses and strains making his life more and more miserable, what is the use of possessing those vast material goods and trying to satisfy ever-increasing wants?

And thus even the Western economists have now been thinking and talking in terms of 'Limits to Growth'. Once it is admitted that there are clear limits to economic growth because of limited amount of land and exhaustible nature of certain essential raw materials and also because of more and more pollution, stresses and strains consequent on additional industrialisation and growth, it follows that there will have to be a clear limit on material wants and pleasures which people as a whole and everyone must seek to satisfy. And thus Gandhiji's ideas regarding containment of material wants stand justified both on moral and economic grounds.

Accent on Physical Labour

According to Gandhiji, there is the divine law that every man must earn his bread by labouring with his own hands. Gandhiji emphasised that every normal and healthy individual must labour enough for his living. According to him, production of every commodity needed to satisfy essential human needs (For example, agricultural commodities, weaving, carpentry, smithy, etc.) and labour in all essential services or occupations like cleaning a well, sweeping a street, scavenging, etc.) may be included under the heading 'bread labour'. For the concept of 'bread labour', Gandhiji was indebted to Ruskin's 'Unto the Last' and another Russian thinker and author T.M. Bondaref. Gandhiji argued that if every individual laboured for his daily bread (*i.e.,* for his essentials) and no more, three would be enough food and enough leisure for all.

"Then there would be no cry of over-population, no disease and no such misery as we see around us today. Man will no doubt do many other things either through their bodies or through their minds, but all this will be labour of love for the common good. There will be no rich and no poor, none high and none low." There is no doubt that intellectual work is important; but Gandhiji wrote: "But what I must insist on is the necessity of physical labour. No man, I claim, ought to be free from this obligation. It will serve to improve even the quality of his intellectual output." Gandhiji strongly believed in the saying of the Gita that "he who eats without offering sacrifice (*i.e.,* labouring), eats stolen food." Gandhiji insisted that everyone must undertake some physical labour and without that he or she is not entitled to his or her food. He urged even millionaires to undertake bodily labour to earn their food.

Gandhiji thus recognised the importance of physical labour in every man's life. He thus emphasised the dignity of labour. All physical labour put in the production of essential goods and services was of the same significance, and there was no higher or lower type of physical labour. In order to stress home this principle, Gandhiji for long undertook the physical work of cleaning latrines at the time of Congress sessions.

Naturally Gandhiji's views on physical labour bring us to his views on machinery and its role.

Gandhiji was generally opposed to machinery and its increasing introduction in modern life especially in countries like India. Machines generally, displace labour and in a country like India where there is immense labour power, created the problems of unemployment which meant that introduction of machinery resulted in increasing unemployment and ever-increasing misery of the masses. While machinery should be a servant of man, Gandhiji was pained to observe that man had become a slave to machine and just a cog in the gigantic machinery. Machine dulled his senses and destroyed his physical, mental and creative powers. Machines helped the unscrupulous elements in society to exploit labourers and accumulate vast wealth dividing society into two classes of the poor and the rich. Machinery enabled the few rich to live luxurious lives without doing any physical work which not only made them parasitic but was detrimental to their own physical and moral health. The craze for using bigger and bigger machines has enabled industrially advanced countries to exploit the developing countries in the Third World where nearly two-thirds of the world's population live a miserable existence.

4. TRUSTEESHIP ECONOMY AS OPPOSED TO STATE-CENTRED ECONOMY

Trusteeship principle is one of the basic ideas of the Gandhian economic system.

Meaning of Trusteeship Principle

Gandhiji was not opposed to the institution of private property. But he was keen to restrict the right of private property to just what was necessary to live a decent life whereas for the private property that was in excess of this required minimum, he prescribed the principle of trusteeship. Gandhiji emphasised that the institution of private property has as its foundation social sanction. Without social sanction the institution of private property just cannot exit. If this is so, then according to Gandhiji, it follows that private property that is in excess of what is required by the property-owner to enable him to live a reasonable standard of life must be held as a trust on behalf of the society of which he is a member. He should regard that the excess private property is a trust and he should behave like a trustee holding the property on behalf of the society and especially those who are poor and have no private property of their own. Gandhiji allowed the capitalist to retain excess private property with himself and if possible exert more to increase his property. But as a trustee of the society on behalf of which he held the property, the capitalist must use the excess property not for his personal benefit of exploiting the poor but for increasing the welfare of the society and especially welfare of those who owned no property.

Gandhiji pointed out to the capitalists that unless they used their excess private property for the benefit of society and for the common good and if they continued to use it for only selfish purposes or for exploitation of the poor, the society would be divided into two classes of 'haves' and 'have-nots' and there would be class struggle resulting in violence. And it is possible that their property would be expropriated, may be without any compensation.

Gandhiji's Trusteeship Principle may be summarised as follows:

Gandhiji believed in the institution of private property. He did not believe in nationalisation of private property and State holding all property. This is because, that would increase power of the State. Gandhiji was extremely apprehensive of concentration of power in the hands of the State. Such concentration of power in the hands of the State would come in the way of development of human personality.

But Gandhiji desired that the private property in excess of what is necessary to satisfy reasonable needs of the capitalist should be held as a trust on behalf of the society and the capitalist should make use of that excess property not as an instrument of exploitation of the poor and dispossessed but for the welfare of society as a whole. The capitalist is free to accumulate more and more property, if all the excess property is held as a trust on behalf of society and for the benefit of society without the sanction of which the institution of private property cannot exist.

In case the capitalists did not adopt and follow the trusteeship principle, society will be divided into two classes of 'haves' and 'have-nots'; there will be class struggle and violence and there is every likelihood that the capitalists would be expropriated of their property.

The trusteeship principle of Gandhiji believed in the goodness of man and his understanding and in persuading him to follow the principle of trusteeship. He believed in the principle of love of man for his brethren and therefore felt that capitalists would be enlightened enough to follow the principle of trusteeship. Gandhiji's trusteeship principle is thus based on the principle of love and reasonableness of man and not on the assumption that man is a wicked creature who would go on accumulating more and more property and use it for exploitation of the poor and dispossessed.

Thus Gandhiji's trusteeship principle has a moral basis and is based on the optimist view of human nature which he felt could be perfected.

According to Gandhiji trusteeship principle is the best instrument of establishing equality among members of society.

Trusteeship Principle as an Alternative to Capitalism and Communism

Gandiji's trusteeship principle, it is claimed, serves as the most satisfactory substitute, both for capitalism on the one hand and centralised and authoritarian communism on the other. Trusteeship principle is the best alterative to both capitalism and communism.

Trusteeship Principle and Capitalism. As already noted, under capitalism (and especially under *laissez-faire* capitalism) people actuated by selfish private profit motive and with a view to satisfy ever-increasing number of wants, go on accumulating more and more wealth. This accumulated wealth, as we have already seen, becomes in the hands of capitalists an instrument of exploitation of the poorer sections of the community. This insensate desire to accumulate more and more wealth splits society into two classes of 'haves' and 'have-nots', the two classes are always in conflict with each other so that most often the result is violence, social and political instability and possibly revolution as in the Soviet Union where capitalists were entirely dispossessed of their property.

Gandhiji's trusteeship principle by holding excess private property as trust on behalf of society and being used for the welfare of the masses avoids split of society into two classes of rich and poor, spreads equality among people, avoids violence and guarantees social stability. Gandhiji warned the capitalists that if they do not follow the trusteeship principle, they will have to face violence and expropriation of all their private property.

Trusteeship Principle and Communism. Communism expropriates all private property and entrusts its ownership and management in the hands of the State. Communism thus believes that evil instincts in man predominate and that man if left to himself will always exploit other fellow human beings. The centralised and authoritarian State therefore takes over all private property and directs its use and distribution of what is produced. Under communism people are therefore deprived of all the initiative and individual freedom. State and its bureaucracy and very often a small powerful clique in the bureaucracy directs all economic activities treating men and women as so many chattels and pawns and with obligations only to obey the dictates of the all-powerful State. This as we have already seen, suppresses human freedom and initiative and is contrary to human nature.

Compared to communism, Gandhiji's trusteeship principle believing in human goodness leaves him to enjoy his freedom, at the same time bringing about abolition of exploitation of the poor masses by the rich and equitable distribution of income and wealth in the most non-violent way as the doctrine is based on the assumption of fundamental goodness residing in human breast. If the main instruments through which communism works are force and punishment, the Trusteeship Principle believes in human goodness and persuasion.

Concluding Remarks

Gandhiji's trusteeship principle is crticised as contrary to human nature, impracticable and idealistic.

If we take a dispassionate view and also note the fact that man is not vicious but has some goodness and compassion in his breast and that man does strive for some ideal, then trusteeship principle appears in a different light.

Capitalism with its unlimited accumulation of wealth by capitalists cannot go on and would definitely result in violence and revolution and expropriation of all private property. Even the capitalists have therefore recognised the limits to private property one can hold. Slowly they are realising to an increasing extent their social obligations and responsibility and the fact that social sanction alone is the basis of private property. With a little more enlightenment, there is no reason why the capitalist class should not in their own interest behave in an enlightened way by accepting the trusteeship principle.

The other alternative, namely, communism is clearly contrary to human nature as it completely suppresses acquisitive instinct, initiative and creativeness and personal freedom. Communism brings its own class structure into existence and its own form of exploitation.

This means that Ganhiji's trusteeship principle, though it appears to savour too much of idealism, is the only satisfactory basis of organising society on the basis of love and non-violence which alone can serve as stable and satisfactory basis for functioning of civilised societies.

CHAPTER 23

LAND GIFT MOVEMENT (BHOODAN) AND SARVODAYA

1. THE LAND-GIFT (BHOODAN) MOVEMENT

Background

It is a well-known fact that ownership of agricultural land in India is extremely unevenly distributed. For example, it is observed that the top 4 per cent of the total number of land-owning class own about 31 per cent of the total cultivated land in the country. The top 15 per cent of the land-owning class in the country own about 61 per cent of the total cultivated land in the country. On the other hand, 51 per cent of the bottom land-owning class own only about 9 per cent of the total cultivated land in the country. It must also be kept in mind that here we are talking about those agricultural classes who own some cultivable land. While considering the pattern of ownership of agricultural land in the country, it ought to be kept in mind that there are millions and millions of people in rural areas who do not own any cultivable land at all. In order to understand the significance and impact of the Bhoodan Movement of Vinoba Bhave, the above background must be kept in mind.

The Land-Gift Movement or Bhoodan Movement was started by Vinoba Bhave, a disciple of Gandhiji, in 1951. The Bhoodan Movement is based on the moral appeal to land-owning classes in the country to voluntarily donate a part of their lands for distribution among their unfortunate brethren, millions of whom own no land at all, or own only small pieces of cultivable land with which they find it impossible to support themselves and their families.

The basic underlying concept or moral values behind the Land-Gift or Bhoodan Movement of Vinoba Bhave are as follows:

1. All land is a free gift of nature like air, water and sunshine and therefore should be equally shared by all.

2. Those land-owning classes who own greater quantities of agricultural land ought to retain only that much land which they can personally cultivate and donate the rest of the land for distribution among their unfortunate brethren who own no land at all or own very small pieces of agricultural land.

3. Since elimination of extreme inequalities is a moral necessity and is also desirable on economic and political grounds as also in the interest of the big land-owning class itself, the Bhoodan Movement makes an appeal to big landlords to share their lands with their unfortunate brethren in rural areas.

It ought to be clear that the Land-Gift or Bhoodan Movement mainly relies on moral appeal and inherent good sense of the land-owning classes to donate part of their agricultural land for being distributed among landless agricultural workers and small and marginal farmers. It is also clear that the movement relies on moral appeal rather than on legislative measures and force to bring about redistribution of land among cultivating classes. One reason is that moral appeal is superior and is in accord with the Indian culture and cultural values whereas resort to legislative measures implies use of compulsion and if necessary violence.

Though initially the Bhoodan Movement only aimed at voluntary donation of land by land-owning classes, in subsequent years some of the State Governments tried to provide legal basis to help transfer of land ownership.

From the Bhoodan Movement, Vinoba Bhave'e movement widened its sphere to include Gramdan (Village-donation Movement). Under Gramdan scheme, the entire village is donated. The idea behind Gramdan is to create an ideal village where all the land in the village is jointly owned and managed by all the villagers.

Achievements of Land-Gift Movement

Of the total net sown area in India of about 328.5 million acres, the Bhoodan Movement fixed the target of collecting by way of donation from land-owning classes 50 millions acres.

Initially there was great enthusiasm; and the missionary zeal with which Vinoba Bhave and his disciples conducted the movement appeared to bear good fruits. As we have seen the Bhoodan Movement was started in 1951. By March 1967, however, only 42.7 lakh acres of land were collected through land-gift or Bhoodan. This means the figure attained during the 16 years was less than 10 per cent of the target of 50 million acres.

It also needs to be noted that of the 42.7 lakh acres donated, nearly half was donated in one State alone, namely, Bihar where for some time Jayaprakash Narayan was working for the Bhoodan Movement.

Also, by August 1967, along with 42.7 lakh acres of land, 39,672 villages were donated under the Gramdan scheme.

Of the 42.7 lakh acres of land donated, only about 12 lakh acres have been distributed so far.

It needs to be noted that of the total of 42.7 lakh acres of land donated, nearly 12.7 lakh acres are unifit for cultivation. Though Bihar donated practically half the land out of the total of 42.7 lakh acres, it also needs to be noted thal nearly 10.5 lakh acres or nearly 50 per cent of the land donated by landlords in Bihar happened to be uncultivable. And then there were several donated lands which were in dispute and the title deeds of which were not clean.

Critical Appraisal of Land-Gift (Bhoodan) Movement

There is no doubt that the Bhoodan Movement has succeeded in collecting by way of land-gifts more land than the amount of surplus land collected under the Land Ceiling Acts of all the State Governments.

And yet the fact remains that the actual realisation has fallen far short of target aimed at by the Bhoodan Movement.

We have also already seen that a substantial amount of land donated has been practically uncultivable land. This means such land-gifts were only of nominal character and not in the true spirit of the Bhoodan Movement, nor of much use to the donees of the movement.

Another feature that has characterised the Land-Gift Movement has been that very often lands donated by landlords have been lands under legal disputes in civil courts or lands about which ownership titles were not clear and clean but were in dispute. Such lands naturally could not be distributed among the poor cultivators in rural areas for whose benefit the movement was launched.

Very often loud and prominent announcements were made by big landlords at important meetings that they are donating a certain amount of their lands; but in fact actual grants of lands were never made. Very often big landlords made donation of some part of their lands with a view to secure some government contracts or a licence or some other consideration. This means often land-gifts were made with some ulterior motive and not out of consideration for the landless and the poor peasants. Such land-gifts therefore were not made in the spirit which inspired the Bhoodan Movement of Vinoba Bhave.

It is widely known that though originally and for some time, there was certain amount of missionary zeal and devoted workers were involved in the movement, that missionary zeal has for all practical purposes disappeared so also the band of devoted and conscientious voluntary workers.

While in the initial stages the collection of donated land proved to be fairly easy, its distribution among the deserving and poor cultivators in the villages proved to be a difficult problem to which no satisfactory answer could be found till the end. How to choose deserving and poor cultivators to whom donated land was to be presented? How much land should be donated to them? Would the land donated be adjacent to the small pieces that the poor cultivators already owned? Would donated lands of differing fertility be appropriately distributed among deserving cultivators? Which is the village body that is to be entrusted with the task of distributing land among poor peasants? Would the distribution of donated land be done impartially? Would the ownership titles etc. be appropriately transferred? The Bhoodan Movement at no stage showed adequate appreciation of the various problems involved in distributing the lands donated by land-holding classes under the Bhoodan Movement.

The most unfavourable aspect of the Bhoodan Movement or the Land-Gift Movement of Vinoba Bhave has been impact of that movement on Land Reforms Legislation. Right from the days of national struggle for independence and also after the country became independent, legislative measures which means the use of government laws, prestige and power had come to be considered as chief instruments of land reforms, namely, abolition of Zamindari system, abolition of intermediaries and absentee landlordism, fixing of ceilings on landholding which a person is authorised to own and so on. After 1937, and especially after 1947, many State Governments passed laws in regard to the above matters and however defective their implementation and whatever their loopholes, these legislative measures by creating awakening among peasants were creating suitable background for much-needed reforms and redistribution of land among agriculturists.

The Bhoodan Movement with its emphasis on moral element and superiority of voluntary surrender of land to the class of poor peasants distracted the attention of policy-makers (especially of those who because of vested interests were lukewarm from the beginning to these legislative land reform measures) and legislators to these legislative measures. Land Reforms Legislation which was gaining momentum during 1950s and 1960s thus received severe setback because of the Land-Gift or Bhoodan Movement of Vinoba Bhave.

Concluding Remarks

With the waning enthusiasm of its leader Vinoba Bhave and more so of his disciples who had shown some missionary zeal in the beginning, the Bhoodan Movement for all practical purposes seems to have petered itself out. It collected, though substantial, only a fraction of its target in view much of which was uncultivable or in legal dispute. While some poor cultivators did get a few patches of lands, the ideal of establishing brotherhood among the landholding classes and poor peasants commonly sharing land which is the free gift of nature, remains as distant as ever. It should be noted that charity and donation cannot become a satisfactory basis of reforming society.

2. EMPHASIS ON VOLUNTARY AGENCIES

Gandhiji had a deep suspicion of Government which mainly relies upon force to bring about any reform. He believed that social or any reforms enforced from above do not represent true reforms and are not lasting. True reforms in any field of human activity must come out of one's inner convictions. This means that voluntary action based on one's convictions are far more superior than reforms enforced by Government. Also, Government action not only means reliance on force but also complex rules and regulations and elaborate governmental machinery all resulting in superficial reforms. This would not be so, if reforms in various fields in India are undertaken by voluntary agencies where action comes out of inner conviction and where labour is labour of love.

Thus limitations of governmental action or reforms introduced by the Government can be easily appreciated, if we consider what is happening in the field of removal of untouchability and prohibition. On paper Government has removed untouchability by law long ago; but since people have not been properly educated and enlightened on the matter and convinced of the inhuman nature of that institution, untouchability continues almost unabated, especially in rural areas whereas yet illiteracy, ignorance and conservatism are all rampant.

Similarly, limitations on Government's power to bring about desirable reforms can again be illustrated by referring to the reform of prohibition through Government legislation. We all know that this has proved a fiasco. Various State Governments introduced total or partial prohibition and recruited additional police and empowered them with vast powers of search and punishment through courts of law. We all know that with all the powers of the Government, the policy of prohibition has not succeeded. On the other hand, bootlegging, illicit distillation and habit of drinking have been spreading more widely than ever before.

The same can be said about the programme of compulsory primary education introduced by Government through legislation. This legal programme and reform has hardly touched the fringe of the problem. At present there are more illiterates in the country than before Government passed the law making primary education compulsory. The same can be said about the abolition of child marriages which by Sarada Act are supposed to be abolished since 1920s. But the institution of child marriage is still widely prevalent in rural areas. Government is an impersonal body without soul and acting within rules and regulations. Such a Government is surely not the most suitable agency to bring about any reforms but only to a limited extent and that also provided suitable environment is created by appropriate steps as a condition precedent to the reform introduced by the Government.

The same can be said about abolition of dowry system by law.

Gandhiji put great faith in voluntary organisations or agencies. In such organisations where compulsion is absent, only those people who are convinced of the cause of reform will enlist themselves. They work because of their deep convictions. Naturally they will work hard and conscientiously. Their chief instruments are persuasion and education of the people among whom reforms, are to be brought about. If devoted workers come forward, money and funds become a secondary consideration and it is observed in India and elsewhere that voluntary organisations composed of sincere and devoted workers have never lacked funds.

Also India has on its hands so many problems that the idea of expanding governmental machinery and to entrust to it various reforms would be unmanageable and hence unthinkable. And therefore India will do well, according to Gandhiji, to build up a network of voluntary organisations and institutions, self-reliant and composed of devoted workers to bring about reforms in various fields.

Gandhiji thus wanted voluntary institutions to work in the fields of communal harmony, removal of untouchability, prohibition, development of Khadi and village industries, village sanitation, upliftment of women, adult education, hygiene and public sanitation and upliftment of Harijans, tribals, Adivasis, the lepers and so on. It is obvious that entire reliance on Government to bring about reforms in some of the above fields would be impracticable. Also work through voluntary organisations would make people self-reliant which enhance the moral dignity of man. Gandhiji did not just go on preaching this doctrine but practised what he preached and built a wide network of voluntary organisations in various fields to bring about desirable reforms in various fields and this he managed to do under the most unfavourable and discouraging atmosphere when the British ruled over India.

Concluding Remarks

There are hardly any instances where the Government could successfully bring about social, economic, political and moral reforms. Government relies mainly upon force and there is inherent contradiction between force and social reform which must come from within. This would mean that voluntary organisations and institutions composed of conscientious and devoted workers and depending upon education and persuasion of the people are the best instruments of social reforms. Government can act in this matter as a support or prop but cannot be the main or the sole instrument of social reforms.

3. SARVODAYA ECONOMIC PHILOSOPHY AND ITS LIMITATIONS

Meaning of the Concept of Sarvodaya

Gandhiji in preference to Benthamite utilitarian philosophy of 'the greatest good of the greatest number', advocated the philosophy of Sarvodaya which means "the welfare of all."

Gandhiji advocated the philosophy of Sarvodaya and later on his eminent disciples J.P. Narayan and Acharya Vinoba Bhave have tried to give it some definite shape and content.

The concept of Sarvodaya is still in the process of evolution and therefore comprehensive definition of that concept cannot as yet be given. But the following six aspects or elements of Sarvodaya would help make the meaning of that concept fairly clear.

Vinoba Bhave explaining the philosophy of Sarvodaya writes : "Sarvodaya means that good of all resides in the good of one. That there could be interests of one person which are against the interest of another, is inconceivable. Similarly, there could be no interests of one community, class or country which would be against the interests of any other community, class or country. The idea of opposition of interests is itself wrong."

J.P. Narayan has defined Sarvodaya as "people's socialism." It seeks "to remove various social evils by developing focus of socialist living through the voluntary endeavour of associations instead of seeking to establish socialism through the use of force and power of the State."

The philosophy of Sarvodaya may be said to be made up of the following elements:

1. Love and not hated is the fundamental basis of social organisation. Human nature is capable of love and affection for other fellow human beings and if there is often hatred and ill-feeling towards others, it is more the result of environment. Naturally the philosophy of Sarvodaya rejects the theory of division of society into two classes of 'haves' and 'have-nots' and the theory of class war advocated by Karl Marx and scientific socialism. Sarvodaya philosophy firmly believes that by changing environment and by creating suitable and appropriate conditions, it is possible to get rid of hatred and such other evil tendencies of man and instead of hatred, competition and class war, love and co-operation among people can be made the basis of social organisation.

2. Sarvodaya philosophy believes in non-violence. It believes that by educating people, it is possible to persuade people to limit their material wants and share their wealth with their fellow-beings and thus establish social and economic equality in society. All this can be done without resort to force or violence.

3. Philosophy of Sarvodaya believes in the least interference by the State in the affairs of the people. J.P. Narayan wrote: "I was and am not sure if the State would wither away completely. But I am sure that it is one of the noblest goals of social endeavour to ensure that the powers and functions and spheres of the State are reduced as far as possible." Gandhiji along with J.P. and Vinoba Bhave firmly believed that the Government is best which governs the least. This is because the State relies on force in bringing about social and individual reforms and these social reformers firmly believed that no reform of permanent value can result by resorting to force to bring about that reform. Social reform must come from within and must result from one's inner convictions, if they are

to be everlasting. Reforms forced upon people by an external agency can never be permanent. Similarly social harmony can come about only by mutual understanding and goodwill among people ; it cannot be forced upon people by an agency like the State whose fundamental characteristic is force. People must be self-reliant. Sarvodaya depends upon willing cooperation among people born out of their convictions. " What is needed to develop people's power is a band of selfless workers prepared to live and move amidst people and help them to reorganise their lives on a self-reliant and self-governing basis." Swarajya literally would and should mean government of individual over himself. This implies that the philosophy of Sarvodaya is fundamentally in conflict with interference by the State to bring about any type of reforms of individuals and of society because State by its very nature comes to depend upon force to bring about reconstruction and reform of the individual and the society. What is achieved by force is not lasting; what is achieved by love is!

It would be observed that this aspect of Sarvodaya is opposed to the communist view. Communism believes that exploitation of the poor by landlords and capitalists can be stopped only by the State using force to expropriate the properties of these classes and for establishing classless society. Thus if communism mainly relies upon force or violence to bring about social and economic reforms and establishing social and economic equality, Sarvodaya aims at the same objective of social and economic equality but relies not upon force but on love and understanding and voluntary cooperation among people and on enlightenment of their mind and rousing of their conscience. Reforms coming from within and not forced from above are true and lasting reforms.

4. Under Sarvodaya self-sufficient and self-governing village communities will form the basis of social and political organisation of the country. Vinoba Bhave wrote: "The villages of India must become self-supporting and they must manufacture finished goods which they require in their villages. All should get food and all must work. The economy of the nation should be-placed on the lines of joint family." This will enable people in villages to get employment and will ensure the use of immense and varied resources in the vast number of villages in India. Such an economy will also avoid concentration of economic and especially manufacturing activities at a few centres creating overcrowding and other socio-political problems. Western-based type of urban-oriented civilisation, is incapable of ensuring social and economic equality and welfare of all.

According to the philosophy of Sarvodaya, there will also be decentralisation of political authority. Each village is to be a self-governing republic. Sarvodaya is opposed to concentration of political authority at the centre because this would result in various restrictions and restraints and to that extent hamper individual initiative and curtail individual freedom.

5. Sarvodaya believes that when the elected representatives of the people take any important decision affecting the welfare of the people in the commu-

nity, the decisions should not be taken on the basis of majority but should be on the basis of consensus. Once we begin to talk in terms of majority and minority decisions, conflicts of various types develop splitting society into groups and factions leading to disagreements and may be to violence. Sarvodaya therefore insists on compromise among different sets of view and on consensus on all important issues. Consensus is possible if there is goodwill on the part of all and the spirit of give-and-take and of mutual trust and cooperation.

6. Sarvodaya is based on the idea of equality of people. This is not the equality enforced by the State as under communism. Gandhiji wrote: "I shall bring about economic equality through non-violence, by converting the people to my point of view, by harnessing the forces of love as against hatred."

Explaining the principle of human equality which is fundamental to the philosophy of Sarvodaya, K.G. Mashruwala gave the following illustration. "An enterprising young man in a joint Hindu family goes abroad and makes money. He has to share it with other members of the family, even as he himself gets a share in the earnings made at home during his absence. Why not extend the bounds of family and include tenant and labourer, indeed the whole village in it? Then there should be no cause for jealousy."

Concluding Remarks

From the above analysis of the fundamental features of the philosophy of Sarvodaya, it becomes clear that Sarvodaya which is based on Indian culture, values and traditions is an original and constructive contribution of Gandhiji. Sarvodaya philosophy, already seen above, is based on several assumptions. It believes that man can be happy not by continual quest for more and more material pleasures and satisfying ever-increasing wants but by limiting them. It assumes that there is innate goodness in human nature and love for fellow human beings and cooperation among men can provide sound foundation for social organisation, and not hatred and violence. It believes in small and self-sufficient village communities with its agriculture and decentralised small-scale and cottage industries which will provide employment and steady income to local people and meet local needs. This would help avoid emergence of crowded cities and towns and various urban problems which are plaguing urban areas in developed countries of the West. Sarvodaya philosophy emphasises self-reliance and self-rule. This implies that under this philosophy there will be no concentration of political authority in the all-powerful central government which is supposed to interfere least in the affairs of the people who are supposed to manage them on the basis of mutual cooperation and understanding. Village community is to be just an extension of family.

Limitations of Sarvodaya Philosophy

The Sarvodaya philosophy on the face of it appears very attractive and an effective alternative to both the economic systems, namely capitalism and communism. Its strength lies in its two main features. In the first place that philosophy is based on ingrained Indian culture and tradition that contentment lies in extinguishing extra and superficial wants and not in multiplying them. Secondly, the Sarvodaya philosophy embodies the ideas of liberty, equality and fraternity made popular by the French Revolution.

But after careful scrutiny of the Sarvodaya philosophy as propounded by Gandhiji, J. P. Narayan and Vinoba Bhave, three questions stare out in the face which must be satisfactorily resolved before the philosophy receives general acceptability. In other terms, the Sarvodaya philosophy suffers from the following three limitations:

1. Sarvodaya philosophy assumes goodness in man and human nature and believes that human nature can be perfected by removing acquisitiveness, jealousy, competitiveness, combativeness and their being replaced by love and cooperation. Sarvodaya assumes the existence of these qualities which however Sarvodaya alone can possibly create. Thus we are caught in the eternal circle. Sarvodaya cannot succeed without the existence of a particular type of human nature; and it so happens that favourable environment can be created only by acceptance and introduction of Sarvodaya.

2. But some would question the very basic assumption of Sarvodaya that human nature is perfectable and that love and cooperation can alone be made, with suitable changes in environment, the dominant features of human nature. Psychologically it is claimed that human nature is a combination of good as well as evil elements and that while sometimes good elements predominate, at other times bad elements would come into their own and that bad elements cannot be completely eliminated, nor human nature be made perfect. This means that Sarvodaya is based on wrong assumptions, and therefore would prove impracticable and unworkable. Sarvodaya is good as an ideal or model ; but it can never be put fully into effective practice.

3. Because of rapid technological progress and annihilation of distance, the world has shrunk into a small unit. Any development anywhere in the world affects everyone's life even in the remotest corner of the world. Modern life has become extremely complex. Would it be practicable under such circumstances to talk in terms of self-sufficient villages, decentralised industries and self-reliance and so on ? What would be the fate of a country based on such concepts in the face of technologically advanced and highly industrialised countries following extremely aggressive policies in the economic and political spheres? Would such a country not succumb to the politically and economically powerful countries? Has that not been the lesson of Indian history? Can we afford to be blind to modern trends prevailing in other countries of the world?

Concluding Remarks

Sarvodaya therefore may be said to be a utopian concept. But then utopias have their uses and values. They set up a model before us, a vision to which we should all aspire. For example, Sarvodaya draws pointed attention to the excesses of modern materialistic civilization and points out clearly its defects and dangers. Sarvodaya thus draws attention to evils flowing from the worship of the mammon, both in capitalist and communist societies; it draws attention to the predominant role which the modern state has come to play suppressing individual initiative and creativeness; it refers to the great inequalities of income and wealth prevalent among people in modern societies and inherent dangers in such an arrangement; it points out the dangers of concentration of political and economic powers in the hands either of a clique of people or even government. This smothers development of personality and creates an environment in which creativity of man does not get adequate scope for its development without which no man can be truly contented and happy. That is why with all the material progress in Western countries, man is feeling completely alienated.

Sarvodaya may be utopian and therefore may prove unworkable. But by pointing out to the dangers of extreme acquisitiveness, concentration of political and economic power, extreme inequality and such other evils besetting modern civilization, both capitalistic and communist, Sarvodaya may persuade men to adopt the middle way whereby dangers from the above defects might be minimised, if not completely eliminated.

There is however no doubt that permanent and lasting peace in the world cannot be ensured by capitalism with its emphasis on acquisitiveness, competitiveness, inequalities and exploitation, division of society into 'haves' and 'have-nots' and an atmosphere of class confrontation and class war, nor by communism with its emphasis on abolition of private property and personal freedom and concentration of economic and political power in the all-powerful State. The vision or utopia of Sarvodaya with its emphasis on love and cooperation, containment of material wants, self-reliance, decentralisation of political power, decentralised type of economy and equality would certainly help people by pointing out the direction along which countries should move if there is to be peace in the world and all people are to live contented and happy life.

CHAPTER 24

THE CHINESE COMMUNIST SYSTEM

The term 'Communism' seems to more appropriately describe the Chinese economic system than those of most other socialist countries (which call themselves communist). This is because the goal of equality and of classless society has been an important factor moulding the economic policy in China since 1949 when the Communist Party came to power.

1. BRIEF HISTORICAL BACKGROUND

Between 1949 and 1952 (or thereabout), the Chinese Communist authorities, along with the work of rehabilitation of the war-damaged economy of the nation, proceeded to gain control of the national economy through measures such as takeover of enterprises previously owned by the Nationalist Government, State trading in major commodities, control over banking, price and wage controls, and taxation. The takeover of enterprises previously owned by the Nationalist Government gave the Communist authorities control over nearly 90 per cent of iron and steel output, over 67 per cent of electric power, 45 per cent of cement output as also control over substantial output of a number of other major industries.

Also during 1949 and 1952, the land, draft animals, implements and houses all belonging to landlords were confiscated. All these agricultural assets were distributed among poor peasants and landless agricultural labourers. This might be said to be an important land reform of this period. The result was not strictly the establishment of communist egalitarianism. This was because "...the rich and middle-class peasants still had greater than average holding as well as more and better equipment and animals. They, too, were more likely to be literate than their poorer fellows..."[1]

2. ATTEMPTS TO ESTABLISH SOVIET-TYPE ECONOMY (1953-56)

It was during 1953 and 1956 that most comprehensive economic planning took place in the Communist China. An attempt was made during this period to establish the Soviet-type economy with the assistance of the Soviet advisers. Agriculture was collectivized and peasants were compelled by the Chinese Communist Party to enter 'agricultural producer cooperatives' which came to be established fairly rapidly. The aim of the Communist Party in doing this was to collect 'surplus' from peasantry as had been done in Russia, as also to prevent the revival of the rich peasant economy in the countryside. The peasant, after working for a specified number of hours on 'the agricultural producer cooperative' was supposed to be free to work on his small plot of land. But these privately cultivated plots were either restricted to small size or such private plots were often abolished; pigs, polutry and equipment on such private plots being often confiscated along with the abolition of those private agricultural plots. It was however observed that rapid establishment of 'agricultural producer cooperatives' did not disorganise agriculture as much as collectivisation of agriculture had done in the Soviet Union.

Also during this period (1953-56) as in the Soviet-type economy, heavy industries in China received the largest share in the total investment in the economy. The comprehensive planning emphasised output targets at the expense of cost reduction or profit objective.

By 1956 the Chinese Communist Party leaders began to realise that the Soviet-type development strategy built on industrialisation with emphasis on basic and heavy industries and comparative neglect of agriculture was not viable and an ideal model, considering the pattern of resource endowment in China.

As result of steps taken during 1953-56, forced-draft industrialisation led to various imbalances and shortages. For example, it led to over-investment in steel accompanied by shortages of cement and timber and even pig iron. The comprehensive type of planning (commandism) resulted in inflexibility (especially at the lower level). During this period, there was neglect of agriculture; there was discontentment among peasants many of whom left 'agricultural producer cooperatives'.

The consequence of the above unfavourable developments consequent on the attempt to adopt Soviet-type planning and strategy during 1953-56 was that in 1957 and 1958 there was severe reaction against the Soviet-type planning and strategy and as a consequence pragmatists and moderates came to the force in Communist China.

Movement Towards Decentralisation

As a reaction to the above developments, there took place considerable decentralisation in the Chinese communist economy. Instead of the Central

Government, many decisions could now be taken at the provincial and enterprise level. There was no more fixation of specific targets in the case of many enterprises, especially those producing consumer goods. The size of 'agricultural producer cooperatives' came to be reduced, while the size of agricultural plots privately cultivated by peasants came to be enlarged; and markets for subsidiary production by agriculturists came to be reopened. During this period even free speech came to be encouraged.

3. 'THE GREAT LEAP' (1958-69)

It became obvious that the Soviet-type bureaucratic model had proved disappointing in China. Also it was feared that capitalist forces were re-emerging in some quarters. And therefore during 1958 to 1960 a move was made in quite a different direction. This has come to be designated as 'The Great Leap Forward'. It included among other things the establishment of People's Communes.

The Communist Party leaders who during these years wielded greater influence thought that the lesson which they had learnt during the days of guerrilla warfare in the countryside should be applied to the economic field. They reacted against the bureaucratic inadequacies as detrimental to people's initiative. Chairman Mao had great faith in the malleability of human nature and potentialities of collective incentives and collective entrepreneurship. It was felt that ideologically committed Communist Party local leaders should seize initiative and move forward with little regard to overall balance in the economy of the nation. The Communist Party local leaders and cadres in agriculture and industry came to be freed from the bureaucratic constraints of central planning. Centrally determined targets did not matter; only that they needed to be much bigger and larger so that there would be 'A Great Leap Forward'. Local Communist Party leaders and cadres were freed from constraints from cost control and profit considerations during this period. It was during this period that small backyard iron and steel furnaces were encouraged. Industrial output rose rapidly during this period but much of what was produced was of low quality or even worthless.

People's Communes

It was during this period (1958-60) that attempts were made to amalgamate 'agricultural producer cooperatives' into large People's Communes. The People's Communes were to be multipurpose units. From the Government point of view, a People's Commune was a basic unit of taxation; from the industrial point of view it was to develop small rural industries and handicrafts; from the financial and commercial point of view, it was to absorb supply and marketing cooperatives and local branches of the People's Bank; and above all it (People's Commune) was to be an agricultural unit. The People's Commune substituted " all-people ownership for collective ownership and they were to distribute part of their income in accordance with need, in particular free meals in communal dining halls." Initially, People's Communes were to be very large units, possibly because of shortage of qualified staff; but subsequently, the emphasis shifted to smaller size People's Communes much diversified in size to suit local conditions. The system of private small agricultural plots came to be abolished so also the free market.

The Great Leap Forward represented an all-out effort to mobilise local resources. But it stretched the organisational and administrative resources beyond their capabilities. There were also a series of bad harvests in 1950, 1960 and 1961 both because of bad weather and also because of institutional weakness of People's Communes. For example, the local leaders of the Communist Party were often out of touch with farm operations and transferred large number of farm-hands at the time of harvesting from farm work to flood control, construction of irrigation projects, mining and steel-smelting. The Great Leap Forward came to be characterised by mismanagement and technical errors in project construction in communes and various other administrative and other deficiencies.

The Retreat

Observing the above undesirable consequences of The Great Leap Forward, the central leadership of the Communist Party effected a retreat in certain respects. The system of private plots of agricultural land came to be reintroduced and limit was put on labour-time which a People's Commune could require from farmers; free market in the form of rural trade fairs were re-introduced. Incentives for increase in collective productivity were restored with reintroduction of piece-rates as also rights of ownership from the People's Commune to the 'Production Brigade' (a unit generally of the size of former 'agricultural producer cooperative') and later down to a 'Production Team'. The peasant household was recognised as a basic unit of consumption and communal dining halls were abolished. Needless to say, the re-emergence of all these capitalistic tendencies or aspects ('sprouts of capitalism') were ideologically suspect to many hard-line Communist Party leaders.

4. THE CULTURAL REVOLUTION (1966-67)

During the years 1966-67, the opponents of capitalistic tendencies in China once again attacked their emergence during the Cultural Revolution of 1966 and 1967. This time the revolution was organised by Mao Tse-tung and in the vanguard were the students and Mao's other followers who were organised into units of Red Guards. The principle theme of the Cultural Revolution was that "Politics must take command", that "Revolutionary principles must not be sacrificed for the ill-wind of economism", that "Bureaucracy and elitism both in Government and Party must be checked", that "masses must be mobilised for attacking development problems", that "class struggle must be relentlessly pursued to prevent re-emergence of bourgeois values", that "socialist objectives must replace material incentives in order that the private plot, the profit motive, and the free market be eliminated."[2]

Though the Cultural Revolution of 1966-67 did not produce as damaging an effect on the Chinese economy as the Great Leap Forward (1958-60), its disruptive effects soon brought again emphasis on "gradual development, material incentives, and functional specialisation". There was retreat from Mao's "revolutionary, mass-oriented, and equalitarian society." Arther G. Ashbrook in his 'China, Economic Review, 1975' writes: "The Cultural Revolution was in part Mao's last great attempt to *(a)* re-impose his authority on an increasing technocratic and independent bureaucracy, and *(b)* re-invigorate the revolutionary movement with its original spirit of unquestioning loyalty, self-sacrifice, plain living and equalitarianism."

Amidst all this volatility, only a faintest trace of what might be called a Chinese model seems to emerge.

5. PLANNING IN CHINA

During China's First Five Year Plan (1953-57), the emphasis was on heavy industry. After that large investments came to be shifted to light industries and rural industries. One reason for the shift was the realisation by the Communist Party leaders that the country was "too near the subsistence level to afford projects with long gestation periods and late returns..."

During subsequent periods, Five Year Plans were more a sort of formality, the focus having shifted to Annual Plans. Economic planning also came to be much decentralised towards provinces and localities. A sort of dualism was emerging, authority being divided between the Centre and Provinces. Generally, the Central Authority using the method of balances worked out targets of important industries and decided upon "Balance Transfers" (involving transfer of commodities from surplus areas of provinces to deficit areas or provinces). "The commodities which one province cannot produce, or produces in insufficient quantities, are supplied by the state through balance transfers from outside the province, and surplus commodities are transferred by the state from the province to outside areas."[3]

It might however be noted that transferees of goods from one area of province to another area or province in China is not practised on as extensive a scale as in the Soviet Union. Lack of adequate and satisfactory means of transport and communications, vastness of the country, varied nature of resources in China have all brought about greater emphasis on provincial or even local self-sufficiency. Also the principle of local self-sufficiency may be a matter, to some extent at least, of ideology as Mao might from the days of guerrilla warfare had emphasised self-reliance which means of less of control from the Central Authority. Or provincial or local self-sufficiency might be due to defective planning and unwillingness to rely on markets, prices and profits to bring about necessary adjustments.

Industrial Planning

During 1950s the Chinese industrial sector and industrial planning, under the influence of Soviet-type planning and advisers, exhibited features characteristics of the Soviet industrial structure. There was over-emphasis on targets of output. This resulted in low quality of goods. The managers of enterprises over-stated their needs of inputs, over-stocked them and discouraged innovations as that would create problems for them by upsetting production of conventional goods in conventional manners.

By 1957, the Chinese planners developed doubts as to whether Soviet-type institutions, strategy, heavy investments and adoption of advanced technology would remove all obstacles to industrialisation. The consequence was that emphasis shifted to small industrial plants and rural industries. The new industrial strategy that came to replace the earlier Soviet-type strategy of rapid industrial development through heavy investment in and development of basic and heavy industries was scaling down of modern large-scale technology and emphasis on development of small-scale and cottage industries such as food-processing industries, repair shops, small mines and so on. The small-scale industries sector which started receiving increasing emphasis included both urban small-scale industries and rural small-scale industries which were as diverse as localities in a vast country like China. This strategy with emphasis on small-scale industries helped to curtail expenditure on building and equipment and at the same time enabled development of manufacturing, managerial and organisational skills among the Chinese peasantry indifferent parts of the country. The small-scale urban and rural industries and small industrial plants received greater emphasis and attention throughout 1960s and 1970s.

Agricultural Planning

As only ten per cent of land in China is arable and her population is relatively large, intensive farming has become a characteristic feature of agriculture in China. The need for intensive cultivation has compelled the Communist Party leaders to adopt suitable strategy for agricultural planning. This also explains decentralisation of decision-making in the agricultural sector leaving powers of decision-making at the levels of provinces, localities, brigades, teams or even peasant households. Thus means in China there is rather loose type of planning in the agricultural sector, Government limiting itself to taxation and procurement by planned purchases. Local Communist Party leaders are given substantial powers so far as the agricultural sector is concerned. It is also observed that private agricultural plots are again and again remerging in spite of efforts on occasions to suppress them on ideological grounds. At present most of China's vegetable, poultry and hogs come from private agricultural plots of peasant households. Subsidiary occupations of peasant households include tending of fruit-trees, collection of firewood, making of ropes, weaving of mats, baskets, etc. It is observed that much of the output produced by peasant households is taken to the market where that is sold for cash, the peasant households having a right to own agricultural implements and their house.

But the major part of agricultural production comes from property of agricultural 'Teams' consisting of 20 to 30 peasant households. The intensive type of agriculture in China makes a Team of this size of 20 to 30 peasant households most suitable for managing and motivating peasants. This means a Team is the most important formally recognised unit of production in the agricultural sector in China.

Agricultural 'Team' members are motivated to work though an appropriate combination of material and non-material incentives. In the long-run, non-material incentives are expected to become preponderant, though the fact remains that at present it is the material incentives that induce a Team to produce more. Within the agricultural Team, distribution of basic labour-points is not too unequal ; for example young and strong farmers getting ten labour-points per day, whereas the elderly and weak ones get about six labour-points. It is also observed that 'While members (or a 'Team') seem willing to share income almost equally with their relatives and close neighbours in this manner, they are not as willing to share it with their compatriots in nearby teams."

The agricultural 'Team' is a fairly autonomous decision-making unit and is also a unit of account. But the Team members are not paid by the State and therefore are not State employees in the strict sense of the word.

With all the increased investment in the agricultural sector and though Chinese agriculture with its intensive cultivation is supposed to be efficient, it is observed that since 1957, the growth rate of the agricultural sector is only about 2 per cent per annum and even in 1970s China has not been in a position to achieve breakthrough in farm technology which would have made possible accelerated agricultural growth rate.

6. CHINESE AND SOVIET ECONOMIC SYSTEMS COMPARED

In China with intensively cultivated smaller plots of land, agriculture is less centralised and controlled than in the Soviet Union. Also, since Chinese peasantry is closer to the level of subsistence, there is less effort in China than in Soviet Union to mobilise agricultural surplus for investment in the industrial sector. Also, China has relied less on turnover-tax on agricultural commodities than the Soviet Union where there is wide difference between prices paid by Government procurement agencies to farmers and prices paid by consumers for agricultural commodities.

The Chinese Communist Party had its roots in rural areas and understood the problems of peasants better than leaders of the Soviet Communist Party which was urban and industry-oriented and had inherited from the former Russian intelligentsia to some extent contempt for rural folk and agriculturists. It is said that the Chinese peasants were as much opposed to people's communes and collectivised agriculture as the Russian peasants; but they accepted the change with possiblly less pain than Soviet peasants because they possibly thought that the Chinese Communist Party is more sensitive to their problems and therefore would do their utmost to solve them; this was because as already noted, the Communist Party of China had its roots in rural areas of the country from where they emerged and functioned.

Another feature that distinguishes the Chinese economic system from the Soviet system is that due to vast size of the country and varied nature of resources, due to under-developed means of transport and communications and possibly due to anarchist tendencies, there is in China greater opposition to centralisation and bureaucratisation. There are fewer interdependencies in the Chinese economy than in the Soviet Union. That explains why in China of today there is less of centralised type of planning than in the Soviet Union and more of decentralisation of authority and decision-making power. It is possible that as the Chinese economy develops and interdependencies among various sectors of the economy and among various firms and enterprises grow, there would be more centralised type of planning along the lines of the Soviet-type and maybe then the Chinese planners may have to depend to greater extent than at present on role of markets, prices, profits, etc. as the Russians have been doing at present.

There appears to be at present a sort of "an unstable equilibrium" in China. There is an uneasy balance between "the desire for central control and recognised need for local initiative, between top leadership (Party and Government) and almost inescapable bureaucracy, and between the respective roles of experts (elitism) and the masses. There is fitful balance between the initiative of Government (and Party) and private initiative — on private plots and in subsidiary household production. There is a wavering balance between preferences for growth in material welfare (but not 'materialism' or consumerism) and preferences for egalitarianism. Finally, there is an uneasy balance between a desire for efficiency (at times labelled 'economism') and belief that 'Politics must be in command'."[4]

7. CHINA AFTER TIANANMEN SQUARE EXPLOSION IN 1989

The Chinese communist party rulers are pragmatic people. They are quick to grasp the long term implications of the world events like the demise of communism in the former Soviet Union and in the East European countries. Also, though the communist rulers of China ruthlessly put down demand for political and economic liberalism and freedom which demonstrated itself in the Tiananmen Square explosion in 1989, they also understood the long-term implications of that explosion in 1989. And therefore, they have been taking gradual steps towards economic liberalism and market economy, though as yet within the broad framework of communist philosophy and communist party rule.

The Chinese communist government is taking cautious steps from communist economy towards free market economy. For example, the Chinese government removed price controls in foodgrains in the country's most populous province of Sichuan and on meat and eggs in Beijing. The Chinese government has decided to watch the impact of the above steps of removing price controls in specified areas and in the case of specified commodities before they move further in the direction of free market economy (i.e., capitalism).

The Chinese government has also withdrawn price subsidies on several consumer goods without encountering unfavourable reaction from the affected people. The Chinese government appears to be preparing people psychologically by announcing government's intention to allow competitive prices as against hereto government-controlled prices and to allow competitive prices in respect of oil, foodgrains and other essential commodities across the country before long. Ground is gradually being prepared before moving forward towards free market economy.

Another aspect of the Chinese economy that indicates its march towards free private enterprise economy is the gradual replacement in the agricultural sector of communes by family farming system. This change to family farming system has resulted in vast increase in agricultural production. This has resulted in rising income of people in both rural and urban areas. As a consequence, there is increase in people's consumption of foodgrains, eggs, pork, edible oil and of consumer durables like T.V. sets, washing machines and refrigerators.

And therefore, these improved living conditions of people in general, both in rural and urban areas of the country, have emboldened the communist party leaders and the government to gradually decontrol prices and move towards free market private enterprise economy.

Foreign capital is not only being freely allowed for investment in China, but is heartily invited. It is noticed that though a communist country for long closed to foreign influences, China is having substantial flow of foreign capital; on the other hand, India with its liberal economic policies announced in July 1991 inviting foreign capital with automatic sanction up to 51 per cent of foreign equity capital in most industries is finding it difficult to get adequate foreign capital.

Another significant development in communist China is the opening and functioning of stock exchanges in the country and citizens freely buying and selling shares and other securities.

As noted already, the Chinese are pragmatic in their approach and therefore they know in what direction world and especially communist countries are moving in the last quarter of the 20th century. They know that China cannot remain in splended isolation which they enjoyed between 1949 and 1990. And therefore, gradual steps are being taken of moving the Chinese economy from tightly regulated communist economy towards free market private enterpise system (*i.e.,* capitalism).

8. SUMMARY AND CONCLUDING REMARKS

India's total geographical area is 3287269 square kilometres while that of China is 9597000 square kilometres which is nearly three times the total area of India. But in respect of cultivable land, in the case of India of the total geographical area nearly 51 per cent which means 168.8 million hectares is cultivable while in the case of China, though its total geographical area is three times that of India, China's cultivable land is only 97.8 million hectares. Thus, though India's cultivable land is nearly 1.7 times the cultivable land in China, yet in 1992 while production of foodgrains in India was around 176 million tonnes, that of China in that year was 442.5 million tonnes (which means nearly 2.5 times that of India).

In China, out of the total population of around 100 crores, nearly 80 per cent (that is nearly 80 crores) depend directly on agriculture. Along with increase in production of foodgrains, production of sugar, tobacco, fruits and vegetables has been increasing by about 5 to 8 per cent per year. China has recognised the fact that stability and progress of her economy depends upon stability and progress of her agricultural sector, a fact which was not recognisd for long by planners in India.

In 1992-93 growth rate of the Chinese economy was around 12 per cent. Compared to India's annual growth rate of her economy of around 5 per cent, China's economic growth rate is truly remarkable. In years to come China expects to attain still higher annual growth rate of her economy.

China expects that her industrial growth rate will be higher by around 20 per cent in 1993 compared to its present growth rate. India's industrial annual growth rate has been around 8 to 10 per cent only.

In 1992 China's exports amounted to 71.9 billion US dollars while India's exports in that year amounted to only 18.1 billion US dollars. This means in 1992 China's exports were four times that of India.

In 1992 foreign investments in China amounted to 58 billion US dollars in 40 thousand projects. This foreign investment in China in 1992 was three times the foreign investment in China in 1991.

In the case of India, with all her announcements of liberal economic policies and automatic approval to projects with 51 per cent equity of foreign capital, foreign investments in 1992 amounted to only 500 million US dollars in 1993.

After the Tiananmen explosion in 1989, Chinese communist party rulers are aware that the country will have to gradually march towards democracy. But communist China is not prepared (unlike the former Soviet Union) to immediately switch over to democracy and free market economy. To avoid another political explosion of the type that brought about disintegration of the former Soviet Union, Chinese communist government appears to be following the policy of gradually raising the standard of living of her people to distract their attention, at least for some time, away from political democracy. In this task China appears to have been fairly successful, at least until now as she has succeeded in avoiding the type of political developments that shook former Soviet Union and East European countries.

The Chinese call their new economic sysem 'Socialist Market Economy'.

REFERENCES

1. 'Chinese Economic System' — Audrey Donnithorne, Pages 36-37.
2. Radical Ideology and Economic Development in China: The Cultual Revolution and Its Impact on the Economy — Robert Derberger in 'Asian Survey', 12 (Dec. 1972).
3. 'China's Economic System' — Donnithorne, Page 463.
4. 'Economic Systems' — Wayne A. Leeman, Pages 265-66.

CHAPTER 25

INDIA AND CHINA

(A COMPARATIVE STUDY OF THE TWO SYSTEMS)

1. INTRODUCTION

India and China are the two biggest countries in Asia. Area of India and China constitute, respectively, 2.5 per cent and 7.16 per cent, of the total area of the world. The total population of India in 1981 was 684 million constituting 15.2 per cent of the total population of the world, whereas the population of China (in 1981) was 983 million constituting 21.8 per cent of the total population of the world. Thus, the two giant countries of Asia contained more than one-third (37 per cent) of the world's population.

India and China have adopted two different political and economic systems. While India has adopted parliamentary democratic type of Government, China has adopted communist and dictatorial type of government. While India has adopted 'a mixed economy' wherein private sector is assigned a very important role in the national economy, China has adopted Communism where private sector plays a negligible role. While India has adopted democratic planning, China has adopted centralised type of communist planning embracing every sector of the economy. While India wants to provide a model that combines both democracy and socialism, China aims at establishing communist society, not through democratic but dictatorial method. While India is following the 'Middle Way', China is following what may be called extreme leftist measures to establish communist society in the country.

India and China have thus adopted different or divergent patterns or economic systems to attain their respective goals and objectives.

India became independent in 1947; the communist regime came to be established in China in 1949. Both therefore may be said to have sarted on their ways to bring economic development and social progress at about the same time. Since India and China have adopted different ideologies and economic systems to attain their respective goals and objectives, and since both are giants in Asia to which smaller nations in Asia which have become independent after World War II, look up for providing suitable models of socio-economic development and political stability, there is a sort of keen rivalry between the two countries. Sometimes this rivalry is explicit while most of the time it is implicit and hidden.

In the face of this competition between the two rival economic systems of India and China, it would be instructive to critically examine achievements of the two respective economic systems, namely that of India and of China. The study of economy systems of the two countries would also enable us to understand in a better way the weaknesses and strengths of the two systems.

Before the comparison is undertaken, one or two points need clarification. There is dearth of comparable statistical data even regarding such important things like GNP, NNP, rates of saving and investment, capital output-ratio and so on in regard to China. Very often Chinese data is not published or not available; often when published, there is no internal consistency. There is often the case of China 'resorting to figure-padding'. It is only in recent years that some objective studies of the Chinese economy are being undertaken and published by the World Bank and scholars like Gunnar Myrdal who has studied in a comparative way economic systems of India and China as part of his 'Asian Drama'.

There is vast difference between China of 1981 and China of 1949 when the communist regime took over. Thus, China of 1949 was feudal and a colonial state, the land being colonised by the Americans, the British and other Europeans. The China of 1940s was characterised by intermittent civil war and lawlessness by a few rich landlords and vast poor peasantry, widespread nepotism, by bribery and corruption, and inefficient bureaucracy. The control of the State over distant provinces was not effective and life of the people moved along traditional and conventional lines.

China of 1981 is fundamentally different from China of 1949. There are no colonial vestiges and no widespread evils of gambling houses, courtesans and brothels, opium dens and recurrent epidemics have been effectively eliminated since the time of liberation in 1949, though new types of crimes, and evils of unemployment characterise the present-day Chinese economy.

Till recently Mao's ideas and ideology dominated Chinese thought and thinking in every sphere of national activity. Economic incentives were frowned upon and discouraged. But over the past four years (*i.e.*, since the death of Mao), Government has learnt that laws of economics have their own logic and those laws can be defied only at great peril. The authorities in China are therefore eager to act in conformity with the basic laws of economics. The authorities are giving some place in the national economy to material incentives, instead of only to moral appeal and resort to force as in the days of

Chairman Mao. The authorities are at present emphasising 'productivity'. There is decreasing regimentation and there is to a certain extent liberalisation. Ultra leftism advocated by 'the Gang of Four' has for all practical purposes been abandoned.

It has to be admitted that the Chinese economic system adopted since the communist party came to power in 1949, has made China a major political, military and economic power, while India is being given only grudgingly the status of a major power in South Asia. China acquired such a position, politically and economically that in one stroke it could cut off its relationship with its main supporter, the U.S.S.R.

2. FOUR MODERNISATIONS

Since 1978 China has been striving to achieve before 2000 A.D. 'Four Modernisations', *i.e.*, modernisation in four vital areas of the nation's economy, namely, agriculture, industry, defence, and science and technology. This achievement is expected to bring China on par with the two super-powers, namely, the United States and the Soviet Union.

In 1978, it was declared that "The four modernisations decide everything." This programme which refers to 'walking on two legs' emphasises simultaneous development of agriculture and industry, of large-scale and light industries, as also decentralisation of economic decision-making and of production.

TABLE 1

Basic Data about India and China

	Item	*Unit*	*India*	*China*	*World*
1.	Area	Million Sq. Km.	3.3	9.6	134
2.	Arable Land	"	1.65	1.29	14
3.	Population	Million (1981)	684	983	4500
4.	Population Growth Rate	Per cent Per Annum	2.4	1.5	1.9
5.	Population Density	Per Sq. Km. (1977)	190	90	31
6.	Persons per Hectare of Arable Land	Number	3.8	6.7	3
7.	G.N.P. (1977)	U.S. $ Million	97	346	7640
8.	Per Capita GNP	U.S. $	150	410	1853
9.	Per Capital Income	U.S. $	190	256	—

From Table No. 1, it would be observed that *(a)* area of China is nearly three times as large as that of India ; *(b)* China's population is nearly 1.44 times that of India; *(c)* China's population growth-rate has been coming down in a marked way and fairly rapidly, whereas India's population growth rate has declined only marginally; *(d)* China's G.N.P. is nearly 3.6 times that of India's, and *(e)* China's per capital GNP is 2.7 times that of India.

But recent World Bank findings cut China's per capita income at U.S. $ 256 and India's per capital income at U.S. $ 190. (This obviously makes nonsense of figures under headings 8 and 9 above derived from Table 1).

If China's per capital income is only $ 256 compared to India's $ 190, the question arises as to whether for less than one hundred dollars, it is worth sacrificing individual freedom and subject oneself to harsh regimentation that obtains in communist China.

TABLE 2

Comparative Growth Rates of India and China (1950-51 to 1977-78)

(In percentages)

Item	*India*	*China*
GNP at Current Prices	8.5	7
Real National Income	3.5	6.1
Per capita National Income	1.4	—
Agricultural Production	2.7	5.3
Industrial Production	6.3	8.6
Foreign Trade	7.3	7.97

From Table 2, it is observed that GNP growth rate (at current prices) of India is almost as good as that of China. But in one sense it is illusory because of differing rates of inflation which is definitely higher in the case of India. And that explains why real national income growth rate of India is only 3.5 per cent per annum compared to China's real income growth rate of 6.1 per cent per year over the entire planning period. Thus China's real growth rate is growing at a little less than twice that of India.

In respect of agricultural production growth-rate of China is much higher than that of India. In respect of foodgrains production growth-rate of China is only marginally higher for China compared to India's.

In respect of industrial production China's annual growth-rate at 8.6 per cent is much higher than India's 6.3 per cent.

Growth-rates in respect of foreign trade are not markedly different for the two countries. But in recent years (last 2 or 3 years) China's foreign trade has gone up sharply, China's exports rising annually by 15 to 20 per cent and imports by 30 to 40 per cent. But it must be kept in mind that China started with a fairly low base due to isolation it practised for long. China's foreign trade annual growth-rate will be substantial in years to come due mainly to her modernisation programme till 2000 A.D.

TABLE 3

Comparative Production of Selected Commodities

Item	*Unit*	*India (1980-81)*	*China (1980)*
Foodgrains	Mill. Tonnes	130	332
Industrial Production	Mill. $	52	297 (1979)
Elec. Generation	Bin. Kwts.	112	312
Crude Steel	Mill. Tonnes	10.1	35
Coal	"	118	620
Crude oil	"	11	106
Cement	"	19	78
Chemical Fertilisers	"	3	9.6
Sugar	"	4.5	2.6

Table No. 3 gives data regarding major sectors or commodities produced in India and China. The production figures put China much ahead of India in the case of most of the commodities. The targets for the coming years will only put China still ahead of India.

India's production exceeds or equals that of China in respect of commodities or goods such as certain heavy chemicals, sugar, motor vehicles, cotton cloth, power generating equipment, oil bearing crops, jutes, locomotives, freight wagons, etc.

As regards structure of nation's economy, since the era of planning commenced in India, it has undergone some important structural changes. Share of agriculture has come down from 59 per cent GDP to 42 per cent at present; share of mining has gone up from 15 to 23 per cent during the same period; the share of service sector has gone up from 26 to around 36 per cent. The share of non-agricultural sector has gone up from 41 per cent to around 58 per cent.

In the case of China, the share of agriculture in GDP at present is around 25 per cent and that of industry about 69 per cent.

This means that whereas in India agricultural sector would continue to be an important sector of the economy for years to come, in China relatively rapid changes have been brought about in the structure of Chinese economy, bringing down steeply share of agriculture in GDP and increasing that of industry.

There is also almost a fundamental difference in the approach to the problem of population control by India and China. Conception of the problem and the implementation of population control programmes differ widely in the two countries.

In India there has been practically no change in population growth-rate. For example, the birth-rate has declined from 24.8 per thousand per year in 1961-71 to only 24.75 in 1971-81.

Till 1960s there was ambiguity in China about need to control population of the country. But change came about during 1960s. Free contraceptions, sterilisation and even abortions facilities were made available. It should be noted that in China certain amount of compulsion has been applied in the case of population control. The consequence is that annual population growth-rate in China has come down from 2.3 per cent in 1971 to 1.2 per cent in 1978. China has fixed target of 1 per cent population growth-rate by 1979 and 0.5 per cent by 1985. Eventually zero population growth rate is the target.

In China compulsion in case of family planning is applied in an ingeneous way. Population control policy includes penalties by way of denial of public facilities in case of excess children in a family, larger quota of food and clothing if there are less children, and 10 per cent cut in salary in case of excess children. There are also some positive incentives for restricting size of a family.

China area-wise is three times the size of India. But as regards arable land, India is more fortunate with 50 per cent of her total area being arable as against only 13 per cent in China. This gives India at present 0.26 hectare per head as against China's figure of 0.15.

Thus China has limited land considering the size of her population. She has also relatively larger unirrigated area. Considering these factors China has followed intensive method of cultivation and achieved better results in the agriculture sector than India which has not yet fully utilised her vast agricultural potentials in terms of arable land, water resources and so on.

But because of comparative sizes of population, while India has achieved foodgrains self-sufficiency, China continues to import foodgrains from the USA and Canada.

In recent years certain aspects of free market economy are being introduced in the Chinese agricultural sector with a view to stimulate agricultural production and to achieve higher yields. Attempts are also being made in recent years to diversify Chinese agriculture. The idea behind additional material incentives and introducing features of free market economy is to stimulate resourcefulness of Chinese cultivators, make them put in more efforts and hard work and secure higher incomes as also diversify their sources of income.

3. INDUSTRIAL SECTORS IN INDIA AND CHINA

Output of industrial sector of China, as seen from Table No. 3, is more impressive than that of India. For example, industrial output of India in 1979 was valued at US $ 51 billion. This was only about one-sixth of value of industrial production for that year in China.

Also compound annual industrial growth rate in the case of India for the period 1951-77 was 6.3 per cent, whereas the rate was around 8 per cent in the case of China. While India's Sixth Plan (1980-85) envisages annual industrial growth-rate of 7.76 per cent and 6.6 per cent for the decade ending 1995, China envisages annual industrial growth rate of around 10 per cent for the years 1978-85. Assuming these industrial growth-rates are realised by both India and China, it is certain that India would further slide down compared to China in the industrial sphere.

In respect of some specific industries, the position is as follows.

While in respect of steel production annual growth-rate in India is around 8 per cent, that of China is around 30 per cent; in respect of cement production, the respective growth rates of India and China are 2.6 per cent and 17 per cent; in respect of coal production, the respective annual growth rates are 4.5 per cent (during 1970s in the case of India), and 12 per cent in the case of China in 1978.

In absolute figures, Chinese coal production is roughly six times that of India; of crude oil 8 times that of India; electricity generation twice that of India.

Weakness of China lies in her lack of management culture. According to the study of J. L. Auerbach, ".... there is an enormous lack of managerial and technical competence in research and development and in particular in the whole concept of engineering and production methodology. The Chine might take years to ingest or absorb the modern US concepts of production scheduling, quality control and manufacturing technology."

On the other hand, due to early exposure of many Indian industrial and commercial establishments to management culture of Western advanced countries, India in regard to management techniques and technical personnel may be said to be much ahead of present-day China. India is said to be much ahead in regards to research and development relating to sciences and technologies compared to China which only recently has suddenly become aware of their significance and is thinking in terms of 'Four Modernisation.' This is broadly true, in spite of China's spectacular progress in certain areas of strategic importance such as nuclear fission, ballistic missiles and rocketry.

As regards problem of introducing equalities, it may be said that in China inequalities have been reduced to the bare minimum, in sharp contrast to India where while paying service to the concept of equality, inequalities in income and wealth, both in rural and urban areas, appear to be continually increasing since the commencement of the era of economic planning.

As regards political freedom, India being a democracy has been regularly going to polls and people have been exercising their fundamental political right to vote and elect government of their choice. Chinese do not enjoy such political freedom. But in a sense there is more democracy in China in the sense there is more economic equality in the country and there is greater opportunity and participation by the broad masses of Chinese people in the task of economic reconstruction of the country. With nearly 50 per cent of total population of India living below the poverty line, it may be said that while there is democratic form in India, the true content of democracy is lacking.

4. CONCLUDING REMARKS

Comparing economic systems of India and China, one view is that China appears to have done better in respect of both economic progress and social justice. No doubt China had to pay some price for this progress in terms of sacrifice by the people of their political and individual freedom and living in a regimented society, though it must be admitted that suppression of individual freedom and regimentation of society in China has never been as severe as in Soviet Union under Stalinst regime.

But considering the fact that a number of other developing countries which have accepted democratic form of government have done better than India, two conclusions emerge. Bread and individual freedom are not necessarily incompatible, and that with vast potentialities that India possesses in men and natural resources, there is every reason why India should not have and should not in future do better than what she has done since 1947 to this day.

CHAPTER 26

MULTI-NATIONAL CORPORATIONS

1. INTRODUCTION

The rise of Multi-National Corporations (MNCs) has become one of the most remarkable phenomenon of post-World War II period. If one wants to know the part which MNCs occupy in daily life of common people, one should just recollect the names of Colgate-Palmolive, Liptons, Brooke Bond, Hindustan Lever, Erasmic, Rexona, Terelene, ICI, Goodyear, Dunlop, Firestone, Bata, Singer, Parker, Dalda, and so on.

MNCs accounted for one-fifth of GNP of all capitalist countries. If their growth continues at the same rate as over the period 1950-75, it is expected that by the end of the century, the share of MNCs will rise to nearly one-half. It is possible that the whole of capitalist economy might very well be dominated by some 200 MNCs of which nearly three-fourths would be from the United States.

It would therefore be instructive to know what MNCs are, how they operate, what role they play in capitalist and world economy, their role in developing countries, the dangers associated with MNCs, especially in developing countries, and the strategy to be adopted by developing countries to take advantage of MNCs but at the same time avoiding the potential dangers from them.

2. DEFINITION OF MULTI-NATIONAL CORPORATION

According to Prof. Kojima, K, "A Multi-National Corporation is a gigantic oligopolistic enterprise which spreads a network of a great many factories and distribution bases in suitable places all over the world, and pursues profit maximisation with the global strategy."

A U.N. Report defines multi-national corporations as "enterprises which own or control production or services facilities outside the country in which they are based. Such enterprises are not always incorporated as private; they can also be cooperative or state-owned entities."

The above general definitions specify multinational corporations as "(*i*) big enterprises, (*ii*) operating in many countries, (*iii*) not limited to export and import only but extend to production, and also (*iv*) with foreign activities attaining a significant proportion of its total sales."

3. PHASES OF EVOLUTION OF MNCs

To begin with a domestic firm extends its sales territory beyond its national boundary. This is the first sign that the establishment is becoming a multinational.

During the second phase MNCs extend their operation and they find that it is better to establish manufacturing or operating units nearer to markets to minimise costs of operation and transportation. This extension may cover production in other country or countries of the entire product or only a part of the product, final assembly taking place in home country.

MNCs reach the third phase when they follow a strategy of managing the money in multinational environment and making advantageous use of different interest rates in different countries. Thus cash and money management assumes significance during this phase.

MNC may be said to have reached the fourth phase in its evolution, when MNC goes beyond the classical factors of production, namely, land, labour, capital and organisation. MNC begins to sell the know-how or management skills like undertaking turnkey projects. Here the emphasis is on MNC's utilisation of its own skills and technical know-how with a view to make maximum profit by making those skills available to other countries.

Thus MNCs command production and distribution of products or services in more than one country. They are big and dynamic enterprises with operations in many countries and often in different continents in a single or many products. Activities of MNC are globally coordinated by groups of persons organised in the head office in the country where the MNC is incorporated. They exercise tight control over money, materials and markets. They derive their strength from their vast capital, high-grade technology and management skills.

4. EMERGENCE OF MULTI-NATIONAL CORPORATIONS

Multi-national corporations (MNCs), as already noted, are large-sized predominantly oligopolistic establishments with sales running into several millions of dollars and with their branches spread over several countries.

It needs to be noted that the United States for all practical purposes accounts for more than half the MNCs having total annual sales of manufacture of more than 2 billion US dollars and also more than half of the total estimated book value of investments which in 1978 amounted to approximately 177 billion US dollars.

The size of modern MNCs is enormous and production on a very large scale. For example, General Motors of the USA had annual sales of 22.8 billion in 1968 and this was larger than the gross national product of countries like East Germany and Argentina. The same way be said about Exxon, Ford and Standard Oil whose gross annual sales exceed gross national product of even countries like South Africa and Pakistan, not to speak of poorer countries in Africa.

MNCs are thus global institutions crossing national boundaries. MNCs arrange to get their inputs from several countries and either assemble the final product in the country of origin or even manufacture final product in several countries.

MNCs thus serve as vehicle for the transfer of capital, technology, latest financial and marketing techniques and all that is latest in the world of business and commerce. MNCs have been operating on a large scale in developing countries and are transferring capital, technology, financial and marketing techniques to several developing countries which stand to benefit from such transfers.

Emergence of multi-national corporations may be traced to several factors.

Rapid technological progress making large-scale production of goods has played an important role in the emergence of MNCs. Equally important has been development of rapid means of communications which enables MNCs to get quickly required inputs from several countries situated in different continents and also help them to move their goods fast from the place of manufacture to various marketing centres.

Development of suitable financial and marketing institutions has also played a vital role in emergence of MNCs.

Thus it may be said that MNCs are a typical product of the rapid scientific and technological progress that has been taking place during post-World War II period.

Some of the important multi-nationals are Exxon, General Motors, Ford, IBM, Unilever, Philips, General Electric, Texaco, Siemens, Chrysler, Hitachi, Mistsubishi Heavy Industries, Volkswagen, Standard Oil, Lipton/Brooke Bond, Massey Fergusson and International Harvestor, Hindustan Lever, Britania Biscuits, Glaxo, Horlicks, Larsen and Toubro, Bata, Enfield and Escorts etc.

5. INTERNATIONALISATION OF PRODUCTION

Centuries ago production of goods was carried out at home by members of the family for satisfying family needs and at the most for local market.

With the arrival of railway and steamship (*i.e.,* with the Industrial Revolution) production began to be carried generally on national basis (though in some cases some raw materials like cotton in the case of English textile industry in the 19th century was obtained from outside the nation) and catered to national markets, some goods entering as they have done for long international markets.

Multi-national corporation represents generally internationalisation of production.

For example, if you take toilet soaps manufactured by Hindustan Lever which is an important MNC, raw material like coconut oil may come from Malaysia, or countries in Africa, machinery from England or the USA, labour from India, capital from practically all over the world, technical personnel also from India and other countries, and soap manufactured will be distributed through thousands of distributors belonging to several nations of the world in practically every country of the world.

Thus MNCs combine labour, raw materials, machinery and technical skills coming from different countries of the world. For this they have established relations with bankers of different countries in the world.

Naturally internationalisation of production has also brought about organisational changes. The head office in the home country has several branches and offices at several places in different countries. These are headed often by locals and these branches have fairly wide powers, the central office mostly deciding important policy matters and providing basic guidelines to branch offices.

It is clear that internationalisation of production in the present century is made possible by several factors such as: rapid means of communications, development of techniques of large-scale production and continual technological progress based on research and development, possibility of collecting huge funds for investment needed by MNCs through shares and stocks, development of the art of co-operation on a very large scale and possibility, again because of rapid means of transport and communications, of distributing goods quickly all over the world.

Internationalisation of production has meant evolving global strategy.

6. CONTRACTUAL RELATIONSHIP

The MNCs have been adopting various evil practices such as bringing pressures on the governments of host countries, influencing their policies, transferring out-dated technology, manipulate prices and make monopoly profits, deny high position to nationals of host countries and so on.

Since MNCs can be an effective instrument of economic development of backward countries and since co-operation between MNCs and Less Developed Countries (LDCs) would be of mutual advantage, it is essential that a code of conduct or a sort of contractual relationship is established between the two, each side strictly adhering to the terms of contract regarding proportions of participating capital, training to be provided to nationals of host countries, local labour to be employed, wages to be paid, profits to be shared and so on. There should be an international agency to enforce the terms of the contract, should either MNC or LDC violate any of the terms.

If on the contractual basis sound relation is established between MNC and LDC, there can be much industrial and commercial activities which will be to the advantage of both parties and to the world as a whole.

7. WHAT CAN MNCs OFFER TO DEVELOPING COUNTRIES?

What can MNCs offer to developing countries like India?

MNCs can offer the following to developing countries:

1. *Help Push up Rate of Saving and Investment.* In the case of less developed countries (LDCs) there is a limit to domestic saving (because of low level of per capita income and mass poverty) and limit to funds which LDCs can obtain for investment purposes from multilateral agencies like the World Bank. The MNCs can help fill the gap, at least partly by tapping the flow of private foreign capital. Thus MNCs can help LDCs to boost up the rate of saving and investment.

2. *Access to Latest Technology.* MNCs bring with them to LDCs latest technology which they continually go on updating. Also, modern technology is brought by MNCs to LDCs in a package form, that is, along with better office management, better marketing and so on.

MNCs generally set up their own research and development section. Nationals of LDCs get training in this important branch. Other native establishments also are influenced and begin to set up their own R and D sections with favourable effect on technology, productivity and general efficiency of the economy of the concerned LDC.

3. *Increase Productivity of Domestic Resources.* When MNCs bring with them latest technology and modern management methods, the efficiency of domestic resources employed or utilised by MNCs naturally increases. The efficiency and productivity of domestic resources also increases because of research and development carried on by MNCs and also because of competition with other international establishments.

4. *More Effective Mobilisation of Domestic Resources.* When an industrial establishment comes to be associated with MNC, it inspires more confidence among nationals of that LDC. People begin to offer their savings by purchasing equity shares or by depositing money which otherwise would have been spent on gold and silver or on luxury items. MNC offer scope to talented people and high grade technicians and management personnel. MNC thus helps more effective mobilisation of domestic resources.

5. *Access to International Markets.* Because of the nature of operations and worldwide markets in which MNCs serve, MNCs help LDCs to get for their products international markets. This would have been difficult otherwise.

MNCs are generally invited predominantly for producing goods for export purposes. Capacity of MNCs to produce goods of quality and standard, availability of international market information to them, confidence of customers in different countries in the products of the MNCs (because of well-known brand names, etc.), all help push up exports of LDCs. Thus MNCs help LDCs to increase their international trade. Without this association with MNCs, LDCs would have found it difficult to push up their exports in foreign markets.

6. *Encouragement to Competition in Domestic Market.* Presence of MNCs in LDCs provides competitive challenge to purely domestic producers to produce goods of quality, both to attract domestic purchasers and for export. Domestic producers begin to aim at producing goods of international quality. This increases efficiency of domestic establishments. This helps domestic consumers also by making available good quality goods at competitive rates, thus helping improve quality of life of people in LDCs.

7. *Professionalisation of Management.* MNCs have been important sources of professional management in LDCs. Foreign big companies inevitably bring with them professional management. Naturally this influences favourably managements of even purely domestic commercial and industrial establishments.

8. INDIA AND MNCs

In 1978 the Government of India noted that there were 833 MNCs operating in India (473 branches and 146 subsidiaries of MNCs and 254 Indian companies with more than 40 per cent non-resident interest).

The MNCs are to be found in India in a number of industries. As for examples the following may be noted: Tea (Lipton and Brooke Bond); Agricultural Machinery (Massey Fergusson and International Harvestor); Insecticides (ICI, IBA and Bayers); Food (Hindustan Lever); Biscuits (Huntly Palmer); Milk Products (Hindustan Lever, Glaxo Laboratories and Horlicks); Dairy Machinery (Larsen and Toubro); Cigarettes (Indian Tobacco and Vazir Sultan); Cotton Textiles (Buckingham and Carnatic, Finlay); Footwear (Bata); Motor Vehicles (Ashok Leyland, Premier Automobiles); Motor Tyres (Dunlop, Firestone, Goodyear and Ceat); Motor Cycles (Enfield and Escorts); Electric Lamps (Philips, Osler); Radio Receivers (Philips), Murphy, GEC); Typewriters (Remington); Cosmetics (Ponds); Toothpaste (Colgate-Palmolive); Soap (Hindustan Lever); Matches (WIMCO); Pharmaceuticals (Glaxo Labs; CIBA, Pfizer, Bayer, Sandoz, Park Davis, Abbot Labs, Boots).

The above companies are well-known international establishments. They have brought with them capital, technical know-how, professional management and have provided opportunities to Indian resources in men and materials to be put to use in producing important goods affecting every aspect of life of people in India.

These MNCs have also set standards in quality, management, work-norms, marketing and professional management which all other companies including purely domestic commercial and industrial establishments are trying to follow. This naturally has favourable effect on employment and efficiency. Under contract these MNCs have trained Indians and have offered them their technical know-how. This has helped India to be self-reliant in respect of technical and professional manpower and also to be among the highly industrialised countries of the world.

9. CRITICISM OF ROLE OF MULTI-NATIONAL CORPORATIONS (MNCs) IN LESS DEVELOPED COUNTRIES (LDCs)

Though multi-national corporations can become an effective instrument of transfer of capital, technological and professional know-how and thus become a catalytic agency of industrialisation and of economic development, MNCs are being criticised by LDCs on many accounts.

Naturally the question arises: Why are MNCs criticised? What are the dangers posed before the LDCs by MNCs? If MNCs are to be used as an effective instrument of industrialisation and of economic development of LDCs, it is necessary to know these defects and dangers associated with MNCs.

Role of MNCs is criticised on the following grounds in many LDCs:

1. Historically MNCs arrived in many backward countries as colonial powers (*e.g.*, the East India Company). Even at present many US multi-national corporations are suspected as mere extension of Western colonial capitalism. The old prejudice against the colonial powers is transferred, justifiably or otherwise, towards MNCs of some Western countries.

2. Local industrial establishments find it difficult or even impossible to successfully compete with MNCs with their huge capital-base, modern technology and world-wide operations. It is feared that MNCs would have adverse effects on development of purely local industries and local talent.

3. MNCs are suspected because of their huge size and success. There is also remoteness of control and therefore mystery associated with MNCs. They do not fully disclose their true picture and nature of activities carried on in LDCs and this gives rise to suspicion and distrust against them.

4. MNCs are accused of charging very high price for transfer of technological know-how. They are suspected of maximising their profits through manipulation of transfer prices, currency movement and tax evasion. Senior posts are often denied to nationals of countries where MNCs are operating.

5. MNCs generally enter those fields or produce mostly those goods which cater to the needs of only richer sections in backward countries. Since MNCs aim at maximising their profits, they tend to produce goods needed in markets. Naturally their products are of elitist nature. MNCs have shown hardly

any interest in producing goods of mass consumption. This has meant diversion of resources of developing countries from essential goods of mass consumption to production of luxury and semi-luxury goods for elitist section of society. This comes in the way of maximising social welfare.

6. MNCs are often accused of neglecting national priorities. It is therefore possible that their policies and activities go contrary to policies and targets envisaged in Five Year Plans of LDCs.

7. MNCs are also accused of transferring only out-dated technology not wanted in their countries. They also tie local collaborators to parent companies and other industrial establishments in their own countries for purchase of essential raw materials, spares, etc. There is rigging of prices.

8. MNCs are accused of interfering in local politics. They are accused of bribing political parties and politicians and influence policies of governments of LDCs in their favour. The best illustration is that of ITT Engineering's successful revolt in Chile in 1969. US multinationals are especially accused of establishing close links with local politicians and build powerful lobby in LDCs in their favour.

9. Altogether, MNCs, it is said, make LDCs highly dependent upon foreign countries. This might be dangerous during times such as wars. They have a depressing effect on purely local business and development of indigenous entrepreneurship. They produce depressing effect on balance of payments position of LDCs. Altogether, they prove, it is stated, an impediment in the way of rapid economic development of developing countries.

10. HOW CAN MULTI-NATIONAL CORPORATIONS (MNCs) IMPROVE THEIR IMAGE IN DEVELOPING COUNTRIES?

MNCs have a positive and constructive role to play in developing countries. This will be to the advantage of both MNCs (*i.e.*, developed countries seeking investment opportunities abroad and making profits) and developing countries in need of investment funds, technological know-how and need to industrialise as rapidly as possible.

With a view to play the role more effectively, MNCs must take some steps to remove suspicion which has rightly or wrongly come to surround them and must make an attempt to present a more favourable and friendly picture of themselves.

MNCs can create a favourable climate in their favour by taking the following steps:

1. MNCs should ensure that their operations result in a net advantage to the host country in the long run. They should ensure maximisation of social benefit to host country. There should be self-assessment and self-regulation on the part of MNCs from this point of view.

2. An important step to create favourable climate in favour of MNCs in host countries would be to induct nationals into management right up to the top level. This would help MNCs to become sensitive to possible criticism in host countries, appreciate their needs and expectations in a better way and evolve and follow policies more satisfying to people in host countries. There would be shared objectives and values of ownership and control would or should become a matter of secondary importance.

3. MNCs may do well to invest at least part of their profits in industries occupying priority in plans of developing countries and thus utilise part of their funds to meet the needs of masses, instead of only those of urban elitist sector of society in host countries. MNCs should diversify their production.

4. MNCs should invite increasing local participation, especially financial participation. They should take steps to provide training opportunities to nationals of host countries.

5. MNCs should strictly keep themselves to business and not enter into politics at any level, much less at the national level and should not try to influence policies of national government through pressures, threats, bribery and so on.

If MNCs can create a better image of themselves in developing countries, MNCs have advantageous opportunities and their role would be beneficial to both MNCs and to developing countries.

11. GUIDELINES TO BE ADOPTED BY DEVELOPING COUNTRIES IN REGARD TO MULTI-NATIONAL CORPORATIONS

On the basis of the role which multi-national corporations have played in the past, the dangers associated with them, and their potentialities to help rapid industrialisation and economic development of backward countries, the following guidelines or principle may be mentioned as basis for sound policy to be followed by developing countries in regard to MNCs:

1. The LDCs, while inviting foreign private capital in the form of MNCs, should see that while certain amount of interdependence among developed and developing countries is inevitable, they do not compromise on the question of their sovereignty and allow their vital national policies to be dictated or influenced by MNCs. There has to be reasonable trade-off between economic interdependence and sovereignty of LDCs.

2. LDCs must consider the limit to which private foreign capital is going to be permitted into their countries. These limits must be carefully weighed. This limit will depend upon factors such as growth rate that is aimed at, strength of indigenous enterprise, absorptive capacity, extent of availability of domestic supplementary resources of various types, etc.

3. There should be proper economic and social evaluation to determine the net gain to the economy from the activities of MNCs. It should be seen that plan policies and targets do not get vitiated by the activities of MNCs. Priorities assigned to different industries must not get altered because of admission and activities of MNCs.

4. MNCs must be carefully watched and should be excluded from local and national politics. They should be, for example, specifically excluded from making contributions to political parties, or supporting particular candidates for elected bodies.

5. It should be seen that MNCs bring appropriate technology that is in tune with the factor endowment of LDCs. Thus in the case of India with surplus labour and 40 per cent of people below poverty line, import by MNCs of capital-intensive technology producing luxury or semi-luxury goods would be found inappropriate and should be discouraged.

12. CONCLUDING REMARKS

In view of the important role which MNCs can play in LDCs, old prejudices against them must be shed. Also MNCs have considerably changed. It is therefore worthwhile having a fresh look at MNCs and make use of them, keeping the above guidelines in view.

CHAPTER 27

ROLE OF THE STATE

1. ROLE OF THE STATE UNDER LAISSEZ-FAIRE CAPITALISM

Laissez-faire capitalism was the economic system that prevailed in capitalist countries of Europe and in the United States in the 19th century or say for labour a century prior to World War I.

Under *laissez-faire* capitalism, individuals are supposed to know what is in their best interest and are free to use their resources as, when and where they like. In such a system the State government takes the least part in the economic activities of people which are guided by personal profit motive.

Under *laissez-faire* capitalism, the role of the State in restricted only to matters like defence of the country, internal law and order some important civil works like construction of roads and bridges because individuals motivated by private profit might not be forthcoming to undertake such civil works.

Thus the State was supposed to keep out and leave individuals to do whatever they wanted to do in the sphere of economic activities because each individual was the best judge of his own interests.

Adam Smith, the founder of *laissez-faire* capitalism, saw no clash of interest of individuals and of society. The interests of individuals and of society, according to Adam Smith, coincided and therefore the State had no role in the economic affairs of the people.

Also in *laissez-faire* capitalism, the State was forbidden to play any active role in the economic affairs of the people, because according to Adam Smith, the State was inherently incapable of undertaking them because of (*i*) spendthrift habits of government, (*ii*) remoteness of control, and (*iii*) inefficiency of management because of negligence and spendthrift habits of government servants.

2. EVILS OF LAISSEZ-FAIRE CAPITALISM

Lassiez-faire capitalism which prevailed in West European countries during the 19th century (say, roughly from the end of Napoleonic War in 1815 to the beginning of World War I) was based on the institution of private property, personal profit motive, freely operating price-mechanism working automatically reflecting market forces of demand and supply, the assumption that there is no conflict between interest of individuals and of society, and, therefore, non-interference by the State in the economic activities of the people.

But in course of time, a number of evils or defects came to be associated with *laissez-faire* capitalism.

The major defects of *laissez-faire* capitalism (which subsequently necessitated increasing role of the State in capitalist countries) were as follows: 1. Recurrent economic crisis which culminated in the Great Depression of 1929-33. 2. Inequality of income and wealth among people because of the principle of free competition. 3. Wastages of resources because of competition and also monopolies which emerged. 4. Emergence of monopoly and monopoly power which was the direct consequence of competition and wastages of monopoly and sacrifice of welfare of the people. 5. Exploitation of workers. 6. Uncertainty and instability in the economic system. 7. Disregard of human and society's welfare. 8. International rivalry and conflicts (due to clash of interest among nations which thus led to World War I and World War II).

It is on account of the above evils that State was called upon to play an increasing role in the economic affairs of the people, especially since the Great Depression of 1929-33 and after the publication of the General Theory of J.M. Keynes in 1936 pleading in favour of abandonment of laissez faire and for positive role by the State.

In this chapter we shall consider increasing role of the State in some important respects such as reduction of inequalities, control of monopoly, to remove unemployment and trade cyclical fluctuations (booms and depressions) and in containing inflation.

3. ROLE OF GOVERNMENT (OR STATE) IN CORRECTING INCOME INEQUALITIES

Under *laissez-faire* capitalism, there appeared increasing inequalities of income and wealth because of 1. unequal inherent abilities and capabilities of different individuals; 2. differences in environment into which different individuals were born; 3. the existing unequal pattern of income distribution under which rich became richer and poor remained poor; 4. law of inheritance and succession which perpetuated inequalities of income and wealth; and 5. illegal gains by certain unscrupulous people in society (for example, black marketers at present, or those who evaded income tax laws or made gains by hoarding and unethical speculation).

Consequences of Unequal Distribution of Income and Wealth

Unequal distribution of income and wealth came to be associated with the following evils: 1. class conflict; 2. inefficient use of society's resources which were used to produce goods needed by the rich, neglecting production of goods wanted by masses; 3. continuance of vicious circle of poverty; 4. enormous wastage as the vast poor for want to income could not develop their productive potentialities; 5. economic insecurity for vast masses of people; and 6. concentration of economic and political power that came to be used in the interest of only certain sections of society, neglecting the welfare of vast masses of people.

Measures to Reduce Inequalities of Income and Wealth

Because of evil social and economic consequences of extreme inequalities of income and wealth, most of the governments in capitalist countries are taking steps to reduce extreme inequalities of income and wealth.

These measures may be classified under two headings:

(A) Measures to reduce income and wealth of richer sections of society, and (B) Measures to increase income and wealth of poorer sections of society.

(A) Measures to Reduce Income and Wealth of Richer Sections of Society

In order to reduce income and wealth of richer sections of society, governments have been taking the following measures:

1. Nationalisation of basic and heavy industries and essential services like iron and steel, railways, air-services, heavy engineering, metals, banking and so on. The idea is that profits from these heavy and essential industries and services should not go into the pockets of a few people in society.

2. Governments have passed death and succession duties taxing inherited property so that with each generation, property inherited goes on decreasing so that there is no perpetuation of inequality of income and wealth on account of law of succession.

3. Imposing progressive direct taxes such as income tax, wealth tax, capital gains tax, gift tax, and divined tax. These taxes are imposed in such a way that as income of an individual goes on increasing, higher proportion of increasing incomes of the rich goes to the State by way of taxation. Thus progressive direct taxation is being increasingly resorted to by governments in capitalist countries to reduce extreme inequalities of income and of wealth.

4. Heavy indirect taxes are levied on luxury and semi-luxury goods consumed by the richer sections of society.

5. Governments have been also taking measures such as fixing a ceiling on incomes of directors, company executives and others. Government has been controlling rents on houses or from land collected by landlords.

(B) Measures to Increase Income and Wealth of the Poorer Sections of Society

While on the one hand taking measures to reduce income and wealth of richer sections of society, on their other hand, governments in capitalist countries have been taking the following measures to increase income and wealth of the poorer sections of the community :

1. Attempts are being made to guarantee employment to poor people by public works, by reservation of seats in government employment (as in the case of Scheduled castes and Scheduled tribes in India).

2. Passing of minimum wage legislation guaranteeing a minimum wage to employees of poorer sections of society.

3. Provision of free education and medical facilities to that earning power of poor people increases.

4. Provision of freeships and scholarships to poor students to enable them to develop their capacities.

5. Provision of government land, house sites, encouragement to start cooperative societies by the poor for which various concessions are offered.

6. Provision of cheap grains through fair price shops, of cheap loans and grants and so on.

7. Provision of social security covering unemployment benefits, accident and sickness insurance, etc.

Practically in all capitalist countries above mentioned direct and indirect steps are being taken by governments, on the one hand to reduce high incomes and wealth of richer sections of society and on the other, increase income-earning capacity and income and wealth of poorer sections of community.

4. STATE AND CONTROL OF MONOPOLIES

Literary meaning of monopoly means a 'single seller' of a commodity or service. But such a situation rarely exists in the real world. And therefore broadly it may be said that a monopoly exists in the sale of a commodity or service, if one seller controls so large aportion of the total supply of a commodity or service that he is in a position, by his own action, to produce a significant effect on the supply of that commodity or service and therefore influence (raise or lower) its price. (On the other hand under conditions of competition, no single producer by varying his supply is in a position to raise or lower the price of his commodity by his own action. He takes the price for granted.

Malpractices of Monopolies

By taking advantage of monopolistic position in the market, a monopolist would reduce his production and supply, if he finds that such an action enables him to raise the price of that commodity so high that it gives him more profits than before. Thus monopolists tend to curtail supplies by keeping productive factors unemployed and raise prices of their commodities and services. While this enables them to make high monopoly profits, welfare of the consumers is sacrificed.

Monopolists often charge discriminatory prices to different class of purchasers or in different markets.

Monopolists often practice unfair practices such as enforcing cut-throat competition to destroy the existing or possible rival in the same line of production; bribing politicians so that rivals are not permitted to enter the same line of production; pressuring government to raise import duties on similar goods so that domestic prices of their commodities rise; bribing employees of rival companies to leak out secrets or win them over for employment; intimidation of consumers, and suppliers of raw materials who are often forced to sell raw materials to monopolist manufacturers at unreasonably low prices; adulteration of quality; forming rings with rival producers to exploit consumers, and so on.

Advantages of Monopolies

Monopolies imply certain advantages. A typical monopoly controls vast resources and produces goods on a very large-scale. It therefore enjoys economies of scale, cut down cost of production and on account of large-scale production is in a position to sell goods at lower prices. This would not have been possible if a large number of producers of the same commodity were to produce goods each on a small-scale. A monopoly thus ensures greater satisfaction to consumers.

A monopoly is generally a stable establishment. It therefore means steady demand for raw materials and steady employment to workers.

Since a monopoly has vast resources, it is in a position to devote part of its funds to research and thus find new commodities or new processes.

But in spite of these advantages, the above-mentioned disadvantages and evils of monopolies are so great and damaging that government in every capitalist country tries to control monopolies.

Methods of Controlling Monopolies

We have seen that under competitive conditions in a capitalist economy, resources are used most efficiently ; there is incentive to save, invest, innovate and increase efficiency ; one's ability gets due reward ; prices of commodities equal average and marginal costs and therefore profits are normal ; all this leads to maximisation of satisfaction of consumers.

Compared to these advantages of competitive market, monopoly is associated with evils such as inefficient use of community's resources, lower output and higher prices, neglect of welfare of the community ; and abnormal monopoly profits at the cost of the community.

Naturally attempts are made to control monopolies in capitalist countries.

The State can control monopolies in a number of ways. In the first place, State can take steps to prevent emergence of monopolies (by, for example, taking over basic and heavy industries where emergence of monopolies is possible) ; secondly, if monopolies do emerge, State can take steps to break up monopolies ; in the third place, if monopolies cannot for some reason be broken up, their power can be adequately curbed by creating competitive conditions in such markets ; fourthly, steps may be taken to build up bargaining power of the parties which are required to deal with monopolies so that there is bargaining between two parties on practically equal terms, thus curbing power of monopolies ; in the fifth place, government might give publicity to the evil practices of monopolies and bring moral pressure or public pressure on them thus making it impossible for them to practise unfair methods of exploiting either employees or consumers ; in the sixth place, government may fix or regulate prices of goods and services produced by monopolies ; and in the seventh place, government may threaten to or even nationalise monopolies to curb market power of monopolies.

We shall now go into certain specific measures taken so far to break up monopolies in capitalist countries notably in the United States.

1. *Prohibition and Break-up of Monopolies.* In the United States, laws such as Sherman and Clayton Acts were passed seeking to prohibit growth of combination of firms resulting in monopolies. Thus the Sherman Act of 1890 provides that "every person who shall monopolise, or attempt to monopolise or combine or conspire with any person or persons to monopolise any part of the trade or commerce among the several States, or with foreign nations, shall be deemed guilty of misdemeanour." Clayton Act of 1914 provides that industrial firms or companies which had formerly been in competition with one another cannot have common directors.

But though legal provisions against monopolies are there, their practical enforcement is found to be very difficult because companies can enter into informal agreement so that on paper the law against monopolies is not violated.

2. *Revival or Maintenance of Potential Competition.* The State can pave the way for entry of potential competitors and thus revive competition in place of monopolies. Thus the United States Federal Trade Commission Act of 1914 provides that "unfair methods of commerce are hereby declared unlawful." The Robinson Patman Act (1936) in the USA forbids any discrimination between buyers of commodities of similarly grade and quality where such discrimination is likely to result in elimination of competition and give rise to a monopoly.

In practice, it is found that monopolies can find a number of easy ways to violate this provision with impunity.

3. *Buyers' or Purchasers' Associations.* If individual buyers are weak in bargaining against monopolies, one way to fight monopoly power would be to form unions of buyers as a countervailing force to match the power of monopolies.

But in practice, it is found very difficult or even impracticable to form buyers' union because of their vast number, their being scattered over wide areas, their indifference and so on.

4. *Bringing Public Pressure on Monopolies.* Giving publicity to anti-social activities of monopolies may help build moral and public pressure against monopolies. In the United States, the Federal Trade Commission makes investigations and regularly publishes its reports. But there is the possibility that monopolies may and do practice anti-social activities in such a subtle manner as not to be noticed by governmental investigating agencies.

5. *Price Control.* To curb monopoly power, government often imposes control over prices of goods traded by monopolies. Price controls may be *(a)* positive, or *(b)* negative.

Positive price control implies " the actual fixation of maximum price" which a monopolist can charge for his commodity.

In the case of negative price control, the monopolist can raise the price of a commodity over the existing price only with the permission of government. Government may grant such permission only if such rise is justifiable due to factors such as rise in cost of production, higher excise duty and so on.

Monopolies may defeat the aim of both positive and negative price control by lowering quality of goods, or reducing quantity as in the case of size of soaps, etc.

6. *Nationalisation.* If various measures to control monopoly power are not successful, at present nationalisation as a means both to control monopoly power and avoid emergence of future monopolies, is being used as an effective check on private monopolies.

But if government takes over, say, iron and steel industry, electricity, railways and airways, etc., that would mean that government monopoly is established in those industries or services. Experience tells us that evils of government monopolies can be as harmful for employees and consumers as private monopolies.

Concluding Remarks

In the face of technological progress and possible advantages of large-scale production, it has become very difficult to effectively curb private monopoly power. Thus at present the entire US economy is dominated by about 200 industrial establishments which are monopolies or oligopolies.

5. STATE AND PROBLEM OF UNEMPLOYMENT

For long Say's Law of Market held sway. According to this law, supply created its own demand and therefore under competitive conditions, a free market economy would automatically reach the level of full employment and stabilise there. Any disturbance and unemployment would be a purely temporary phenomenon that would soon get removed automatically restoring the economy back to the position of full employment equilibrium.

But cyclical fluctuations with their succession of booms and depressions have been regularly visiting free economies right from 1793 onwards. But for long these trade cycles were considered as abnormal happenings. But the Great Depression of 1929-33 changed the entire scene and shattered the faith in Say's Law of Market.

J. M. Keynes explained that the rate of saving and investment in an economy could be such as would enable economy to stabilise at a low level — low level equilibrium. The aggregate demand might be such as would not result in full employment because of demand deficiency which would not enable people in the community to purchase full-employment output at remunerative prices.

J.M. Keynes therefore advocated that government will have to take active steps to realise the goal of full employment and just not suppose that *laissez-faire* policy would automatically lift the economy to full employment level and stabilise it.

J. M. Keynes suggested monetary and fiscal measures to ensure full employment in an economy. In case of depression or prevalence of unemployment, J. M. Keynes advocated cheap money policy. Lowering the bank rate would result in lowering market rate of interest. This would result in increase in investment, level of income and demand, in rise in prices and level of employment. By suitable deficit financing, Keynes wanted the level of aggregate demand to be maintained at a level that would result in people having adequate disposable income to purchase full employment output at remunerative prices.

Subsequently Keynes relied more on fiscal policy — policy of varying rates of taxation and amount of government expenditure — to deal with the problem of unemployment and to ensure full employment. Thus during depression, lowering of rates of taxation would leave more disposable income with people. This would push up demand, price, output and level of employment. This can also be achieved by government increasing public expenditure by deficit financing (*i.e.*, by creation of addition money).

J. M. Keynes also pleaded in favour of a substantial public sector as a key factor in maintaining aggregate demand at appropriate level.

During post-World War II period, most governments in capitalist countries have recognised maintaining full employment as one of the important objectives of their economic policy. Thus the U.S. Government passed an Act in 1946 ensuring full employment and providing unemployment benefits in case government for any period of time is unable to provide to any one employment directly or indirectly.

Maintaining full employment and ensuring stable income have become in free economies important objectives of economic policy during post-World War II period.

6. STATE AND PROBLEM OF INFLATION

Inflation is defined as persistent and abnormal price rise in an economy. Since the commencement of World War II, inflation has become a global phenomenon. Not only it has not abated during post-World War II period, as was anticipated by many experts on the ground that end of war would mean shrinkage of demand for all types of goods and services because of fall in employment and income and vast number of people no longer needed in defence industries which will have to be dismantled. Not only did this prediction not come true, but with the passage of every decade since the end of World War II, inflationary pressures are gathering increasing force in both developed and developing countries excluding the communist countries. Inflation has not spared even highly prosperous countries like the United States, West Germany and Japan, not to speak of other developed countries and developing countries of the Third World. Two-digit inflation has appeared in unplanned capitalist economies which have adopted some type of planning (such as indicative planning in France) and in mixed economies like Sweden and India. It has truly become a global phenomenon. (The only exceptions are the centrally planned communist economies, namely, those of the USSR, China and East European countries).

The matter for greater worry is that contrary to Keynesian thesis, rising price level is being accompanied by lack of growth or very slow growth, and increasing unemployment — a phenomenon which has come to be designated as 'Stagflation.'

Adverse Effects of Inflation

It is observed that continual inflation (which has now prevailed for over 50 years) produces adverse effects on production. During period of continually rising prices, instead of investing money in industrial ventures which are productive, entrepreneurs prefer to make quick speculative gains by hoarding commodities. Thus trading activities are preferred to manufacturing activities.

Inflation also produces adverse effect on the rate of saving by the community and hence on investment. This has adverse effect on production.

During period of inflation, pattern of production and allocation of community's resources get distorted. Increasing amounts of resources come to be diverted to production of luxury and semi-luxury articles which are in increasing demand by rich sections of the community as their income in the form of profit rises fast compared to those of other sections of the community.

Inflation also affects exports of commodities which decline due to rising prices. This both adversely affects production of export-goods and also balance of payments position of the country.

More serious are the adverse effects of inflation on distribution of income and wealth. Majority of people belong to what is called 'fixed income groups' (*i.e.,* wages and salary earners) and their income either do not rise or rise very slowly when price level is rising faster. Fixed income group people are therefore the worst sufferers as their income purchases less and less. Inflation has thus positively adverse effect on the welfare of the community. Those who are unemployed and living on fixed income (like contractual house-rent) are the worst affected by inflation.

Types of Inflation

It has become customary to classify inflation in the following way:

(*a*) *Creeping Inflation.* Under this type price rise is gradual. And therefore danger from inflation that is creeping (moving up gradually) to the economy is not great. On the contrary, creeping inflation over a period of time may provide stimulus to production and may push up the growth-rate.

(*b*) *Walking Inflation.* When price rise is a little more quicker than in the case of creeping inflation, it is known as 'Walking inflation'.

(*c*) *Runaway Inflation.* Under 'runaway inflation', the price level rises much faster so much so that government or monetary authority finds it increasingly difficult to control further rise in price level.

Under this type of inflation, people in general also expect further quick rise in prices and therefore there is rush to buy commodities and store them rather than holding and storing cash and bank balances.

(*d*) *Hyper Inflation or Galloping Inflation.* Under this type of inflation price rise is fantastic. Very quick price rise takes place daily or even hourly. The consequence is that under this type of inflation, people for all practical purposes lose faith in money of their country and begin to get rid of it by converting whatever cash or bank balance the have in goods or foreign currencies. Even transactions begin to be carried in goods without the intervention of money (as in the case of barter-exchanges). Naturally hyper or galloping inflation has the most upsetting and damaging effects on the economy which gets completely disrupted as during the days of hyper inflation in Germany during early 1920s.

(*e*) *Repressed or Suppressed Inflation.* When during period of rising prices, government steps in and imposes price control, wage and profit freeze so that price rise which otherwise would have taken place if there were no government intervention, is not allowed to take place.

But it is observed that such price controls result in appearance of long queues in front of shops, black-marketing, and diversion of community's resources from the production of goods the prices of which are controlled to production of those goods the prices of which are not controlled by the government. Since prices of all goods and services cannot be controlled due to administrative and practical reasons, price controls are always partial. This results in various distortions in the economy.

It should be noted that these different types of inflation — creeping, walking, runaway and hyper — get mixed in one another and the distinction becomes a matter of degree. One gets merged into the other so that one cannot definitely say when creeping inflation has become walking inflation or the latter runaway inflation.

Inflation is also classified as : (*a*) Demand-Pull Inflation, and (*b*) Cost-Push Inflation.

(*a*) *Demand-Pull Inflation.* Demand-pull inflation is that when price rise takes place because demand for goods and services is rising due to factors such as increase in population, rise in level of income of people or due to some psychological factors whereby people begin to spend more and more of their income (as when for example war is expected) instead of holding and saving money.

(*b*) *Cost-Push Inflation.* Cost-push inflation is that where price rise takes place because of continual rise in cost of production either because trade unions have forced substantial wage rise or prices of raw materials have been rising or because government has raised taxes such as excise duties and so on.

It should be noted that whatever the origin of inflation — demand-pull or cost-push — later on these forces act and react upon each other. Thus demand-pull inflation results in rise in cost of production which pushes price level further; similarly cost-push inflation pushes up prices and people begin to purchase more and more before prices have risen still further.

Measures to Control Inflation

Since inflation produces harmful effects on production and distribution results in great injustice to the vast majority whose incomes are fixed and generally damages the economy by creating uncertainty and instability in the economy which hamper steady long-term economic progress, governments in non-communist countries are fighting a continual battle to devise policies and strategies that would help restrain inflation.

The following are the major policy-instruments which are generally used (in combination and not in isolation) to combat inflationary pressures in the economy.

1. *Monetary Policy and Measures.* Since quantity of money (*i.e.,* cash plus saving account deposits in commercial banks) has influence over price

level, during period of inflation attempt is made to reduce the total quantity of money in circulation by taking the following measures:

(*i*) Raising of the Bank Rate;

(*ii*) Selling of government and other securities with the Central Bank of the country to the public;

(*iii*) Raising the Reserve Ratio (*i.e.*, amount of cash which commercial banks keep with the Central Bank of the country) as also the liquidity ratio.

Along with these quantitative monetary control measures, government also employs selective control measures such as raising margin requirements, prohibiting loans on security of some goods, moral persuasion, direction to commercial banks to restrict granting of credit and, if necessary, rationing of credit.

These monetarist measures to control inflation have been receiving increasing attention especially in the United States and the United Kingdom since President Regan and Mrs. Thatcher came to power in those countries.

But unfortunately monetarists (as these people are called) have yet not been successful in containing effectively inflationary pressures in their countries. Price level in both the countries continues to rise and so is number of unemployed people.

The argument of those who are opposed to above monetarist measures is that such restrictive monetary policy by raising the rate of interest will hamper investment and have adverse effect on growth rate. This would only succeed in pushing price level upwards.

2. *Fiscal Policy and Measures.* During inflationary period government tries through fiscal policy (*i.e.*, government taxation and expenditure policy) to reduce overall demand for goods and services to restrain inflationary forces in the economy. This the government tries to do by the following fiscal measures:

(*i*) Reducing government expenditure, especially unproductive government expenditure;

(*ii*) Imposing additional taxation, especially on richer sections of the community with a view to curtail their consumption expenditure;

(*iii*) Raising public debt from the people with a view to reduce their consumption expenditure during present times; and

(*iv*) Adopting measures such as compulsory deposit schemes with a view to freeze part of disposals income in the hands of especially rich people.

3. *Other Measures to Control Inflation.* Along with the above monetary and fiscal measures, government has been adopting some or all of the following measures to restrain inflationary pressures:

(*i*) *Expansion of Output.* Final answer to inflation is to expand output of all types of goods in the economy to correspond with increasing demand for them. Government takes various steps to increase output of goods by granting various tax and other concessions and by providing various infrastructure facilities needed by the agricultural and industrial sector.

(*ii*) *Wage Policy.* During inflationary times attempt is made to regulate wage rise and sometimes even adopting wage freeze for stated period of time.

(*iii*) *Price Control and Rationing.* Another policy which government has been following to lessen the impact of inflation is to adopt the policy of price control and rationing.

Government tries to control prices of essential commodities especially consumed by the poorer sections of society, make compulsory procurement of essential commodities from agriculturists and factories and distribute these essential goods especially among poorer sections of the community through ration or fair price shops.

In spite of all these measures being used in a package, inflationary forces in the economy appear to be defying all attempts to control inflation. Inflationary pressures in practically all non-communist countries are getting more powerful especially since the oil-crisis of 1970s and fourfold increases in prices of petrol and petroleum products. Along with rising prices, it is observed that level of unemployment in most non-communist countries is also rising. This phenomenon of rising prices along with rising unemployment is known as 'Stagflation'.

It is observed that developing countries like India with rapidly increasing population and rigidity on the supply side of commodities are finding it all the more difficult to control inflation and level of unemployment.

Effects of Price Control and Rationing

When government resorts to price control of essential commodities especially those entering consumption pattern of poorer section of the community leaving prices of other commodities, especially luxury and semi-luxury goods, the following consequence are likely to take place:

1. The welfare of the poor is protected insofar as they get essential commodities at low controlled prices. If everyone is allowed a definite quota in the rationed commodity (*e.g.*, sugar), black market is likely to develop. Those poor people not in a position to consume such articles or not wanting such articles would purchase their quota and sell it to the needy at higher prices. (This was what used to happen in the case of sugar when it was rationed and was not available in the open market).

2. Since profits from price-controlled goods would be lower than in the case of uncontrolled goods, unless government compels producers to produce price controlled goods as before, there will be tendency on the part of producers

to move away from the production of price-controlled goods giving lower rate of profit to the production of those goods prices of which are not controlled and therefore where profit margin is higher than in controlled goods. Thus price controls would bring about reallocation of community's resources not always of desirable type.

3. Price control and rationing to be successful, will have to be accompanied by regulation of production and compulsory procurement. One control would automatically lead to other controls. The whole thing would logically have to end up in comprehensive planning.

While such comprehensive planning with complex mechanism of controls might be desirable during emergencies like war, in normal times it would undermine democratic form of government and individual freedom.

7. MANAGEMENT OF PUBLIC DEBT

During the 19th century when governments followed *laissez-faire* policy, the concept of balanced budget was prevailing. Public debt was to be avoided and was disfavoured. If governments were compelled during emergencies like war and drought to raise public debt, governments were expected to pay back public debt as early as possible, returning back to normal budgeting when revenue raised matched normal expenditure of the government.

All this changed especially after the publication of The General Theory of J. M. Keynes. Management of public debt at present has become an important fiscal instrument to control inflationary pressures as also of influence level of activity in the community.

For example, during times of depression, government raises loans from the people and spends it on productive activities. Thus money or savings lying idle with people is activised and begins to circulate providing income to people now employed on public works undertaken by government with funds raised through public debt. Prices begin to rise and so does the level of employment which after sometime gathers momentum and pulls the whole economy out of depression.

During times of inflation government raises loans from the people and keeps the amount so raised frozen for the time being. Quantity of money with the people is reduced. This reduces demand of the people for goods thus pushing down the price level. Thus public debt can be an important instrument to control inflationary forces.

In developing countries where only limited amount can be raised through taxation, public debt can serve as useful and effective instrument in government hands to put to use productive resources otherwise lying idle and raise level of employment and production of wealth. Thus if public debt is managed skilfully, it can serve as an important instrument to [illegible] various objectives like controlling cyclical booms and depression, to control inflationary forces, to influence level of activity in the community, to bring about upliftment of economically backward regions and so on.

And therefore at present public debt is not frowned upon as during the 19th century. Practically every government in capitalist and democratic countries including USA has raised immense public debt which is being managed to attain various economic and other objectives.

CHAPTER 28

CONVERGENCE OF DIFFERENT ECONOMIC SYSTEMS

1. MEANING OF CONVERGENCE THESIS

Since Jan Tinbergen wrote in 1961 his famous paper on 'Convergence hypothesis', that idea has attracted a good deal of attention and a number of writers like J. K. Galbraith, Harry C. Haffer, Jan S. Prybyla and socialist writers like L. Leoritier, A. P. Buteriko, G. Gallai and most of others have written on the topic of "The Convergence of Market-oriented and Command-oriented Economic Systems." It would be instructive to know the thesis and the pros and cons and the political and practical implications of the convergence thesis.

According to the convergence thesis, "Socialist and capitalism economies are departing more and more from centralised economic planning and from *laissez-faire* private enterprise respectively, and instead are evolving patterns of thinking, institutions, methods and practices, which are increasingly similar." This advanced form of capitalist economy and advanced type of socialist economy are converging towards each other. Each system is borrowing some features from the other economic system. This is resulting, as stated above, into some patterns of thinking, institutions and procedures which appear to be common to both the capitalist and socialist economic systems.

2. FACTORS RESPONSIBLE FOR BRINGING ABOUT THE CONVERGENCE

The following factors are said to be responsible for bringing about convergence of capitalist and socialist systems:

1. *Technological Factor.* Whether a factory is in the private sector or in the public sector, it experiences the same impact of rapid technological progress that is taking place. The large-scale production made possible by technological advance poses the same problems of division of labour and its coordination, organisation of the factory, continuous supply of raw materials

and disposal of output, irrespective of whether the factory is in the private or public sector or in the USA or the USSR. Thus a number of organisational and technological problems faced by Ford Motor company in the U.S.A. and public sector motor-car manufacturing factory in the U.S.S.R. are similar.

2. *Better Understanding of Each Other's System.* Initially (*i.e.*, right from the October Revolution in 1917 till 1959) each system viewed the other system with great amount of suspicion or even animosity. There were strong and blind prejudices about the opposite system and possibly there were historical reasons for that (namely, Marxist idea of destroying capitalism every where and establishment of the Third International, and attempt by capitalist countries to destroy the Communist regime installed in the U.S.S.R. after the October Revolution by militarily invading the country). But the days of blind prejudice are over. Scholars from both the countries are objectively studying the other system and its merits and defects. Naturally this had led to adoption by each system of the good aspects or devices or institutions from the other economic system.

3. *Keen Rivalry.* Keen rivalry between the two systems, especially during the days of Cold War following the end of World War II, and desire to outdo and outpace each other has resulted in each system borrowing from the other some of the features and institutions that might help the system push it ahead of its rival system.

4. *Threat of Nuclear War and Necessity of Co-existence.* Since any more international war would mean nuclear conflict and destruction of entire humanity, that has forced co-existence of the two rival systems. If co-existence is inevitable, each is trying to learn as much as possible from the other to prove in the atmosphere of peaceful competition and rivalry that their system is superior to its rival system.

3. CONVERGENCE THESIS EXPLAINED

Attempt is made first to explain the convergence thesis in the following paragraphs :

1. *Micro-Macro Tendencies.* If at one time capitalist countries concentrated only on micro-economic analysis, as a consequence of the writings of J. M. Keynes, they are looking at the problems of aggregate saving and investment, aggregate demand, unemployment, inflation etc., in the economy which has compelled them to take greater interest in macro-economic studies.

On the other hand, if at one time socialist countries concentrated mostly on macro-economic analysis, they are now turning more and more of their attention to micro-level studies like problems of firms, farms, and of individual establishments.

2. *Economic Planning.* While at one time the term 'planning' was an anathema to capitalist countries, because of increasingly complex nature of modern economy, impact of socialist thought and remarkable achievements of planned economies of socialist countries, capitalist countries have come to accept some sort of planning (indicative planning, democratic planning, planning from below or regional planning and so on).

On the other hand socialist countries have been departing more and more from authoritarian and highly centralised type of planning in favour of decentralisation and planning from below and with greater authority to firms factories and individual establishments.

3. *Economic Administration.* It is observed that instead of following *laissez-faire* policy, governments in capitalist countries of Western Europe are intervening to a greater and greater extent in the economic affairs of the people. Thus we observe anti-monopoly legislation, State marketing organisations, public undertakings, control and regulation of basic and heavy industries, of their location and output, policy of protection to some industries and policy of social security — all indicating the extent of departure from *laissez-faire* policy once followed by capitalist countries which are now required to maintain huge administrative structures for supervision and management.

On the other hand, in the case of socialist countries, centralised control practiced up to 1950s is gradually giving place to decentralisation of authority and allowing greater scope of decision-making and executive action to bodies at lower level thus relieving the central planning body of much of its responsibility.

4. *Management.* At one time in capitalist countries management was concentrated in the hands of top managerial personnel, workers having absolutely no voice in the management of the establishment. Things have changed now and trade unions are playing increasing part and there is also greater participation of labour in management through devices such as Works Committees, Joint Management Councils and sometimes director labour participation in management both in private sector and public sector establishments.

On the other hand, in socialist countries, there is greater realisation that workers on their own cannot manage factories or other industrial and commercial establishments as was assumed by the socialist theory. "The position of local management has been recently strengthened, and a 'director' of a socialist enterprise in several respects now resembles a 'manager' in capitalist countries."

5. *Role of Money and Banking.* In capitalist countries the role of money is not as great as it used to be once; and monetary policy is being increasingly supplemented by wage and income policies and even direct price controls and rationing.

On the other hand, while orthodox socialism started its career by condemning money as a capitalist device of exploitation, advanced socialist countries are now using to a considerable extent money, monetary and fiscal incentives, and banks are now playing increasingly important role of selecting economically sound and viable projects, instead of entirely relying on administrative directives as before.

6. *Role of Profits.* As one time under capitalism maximisation of private profit was the sole factor determining entrepreneurs' actions. At present many firms in capitalist economy are attaching much importance to goodwill of the public ; entrepreneurs who are more professional in their approach are showing greater sense of social responsibility. In public sector enterprises profit maximisation is not the main consideration. In private enterprise, entrepreneurs are seeking job-satisfaction. There are profit-sharing schemes. Thus unlike in olden days, private profit-maximisation has ceased to be of the same importance at present in capitalist economic system.

On the other hand in European socialist countries, profit has come to play increasingly important role. Profit has come to be regarded as the test of efficiency of public enterprises, and part of profit is being shared by workers and management. All these were once a taboo in socialist countries.

7. *Private Ownership of Property.* Under advanced capitalist countries, there is increasing extent of state ownership and nationalisation of basic and heavy industries, banking and so on, though at one time such State interference and ownership was unthinkable. There are also heavy death duties and succession duties on big private estates and properties.

On the other hand, in advanced socialist countries there is some degree of de-collectivisation. Individual farm-units are playing increasingly important role even in the U.S.S.R. Individual farmers can own livestock and individual enterprises are allowed to play significant role in retail trade, catering, fishing, etc.

8. *Distribution of National Income.* Inequalities of income and wealth in capitalist countries are increasingly being reduced by devices such as expanding public sector, progressive direct taxes, taxes on luxury and semi-luxury goods and increasing expenditure on social security, minimum wages for workers, etc., and expansion of other social services all with a view to protect and increase welfare of workers.

On the other hand, the dream of equalisation in the distribution of income has been given up in advanced socialist countries. Rewards are being related to quantity and quality of work and more and more material rewards are being provided to workers. As a consequence increasing inequalities in income are arising and technocrats, skilled workers, engineers and higher bureaucrats are getting much higher incomes than unskilled workers and lower-grade public sector employees.

9. *Social Structure.* In capitalist countries, former class distinctions are gradually getting reduced because on the one hand personal incomes and wealth are getting reduced, as we saw, by various devices including progressive taxes.

On the other hand, class distinctions are arising in socialist countries because of increasing income differentials. Thus class distinctions can be observed in the case of peasants, workers, intelligentsia is and Communist Party elites.

10. *Role of Prices.* Freely fluctuating price-mechanism which was once the basic and fundamental feature of capitalism is now found only in textbooks. Under modern capitalism prices of commodities and services are now being increasingly manipulated by giant monopolies, public sector enterprises, price policies, indirect taxes, Government fixation of prices directly and by subsidisation as in the case of agricultural commodities in the USA.

On the otherhand; in socialist countries price-mechanism is being allowed increasing role to reflect consumer preferences.

11. *Role of Consumers.* In capitalism consumer has ceased to be 'sovereign.' Monopolies, price fixation in the case of public sector enterprises and regulation of prices in the case of public utilities, price fixation in some cases by Government and rationing, and high pressure advertisement by giant industrial concerns have all reduced the power of consumers to dictate production of goods and services.

On the other hand, in advanced socialist countries pries are being assigned increasing role with continually rising standard of living : prices are being used increasingly to reflect consumer preferences.

12. *Increasing Mutual Trade.* Until 1950s the capitalist and socialist countries viewed each other with great suspicion and avoided trading with each other. But since 1960s and especially in recent years trade between the two blocks is continually increasing. Thus between 1953 and 1976, trade between these two blocs of countries increased at an annual average rate of about 18 per cent. Solutions are being found to overcome obstacles to trade between capitalists countries with dominant private sector and socialist countries with the public sector.

4. CRITICAL EXAMINATION OF CONVERGENCE THESIS: ARE THE TWO SYSTEMS TRULY CONVERGING?

Are the two economic systems, namely, capitalism and socialism, truly converging ?

Divergent views are held on this matter.

One view is that the two systems are converging and are borrowing important and useful features from the other system. This is reducing former antagonism between them. This has opened the way to political detente and possible peaceful co-existence between the two blocs of countries.

Then there is other view which is not so hopeful. According to this view fanatical socialist thinkers think that basic tenets or principles of *laissez-faire* capitalism have been shown to be defective and inoperative and therefore capitalism is being forced to accept more and more devices of socialist system (as noted already). On the other hand, the ardent advocates of capitalism believe that socialism has realised the weaknesses of its basic principles and therefore is being forced to accept many of the important devices of capitalism.

A view is expressed that 'Most of the modifications accepted on each side are not conscious imitation but rather selective adaptations to a variety of economic and technical changes, independent of the other system." As J. Kleer, a Polish author, wrote : " The reforms being carried out in socialist countries have nothing in common with the convergence of socialism and capitalism. They are merely used to perfect our system of planning and management whereby the objectives of the socialist society can be attained in a more effective way."

Socialist countries appear to borrow from capitalist system some of their devices such as 'profit', 'market mechanism', 'decentralisation', 'consumer freedom', etc., etc. In this connection, L. Leontier, a noted critic of the 'Convergence Thesis', has the following things to say.

"First, socialisation of the means of production remain in force in the socialist countries. This is why there is little point in comparing the status of economic executive in the socialist countries with the role of capitalist managers. Secondly, centralised planning is preserved in the socialist countries while 'economic market' methods are made to serve it. Third, prices are fixed by State bodies. Due to this, prices do not play the role of indicators of 'economic insufficiency' and cannot serve as a reliable basis for making decisions concerning capital investment. Fourth, real competition is out of question, for enterprises arise and disappear 'not from the angle of competition.' Finally, the economic goals in the socialist countries are determined by political institutions."

It is therefore maintained that since the basic philosophies of the two systems are totally different, "Convergence is out of question." They theory of 'Convergence', it is maintained, remains nothing but an illusion both in the theory and in practice.

CHAPTER 29

SOME IMPORTANT DEVELOPMENTS

1. 'INDICATIVE PLANNING' IN FRANCE

France has become famous during the post-World War II years for what has come to be called 'Indicative Planning'. This 'Indicative Planning' has been in operation in France since 1947 and that has become a basic feature of the French economic system. It is observed that success of the French 'Indicative Planning' has stimulated interest in that type of economic planning in countries like the U.S.A., Belgium, Italy and even Great Britain. It would therefore be instructive to have a broad idea of 'Indicative Planning' adopted in France.

France happens to be a highly industrialised country in Western Europe, ranking next to West Germany and the United Kingdom. The industrial units in France however tend to be smaller than in the other two countries mentioned above. What is remarkable about France is that because of its varied natural resources, France happens to be both a leading industrialised country as also the largest agricultural producer among the West European countries.

In France most of the productive activities are in the private sector. For example agriculture is in the private sector so also distribution. But what is remarkable about France is growing participation of the State in the economic sphere. The State has been since 1947 increasingly participating in business, industry and finance. Thus in France the State controls all railroads, nearly 70 per cent of airlines, practically whole of coal production and nearly 93 per cent of electrical power. The Government of France also commands a large share in natural gas and petroleum industries as also in the production of motor vehicles and airplanes. The Bank of France and four major commercial banks in the country are nationalised concerns. Nationalised commercial banks have about 60 per cent of total deposits in the country whereas nationalised insurance companies receive about 25 per cent of total insurance premiums paid by insurance policy-holders in the country. It is observed that broadly nationalised

industries in France employ about 13 per cent of all the employed industrial workers in the country and the public sector enterprises account for about 25 per cent of total gross fixed investment in the country. Thus the French economy, like the U.K. economy, has a fairly large public sector so that the Central Government along with the Local Governments and nationalised industries account for roughly half of the nation's gross domestic fixed investment.

The French Indicative Planning

France has attracted world-wide interest, especially among capitalist democratic countries, because it has developed what is commonly referred to as 'Indicative Planning'. Indicative Planning may be regarded as 'The Middle Way' between unregulated capitalist economy and centrally controlled and planned communist or socialist economy.

French economic planning is called 'indicative planning' because the Government after going through the planning process (described below) and after formulating a National Plan indicates the directions in which the economy and different sectors of the economy should broadly move or progress within the next five years or so. The national plan does not provide specific targets for different sectors or for firms and enterprises. In order to make the economy move in the indicated directions decided by the national plan, the Government relies on policies of selective promotion or protection to selected sectors, or industries or regions. It is observed that in France capital market is not as well developed as in the U.K. and West Germany. Government therefore has an important instrument of providing finance to enterprises in the private and public sector in a selective way to promote their growth and development. The Government sells treasury bills and bonds to public and uses loan proceeds of these sales to provide finance to enterprises both in the private and public sectors.

The selective growth is brought about not by direction or using compulsion, but by devices such as provision of credit to favoured areas or segments of the economy which according to the national planned need more rapid development, special depreciation allowances to selected industries, more favourable treatment of exports under the value-added tax and preferential treatment in Government's purchases. By its various polices (and not directly), the Government is in a position to influence pattern of investment, plant location and prices in the French economy.

Though the French Government is committed to planned economic and social development, private economy is the backbone of the French economy and the whole of agriculture continues to be dominated by small-scale family farms.

It may be said that during post-World War II years, France has developed the most elaborate and detailed planning system among the West European countries.

France has developed a fairly comprehensive institutional framework of planning, involving a number of interested parties as also professional experts in various fields.

At the centre of the French planning structure is the General Commissariat for Planning (popularly known as Planning Commission). This is an autonomous Government agency. The Planning Commission' functions with the help of Economic and Financial Research Commission and prepares various studies regarding current situations as also medium-term and long-term possibilities in different sectors of the French economy. Though Planning Commission takes initiative in suggesting or evolving planning policy in the initial stages and also draws the final draft of the national plan, the spade-work is carried on by a number of specialised committees involving both Government personnel as also a number of experts from outside the Government. Civil servants do the job of coordinating the work done in every sector by a vast number of individuals inside and outside the Government. What is characteristic about the French procedure of drawing up a national plan made up of several sectorial plans is that cooperation of experts from various sectors is sought and the plan is based on consensus of all the people in the different sectors concerned.

Then there are Modernisation Committees about 25 in number. After the Government has laid down the broad framework of the national plan made up of several sectoral plans, these Modernisation Committees composed of people from various institutions and sectors of the economy take over and work out the details concerning different sectors and problem areas. Modernisation Committee membership consists of heads of business and management organisations, Government officials and experts in various fields from interested ministries. Their proposals are coordinated by the Planning Commission in such a manner that a consistent national plan is evolved which finally comes before the legislature and Government for approval.

As regards the execution of the national plan, after it is evolved, it may be noted that the plan is not strictly binding. There is no formal mechanism for its execution. The national plan serves only to provide voluntary guidelines to the private sector, enterprises and for that matter even to enterprises in the public sector which can disregard the guidelines, if they so choose. But as we have already seen, the Government is not so powerless as it apparently appears and it has various indirect instruments such as supply of credit, tax concessions and so on with which it can ensure broad cooperation of enterprises in the private and public sectors in fulfilling the objectives of the national plan.

As noted above, great emphasis is placed on experts and individuals outside the Government and from trade and industry while formulating the plan which generally is the result of consensus. This itself ensures voluntary cooperation from individual business firms and farms in the successful implementation of the plan. And as we have seen there are various indirect instruments such as monetary and fiscal policies that can ensure co-operation of various sectors and firms in successful implementation of the plan which broadly indicates the direction of progress without setting down specific targets either for the national economy or for any specific sector or an enterprise. That is why planning in France is called 'Indicative Planning' and not planning by direction or prescriptive planning.

Evaluation of French Indicative Planning

The efficiency or effectiveness of the French indicative planning has been often debated. The supporters of the French indicative planning point out to the high rate of growth of the French economy as conclusive proof of its success. Another merit of this type of planning has been that it is evolved and executed with consensus and within the democratic framework with no loss of political rights or individual freedom of French citizens. The French guided capitalism has not only attained high and sustained growth rate of the national economy with very low rate of unemployment but it has also won the confidence of the managers of enterprises in the private sector.

But the critics of French indicative planning point out many shortcomings of the system. For example, the critics point out that without any type of economic planning, West Germany and to a certain extent Italy achieved higher rates of growth than France has done with its indicative planning. Another point of criticism is that French type of planning perpetuates the existing concentration of economic power and is incapable of bringing about equitable distribution of income and wealth. There is failure to work out wage and income policy. Further, the French type of planning has failed to effectively control inflationary pressures emerging in the economy. This means the so-called French planning failed to so distribute income that aggregate demand for goods and services equals aggregate supply of them at the level of full employment in the economy.

The French type of planning has also so far failed in some specific fields or failed to attain certain desirable objectives. Thus it has failed to bring about balanced regional development. It has also failed to remove deficiencies in housing and educational facilities. On the whole, trade union movement in France has not strongly supported the French planning. That is why J. A. Hackett writes : "French planning is more business sponsored than labour-supported activity."[1]

2. REFORMS IN SOCIALIST COUNTRIES SINCE 1960s

It would be instructive to analyse various reforms which have been taking place in the socialist countries in Europe.

Broadly, it can be said that up to 1960 some reforms were effected only in Yugoslavia which was expelled from Cominform in 1949 for deviating from the Stalinist line. Thus in Yugoslavia detailed annual plans were discontinued since 1952 when substantial independence also came to be granted to industrial enterprises; also greater role came to be assigned to price-mechanism and decollectivisation of land came to be permitted. In Yugoslavia reforms along the above lines were further carried out after 1958.

In most socialist countries of Eastern Europe, namely, the U.S.S.R., Poland, Hungary, Rumania, German D.R., Czechoslovakia, Yugoslavia, Bulgaria, a number of reforms came to be implemented after 1960. The main idea behind these reforms in these countries (which had reached fairly advanced stage of economic development along socialist line) has been to increase efficiency of the economy and further increase social welfare.

An outline of reforms (common to all the socialist countries) which have been taking place since 1960 and through 1970s is given below.

1. *Liberalisation of Economic Planning.* After 1960, there has been taking place what may be called, 'liberalisation' of planning. Economic planning in socialist countries is becoming less prescriptive; it is becoming less detailed. Planning has been laying down broad directions and targets; there is now greater emphasis on long-term planning than on short-term planning as before. Attempt is also increasingly being made to establish closer correspondence between the central planning authority and individual enterprises.

2. *Greater Independence to Enterprises.* In the place of former authoritarian, rigid and hierarchical system, the trend since 1960 is to give greater freedom, to industrial, agricultural and trading enterprises of choosing ways and means of fulfilling targets which are laid down in broad terms and in consultation with the enterprises themselves.

3. *Changed Role of Profits.* Before 1960 an enterprise was supposed to be functioning efficiently, if it followed the directive from the central planning authority. This meant that profit had no place in the socialist economy as it was thought that it was a typical phenomenon in a capitalist economy. Since 1960 the criterion of profit (which however goes to the State, though part of it may be made available for the collective benefit of the employees of the enterprise making the profit) has come to accepted as an indicator of the performance and efficiency of an enterprise.

4. *Provision of Increasing Material Incentives for Workers.* Before 1960 material incentive were criticised as typical capitalist device and socialism then gave emphasis on moral incentives such as social approbation and praise by the community, working for the community and job-satisfaction, etc. But since 1960 there is greater recognition of the effectiveness of material incentives under socialism. As a consequence, since 1960 a portion of profit made by an enterprise is being distributed individually and collectively to workers of the enterprise according to the quantity and quality of work performed by individual workers. Thus provision of material incentive (which plays such a predominant role under capitalism) has come to be accepted to some extent by socialism.

5. *Price Reforms.* Prices of commodities are being brought in closer correspondence with cost of production in socialist countries — cost including elements of rent, profit and interest. The idea is to reduce or even abolish State subsidies and enable State enterprises to make reasonable profits.

In many socialist countries where the agricultural sector has lagged behind, prices of agricultural commodities have been raised in relation to prices of industrial goods with a view to raise income of workers in the agricultural sector as also agricultural production.

In many socialist countries prices of commodities and services are not being fixed with the same rigidity as before. On the other hand, prices are increasingly being allowed to be influenced by forces of demand and supply in the market with the consequence that prices these days are more flexible reflecting the changing preferences of consumers.

6. *Greater Role Assigned to Finance and Credit.* At one time, money had come to be considered in socialist countries as a capitalist device through which employers exploit workers. All this is changed since 1960. Money is assigned a vital role in a socialist economy. "Enterprises have been charged with greater financial responsibility. Capital charges (on capital supplied directly by the State) have been introduced. Instead of directives, the authorities are increasingly relying on a flexible use of interest rates, credit and taxes."[2]

7. *Establishment of Closer Link between Production and Distribution.* Wholesale and retail trade have come to be overhauled. The idea behind is to serve consumers better and to see that changing consumer preferences are appropriately made known to producers. "Profit is now generally calculated on the basis of output sold, not merely produced or handled so that it is in the interest of both industry and trade to supply customers what they want."[3]

8. *Increasing Role Assigned to Foreign Trade.* There was a time when socialist countries considered trading with capitalist countries morally injustifiable; they therefore for some time though more or less in terms of self-sufficiency, if not of each socialist country, certainly in terms of self-sufficiency of a group of socialist countries like Cominform. But since 1960 foreign trade with other countries including capitalist countries is being encouraged. Increasing emphasis is being given on promoting exports. The socialist countries in return for their exports want to import sophisticated technology from advanced capitalist countries. They also want to import raw materials from the Third World countries in return for exports of capital goods to help industrialise them with emphasis on manufacture of capital goods.

Concluding Remarks

It would be observed from the above description that socialist countries have been trying to reform their system by accepting some of the so-called features of capitalism such as freedom of enterprise, role of profit and material incentives, price mechanism, increasing role of money and credit and so on.

But one or two consideration musts be kept in mind.

The socialist authorities are very cautions in introducing reforms such as market mechanism so that it is not allowed to play the role which it plays under capitalism. The above reforms are being gradually introduced, a little of this and a little of that being grafted on the socialist system, instead of effecting radical departure from central planning which is the core of socialism. The reason is that the above reforms impinge not only on economics but also on social and political ideology of socialism.

It must also be noted that there are still many Stalinist hardliners who are critical of these reforms and condemn them as 'economic revisionism'.

3. INTERNATIONAL ECONOMIC CO-OPERATION

Up to mid-1950s, the socialist countries in Eastern Europe adopted highly critical attitude to most of the international organisations which for all practical purposes were then dominated by the capitalist countries, and especially by the U.S.A. It was observed that most of the socialist countries either refrained from joining international organisations or obstructed their functioning or used those organisations as forums for propaganda work on behalf of communism.

But since mid-1960s, the attitude of the European socialist countries has considerably changed. Many of them have joined relevant economic organisations such as Baltic International Maritime Conference, Food and Agricultural Organisation (FAO), the General Agreement of Tariffs and Trade (GATT), the World Energy Conference, and of course, the United Nations Organisation. There are about twenty international organisations of which the European socialist countries have become members. They have been taking part in their deliberations generally in a co-operative spirit. Of all the international organisations, the European Commission for Europe has become "the most fruitful platform for identifying and solving the economic problems arising between the capitalist and socialist countries."[4]

Experts from capitalist and socialist countries who are the members of the above international organisations have deliberated on questions of mutual interest such as "nature of economic growth, the criteria for investment policies, regional and intra-regional planning, macro-economic models, technological progress as a factor in economic growth and long-term problems of international trade."[5]

It is a hopeful sign that capitalist and socialist countries in Europe have succeeded to a smaller or greater extent in finding some common solutions such as standardization of commercial documents, reciprocity in respect of the Most-Favoured Nation treatment, rules regarding avoiding discriminatory surcharges on imports and exports, conditions regarding insurance in respect of international trade, mutually acceptable procedures for settlement of disputes in the sphere of foregin trade, etc.

Co-operation between Socialist Countries and Capitalist Countries

Declaration of 'Peaceful Co-existence' formulated by the socialist countries and reaffirmed at the 1961 Congress of the Communist Party of the U.S.S.R. may be said to have provided broad basis for co-operation between the socialist and capitalist countries. These two declarations emphasised peaceful co-existence and its other postulates such as respect for national sovereignty, non-interference in the internal affairs of other countries and renunciation of war as an arbiter of international disputes. The two declarations also gave a call for "promotion of economic and cultural co-operation on the basis of equality and mutual benefit" between capitalist and socialist countries.

Proponents of socialist countries point out that socialist countries have shown conciliatory attitude towards capitalist countries. This is evident from increasing trade of socialist countries with capitalist countries, their strict adherence to terms of contracts and payments, increasing imports of consumer goods from capitalist countries, relaxation of restrictions on foreign travel, and increasing meetings of officials, engineers, and traders of socialist and capitalist countries. Also, many socialist countries have signed bilateral agreements with a number of capitalist countries on industrial, scientific, technical and cultural co-operation. Most of the European socialist countries have been maintaining permanent trade missions in important trading centres in the capitalist countries. There has also been remarkable development of co-operation at the micro-economic level as evidenced by socialist-capitalist industrial co-operation agreements which by 1976 exceeded 1,700. There are integrated enterprises where capitalist and socialist countries have co-operated by jointly sharing capital, management and risk.

In addition to the initiative which the European socialist countries have taken in co-operating in the above manner with capitalist countries, socialist countries are strengthening their links with the developing countries by extending economic aid, by negotiating trade agreements and by expanding trade with them. It may be noted that share of developing countries in the foreign trade of East European socialist countries has increased from 3 per cent in 1953 to 11 per cent in 1975.[6]

REFERENCES

1. *'Economic Planning in France'* — J. A. Hackett, page 342.
2. *'The Economics of Socialism'* — J. Wilezynski, page 28.
3. *Ibid*, page 28.
4. *'The Economics of Socialism'* — J. Wilezynski, page 192.
5. *Ibid*, page 192.
6. The process of co-operation between the two economic systems — capitalism and socialism — may be said to have preceded by co-operation among the socialist countries themselves.

   Broadly, it might be said that systematic economic co-operation (as distinct from political) among the European socialist countries began with the formation of the Council for Mutual Economic Assistance (COMECON) in 1949.

   Broadly, till the middle of 1950s co-operation among the socialist countries was limited to mutual co-ordination of trade. After the middle of 1950s, this co-operation has come to be extended to broader economic fields which include such aspects as economic integration through co-ordination of investment plans, specialisation, joint undertakings, and financial, scientific and technical co-operation.

   Of course, this co-operation among European socialist countries has and has been facing certain difficulties such as national differences, the question of Supra-National Authority, the pricing conundrum and suspicion of exploitation (by the U.S.S.R., a giant among the small East European socialist States). But many of these obstacles are being gradually overcome to the mutual advantage of participants and increasing co-operation is also being forced upon them by the commonly shared fear of NATO which perpetually is staring them in the face.